The Coming Forth of the
BOOK OF MORMON

A Marvelous Work and a Wonder

The Coming Forth of the BOOK OF MORMON

A Marvelous Work and a Wonder

edited by

Dennis L. Largey

Andrew H. Hedges

John Hilton III

Kerry Hull

THE 44TH ANNUAL

BRIGHAM YOUNG UNIVERSITY

SIDNEY B. SPERRY SYMPOSIUM

RSC BYU

DESERET BOOK

The Sperry Symposium is sponsored annually by Brigham Young University and the Church Educational System in honor of Sidney B. Sperry. In the course of his forty-five-year career as a religious educator, Dr. Sperry earned a reputation for outstanding teaching and scholarship. The symposium seeks to perpetuate his memory by fostering continuing research on gospel topics.

Copublished by the Religious Studies Center, Brigham Young University, Provo, Utah, and Deseret Book Company, Salt Lake City, Utah.

Interior layout by Shanna Clayton.

Library of Congress Cataloging-in-Publication Data

Sperry Symposium (44th : 2015 : Brigham Young University), author.

The coming forth of The Book of Mormon : a marvelous work and a wonder : the 44th Annual Brigham Young University Sidney B. Sperry Symposium / Dennis L. Largey, Andrew H. Hedges, John Hilton III, and Kerry Hull, editors.

pages cm

Includes bibliographical references and index.

ISBN 978-1-62972-114-9 (hardbound : alk. paper)

1. Book of Mormon—Evidences, authority, etc.—Congresses. 2. The Church of Jesus Christ of Latter-day Saints—Doctrines—Congresses. 3. Mormon Church—Doctrines—Congresses. I. Largey, Dennis L., editor. II. Hedges, Andrew H., 1966– editor. III. Hilton, John, III, editor. IV. Hull, Kerry, editor. V. Title.

BX8628.S72 2015

289.3'22—dc23 2015019222

Printed in the United States of America

Publishers Printing, Salt Lake City, UT

10 9 8 7 6 5 4 3 2 1

Contents

Introduction

"With other latter-day prophets," President Thomas S. Monson said, "I testify of the truthfulness of this 'most correct of any book on earth,' even the Book of Mormon, another testament of Jesus Christ. Its message spans the earth and brings its readers to a knowledge of the truth. It is my testimony that the Book of Mormon changes lives."[1] Over the years many prophets have spoken of the book's importance. For example, President Ezra Taft Benson spoke of the Book of Mormon as a gift "more important than any of the inventions that have come out of the industrial and technological revolutions. This is a gift of greater value to mankind than even the many wonderful advances we have seen in modern medicine. It is of greater worth to mankind than the development of flight or space travel."[2] Although this book has blessed many lives from its publication to the present, it was not an easy gift to obtain. The chapters in this volume tell the story of how this remarkable gift came to pass.

This volume tells the story of a modern miracle, sharing details behind the translation and publication of the Book of Mormon, which the Prophet Joseph Smith described as "the keystone of our religion."[3] This remarkable book has been a critical element of the Church since its inception, but not every member realizes the challenges faced by those who worked so hard to bring it forth. While many of us are familiar with the narratives and doctrines the book contains, we often disregard the importance of its history. We hope that this volume will be an invaluable resource to those seeking to understand the importance of the Book of Mormon's background, whether for individual study or for teaching purposes.

In the opening chapter, President Merrill J. Bateman, Emeritus Seventy, addresses a major purpose of the coming forth of the Book of Mormon: to restore plain and precious truths. The doctrines and principles contained in the book augment, clarify, and complement those taught in the Bible and testify of the reality and divinity of Christ. The accounts written by ancient prophets in the Americas have been critical to the restoration and understanding of plain and precious truths contained within the book.

Other chapters discuss the experiences of Joseph Smith and those closest to him in obtaining and protecting the gold plates and other objects associated with the Book of Mormon translation. The witnesses provided evidence, both for their contemporaries and for us today, that Joseph Smith did obtain the physical objects associated with the book's emergence. These chapters draw on primary accounts from the period of Joseph's life during which he grew from a teenage boy who saw God the Father and His Son to a chosen seer who was entrusted by the angel Moroni with the care and protection of the sacred record that would become the Book of Mormon.

We next move to the translation and publication of the Book of Mormon. Chapters in this section discuss the translation process (which many Latter-day Saints may not have an accurate knowledge of), as well as the arduous journey of getting the book published. From seer stones to lost pages, readers can learn of the trials endured, miracles witnessed, and prophecies fulfilled during this pivotal period of the Book of Mormon's life story. These essays include excerpts from primary accounts as well as scriptural texts that describe and confirm the miraculous reality of the Book of Mormon's translation. Many accounts include testimonies of various witnesses of the book—the Eleven Witnesses and others who simply had the faith to believe in Joseph's prophetic calling and his role in bringing forth an inspired and true record.

The next chapters evaluate how the Book of Mormon has gained prominence and acceptance as a testimony of Jesus Christ from its publication to the present day. Both within and without the Church, the Book of Mormon has endured times of scorn and doubt, but it has also gained unfaltering support by those who have sought their own witness of the book's truth. And as the Church has grown, the book has become available to millions of members who would not have been able to read the original English manuscripts. Since its original printing of five thousand copies, the Book of Mormon has been able to serve as a missionary tool both in America and dozens of other nations, being translated into nearly one hundred languages.

This volume concludes with two chapters highlighting two central purposes of the Book of Mormon. Besides containing inspiring stories and comforting messages, the Book of Mormon plays a critical role in spreading the gospel to all the world. The Lord's purpose in bringing forth this record was not simply to educate and inspire, but to "show unto the remnant of the house of Israel what great things the Lord hath done for their fathers; and that they may know the covenants of the Lord, that they are not cast off forever—and also to the convincing of the Jew and Gentile that JESUS is the CHRIST, the ETERNAL GOD, manifesting himself unto all nations."[4] The Book of Mormon repeatedly invites readers to "come unto Christ" (Moroni 10:30, 32; see also 1 Nephi 6:4).

In addition, the Lord brought forth this book for other purposes. For example, President Benson declared, "The Book of Mormon exposes the enemies of Christ. It confounds false doctrines and lays down contention. (See 2 Ne. 3:12.) It fortifies the humble followers of Christ against the evil designs, strategies, and doctrines of the devil in our day."[5]

Whether we are seeking tangible evidence of the Book of Mormon or spiritual witnesses of the book's divinity, this volume will provide insightful and educational information that will aid us in our search. The chapters in this volume testify of the reality of the book's origin and history, as well as the reality of the testimonies and doctrines it provides. While some articles provide historical evidence of the book's existence and translation process, others testify of the inspired messages contained within the book's text. Both forms of evidence will be useful to us as we seek to develop our knowledge and testimony of the book and as we seek to share that light with others.

Finally, we emphasize that while this volume does provide significant evidence of the book's truth, gaining a witness that the Book of Mormon is true is an individual and lifelong process. As Moroni has promised, those who seek their own confirmation of the Book of Mormon will receive a personal answer from the Lord (see Moroni 10:4). The Book of Mormon supports biblical testimonies of Christ and provides additional messages of his divine sonship. We encourage all readers of this volume to build on their current testimonies of the Book of Mormon by learning of its incredible history and origins. We hope this volume will be a valuable supplement to your Book of Mormon study and provide an additional source of the book's light and truth. As editors of this volume, we add our personal testimony that the Book of Mormon is true. It is an ancient record brought forth in our day, translated by the gift and power of God through Joseph Smith, the Lord's prophet.

Dennis L. Largey
Andrew H. Hedges
John Hilton III
Kerry Hull
Patty Smith
Sperry Symposium Committee

Notes

1. Thomas S. Monson, "Precious Promises of the Book of Mormon," *Ensign*, October 2011, 5.
2. Ezra Taft Benson, "The Book of Mormon—The Keystone of Our Religion," *Ensign*, November 1986.
3. Introduction to the Book of Mormon.
4. Title page of the Book of Mormon.
5. *Teachings of Presidents of the Church: Ezra Taft Benson* (Salt Lake City: The Church of Jesus Christ of Latter-day Saints, 2014), 125–35.

Acknowledgments

We extend our sincere appreciation to all those who have contributed to this year's Sperry Symposium in every stage of its production and presentation. In addition to those already recognized herein, we would like to thank Patty Smith and the support staff of Religious Education and the blind reviewers who carefully vetted each submission and made helpful suggestions for all of the papers. In addition, we are grateful to the staff of BYU's Religious Studies Center: Thomas Wayment, Devan Jensen, Brent R. Nordgren, Joany O. Pinegar, Alison Brimley, Shanna Clayton, Rachel Gessel, Hadley Griggs, Rebecca Hamson, and Leah Welker, who have contributed significant time and effort in reviewing, editing, and revising the papers, enhancing the book's professional and scholarly value. Additionally, we would like to thank Elder Merrill J. Bateman, Emeritus Seventy, for presenting his article "The Coming Forth of Plain and Precious Truths" at the symposium and allowing us to publish it herein.

1

The Coming Forth of Plain and Precious Truths

Elder Merrill J. Bateman

Elder Merrill J. Bateman is an emeritus member of the First Quorum of the Seventy.

The Book of Mormon's primary purpose is to be another witness of the Lord Jesus Christ.[1] In this regard the book includes prophetic visions of Christ's birth and life in Jerusalem, the global calamity that accompanied His atoning sacrifice and crucifixion, and His ministry among the people of the Americas following His resurrection. Yet the Book of Mormon has another major purpose. The prophet Nephi records what an angel explained to him—that the coming forth of the book of Mormon in the latter days would restore "many plain and precious things" that were "taken away from the gospel of the Lamb . . . and also many covenants of the Lord" (1 Nephi 13:26, 28). Changes in doctrine by various sects and councils after the time of Christ and His Apostles, together with translations and retranslations of the Bible from the time of Christ to the present resulted in parts of the gospel being lost (see 1 Nephi 13:27). The angel further explains to Nephi that the lost covenants (doctrines and principles) cause many people to stumble and lose their way (see 1 Nephi 13:29). Without key doctrines, people fail to understand the Lord's plan for His children on this earth, their spiritual heritage, the purpose of life, and their eternal potential.

With the coming forth of the Book of Mormon, these essential truths were again available and clear. Here we will examine the plain and precious truths restored with respect to the plan of salvation. These restored truths clarify one's understanding of life's purposes.

The Plan of Salvation

An important truth restored by the Book of Mormon is that the Father has a plan for His children—a plan that operated before we came to earth, a plan for this life, a plan that extends beyond the grave. The plan tells us how to live on this earth so that we will experience joy and happiness both here and hereafter. It discusses the environment in which we live and the actions we must take in order to achieve God's purposes for us. The plan, as outlined in the Book of Mormon, gives direction and order to our lives, and increases our understanding of life and the steps required to achieve the goal of eternal life.

The Bible, on the other hand, contains elements of the plan, but the elements are outlined less clearly. The plan's framework is missing, which results in confusion regarding the necessity of various elements, as will be discussed later.

The plan is known by a number of names in the Book of Mormon, but it is the same regardless of the name. It is called the "plan of salvation" (Alma 42:5), the "plan of mercy" (Alma 42:15), the "merciful plan of the great Creator" (2 Nephi 9:6), the "plan of our God" or the "great plan of the Eternal God" (2 Nephi 9:13; Alma 34:9), the "plan of redemption" (see Alma 12:25 33; 22:13), the "plan of restoration" (Alma 41:2), and the "plan of happiness" (Alma 42:16). A key part of the plan is called the doctrine of Christ or the gospel of Jesus Christ (see 2 Nephi 31:5–21; 3 Nephi 27:13–21). The plan is mentioned approximately thirty times in the Book of Mormon. The word "plan" as it relates to the plan of salvation does not appear in the King James Bible, and no phrase resembling "the plan of salvation" appears in any biblical translation.

The main elements of the plan include:

- A **council in heaven** of premortal spirit beings who were given agency to choose whether or not they would come to earth as part of their progression (see 2 Nephi 2:17; Alma 13:3).
- The **creation of an earth** for God's children to experience mortality (see 1 Nephi 17:36; 2 Nephi 2:14; Mosiah 4:9; 3 Nephi 9:15).
- The **Fall of Adam and Eve** that opened the door for humankind to be born on earth, to grow spiritually through the use of agency, and to experience temptation and ultimately death. The Fall resulted in two types of death: physical and spiritual. Physical death occurs when the spirit and body separate at the end of our mortal lives. The spiritual death brought about by the Fall is a separation from God. When men and women enter mortality they separate from God and experience spiritual death. This is called the first spiritual death. A second spiritual death also may occur as a result of disobedience to one or more of God's laws (see 2 Nephi 2; Alma 12).
- The **Savior's Resurrection and Atonement**. The Book of Mormon teaches that the Atonement had to be infinite and eternal. Therefore, it had to be performed by an infinite and eternal being. The Lord's atoning sacrifice makes it possible to overcome all these deaths mentioned above (see Alma 34:10, 14; Mosiah 3; 3 Nephi 11; Helaman 14:17).
- The **doctrine of Christ**, which includes His teachings and the covenants and ordinances that link us to the Atonement. The doctrine of Christ is also known as the gospel of Jesus Christ.
- The **resurrection of the physical body** and its reuniting with the spirit. The resurrection makes possible exaltation and eternal life (see Mosiah 15:20–24; Alma 40:16–18).
- A final step in the plan is a **righteous judgment** and assignment to a kingdom, one of the Lord's many mansions (see John 14:2; Enos 1:27; Ether 12:32).

The Book of Mormon brings new insights and clarity to these key elements of the plan that the Bible lacks.

The Council in Heaven and Our Premortality

A plan of salvation was presented by our Heavenly Father to His children in a premortal council. The plan called for the creation of an earth where Heavenly Father's spirit children could obtain a physical body, experience the challenges of mortality, and be tested regarding their willingness to follow the plan. The Father's children would have agency to choose for themselves (see Alma 13:3). The plan provided for a Savior to open the way for all of God's children to return to His presence and be judged according to their faithfulness. Those who strive to follow the plan are blessed with the companionship of the Holy Ghost. Without destroying agency, the Lord through the Holy Ghost helps individuals live the commandments prescribed by the plan. The ultimate reward is to be lifted up to the Father to receive eternal life.

Premortal Existence of Jesus Christ

An important truth to come forth through the Book of Mormon is the premortal existence of Jesus Christ as a separate personage from the Father. The appearance of the Savior to the brother of Jared in Ether chapter 3 makes clear that Christ existed before His birth, that He was a person of spirit, and that He was Jehovah, the God of the Old Testament.

Although the Bible suggests that Christ was Jehovah, many people have a concept of the Trinity that does not allow for a clear understanding of who Jehovah was and is and the role He played during Old Testament times as the Son of the Father.

One biblical passage pertaining to the Savior indicating that He was Jehovah occurs in John 8:56. Christ, speaking to the Jews in the temple, says: "Your father Abraham rejoiced to see my day: and he saw it, and was glad." The saying upset those listening and they then said, "Thou art not yet fifty years old, and hast thou seen Abraham?" Jesus said unto them, "Verily, verily, I say unto you, Before Abraham was, I am" (John 8:57–58). The Jews then took up stones to kill Christ because He stated that He was the Great I Am, the Jehovah of the Old Testament. Other biblical and Book of Mormon passages are plentiful, indicating that both Christ and we lived before life on earth.[2] In spite of these passages, many do not accept the notion that Christ and the Father are separate personages and that we lived as spirits before coming to earth.

People Foreordained to Callings

Another of the doctrines mentioned in the Bible and the Book of Mormon regarding premortality is the foreordination of individuals to various earthly roles when they came to earth. The Bible is explicit in stating that Christ was foreordained to be the Savior of the world before He was born (see 1 Peter 1:18–20). The Bible suggests the foreordination of others as well (see Jeremiah 1:5; Ephesians 1:4), but the Book of Mormon is clearer on the matter. The prophet Alma in the Book of Mormon states clearly that spirits living in the antemortal world were "called and prepared from the foundation of the world according to the foreknowledge of God" to serve in holy callings when they came to earth (Alma 13:3). Again, there is disagreement in the religious world concerning this truth.

The same Book of Mormon passage in Alma also indicates that men and women were free to choose in premortality—i.e., they were given agency to act according to their own wills. The fact that spirits have agency helps one understand the war that took place in heaven when Lucifer rebelled against the Father's plan when it was presented in the Grand Council and Satan and the angels that followed him were cast out (see Revelation 12:7–11).

Nature of Spirits

Another clarifying doctrine of the Book of Mormon with respect to premortality is an explicit statement regarding the nature of a spirit person. Although the Bible alludes to the form and substance of a person of spirit (see Luke 24:36–39), it is not clearly addressed.

Knowing that we lived as spirits prior to earth life, we may wonder, what were we like? Adherents of many faiths confuse the spiritual force used by God to govern the earth with the spirit of a person. In many faith traditions, the word "spirit" is often defined in one of three ways—an incorporeal being, a fiery essence of breath, or a liquid substance that connects the brain and the body.[3] In all three cases there is no material body or form. There are those within Christianity who believe that the resurrected Lord laid aside his physical body when he ascended to heaven and assumed an immaterial, noncorporeal existence with the Father and the Holy Spirit. Consequently, for them the spirit of man is also non-corporeal and immaterial. But what does it mean to be made in the image of God if God has no image?

The Book of Mormon clarifies misunderstandings on this matter. In Ether chapter 3, Jehovah appears to the brother of Jared on the mountain and uses his finger to give light to a set of stones. This event occurred thousands of years before Christ's birth. Upon seeing the Lord's finger, the brother of Jared exclaims, "I knew not that the Lord had flesh and blood." The Lord then says to him, "Because of thy faith thou hast seen that I shall take upon me flesh and blood; and never has man come before me with such exceeding faith as thou hast; for were it not so ye could not have seen my finger. Sawest thou more than this?" (Ether 3:8–9).

The brother of Jared says, "Nay; Lord, show thyself unto me" (Ether 3:10). The veil is then parted, and the brother of Jared sees the Lord in His fulness. The Savior then says, "Behold, I am he who was prepared from the foundation of the world to redeem my people. Behold, I am Jesus Christ. . . . This body, which ye now behold, is the body of my spirit; and man have I created after the body of my spirit; and even as I appear unto thee to be in the spirit will I appear unto my people in the flesh" (Ether 3:14, 16).

In one short passage, the Book of Mormon makes clear that the spirit body has the same form as the physical body. It is made of substance, but substance so refined that the natural eye cannot see it (see D&C 131:7). Knowing the form of one's spirit gives meaning to Genesis 1:26–27, which states that men and women were created in the image of God. That is true both spiritually and physically.

The creeds of Christianity have exacted a heavy toll on the most important truths one can know. Who is God? What is He like? Who am I? What is my spirit like? What is my relationship with the Father and the Son? What does it mean to be the offspring of God, to be His son or daughter? The truths needed to answer these questions are provided in the Book of Mormon.

Why the Fall of Adam?

The Bible describes the events that constitute the Fall of Adam, but it does not explain why the Fall was necessary. In the Book of Mormon, Lehi explains to his son Jacob why the Fall was necessary for humankind to progress and how the Atonement was prepared before the foundation of the world to mitigate its effects (see 2 Nephi 2).

Lehi gives two reasons for the Fall. The first is that Adam and Eve would have had no children in the Garden of Eden, given their state of innocence. Partaking of the fruit resulted in a change in which Adam and Eve recognized their nakedness and their physical bodies became mortal subject to death. In Eden, "they would have had no children; wherefore they would have remained in a state of innocence, having no joy, for they knew no misery; doing no good, for they knew no sin" (2 Nephi 2:23). The Bible supports the notion of innocence and the impossibility of having children as it states that they did not recognize their nakedness until their eyes were opened after partaking of the forbidden fruit (see Genesis 3:7). The Bible indicates that Eve was deceived, but Adam partook of the fruit knowingly (see 1 Timothy 2:14). Why did Adam partake? He came to understand that in order to fulfill the greater commandment of multiplying and replenishing the earth, he needed to remain with Eve. Lehi explained that without the Fall of Adam, the rest of God's children could not have come to earth (see 2 Nephi 2:25). Both Adam and Eve needed to partake of the fruit and enter into mortality in order to have children.

The second reason for the Fall was to provide an environment of opposites outside God's presence where men and women could grow spiritually by exercising their agency. Lehi explains why there must be opposites in all things. "If not so," Lehi says, "righteousness could not be brought to pass, neither wickedness, neither holiness nor misery, neither good nor bad." Lehi further states that if opposites did not exist, "all things must needs be a compound in one." This means there is "no life neither death, nor corruption nor incorruption, happiness nor misery, neither sense nor insensibility" (2 Nephi 2:11). Without opposites there would be no purpose in God's creation (see 2 Nephi 2:12–13). Spiritual growth occurs when one makes righteous choices. A person can only act for himself or herself if a choice exists (see 2 Nephi 2:16).

Elder Bruce R. McConkie said, "The whole plan of salvation, including both immortality and eternal life for all the spirit hosts of heaven, hung on their [Adam and Eve's] compliance with this command" to multiply and replenish the earth (see Genesis 1:28; Moses 2:28). This could only be accomplished if they partook of the fruit and fell. Elder McConkie continues, "[Adam] fell by breaking a lesser law—so that he too having transgressed, would become subject to sin and need a Redeemer and work out his own salvation, as would be the case upon whom the effects of his fall would come."[4]

The Atonement and Resurrection of Jesus Christ

The Atonement of Jesus Christ is the greatest event in the history of humankind. The Atonement reconciles men and women with God by making faith, repentance, and baptism efficacious. Whereas the Fall allowed for the spirit hosts of heaven to come to earth, the Atonement makes possible their return to the Father's presence. Through the Atonement, mortals become immortals, incorruptible—i.e., they rise from the grave and overcome physical and spiritual death through the Savior's sacrifice and Resurrection (see 1 Corinthians 15:42–44).

The New Testament clearly teaches that Jesus Christ experienced a literal bodily resurrection, and so will every other son and daughter of God (see Luke 24:36–39; 1 Corinthians 15:21–22). There are numerous biblical scriptures that indicate a resurrection of the physical body. Job bore testimony that "though . . . worms destroy this body, yet in my flesh shall I see God" (Job 19:26). When Christ appeared to his disciples after His Resurrection, He made clear that His body was composed of "flesh and bones" (Luke 24:39). When the Savior appeared to the Nephites following His ascension, He invited them to come one by one "that ye may thrust your hands into my side, and also that ye may feel the prints of the nails in my hands and in my feet" (3 Nephi 11:14). The prophet Zechariah indicates that when Christ returns for the Second Coming, people will see the wounds in His hands and feet (see Zechariah 13:6). In other words, He will come with a resurrected, physical body.

The Book of Mormon makes clear that it is flesh and bone that is resurrected and combined with the spirit that will stand before God to be judged (see 2 Nephi 2:8). Alma in speaking to his son, Corianton, indicated that there is a time between death and the resurrection in which the soul or spirit of man is taken home to God with the righteous received into a state of paradise and the wicked separated and assigned to a state of fearfulness (or spirit prison). Alma states that some have called the assignment to paradise the first resurrection. Alma then proceeds to clarify that this is not a resurrection in the true meaning of the word. He states that the Resurrection is "the reuniting of the soul with the body" (Alma 40:11–18).

The Atonement also makes possible men and women overcoming the two spiritual deaths. The Book of Mormon is clear in explaining the first and second spiritual deaths. The Bible is not clear. It speaks of a second spiritual death (see Revelation 20:6), but does not mention the first or differentiate between the two. Fortunately, the Book of Mormon describes what is meant by the different spiritual deaths and their relationship to the Atonement.

Overcoming the Physical Death Associated with Adam's Fall

The plan of salvation has a number of objectives that are accomplished through the Redeemer's sacrifice. The first is overcoming the effects of the Fall. As a result of the Fall, men and women receive mortal bodies that decay and ultimately die. In order to achieve eternal life, a resurrection or reuniting of an immortalized physical body with the spirit is necessary. The Savior's Atonement and Resurrection allow everyone to come forth from the grave in a newness of life. Everyone will be resurrected and overcome physical death. The Apostle John records, "all that are in the graves . . . shall come forth" (John 5:28–29), and the Apostle Paul confirms John's statement when he says that "there shall be a resurrection of the dead, both of the just and unjust" (Acts 24:15).

The First Spiritual Death

The Fall also caused a separation of Adam's and Eve's family from the presence of God. This is known as the first spiritual death. The prophet Samuel the Lamanite speaking of Christ's death says, "Yea, behold, this death bringeth to pass the resurrection, and redeemeth all mankind from the first death—that spiritual death; for all mankind, by the fall of Adam being cut off from the presence of the Lord, are considered as dead, both as to things temporal and to things spiritual" (Helaman 14:16). The prophet Samuel's statement makes clear that Christ's Atonement and Resurrection not only overcome physical death for all mankind, but also overcome the spiritual death brought about by the Fall. To use the prophet Samuel's words again, Christ's death and Resurrection "redeemeth all mankind from the first death—that spiritual death . . . and bringeth them back into the presence of the Lord (Helaman 14:16–17).

As noted above, the Bible is not clear on the two spiritual deaths. It mentions the second spiritual death in the Book of Revelation and implies the first spiritual death in 1 Corinthians 15. John the Revelator speaking of the last days states, "Blessed and holy is he that hath part in the first resurrection; on such the second death hath no power, but they shall be priests of God and of Christ, and shall reign with him a thousand years" (Revelation 20:6). Although the Bible teaches that those who come forth in the first resurrection will not suffer the second spiritual death, it still leaves us asking, "What is it? What is the difference between the first and second deaths?"

The first spiritual death is implied in the Apostle Paul's statement to the Corinthians when he links the consequences of Adam's Fall to the effects of the Atonement. He said, "For since by man came death, by man came also the resurrection of the dead. For as in Adam all die, even so in Christ shall all be made alive" (1 Corinthians 15:21–22). This statement is a reference to Christ overcoming physical death for everyone plus overcoming the spiritual death brought about by Adam's Fall—the first spiritual death. Adam's children are not responsible for physical death or the first spiritual death. The Savior's Atonement removes the burden of these two deaths.

Elder Tad R. Callister describes the power of the Atonement to overcome the first spiritual death in these words:

> The scriptures teach that every person, saint or sinner, will return to the presence of God after the resurrection. It may be only a temporary reunion in his presence, but justice requires that all that was lost in Adam be restored in Jesus Christ. Every person will return to God's presence, behold his face, and be judged for his own works. Then, those who have obeyed the gospel will be able to stay in his presence, while all others will have to be shut out of his presence a second time and will thus die what is called a second spiritual death.[5]

The Second Spiritual Death

Men and women are on earth with the expectation that they will learn how to make wise choices and grow spiritually. However, mistakes are made and sins are committed. The Apostle Paul told the Romans, "All have sinned, and come short of the glory of God" (Romans 3:23). Nephi noted that "no unclean thing can dwell with God" (1 Nephi 10:21; 15:34). Alma taught that men and women will suffer a "second death, which is a spiritual death" unless they become clean from their own sins (Alma 12:16).

The great plan of mercy called for the Savior to pay the price for sin, to take upon Himself the sins of all if they would exercise faith in Him and repent. The great prophet Isaiah stated that Christ would "[bear] our griefs and [carry] our sorrows," that he would be "wounded for our transgressions, [and] bruised for our iniquities," and that "with his stripes we are healed" (Isaiah 53:4–5). Upon seeing the Savior, John the Baptist exclaimed, "Behold the Lamb of God, which taketh away the sin of the world" (John 1:29).

Overcoming the first spiritual death is a free gift. Triumph over the second is conditional. Lehi explained to his son Jacob that Christ "offered himself a sacrifice for sin, to answer the ends of the law, unto all those who have a broken heart and a contrite spirit; and unto none else can the ends of the law be answered" (2 Nephi 2:7). The Apostle Paul explained to the Hebrews that Christ "became the author of eternal salvation unto all them that obey him" (Hebrews 5:9). The prophet Nephi explained to his people, "we know that it is by grace that we are saved, after all we can do" (2 Nephi 25:23). In order for people to overcome the second death, they have a part to play. A later section of this paper discusses the process by which one overcomes the second spiritual death through Christ's Atonement.

The Infinite and Eternal Atonement

An important truth clarified by the Book of Mormon concerns the type of sacrifice that must be made and the nature of the person required to perform it. In Amulek's sermon to the poor Zoramites, he describes the dimensions of the sacrifice required thus: "For it is expedient that there should be a great and last sacrifice; yea, not a sacrifice of man, neither of beast, neither of any manner of fowl; for it shall not be a human sacrifice; but it must be an infinite and eternal sacrifice" (Alma 34:10). He then goes on to say, "And behold, this is the whole meaning of the law, every whit pointing to that great and last sacrifice; and that great and last sacrifice will be the Son of God, yea, infinite and eternal" (Alma 34:14).

The Atonement must be infinite—that is, without end. Its effects must go on into the eternities. It covers all sin, all sorrow, all grief, all death. It must be timeless—that is, it must cover all those who lived before Christ came to earth as well as everyone thereafter. Alma, speaking to his son

Corianton, states that the souls who lived before Christ's earthly sojourn are as precious to the Lord as those who lived during and after His time (see Alma 39:16–19). Since man had agency in the antemortal world, the Atonement must reach back to a time before the foundations of this world were laid (see Alma 13:3). It also reaches forward into the spirit world where Christ directed the preaching of the gospel to the spirits in prison during the three days His body was in the tomb (see 1 Peter 3:18–20; 4:6). There would be no reason for the Savior to preach to the spirits in prison who lived on earth during the time of Noah if they could not repent and receive the blessings of the Atonement. The great and last sacrifice must encompass all of God's children, both before the time of Christ and after, both before the mortal life and after.

Infinite in Power

The Atonement must be infinite in power because of the coverage, reach and change required to qualify human beings for salvation. The Atonement covers every man, woman, and child who has lived, now lives, or will live on the earth. The Atonement brings forth all of God's creations from the grave. The apostle Paul taught that the Savior's sacrifice covers the resurrection of animals, beasts, fish, and birds (see 1 Corinthians 15:37–44; D&C 29:23–25).[6] Modern-day revelation teaches that God's creations cannot be numbered: "And as one earth shall pass away, and the heavens thereof even so shall another come; and there is no end to my works" (Moses 1:37–38). Moreover, the inhabitants of those other worlds are "begotten sons and daughters unto God," i.e., the Atonement covers them as well (D&C 76:23–24). A poetic version of section 76 states the infinite reach and power of the Atonement:

> And I heard a great voice, bearing record from heav'n,
> "He's the Savior, and only begotten of God—
> By him, of him, and through him, the worlds were all made,
> Even all that careen in the heavens so broad.
>
> "Whose inhabitants too, from the first to the last,
> Are sav'd by the very same Saviour of ours;
> And, of course, are begotten God's daughters and sons,
> By the very same truths and the very same pow'rs."[7]

No wonder Amulek stated that the Atonement had to be infinite.

Infinite in Love

There are numerous Book of Mormon passages that speak of the Father's and the Son's love. One of the most poetic, symbolic stories occurs in Nephi's and Lehi's dreams of the tree of life. In Nephi's dream, an angel shows Nephi a tree whose beauty is beyond description, whose "whiteness . . . did exceed the whiteness of the driven snow" (1 Nephi 11:8). Nephi wants to know the meaning of the tree. He is shown a man descending out of the heavens and is told to bear record that the person is the Son of God (see 1 Nephi 11:7). He is then shown a virgin in the city of Nazareth with a baby in her arms. The angel explains to Nephi that this baby is "the Lamb of God, yea, even the Son of the Eternal Father" (1 Nephi 11:21). Eventually, Nephi is shown the crucifixion. Nephi explains, "I looked and beheld the Lamb of God, that he was taken by the people; yea, the Son of the everlasting God was judged of the world; and I . . . saw that he was lifted up upon the cross and slain for the sins of the world" (1 Nephi 11:32–33). Helping Nephi to interpret the images he has seen, the angel asks: "Knowest thou the meaning of the tree?" Nephi's response: "Yea, it is the love of God, which sheddeth itself abroad in the hearts of the children of men; wherefore, it is the most desirable above all things" (1 Nephi 11:22). The tree is a symbol of God's love, and the greatest manifestation of that love is that He sent His Only Begotten Son, to suffer, die, and atone for the sins of all humankind (see 1 Nephi 11:13–33; John 3:16).

Lehi, in his dream, partakes of the tree's fruit and discovers its sweetness and wants his family to partake. The fruit represents the gifts of the Atonement—forgiveness, mercy, patience, kindness, love, hope, faith, temperance, immortality, glory, and eternal life (see 2 Peter 1:3–8). When one understands the depth and breadth of the Atonement, one comes to understand the infinite love and power that constitute its foundation.

A Witness of God's Eternal Power

Notice that Amulek also indicated that the Atonement had to be eternal in nature, meaning not only that it is without end, but that it is godlike power. Not only is the physical body raised from the grave, but the flesh is changed from a corruptible to an incorruptible state, from a natural to a spiritual body, never to die again (see 1 Corinthians 15:42; Romans 6:9).

In this same context, one should note that a "spiritual" body is not a "spirit" body. Christ made that clear when He explained to His disciples following His resurrection that "the spirit hath not flesh and bones, as ye see me have" (Luke 24:39). Amulek, in the Book of Mormon, teaches what a "spiritual" body is. He said, "The spirit and the body shall be reunited again in its perfect form; both limb and joint shall be restored to its proper frame" (Alma 11:43; see also v. 44). Thus, the "spiritual" body mentioned by Paul is a resurrected body of flesh and bones that has been immortalized and perfected. The power to change the body from a corruptible state to an immortal state is "eternal," or godly in nature.

The Book of Mormon teaches that the Atonement has the power to not only change the physical body but also to change the nature of man's spirit. King Benjamin taught that "the natural man is an enemy to God, and has been from the fall of Adam, and will be, forever and ever, unless he yields to the enticings of the Holy Spirit, and putteth off the natural man and becometh a saint through the atonement of Christ" (Mosiah 3:19). The Atonement, combined with the influence of the Holy Spirit, has the power to change man's character and behavior from its earthly nature to a saintly or Godlike nature.

Third Nephi records that the Savior also received power through the Atonement to draw all men to Him that they may be lifted up to the Father to be judged (see 3 Nephi 27:14).

As one comes to understand the Savior's sacrifice, its effects and its coverage, one realizes that the Atonement must be infinite and eternal in its power to save and exalt humankind. It has power to overcome the consequences of Adam's sin, it has the power to save men from their own sins, it has the power to change the nature of one's character as well as the physical body, and it has power to sanctify men and women that they may be lifted up to the Father. No wonder it took the power of a God, the Son of God, to accomplish it.

The Great and Last Sacrifice Must Be the Son of God

Only a God has the power and endurance to perform the Atonement (see D&C 19:18). King Benjamin in the Book of Mormon describes the Savior's suffering in these words: "And lo, he shall suffer temptations, and pain of body, hunger, thirst, and fatigue, even more than man can suffer, except it be unto death; for behold, blood cometh from every pore, so great shall be his anguish for the wickedness and the abominations of his people" (Mosiah

3:7). The Book of Mormon confirms the historicity of these events and clarifies that He actually sweat blood and suffered for our sins. Therefore, the Book of Mormon restores vital truths that the Atonement began in the Garden of Gethsemane.

As noted above, Christ achieved Godhood before coming to earth. He was Jehovah, the Almighty God of the Old Testament. His creations included the heavens and the earth. He was foreordained to be the Savior. His powers and Godhood continued into mortality through His birth. His mother was mortal. His Father was immortal. He was the Only Begotten Son of the Eternal Father (see 1 Nephi 11:21). That is why He stated near the end of His life, "Therefore doth my Father love me, because I lay down my life, that I might take it again. No man taketh it from me, but I lay it down of myself. I have power to lay it down, and I have power to take it again. This commandment have I received of my Father" (John 10:17–18). Speaking of Christ, the prophet Abinadi in the Book of Mormon, sums up His power with the following: "He is the light and life of the world; yea, a light that is endless, that can never be darkened; yea, and also a life which is endless, that there can be no more death" (Mosiah 16:9). Because he was an eternal being who lived without sin in mortality, he did not have to die. He chose to die, and therefore had the power to rise from the tomb.

The Intimate Atonement

The Book of Mormon teaches not only that the Atonement was infinite, but also intimate. Christ experienced the pain, suffering, grief, and death of every person. One of the great passages in the Book of Mormon is Alma's teachings to the people in Gideon in Alma chapter 7. His sayings concerning Christ not only teach the elements of the Atonement, but also describe the intimate nature of it. Alma teaches that Christ "shall go forth, suffering pains and afflictions and temptations of every kind; and this that the word might be fulfilled which saith he will take upon him the pains and the sicknesses of his people. And he will take upon him death, that he may loose the bands of death which bind his people; and he will take upon him their infirmities, that his bowels may be filled with mercy, according to the flesh, that he may know according to the flesh how to succor his people according to their infirmities" (Alma 7:11–12).

The Son of God performed the Atonement in the flesh in order to know fully how to succor His brothers and sisters in their extremities. He descended below all things that He might comprehend all things (see D&C 88:6). In the garden and on the cross, Christ experienced the deepest feelings of each human being. He felt our pains and sufferings, our sicknesses and griefs. His sojourn in mortality and his atoning experience gave him unique insights regarding our challenges, sorrows, and weaknesses. Those insights make it possible for him to come to our aid and help us through our trials and afflictions. It was not a collective mass of sin that He experienced, but the sins, wounds, and sufferings of an infinite stream of individuals. As Alma said, He knows according to the flesh how to succor each soul.

The Doctrine of Christ

The gospel of Jesus Christ is the good news, the good tidings or glad tidings that Christ restored during His ministry on earth. What are those good tidings? Here is one definition of the gospel accepted by many using the Bible: "That Christ died for our sins according to the scriptures, and that he was buried, and that he rose again on the third day" (1 Corinthians 15:3–4). Christ Himself adds to that definition in the Book of Mormon. He defines the gospel, or doctrine of Christ, as the Atonement, Resurrection, and Judgment, and then expands the definition to include the responsibilities that men and women have in the salvation process. In 3 Nephi chapter 27, Christ outlines the gospel for the righteous Nephites. His definition begins with the role He plays in the good news:

> Behold I have given unto you my gospel, and this is the gospel which I have given unto you—that I came into the world to do the will of my Father, because my Father sent me.
>
> And my Father sent me that I might be lifted up upon the cross, and after that I had been lifted up upon the cross, that I might draw all men unto me, that as I have been lifted up by men even so should men be lifted up by the Father, to stand before me, to be judged of their works, whether they be good or whether they be evil. (3 Nephi 27:13–14)

After explaining His role, Jesus outlines the principles of the gospel that men and women must live in order to be full beneficiaries of His Atonement (see 3 Nephi 27:16–21). The Savior states the following:

1. We must have faith in the Lord Jesus Christ.
2. We must repent of our sins.
3. We must be baptized in the name of Jesus Christ.
4. We must receive the gift of the Holy Ghost and be sanctified by it.
5. We must endure to the end.

Each step leads naturally to the next. For example, Mormon teaches, "The first fruits of repentance is baptism; and baptism cometh by faith unto the fulfilling the commandments . . . and because of meekness and lowliness of heart cometh the visitation of the Holy Ghost, which Comforter filleth with hope and perfect love, which love endureth by diligence unto prayer, until the end shall come, when all the saints shall dwell with God" (Moroni 8:25–26; see also 2 Nephi 31:5–20). Let me highlight just a few of the contributions of the Book of Mormon with respect to the doctrine of Christ.

Developing Faith in Christ

The Bible teaches the importance and necessity of faith in Christ but does not explain the process by which one obtains and builds faith. One reads in the Bible about events that establish faith in individuals. An example is the apostle Paul on the road to Damascus (see Acts 9). But for most people, and even for Paul, developing faith in Christ is a process that takes place over one's lifetime.

The Book of Mormon explains the manner in which people can build faith in Christ. Alma's discourse to the Zoramites on how faith develops is profound and unique. The path Alma outlined begins with a "desire to believe." The person must then act on that desire by conducting an experiment. The experiment is to plant a seed in one's heart. What is the seed? It is the "word of God." What is the word of God? It is the holy scriptures; it is the words of the prophets. Ultimately, "the word" is Christ. One must give place for Christ in one's heart. One must be willing to follow the Master. Alma then makes a promise. If we diligently strive to apply "the word" in our lives, the Holy Spirit will cause feelings to come into our souls. The seed will sprout and grow, and we will come to know that the seed is good and the gospel is true.

Alma then asks, "Because ye have tried the experiment, and planted the seed, and it swelleth and sprouteth . . . is your knowledge perfect?" (Alma

32:33–34). The answer is no, you have just begun. The seed is now a small seedling that requires further nourishment and care. It must continue to take root, grow, and mature before the tree yields fruit. As the tree continues to grow, our belief, faith, and hope in the Savior deepen because we feel the swelling motions that come through the Holy Ghost. Our commitment to action expands from wanting to know for ourselves to wanting to serve and help others. Service and consecration become part of one's life. As we serve others, the Holy Spirit provides additional witnesses that the seed is good and that forgiveness can be obtained. If with diligence, patience, and faith we continue to nourish the tree, it becomes fully rooted inside our souls and we can pluck the fruit thereof. A person filled by the fruit will "hunger not, neither . . . thirst" (Alma 32:42; see also vv. 41, 43). The fruits are the blessings of the Atonement—forgiveness, sanctification, and eternal life.

Baptism

First, as Mormon noted, faith leads to baptism. Amongst Christian denominations there is disagreement about how baptism is to be performed and whether it is necessary, but the necessity and mode of baptism are clearly outlined in the Book of Mormon. Jesus was emphatic with respect to the necessity of baptism. He told Nicodemus, who came by night inquiring what he needed to do to be saved, "Verily, verily, I say unto thee, Except a man be born of water and of the Spirit, he cannot enter into the kingdom of God" (John 3:5).

Second, after the Savior defined the gospel in 3 Nephi, He expounded on the necessity of baptism by saying:

> And no unclean thing can enter into his [the Father's] kingdom; therefore nothing entereth into his rest save it be those who have washed their garments in my blood, because of their faith, and the repentance of all their sins, and their faithfulness unto the end.
>
> Now this is the commandment: Repent, all ye ends of the earth, and come unto me and be baptized in my name, that ye may be sanctified by the reception of the Holy Ghost, that ye may stand spotless before me at the last day.
>
> Verily, Verily, I say unto you, this is my gospel. (3 Nephi 27:19–21)

Third, the Lord also gave the Nephites the mode of baptism. Shortly after His appearance, He called Nephi and gave him power to baptize and then instructed him to go down into the water with the person to be baptized. After saying a baptismal prayer, the person was to be immersed in the water (see 3 Nephi 11:23–26).

Fourth, the Book of Mormon is specific with regard to the baptism of little children. This is a significant doctrinal contribution of the Book of Mormon; while Christians for centuries have worried over the souls of deceased but unbaptized children, the Book of Mormon teaches that "little children need no repentance, neither baptism." The Lord revealed to the prophet, Mormon, that Christ "came into the world not to call the righteous but sinners to repentance; the whole need no physician, but they that are sick; wherefore, little children are whole, for they are not capable of committing sin; wherefore the curse of Adam is taken from them in me. . . . Behold I say unto you that this thing shall ye teach—repentance and baptism unto those who are accountable and capable of committing sin" (Moroni 8:8, 10).

The Gift of the Holy Ghost

The Book of Mormon also makes clear that every person is entitled to the gift of the Holy Ghost if they follow the path of faith, repentance, and baptism (see 2 Nephi 31:12). On the day of Pentecost, Peter promised the multitude the gift of the Holy Ghost if they would "repent, and be baptized . . . in the name of Jesus Christ" (Acts 2:38). The Book of Mormon is more explicit in stating that the gift of the Holy Ghost is given by the laying on of hands by those who have authority given to them by Jesus Christ (see 3 Nephi 18:36–37; Moroni 2:2).

The Power of the Book of Mormon

Let me conclude with a story about the power of the Book of Mormon. The plain and precious truths found in Alma's sermon in Alma 32 impacted a young soldier in Afghanistan. As a teenager from an active LDS family, he determined to leave the Church even though his faithful parents had given him "every opportunity to learn the gospel of Jesus Christ."[8] In order to escape his parents' disapproval, he joined the military where he became a medic. In the ensuing years, he worked hard and played hard. Eventually he married, and the couple was blessed with children.

A time came when his unit was sent to Afghanistan. Although he adapted well in the beginning to the extraordinary demands, eventually "exposure to death and the destruction of war began to take its toll," he said. "While I continued to perform my duties as required, fear ruled my thoughts. I feared death and the justice of God, and I questioned whether I would see my wife and children again. The sins that I had so flippantly committed were now unbearable, but I had nowhere to turn for relief."[9]

A close brush with death and spiritual promptings caused him to begin reading a copy of the Book of Mormon that his mother had given him. Over time he realized that the fear of death had diminished, but he still vowed not to return to the Church. One day he read Alma's discourse on faith and it changed his life. The passage begins, "Now, as I said concerning faith—that it was not a perfect knowledge—even so it is with my words. Ye cannot know of their surety at first, unto perfection, any more than faith is a perfect knowledge. But behold, if ye will awake and arouse your faculties, even to an experiment upon my words, and exercise a particle of faith, yea, even if ye can no more than desire to believe, let this desire work in you, even until ye believe in a manner that ye can give place for a portion of my words" (Alma 32:26–27).

Although he had almost no faith or hope, he did have a "desire to believe" that his sins could be forgiven through the Atonement of Jesus Christ. He continued studying the Book of Mormon in Afghanistan and continued when he returned home. He said that it took many months after he returned home to gain a testimony of the gospel and follow the steps necessary to receive forgiveness, but he committed himself to Alma's pattern, and peace and forgiveness came.[10] This story is an example of the clear and powerful truths that have come forth through the Book of Mormon and the effect they can have on the lives of individual seekers of truth.

Conclusion

The Book of Mormon came forth as not only another witness for the Lord Jesus Christ but also a restoration of plain and precious truths necessary for a full understanding of the Lord's plan, including the premortality and foreordination of Jesus Christ, the preexistence of God's spirit children, the infinite and eternal nature of Christ's Atonement, and the principles of the gospel we must live in order to fully access that Atonement. There are other plain and precious truths restored by the book that have not been considered. Their exegesis is left to others. The Book of Mormon is like a box of jewels—plain and precious truths for the fulness of times. Those truths, omitted from or not clearly explained in the Bible, have been restored in the last days to teach us where we came from and how to live.

Notes

1. The title page of the Book of Mormon.
2. Bible scriptures indicating a premortal existence for Christ and His role as Jehovah include John 1:1, 3:13, 6:62, 8:58, 16:28, and 17:5. Book of Mormon passages that indicate that Christ lived in an antemortal world and was Jehovah include 1 Nephi 21:26; Mosiah 3:5; 3 Nephi 1:13; 26:5; Ether 3:16; and Moroni 10:34. Biblical references regarding the premortality of men and women include Numbers 16:27; Job 38:7; Jeremiah 1:5; John 9:2; Acts 17:28; Romans 8:29; Ephesians 1:4; Hebrews 12:9; Jude 1:6; and Revelation 12:7. Key Book of Mormon passages regarding man's premortality are Alma 13:3 and Helaman 14:17.
3. Michael Maher and Joseph Bolland, "Spirit," in *The Catholic Encyclopedia: An International Work of Reference on the Constitution, Doctrine, Discipline, and History of the Catholic Church*, ed. Charles George Herbermann and others (New York: Robert Appleton Company, 1912), 14:220.
4. Bruce R. McConkie, *The Promised Messiah* (Salt Lake City: Deseret Book, 1978). 220–21.
5. Tad R. Callister, *The Infinite Atonement* (Salt Lake City: Deseret Book, 2000), 46.
6. See Bruce R. McConkie, *Mormon Doctrine*, 2nd ed. (Salt Lake City: Bookcraft, 1958), 578.
7. "The Answer," *Times and Seasons*, February 1, 1843, 82–83.
8. Eric Carter, "Book of Mormon in the Battlefield," *Ensign*, January 2015, 28–29.
9. Carter, "Book of Mormon," 28.
10. Carter, "Book of Mormon," 29.

2

The Probation of a Teenage Seer

Joseph Smith's Early Experiences with Moroni

Steven C. Harper

Steven C. Harper is a historian at the Church History Department, The Church of Jesus Christ of Latter-day Saints.

Millennia before Joseph Smith reached his teen years in rural New York, the God of Israel revealed that he would raise a choice seer from among the descendants of Joseph of Egypt and command him and give him "power to bring forth my word" (see 2 Nephi 3:6–13). Although Joseph Smith was foreordained to be a seer, he had to learn and grow through his life experiences and rise to his calling to bring forth the Lord's word—the Book of Mormon. His early experience with seer stones seemed to provide some foundation for this later work, and the angel Moroni offered valuable tutoring through a four-year probationary period.

Joseph's Early Years

Joseph Smith's 1838–39 history says that after his First Vision in the spring of 1820, he "continued to pursue [his] common vocation" (Joseph Smith—History 1:27), meaning that he farmed with his father and took odd jobs to supplement the family income. Joseph talked about his teenage struggles and sins and his efforts to overcome them: For instance, an early draft of his manuscript history reads:

> During the space of time which intervened between the time I had the vision and the year Eighteen hundred and twenty three, (having been forbidden to join any of the religious sects of the day, and being of very tender years, and persecuted by those who ought to have been my friends and to have treated me kindly and if they supposed me to be deluded to have endeavoured in a proper and affectionate manner to have reclaimed me) I was left to all kinds of temptations, and, mingling with all kinds of society I frequently fell into many foolish errors and displayed the weakness of youth and the corruption of human nature which I am sorry to say led me into divers temptations to the gratification of many appetites offensive in the sight of God.[1]

A few years later, while preparing the history for publication under Joseph's direction, Willard Richards clarified Joseph's confession by deleting some words and by adding the following ones:

> In making this confession, no one need suppose me guilty of any great or malignant sins. A disposition to commit such was never in my nature. But I was guilty of levity, and sometimes associated with jovial company, etc., not consistent with that character which ought to be maintained by one who was called of God as I had been. (Joseph Smith—History 1:28)[2]

Joseph was not guilty of sins that unalterably shaped his destiny, but evidence indicates that he was troubled by a nagging covetousness, complicated by his family's often being on the verge of, but never finally attaining, a comfortable living. God had work for Joseph Smith to do, but Satan determined to thwart it. Joseph's autobiographies, his mother's memoir, Oliver Cowdery's historical letters, and Joseph Knight's autobiography enable us to watch the teenager struggle to choose between God's plan for him and Satan's efforts to undermine the acquisition and translation of the gold plates. These records make it possible to observe how God sent a messenger (Moroni) to tutor, chasten, and empower Joseph, finally enabling the vulnerable, unlearned farmer to begin a most marvelous work and a wonder: the translation and publication of the Book of Mormon.

To identify Joseph as a tempted—even at times a foolish—teenager may seem antithetical to the justified praises sung to "the man who communed with Jehovah."[3] But this is the story of how he became such, so it must first establish what he candidly admitted about his flawed beginnings and need for development.

Aside from his aforementioned confession, he wrote in 1832 that many days after his First Vision in 1820, "I fell into transgressions and sinned in many things which brought a wound upon my soul." He said further, "When I was seventeen years of age I called again upon the Lord and he shewed unto me a heavenly vision for behold an angel of the Lord came and stood before me and it was by night and he called me by name and he said the Lord had forgiven me my sins."[4]

Joseph's faith in Jesus Christ, humility, and resulting repentance, including his choice to respond positively to chastisement, suggest why the Lord called Joseph to be the seer to bring forth the Book of Mormon. Relying on the Lord and responding faithfully to his instructions, he overcame these sins and struggles to indeed bring forth a marvelous work.

Context for Joseph Smith the Seer

Knowing about Joseph's activities and surrounding culture between 1820 (when he received the First Vision) and 1823 (when Moroni appeared to him) helps to clarify his growth and experiences with the gold plates.

Joseph's world was shifting rapidly from an agrarian economy to an industrialized, capitalistic marketplace. For many, that meant opportunity and wealth. But for many others, including the Smith family, it meant one setback after another. Like the markets, churches were becoming more free and open, competing for converts the same way that shoemakers or whiskey distillers were competing for consumers. Many, including Joseph Smith, struggled with the twin developments of market revolution and the multiplication of churches from which to choose. His family experienced these developments as pressure, an escalation of stress and anxiety about both their home economy and their eternal salvation.

This financial stress drove a substantial group of settlers to "an unconquerable expectation of finding buried treasure in the earth."[5] There is evidence that both Joseph and his father joined in some of the activities of a group of neighborhood treasure seekers who looked for buried riches in nocturnal rituals.[6] For them and many other Christian people, treasure seeking made good sense, though most "respectable" folks, the type Joseph thought ought to have befriended him if they were good Christians, thought treasure seeking was beneath them.[7] But historian Alan Taylor explained why treasure seeking made sense in that time and place: it met the needs of some people who felt pressured by the culture's demand to get more possessions and more religion. In other words, treasure seeking promised "both quick wealth and a sense of power over the supernatural world."[8]

Many treasure seekers appealed to guardian spirits or charted the cycles of the moon to increase their chances of discovering riches. They also "turned increasingly to 'seer stones' or 'peep stones'" in order to find riches.[9] While such a practice may seem odd today, this skepticism is an assumption of modern culture. It has not always been the dominant idea. As the Bible attests, in ancient Israel, certain stones were associated with the priestly or prophetic office and considered a means of revelation.[10] The Bible says that Jacob, Moses, and Aaron had powerful rods and that Joseph of Egypt had a cup "whereby indeed he divineth" (Genesis 44:5).[11] In the Book of Mormon, Alma taught his son Helaman a prophecy from the Lord, saying, "I will prepare unto my servant Gazelem, a stone which shall shine forth in darkness unto light" (Alma 37:23). And the Lord prepared two stones for Jared's brother to bury with his records, stones that could be used to translate (see Ether 3:22–24). Perhaps basing their hopes and ideas on biblical precedents like these, several magician-mathematicians, including Isaac Newton, sought after or used marvelous stones in Renaissance and early modern Europe. John Dee, for example, taught algebra and navigation, sought to commune with angels, and used a translucent stone that has been on display in the British Museum.[12]

Joseph evidently discovered one or more seer stones after his First Vision and before he knelt to pray for forgiveness before Moroni's first visit in September 1823.[13] There is no reason to reject the basic assertion that Joseph searched for buried treasure using a marvelous stone, even though the claim is made by some of his antagonists. Joseph did not dispute that claim, and people who loved, trusted, and followed him confirmed that he had such a stone.[14] A man who hired Joseph reported that Joseph's search for a seer stone was inspired by an earlier experience of seeing it through a stone that belonged to a neighbor girl.[15] Another neighbor said that Joseph could see in a stone they found while digging a well.[16] Joseph's mother also acknowledged his gift of seership, saying that Joseph "was in possession of certain means, by which he could discern things that could not be seen by the natural eye."[17] Joseph Knight, who employed Joseph in 1826 and who converted shortly after the Church was organized, wrote that Joseph "looked in his glass," meaning his stone.[18] Brigham Young later used the term *seer stone* to describe this object, called "means" by Lucy and "glass" by Joseph Knight.[19] (For more about Joseph Smith's use of seer stones, see chapter 4 in the present volume.)

However, the most important point here is not the revelatory object, or what the scriptures repeatedly call the "means" (Mosiah 8:18; 28:13; Alma 37; D&C 8:9; 10:4; 20:8). The point of emphasis here is the gift of revelation itself. As evidenced by the above accounts, Joseph had a gift similar to the one described in this Book of Mormon passage:

> A seer is a revelator and a prophet also; and a gift which is greater can no man have. . . .
>
> But a seer can know of things which are past, and also of things which are to come, and by them shall all things be revealed, or, rather, shall secret things be made manifest, and hidden things shall come to light, and things which are not known shall be made known by them, and also things shall be made known by them which otherwise could not be known.
>
> Thus God has provided a *means* that man, through faith, might work mighty miracles; therefore he becometh a great benefit to his fellow beings. (Mosiah 8:16–18; emphasis added)

Thus Joseph, as a teenager, had the "means" that, through faith, he could "work mighty miracles." But although he evidently had the ability of seership early on, he was in the process of becoming the Lord's seer, learning how to apply the gift of revelation (see D&C 8:2–4).

Moroni's Instructions

On September 21, 1823, Joseph went to bed but not to sleep. "I was verry conscious," he later said of that night, "that I had not kept the commandments, and I repented hartily for all my sins and transgression, and humbled myself."[20] Then light flooded the room, making it brighter than at midday, and an angel appeared, striking, luminous, and standing in the air. Joseph shrank in fear for a moment before the messenger spoke his name, introduced himself as Moroni, and announced that God had work for Joseph to do.[21]

"He told me of a sacred record which was written on plates of gold," Joseph remembered, adding, "I saw in vision the place where they were deposited."[22] It was the sacred history of a lost civilization, Christians the Savior had visited, Moroni said, and with it were two stones—means God had prepared for its translation. The golden plates were now concealed in a nearby hill with these seer stones.[23]

Moroni told Joseph that whoever had the stones and could see in them was a seer, and to Joseph the news was both fascinating and somewhat familiar. He knew that he had the gift of which Moroni spoke because he had already discovered it through his use of seer stones. Now, the Lord had sent the angel as a mentor to help Joseph rise to the gift's innate potential to perform a marvelous work.

Then Moroni "commenced quoting the prophecies of the Old Testament," first from Malachi, who described the coming day "that shall burn as an oven" and said that the wicked would be left without root or branch. He then made Malachi's distant prophecy proximate: "I will reveal unto you [Joseph] the Priesthood, by the hand of Elijah the prophet, before the coming of the great and dreadful day of the Lord. . . . And he shall plant in the hearts of the children the promises made to the fathers, and the hearts of the children shall turn to their fathers. If it were not so, the whole earth would be utterly wasted at his coming" (see Joseph Smith—History 1:36–39).

How much Joseph Smith understood is not clear, but over time he learned of Moroni's meaning: God had chosen Joseph to restore the powerful priesthood ordinances in which solemn covenants could bind families to God and, by leading them to eternal lives, fulfill the plan of redemption that this earth was created to facilitate. Otherwise all the effort and energy put forth in creating this earth would be wasted at the Lord's coming.[24]

That was heady stuff for a seventeen-year-old. And there was more. Moroni quoted from Isaiah chapter 11, which foretells that Christ will come in glory, might, and vengeance to separate the righteous from the wicked. But not before setting "his hand again the second time" and gathering "the outcasts of Israel" by setting up an "ensign for the nations," a standard, or in other words, a church with a commission to preach the gospel to the whole world.[25]

Moroni continued by quoting Acts 3:22–23, prophesying that all who failed to hear the Lord's warning voice and gather to his ensign would "be destroyed." He then cited Joel 2:28–32: "I will pour out my spirit upon all flesh; and your sons and your daughters shall prophesy, your old men shall dream dreams, your young men shall see visions." Moreover, cataclysms and terrible judgments would be visited upon all who failed to build Zion. In the end, Zion builders alone would be delivered. Moroni told Joseph "that the fullness of the gentiles was soon to come in," meaning that the large-scale spread of the gospel to all nations loomed imminently in the future. Then, Joseph explains, "[Moroni] quoted many other passages of scripture and offered many explanations which cannot be mentioned here."[26]

Now, standing midair in Joseph's room, Moroni explained that Joseph could not have the plates or seer stones yet, and warned that if he showed them to others without permission once he received them, he would be destroyed. Joseph envisioned the hillside in which Moroni deposited the plates over a millennium earlier. Then the light gathered around the messenger and he ascended through a conduit "right up into heaven," leaving Joseph in a dark, still room, "marvelling greatly at what had been told to me by this extraordinary messenger."[27]

"I lay musing on the singularity of the scene," Joseph remembered, "when in the midst of my meditation," Moroni reappeared. He "again related the very same" message, then added more detail on the "great judgments which were coming upon the earth" before ascending again. "Sleep had fled from my eyes," Joseph wrote, "and I lay overwhelmed in astonishment at what I had both seen and heard."[28]

Then Moroni appeared a third time, relayed the same message, and cautioned Joseph "that Satan would try to tempt me (in consequence of the indigent circumstances of my father's family) to get the plates for the purpose of getting rich, This he forbid me, saying that I must have no other object in view in getting the plates but to glorify God, and must not be influenced by any other motive but that of building his kingdom, otherwise I could not get them."[29]

Joseph's mother wrote later that Moroni added "a few words of caution and instruction: thus, that he must beware of covetousness; and he must not suppose the record is to be brought forth with the view of getting gain; for this was not the case; but that it was to bring forth light and intelligence, which had for a long time been lost to the world: and, that when he went to get the plates, he must be on his guard, or his mind would be filled with darkness."[30]

As scholar Terryl Givens summarized Joseph's situation, "He was neither to exhibit the plates to anyone nor to think of alleviating his family's acute impoverishment by selling them" or by selling the book he could publish from them.[31] Seeking fame and fortune—two of the most potent temptations—was explicitly, absolutely forbidden by God's messenger. Warned against the temptations he would face, Joseph had to choose whether or not he would follow God's plan. In fact, during his mortal life, Moroni had written of a young Joseph, chosen to translate the sacred records and potentially covetous of the wealth embedded in a stack of precious metal: "The plates . . . are of no worth because of the commandment of the Lord. For he truly saith that no one shall have them to get gain; but the record thereof is of great worth; and whoso shall bring it to light, him will the Lord bless" (Mormon 8:14–16).

When Moroni ascended again, Joseph "was again left to ponder on the strangeness of what I had just experienced" but was interrupted by a rooster announcing the break of dawn. Joseph arose and went to work as usual.[32]

Attempt to Take the Plates

Joseph, Alvin, and their father began harvesting together, but Joseph seemed preoccupied. "Joseph," Alvin told him, "we must keep to work or we shall not get our task done." Joseph tried to get back to work, but when his father saw how weak he was, he sent Joseph home.[33] "I started with the intention of going to the house;" Joseph wrote, "but, in attempting to cross the fence out of the field where we were, my strength entirely failed me, and I fell helpless on the ground," unconscious. As he woke, Joseph saw "the same messenger" whom he had seen the night before.[34]

According to Joseph's mother, Moroni told Joseph the night before to tell his father what he had heard and seen, but Joseph had not.[35] "Why?" the angel asked him. "I was afraid my father would not believe me," Joseph replied. Moroni then promised that Joseph's father would believe every word.[36] "I obeyed," Joseph wrote, tellingly. "I rehearsed the whole matter to him. He replied to me that it was of God, and told me to go and do as commanded by the messenger."

Joseph reported to a hill known simply to the Smiths as "a hill of considerable size." There, near the top, on the west side, Joseph found the stone which concealed the box in which the plates were deposited. Joseph found a tree branch, jammed one end of it "under the edge of the stone, and with a little exertion raised it up." He remembered, "I looked in and there indeed did I behold the plates, the Urim and Thumim and the Breastplate as stated by the messenger."[37]

Here Joseph's Manuscript History is terse: "I made an attempt to take them out but was forbidden by the messenger."[38] Oliver Cowdery wrote in 1835 that Joseph had experienced "the visions of heaven during the night, and also seeing and hearing in open day; but the mind of man is easily turned, if it is not held by the power of God through the prayer of faith," and as Joseph walked to the hill, "two invisible powers were operating upon his mind . . . one urging the certainty of wealth and ease in this life, [which] had so powerfully wrought upon him" by the time he arrived that the angel's instructions "had entirely gone from his recollection." Oliver didn't blame Joseph. "He was young, and his mind easily turned from correct principles," but also, Oliver acknowledged, he was teachable and ready "to be lead into the great work of God, and be qualified to perform it in due time."[39]

According to Oliver, Joseph "had heard of the power, of enchantment, and a thousand like stories, which held the hidden treasures of the earth, and suposed that physical exertion and personal strength was only necessary to enable him to yet obtain the object of his wish." Oliver had earlier stated, "On attempting to take possession of the records a shock was produced upon his system, by an invisible power, which deprived him in a measure, of his natural strength."[40]

Agonizing that he was powerless to take the plates, Joseph cried out to the Lord, "Why can I not obtain them?" Moroni's reply came: "You have not kept the commandments of the Lord which I gave unto you." He explained to Joseph how succumbing to temptation could teach him of "the power of the advisory [*sic*]," commanded him to repent, and promised the Lord's forgiveness if he would. Joseph remembered what he had been taught and began to pray, and the Spirit returned.[41]

Joseph was teachable, and Moroni said to Joseph, "Now I will show you the difference between light and darkness and the operation of a good Spirit and an evil one[.] an evil spirit will try to crowd your mind with every evil and wicked thing to keep every good thought and feeling out of your mind but you must keep your mind always staid upon God that no evil may come into your heart."[42] According to Oliver Cowdery, Moroni showed Joseph a vision of "the prince of darkness, surrounded by his innumerable train of associates," and taught, "all this is shown, the good and the evil, the holy and impure, the glory of God and the power of darkness, that you may know hereafter the two powers and never be influenced or overcome by that wicked one."[43]

So Joseph returned home from the hill empty-handed but full of knowledge. He admitted in his 1832 autobiography, "I had been tempted of the advisary and saught the Plates to obtain riches and kept not the commandme[n]t that I should have an eye single to the Glory of God therefore I was chastened."[44] According to Lucy, the angel told Joseph "that he could not take them from the place wherein they were deposited, until he had learned to keep the commandments of God," clarifying that Joseph needed to become "not only willing, but able to do it."[45]

In his later history, Joseph rendered the story more matter-of-factly and said simply that he learned on that first visit to the hill

> that the time for bringing them forth had not yet arrived, neither would untill four years from that time; but he told me that I should come to that place precisely in one year from that time, and that he would there meet with me, and that I should continue to do so untill the time should come for obtaining the plates. Accordingly as I had been commanded I went at the end of each year, and at each time I found the same messenger there and received instruction and intelligence from him at each of our interviews respecting what the Lord was going to do, and how and in what manner his kingdom was to be conducted in the last days.[46]

Readers of this passage in Joseph's history often assume that he knew at the time that it would be four years before he received the plates, but he did not. All he knew was that the time was not yet, and that he should return in exactly one year and continue faithful until the unspecified time came. Joseph was not simply to pass time until he got the plates regardless of his behavior. He was to prepare himself by gaining experience in keeping the commandments of God and gaining strength to resist temptations; he was to prove himself faithful to the Lord's instructions and get the plates because of his obedience.

A Four-Year Probation

Joseph's four-year probation was characterized not only by divine visitations and adversarial interferences, but also by the vicissitudes of everyday family responsibilities as he sought to make ends meet at home, and later with his bride, Emma Hale. Throughout these years, God, largely through the angel Moroni, mentored Joseph to fulfill his potential as the seer who would obtain and protect the buried golden plates, translate them through the gift of God, and ultimately shepherd the sacred writings into print.

Joseph farmed and helped his brother Alvin build a respectable middle-class frame home for their aging parents. After a day's work Joseph's family gathered, "all seated in a circle . . . listening in breathless anxiety to the religious teachings of a boy eighteen years of age." He urged them not to tell others, fearing rejection and even violence against him.[47] Covetous neighbors—treasure seekers—might get word and demand the treasure. The Smith family members were to keep confidential that which Moroni had revealed in order to prove themselves trustworthy of obtaining further knowledge. "If we are wise and prudent in that which [is] revealed to us," Joseph taught them, "God is able to make all things known to us." His father agreed and promised that they would try to live worthily to be so trusted by God.[48]

But life was not without hardship. "On the 15 of Nov[ember 1823]," Lucy remembered, "Alvin was taken very sick." The family doctor was summoned but unavailable. Another came instead and "administered to him although the patient objected much against it[,] a heavy dose of Calomel." Alvin soon recognized that he would not survive. He charged Hyrum to finish the frame home and take care of his parents in their old age. He spoke to each of his siblings in turn, telling Joseph, now nearly eighteen, "I am going to die now[.] The distress which I suffer and the sensations that I have tell me my time is very short[.] I want you to be a good boy & do everything that lays in your power to obtain the records[.] Be faithful in receiving instruction and in keeping every commandment that is given you." After an affectionate farewell to two-year-old Lucy, Alvin died.[49]

By the following spring, 1824, family routines returned to normal. A new preacher in town taught the need for the different denominations to agree and "worship God with one mind and one heart." Lucy Mack Smith "wished to join them, and I tried to persuade my husband to do so." Joseph Sr. attended a few times, and the children—except Joseph—followed Lucy. Joseph assured his mother that he could take his Bible "and go out into the woods and learn more in two hours than you could if you were to go to meeting two years." Joseph was growing confidently into his calling. He told his mother that it would not hurt her to join, but prophesied that though the leader of the church preached piously, within one year he would take the last cow of a widowed mother of eight to satisfy a debt. Lucy, who had long since perceived that her son had a gift, was even more impressed when the fellow fulfilled Joseph's prophecy.[50]

Such religion could not satisfy Joseph. Though many came preaching various doctrines, he remained apart, waiting for more instruction by a messenger sent from the presence of God. According to Lucy, Moroni finally told Joseph he could obtain the plates on September 22, 1824, if he would keep them in his hands, take them straight home, and immediately secure them there in a trunk with a good lock and key. The whole family, most of all Joseph, anxiously anticipated that he would return home with them.[51]

He went to the hill on the appointed day, pried up the stone that covered the plates, and looked down on them. He reached down and lifted the plates from their stone box when, according to his mother, "the thought flashed across his mind that there might be something more in the box," something he could profit from after all. Excited, Joseph laid the plates down to cover the box, planning to come back later for the rest. When he turned back to pick up the plates, they were gone, "but where he knew not nor did he know by what means it had been taken away." Alarmed, Joseph knelt and prayed. The angel appeared "and told him that he had not done as he was commanded," that he was still tempted "to secure some imaginary treasure," that he was still too easily overcome by the powers of darkness, not yet vigilant enough, not yet motivated solely by the glory of God.[52]

After the rebuke Moroni allowed Joseph to raise the stone again and see that the plates were safe in their stone box. Joseph reached for them again but was hurled back. The angel left, and Joseph rose and returned to the house, weeping, disappointed, and fearing that his family would no longer believe him.[53]

Joseph was no sooner in the door than his father asked whether he had obtained the plates. "No, Father," he said. "I could not get them."

"Did you see them?" his father asked.

"Yes," replied Joseph, "I saw them, but could not take them."

"I would have taken them," his father said earnestly, "if I had been in your place."

Subdued, Joseph said, "You do not know what you say. I could not get them, for the angel of the Lord would not let me."[54]

Joseph then related the whole story, causing his parents to fear that he may never qualify to get the plates. "We therefore," Lucy remembered, "doubled our dilligence in prayer and supplication to God, in order that he might be more fully instructed in his duty, and be preserved from all the wiles and machinations of him 'who lieth in wait to deceive.'"[55] Though it was emotionally painful, Joseph's 1824 attempt to obtain the plates was yet another learning opportunity that helped train him into a steward of the Book of Mormon plates, and into a seer who could translate the sacred writings inscribed on them.

There are no detailed records of what happened the next September, in 1825. There is evidence, however, that the temptation for Joseph to use his gift for material gain intensified rather than diminished. With Alvin's death, the burden of finishing the frame home and meeting the annual mortgage payment fell increasingly to Hyrum and then, when he married, to Joseph. They scoured the countryside for odd jobs. In October of 1825, Josiah Stowell, a farmer from southeastern New York, enticed Joseph and his father to come to work for him. Stowell had, according to Joseph, "heard something of a silver mine having been opened by Spaniards in Harmony, Susquahanah County, State of Pennsylvania, and had previous to my hiring with him been digging in order if possible to discover the mine."[56] Stowell had also heard of Joseph's gift. He had learned, as Lucy put it, "that he was in possession of certain means, by which he could discern things, that could not be seen by the natural eye." Stowell "offered high wages" for such skill, appealing to the struggling Smith family.[57]

Now Joseph had a dilemma: Should he sell his reputation as a seer for fourteen dollars a month to help his family make the mortgage payment on the farm they had worked awfully hard to improve? It seemed like a harmless decision, and Joseph decided to follow Stowell to Susquehanna County. But in the winter of 1826, Stowell's nephew, Peter Bridgeman, filed a complaint against Joseph with a justice of the peace in South Bainbridge, New York. Joseph was evidently arrested and tried for disorderly conduct that probably stemmed from using his stone to search for buried treasure. One account of the trial reports that the Smiths were "mortified that the wonderful power which God had so miraculously given . . . should be used only in search of filthy lucre."[58]

The digging stopped after a month, and Joseph Sr. returned home while Joseph Jr. stayed to work for the Knight family of Colesville, New York. According to Joseph Knight Jr., Joseph told the Knights "that he had seen a vision, that a personage had appeared to him and told him where there was a book of ancient date buried." They believed and encouraged Joseph.[59]

While digging for Stowell, Joseph boarded with the family of Isaac Hale in Harmony, where he met their tall, dark-haired daughter, Emma. Encouraged by his parents, Josiah Stowell, and the Knights, Joseph courted Emma and sought her hand. On January 18, 1827, Emma Hale married Joseph Smith in South Bainbridge, New York, in a simple ceremony by a justice of the peace. Emma and Joseph then went directly to Manchester, where they lived with Joseph's parents.[60]

But just as Lucy finished getting the new house ready for their arrival, and while she was thanking the Lord for the "prospect of a quiet and comfortable old age," their contractor came to the door to tell her that he had agreed with the mortgage agent to purchase the home and farm. Friends circulated a petition, protesting the sale. Finally the Smiths persuaded Lemuel Durfee to buy the place and let them continue there. "We were now renters," Lucy remembered, deeply discouraged. Once more their fortunes had failed.[61]

"Soon after this," Lucy wrote, Joseph went to town on an errand for his father. Lucy remembered that "he did not return home until the night was considerably advanced," and she worried because she was "aware that God intended him for a good and important work; consequently we expected that the powers of darkness would strive against him more than any other."[62]

"Joseph, why have you stayed so late," his father asked when he finally arrived. "Father," he answered after a while, "I have had the severest chastisement that I ever had in my life." Joseph's father wished to know who presumed to find fault with his son. "Father," Joseph said, "it was the angel of the Lord. He says I have been negligent that the time has now come when the record should be brought forth and that I must be up and doing that I must set myself about the things which God has commanded me to do but Father give yourself no uneasiness as to this reprimand for I know what course I am to pursue, and all will be well."[63]

That summer Emma wrote home, seeking permission to retrieve her clothes, cows, and furniture. Her father agreed and Joseph set out with a neighbor for Harmony, Pennsylvania. Through tears Isaac Hale accused Joseph of stealing his daughter, pled with him to bring her back, and promised to help Joseph get a start in farming. Evidently Joseph wept too and promised to stop using his gift for money and to move to Harmony with Emma. But even as Joseph rolled along in the wagon toward his parents' home, he knew it would be hard for him. "They will all oppose," he said to a neighbor. "They want me to look in the stone for them to dig [for] money." The neighbor testified that "in fact it was as he predicted. They urged him, day after day, to resume his old practice of looking in the stone. He seemed much perplexed as to the course he should pursue."[64] In that dilemma, Joseph received an ultimatum from Moroni. According to Joseph Knight, during Joseph's September 1826 meeting with the angel, he learned that "if he would Do right according to the will of God he mite obtain [the plates] the 22nt Day of September Next and if not he never would have them."[65]

As the time drew near, Joseph Knight and Josiah Stowell made an ostensible business trip upstate in order to be in Manchester on September 22, 1827. At about midnight, Joseph asked his mother if she had a chest with a lock and key. Suspecting his purposes, she fretted that she had nothing of the sort. Joseph assured her all would be well, but Lucy remained sleepless through the night, remembering what she called the "first failure" to return with the plates. Emma appeared in her riding dress and bonnet, and she and Joseph left in Joseph Knight's wagon. That night Moroni entrusted the plates to Joseph, now age twenty-one.[66] Joseph was still prone to mistakes and some sins even after his probationary period, but clearly he gained the Lord's trust and Moroni's confidence. He had faced difficult temptations, overcoming many and repenting when he fell to others. "He had learned to keep the commandments of God" and had become "not only willing, but able" to be the keeper of the sacred record.[67]

The next morning Lucy made breakfast and, when his father requested his company, excused Joseph, who had not yet returned home. Lucy also calmed Joseph Knight when he thought his wagon had been stolen. When Joseph Smith arrived, he assured his mother that all was well but could not resist the chance to prolong the anxiety others felt. After eating breakfast, he called Knight aside, "set his foot on the Bed and his head in his hand and says, 'Well I am Dissopinted.' 'Well,' says I [Knight], I am sorrey.' 'Well,' says he, 'I am grateley Dissopinted: it is ten times Better then I expected.'"[68] Joseph had finally obtained the plates, and with them, ostensibly, some relief from the struggle.

Conclusion

Joseph Smith's journey from 1823 to 1827, from a gifted teenager to the Lord's chosen seer, was marked by the trials of helping provide for his struggling family, as well as the temptations and subsequent reproof and repentance rooted in the Lord's efforts to train him to bring forth his word and the adversary's attempt to upset that trajectory. Joseph learned humility, penitence, and persistence from his temptations and trials. Moroni chastened him several times, and he responded by striving to repent and improve and become what God knew he could be. He was faced with intense financial pressure within his families—both the family that he grew up in and his own new union with Emma—which created a natural desire to provide in the best possible way. Yet he learned to control his passions and desires and to not set his heart on riches.

Joseph's teenage years show him struggling, choosing, and becoming what he was called to be, all in the context of his assignment to bring forth the Book of Mormon. There is no need to avoid or apologize for Joseph's confessed foibles. A nurturing God fashioned them into learning experiences that helped Joseph see "the difference between light and darkness and the operation of a good Spirit and an evil one."[69]

As the summer of 1827 ended, Joseph Smith, still far from perfect, had nevertheless qualified himself to obtain the sacred plates. In short, Joseph had four *years* to "choose . . . this *day*" whom he would serve (see Joshua 24:15). He had faced dilemmas, been sorely tempted, been rebuked by an angel, and now, at last, reached a turning point in his life as the Lord's seer. Elder Dallin H. Oaks described this process. He said "that no prophet is free from human frailty, especially before he is called to devote his life to the Lord's work. Line upon line, young Joseph Smith expanded his faith and understanding and his spiritual gifts matured, until he stood with power and stature as the Prophet of the Restoration."[70]

Notes

1. Karen Lynn Davidson, David J. Whittaker, Mark Ashurst-McGee, Richard L. Jensen, eds,, *Joseph Smith Histories, 1832–1844,* vol. 1 of the Histories series of *The Joseph Smith Papers,* ed. Dean C. Jessee, Ronald K, Esplin, and Richard Lyman Bushman (Salt Lake City: Church Historian's Press, 2012), 220–21 (hereafter *JSP*, H1).
2. *JSP*, H1:221n55.
3. William W. Phelps, "Praise to the Man," in *Hymns* (Salt Lake City: The Church of Jesus Christ of Latter-day Saints, 1985), no. 27.
4. *JSP*, H1:13–14; original spelling and punctuation has been preserved in all *JSP* references.
5. Alan Taylor, "The Early Republic's Supernatural Economy: Treasure Seeking in the American Northeast, 1780–1830," *American Quarterly* 38, no. 1 (Spring 1986): 7.
6. See Appendix I: Agreement of Josiah Stowell and Others, November 1, 1825, in Michael Hubbard MacKay, Gerrit J. Dirkmaat, Grant Underwood, Robert J. Woodford, and William G. Hartley, eds., *Documents, Volume 1: July 1828–June 1831,* vol. 1 of the Documents series of *The Joseph Smith Papers,* ed. Dean C. Jessee, Ronald K. Esplin, Richard L. Bushman, and Matthew J. Grow (Salt Lake City: Church Historian's Press, 2013), 345–52. For additional evaluation of the agreement, see Larry C. Porter, "A Study of the Origins of the Church of Jesus Christ of Latter-day Saints in the States of New York and Pennsylvania, 1816–1831" (PhD diss., Brigham Young University, 1971), 48–49.
7. For example, in 1831 a Palmyra newspaper reported, "The MANIA of money digging soon began rapidly to diffuse itself through many parts of this country; men and women without distinction of age or sex became marvellous wise in the occult sciences, many dreamed, and others saw visions disclosing to them deep in the bowels of the earth, rich and shining treasures, and to facilitate those *mighty* mining operations . . . divers devices and implements were invented, and although the SPIRIT was always able to retain his precious charge, these discomfited as well as deluded beings would on a succeeding night return to their toil, not in the least doubting that success would eventually attend their labors." *Reflector* (Palmyra, NY), February 1, 1831.

8. Taylor, "Supernatural Economy," 8. More evidence for and analysis of this idea are in Mark Ashurst-McGee, "A Pathway to Prophethood: Joseph Smith Junior as Rodsman, Village Seer, and Judeo-Christian Prophet" (master's thesis, Utah State University, 2000).
9. Taylor, "Supernatural Economy," 10.
10. The best study of this subject is Cornelius Van Dam, *The Urim and Thummim: A Means of Revelation in Ancient Israel* (Winona Lake, IN: Eisenbrauns, 1997), 216.
11. See Genesis 30; Exodus 7, 14. For more on the gift of Aaron in latter-day scriptures, see Dennis L. Largey, ed., *Doctrine and Covenants Reference Companion* (Salt Lake City: Deseret, 2012), s.v. "Gift of Aaron."
12. Peter French, *John Dee: The World of an Elizabethan Magus* (London: Routledge, 1984).
13. All of the evidence for this claim is presented and analyzed carefully in Ashurst-McGee, "Pathway to Prophethood." The largest collection of documents relative to Joseph Smith's treasure seeking includes several controversial statements by neighbors and some acquaintances of the Smith family who believed that Joseph's ability to discern involved a stone or stones. Many of these statements were gathered in 1833 by a man named Doctor Philastus Hurlbut, an excommunicated Latter-day Saint who was antagonistic to Joseph Smith and the Church. The statements he gathered were published by another critic, Eber D. Howe, in *Mormonism Unvailed* (Painesville, OH: E. D. Howe, 1834), one of the earliest anti-Mormon books. Scholarly analysts of the statements have made strong arguments for and against their reliability. For example, Richard L. Anderson argued against the reliability of the statements in "Joseph Smith's New York Reputation Reappraised," *BYU Studies* 10, no. 3 (Spring 1970): 283–314. Rodger I. Anderson argued for the general reliability of the statements in *Joseph Smith's New York Reputation Reexamined* (Salt Lake City: Signature Books, 1990). Marvin S. Hill evaluated the strengths and weaknesses of these arguments in his review of Rodger I. Anderson's book in *BYU Studies* 30, no. 4 (Fall 1990): 70–74.
14. Editorial, November 1837, Far West, Missouri, *Elders' Journal* 1 (November 1837): 27–29. Editorial, July 1838, Far West, Missouri, *Elders' Journal* 1 (July 1838): 42–44. Testimony reportedly given by Joseph Smith before justice of the peace Albert Neely in March 1826, according to William D. Purple, "Joseph Smith, The Originator of Mormonism," *Chenango Union* (Norwich, NY) 30, no. 33 (May 2, 1877).
15. See testimony reportedly given by Joseph Smith, according to Purple, "Joseph Smith, The Originator of Mormonism": "He [Joseph Smith] said when he was a lad, he heard of a neighboring girl some three miles from him, who could look into a glass and see anything however hidden from others; that he was seized with a strong desire to see her and her glass; that after much effort he induced his parents to let him visit her. He did so, and was permitted to look in the glass, which was placed in a hat to exclude the light. He was greatly surprised to see but one thing, which was a small stone, a great way off. It soon became luminous, and dazzled his eyes, and after a short time it became as intense as the mid-day sun....

This singular circumstance occupied his mind for some years, when he left his father's house, and with his youthful zeal traveled west in search of this luminous stone. . . . After traveling some one hundred and fifty miles he found himself at the mouth of the creek. He did not have the glass with him, but he knew its exact location. He borrowed an old ax and a hoe, and repaired to the tree. With some labor and exertion he found the stone, carried it to the creek, washed and wiped it dry, sat down on the bank, placed it in his hat, and discovered that time, place and distance were annihilated; that all intervening obstacles were removed, and that he possessed one of the attributes of Deity, an All-Seeing-Eye. He arose with a thankful heart, carried his tools to their owner, turned his feet towards the rising sun, and sought with weary limbs his long deserted home."

16. See Willard Chase's statement in Howe, *Mormonism Unvailed, 240–48.*
17. Lucy Mack Smith, History, 1845, handwriting of Howard Coray and Martha Jane Knowlton Coray, [95], Church History Library, Salt Lake City.
18. Dean C. Jessee, ed., "Joseph Knight's Recollection of Early Mormon History," *BYU Studies* 17, no. 1 (1976): 29–58. Quote is on page 3 of online pdf version at byustudies.byu.edu.
19. "History of Brigham Young," *Deseret News*, March 10, 1858, 3.
20. Dean C. Jessee, Mark Ashurst-McGee, and Richard L. Jensen, eds., *Journals, Volume 1: 1832–1839*, vol. 1 of the Journals series of *The Joseph Smith Papers*, ed. Dean C. Jessee, Ronald K. Esplin, and Richard Lyman Bushman (Salt Lake City: Church Historian's Press, 2008), 88–89.
21. *JSP*, H1:220–30.
22. *JSP*, J1:88–89.
23. See *JSP*, H1:13–14.
24. See *JSP*, H1:220–30.
25. See Isaiah 11; *JSP*, H1:220–30.
26. *JSP*, H1:224.
27. *JSP*, H1:226.
28. *JSP*, H1:220–30.
29. *JSP*, H1:230.
30. Lucy Mack Smith, History, 1845, [82]. See also *JSP*, H1:69, 74–75.
31. Terryl L. Givens, *By the Hand of Mormon: The American Scripture That Launched a New World Religion* (New York: Oxford University Press, 2003), 13; *Latter Day Saints' Messenger and Advocate*, April 1835, 157.
32. *JSP*, H1:230–31.
33. Lucy Mack Smith, History, 1844–1845, book 3, [11].
34. *JSP*, H1:230–32.
35. See Lucy Mack Smith, History, 1845, [82].
36. Lucy Mack Smith, History, 1845, [83].
37. *JSP*, H1:232.
38. *JSP*, H1:232.
39. *JSP*, H1:82; see also p. 76.
40. *JSP*, H1:82–83.
41. *JSP*, H1:14; see also pp. 82–83.

42. Lucy Mack Smith, History, 1844–1845, book 3, [11–12].
43. *JSP*, H1:83; see also Moses 1.
44. *JSP*, H1:14.
45. Lucy Mack Smith, History, 1845, [85].
46. *JSP*, H1:232–34.
47. Lucy Mack Smith, History, 1844–1845, book 4, [1].
48. Lucy Mack Smith, History, 1844–1845, book 4, [1].
49. Lucy Mack Smith, History, 1844–1845, book 4, [3–5].
50. Lucy Mack Smith, History, 1844–1845, book 4, [7–8].
51. See Lucy Mack Smith, History, 1844–1845, book 4, [2].
52. Lucy Mack Smith, History, 1844–1845, book 4, [2].
53. See Lucy Mack Smith, History, 1845, [89]; Lucy Mack Smith, History, 1844–1845, book 4, [3].
54. Lucy Mack Smith, History, 1845, [89]; see also Lucy Mack Smith, History, 1844–1845, book 4, [3].
55. Lucy Mack Smith, History, 1845, [89]; see also Lucy Mack Smith, History, 1844–1845, book 4, [3].
56. *JSP*, H1:234.
57. Lucy Mack Smith, History, 1845, [95].
58. Purple, "Joseph Smith, the Originator of Mormonism." There are five different contradictory accounts of Joseph's appearance before the justice of the peace, published anywhere from five to fifty-seven years after the event. Only the one cited above claims to be the record of an eyewitness, a fellow named William Purple, who wrote that he kept the records for the justice of the peace. This account includes quite a bit of testimony reportedly from Joseph and claims that he was discharged, meaning released without being cleared or condemned.
59. Joseph Knight Jr., as quoted in Larry C. Porter, "The Colesville Branch and the Coming Forth of the Book of Mormon," *BYU Studies* 10, no. 3 (Spring 1970): 369.
60. See *JSP*, H1:236–37.
61. Lucy Mack Smith, History, 1845, [98]; Lucy Mack Smith, History, 1844–1845, book 4, [11].
62. Lucy Mack Smith, History, 1844–1845, book 5, [4–5].
63. Lucy Mack Smith, History, 1844–1845, book 5, [5].
64. Peter Ingersoll Statement, December 2, 1833, in Howe, *Mormonism Unvailed*, 232–37, 248–49.
65. Dean C. Jessee, ed., "Joseph Knight's Recollection of Early Mormon History," *BYU Studies* 17, no. 1 (Fall 1976): 33.
66. Lucy Mack Smith, History, 1844–1845, book 5, [6].
67. Lucy Mack Smith, History, 1845, [85].
68. Jessee, "Joseph Knight's Recollection," 33.
69. Lucy Mack Smith, History, 1844–1845, book 3, [11–12].
70. Dallin H. Oaks, "Recent Events Involving Church History and Forged Documents," *Ensign*, October 1987.

3

Hefted and Handled
Tangible Interactions with Book of Mormon Objects

Anthony Sweat

Anthony Sweat is an assistant professor of Church history and doctrine at Brigham Young University.

In his 1839 history, Joseph Smith said that he found the Book of Mormon plates "under a ~~stound~~ stone of considerable size." The plates were "deposited in a stone box" along with "the Urim and Thummin and the Breastplate as stated by the messenger."[1] These plates would be unearthed by Joseph Smith on September 22, 1827, and be carried from Manchester, New York, to Harmony, Pennsylvania, where Joseph would begin to translate the plates in the winter of 1828 and produce the sacred text called the Book of Mormon. Although Joseph begins his narrative of the Book of Mormon's origin by telling us of actual physical relics, some dismiss the physical reality and factual historicity of the Book of Mormon record by consigning the text to the status of an extraordinary work of mystical mythology.[2] They claim the Book of Mormon could be inspired truth—a supernatural, magical work of revealed religious fiction—yet still not be factual, historical truth. However, this position overlooks Joseph Smith's foundation story of the physical origins of the Book of Mormon: actual relics hefted and handled, touched and transported, from one place to another and by one person to another. Joseph Smith did not describe the coming forth of the Book of Mormon the way he described many of his revelations found in the Doctrine and Covenants: as inspired words of the Lord that came to his mind and that he then dictated to a scribe.[3] No, Joseph said the Book of Mormon came forth from a nearby hill, by removing dirt, using a lever to lift a large stone, and removing actual engraved plates and sacred interpreters for the translation of its inscriptions. The Book of Mormon text didn't just pass through Joseph's trance-induced revelatory mind; its palpable relics passed through a clothing frock, hollowed log, cooper's shop, linen napkin, wooden chest, fireplace hearth, and barrel of beans. As historian Terryl Givens has insightfully deduced, "This continual, extensive, and prolonged engagement with a tangible, visible, grounding artifact is not compatible with a theory that makes him an inspired writer reworking the stuff of his own dreams into a product worthy of the name scripture. . . . The story of the gold plates could not be fanciful mythology and the Book of Mormon still be scripture."[4]

It is logically inconsistent to claim that Joseph Smith disingenuously contrived the explicit origin story of the Book of Mormon and then expected its readers to implicitly accept the very story and teachings that the book contains. How can one accept Joseph Smith's revelation of truth if the story that produced it was a complete fabrication? Either the physical origin story of the Book of Mormon as told by Joseph Smith is true, or it is not. The truthfulness of its text is inextricably linked to its inception report.

The purpose of this article is to examine multiple historical accounts of persons who interacted with actual, physical, tangible objects related to the coming forth of the Book of Mormon—persons who could substantiate the reality of these origin objects. Taken collectively, these material experiences with Book of Mormon relics provide compelling evidence to the truthfulness of Joseph Smith's account of the Book of Mormon's ancient origins. Building upon prior research by Andrew Hedges[5] and emerging research by Michael MacKay and Gerrit Dirkmaat,[6] this paper will describe multiple independent accounts from perhaps the most material time period of the book's coming forth: the protection period from when the plates were unearthed in September of 1827 in Manchester, New York, to when they began to be translated in early winter of 1828 in Harmony, Pennsylvania.

(For more about the witnesses, see chapter 2 by Steven C. Harper and chapter 8 by Amy Easton-Flake and Rachel Cope in this volume.)

Taken from a Stone Box

After four years of anxious personal preparation following Joseph Smith's First Vision, the time had come for Joseph to unearth and retrieve the Nephite record. Around midnight on the evening of September 21, 1827, Joseph asked his mother, Lucy, "if [she] had a chest with a lock and key,"[7] to store the plates in once he retrieved them, but she did not have anything to offer him. Lucy noticed that Joseph's wife, Emma, was in her riding apparel, and although Joseph didn't mention it specifically, Lucy deduced that he was taking Emma and leaving to get the plates. Without obtaining consent,[8] Joseph took Joseph Knight's horse and wagon, and he and Emma left for the Hill Cumorah. Leaving Emma at the bottom of the hill to wait, Joseph went to retrieve the plates from their ancient burial place.

Often overlooked, the stone box from which the plates were retrieved is one of the first physical evidences of Joseph's origin story of the Book of Mormon plates and text. Joseph described the box in which the plates and interpreters were interred: "The box in which they lay was formed by laying stones together in some kind of cement, in the bottom of the box were laid two stones crossways of the box, and on these stones lay the plates and the other things with them."[9] Meeting the angel Moroni at the site of the stone box, and after having received a sacred charge from the angel that Joseph was now responsible for the plates' care, Joseph removed the plates from their tomb. Because he had not yet prepared a secure place to lock the plates at home, he initially stored the plates in a hollowed-out birch log on the hill.[10] A few days later, after having obtained a wooden chest from his brother Hyrum to secure the plates, Joseph returned to the Hill Cumorah and took the plates home.

Ironically, while much of Joseph's later persecution may have arisen out of others doubting the existence and possession of golden plates, originally the difficulty was due to the exact opposite: certain persons were convinced he had actually retrieved the record.[11] Part of their certainty was due to their interaction with the place where the plates were buried. Willard Chase and Samuel Lawrence, two local friends of Joseph's and associates in some of his previous treasure-seeking ventures, were particularly attuned to

Joseph's retrieval of the plates. According to an account by Willard Chase, prior to Joseph's obtaining the record Joseph had taken Samuel Lawrence to the Hill Cumorah and shown him the spot where the Book of Mormon plates were concealed in the stone box. Lawrence asked Joseph "if he had ever discovered anything with the plates of gold; he said no; he then asked him to look in his stone, to see if there was anything with them. He looked, and said there was nothing; he told him to look again, and see if there was not a large pair of specks with the plates; he looked and soon saw a pair of spectacles, the same with which Joseph says he translated the Book of Mormon."[12] Although portions of Chase's account must be read skeptically, Joseph Knight Sr. shared a similar story in his reminiscence, saying Samuel Lawrence "had Bin to the hill and knew about the things in the hill and he was trying to obtain them."[13]

Lawrence and other local treasure hunters, such as Willard Chase, are likely some of those who, because they had seen the place from which the plates came forth, later convinced an inquiring man named David Whitmer that Joseph had obtained the plates from the hill. David Whitmer would later remember:

> I had conversations with several young men who said that Joseph Smith had certainly golden plates, and that before he attained them he had promised to share with them, but had not done so, and they were very much incensed with him. Said I, 'how do you know that Joe Smith has the plates?' They replied: '*we saw the plates [place] in the hill that he took them out of just as he described it to us before he obtained them*.' These parties were so positive in their statements that I began to believe there must be some foundation for the stories then in circulation all over that part of the country.[14]

In another interview Whitmer told a reporter that "the community in which he [Whitmer] lived . . . was alive with excitement in regard to Smith's finding a great treasure, and they informed him that they knew that Smith had the plates, *as they had seen the place that he had taken them from, on the hill Cumorah*."[15]

Shortly after Joseph had obtained the plates, Martin Harris and two others also went to the Hill Cumorah to "hunt for some more [stone] boxes." While this is a later reminiscence and he doesn't state with certainty whether or not this was the very box the Book of Mormon plates were removed from, Harris claimed, "indeed we found a stone box" that he and the other two persons were excited about. After unsuccessfully trying to remove the box from the hill, they took a crowbar and "broke one corner off the box." Harris concluded, "Sometime that box will be found, and you will see the corner broken off, then you will know I have told you the truth. Again Brethren as sure as you are standing here and see me just that sure did I see the angel with the golden plates."[16]

The stone box from the Hill Cumorah was also apparently left exposed for the display of residents and visitors to Palmyra for decades. In 1893, Elder Edward Stevenson wrote that during a trip to Palmyra "early on a summer's morning in the year 1870," he had been shown where the stone box once was by a local resident who lived near the Hill Cumorah. Stevenson said, "Questioning him closely he [the local] stated that he had seen some good sized flat stones that had rolled down and lay near the bottom of the hill. This had occurred after the contents of the box had been removed and these stones were doubtless the ones that formerly composed the box. I felt a strong desire to see these ancient relics and told him I would be much pleased to have him inform me where they were to be found. He stated that they had long since been taken away."[17] Testimonies and affidavits of local Palmyra residents such as this man, Martin Harris, Samuel Lawrence, and others corroborate Joseph Smith's testimony of the Book of Mormon relics being found and removed from a stone box he unearthed on the Hill Cumorah.

Responsible for a Relic

Returning to the evening of Joseph's retrieval of the plates from the Hill Cumorah, Joseph recounted that the angel Moroni gave him a strict charge regarding their care. Joseph recorded, "The same heavenly messenger delivered them up to me with this charge that I should be responsible for them. That if I should let them go carelessly or through any neglect of mine I should be cut off, but that if I would use all my endeavours to preserve them untill he (the messenger) called should call for them, they should be protected."[18] Because he had nowhere to protect the plates at home, Joseph left the plates hidden in a Cumorah birch tree "3 miles"[19] from the Smith home and went west to Macedon to take a job digging a well in order to earn money to have a wooden chest made in which to secure the plates.

While Joseph was gone, word apparently spread that he had obtained the record. Samuel Lawrence, Willard Chase, and others had gathered a group of about a dozen men together (including a conjurer from sixty to seventy miles away)[20] to find the place where Joseph had secreted the plates. Joseph Smith Sr. learned of their plans and alerted Emma, and she rode on a stray horse to Macedon to alert Joseph that the plates were in danger. Joseph miraculously knew of Emma's coming and went out and met her on the road. Upon hearing the plates may be in danger, Joseph consulted the "Urim and Thummim, and saw that the Record was as yet safe; nevertheless, he concluded to return with his wife."[21] Upon arriving in Palmyra, Joseph went to the Hill Cumorah to retrieve the record, still dressed in his linen working frock. Joseph retrieved the plates from the hollowed log, wrapped them in his frock, and began on his way home through the woods with the record. He was attacked three times on his way home, dislocating his thumb fighting off one of the attackers. Arriving at his parents' home, according to Joseph's sister Katherine, Joseph "came in nearly exhausted, carrying the package of gold plates . . . clasped to his side with his left hand and arm, and his right hand was badly bruised."[22] Family friend Josiah Stowell, who was visiting the Smith's, reported that Joseph then handed him the plates, wrapped in his linen frock, through an open window.[23] Similarly, Martin Harris recounted that upon arriving home, Joseph "handed the plates in at the window," although according to his recollection, the plates "were received from him by his mother [Lucy Smith]."[24]

Josiah Stowell, the First Unintentional Witness

Josiah Stowell claimed he was the "first person that took the Plates out of [Joseph Smith's] hands the morning [he] brought them in."[25] Thus Josiah Stowell would have been the first witness to validate Joseph's claims of obtaining tangible plates. However, although Stowell's experience hefting the plates as they were passed to him—feeling of their weight, mass, and shape—constitutes a witness in itself, Josiah Stowell also claimed that he *saw* (albeit unintentionally) the exposed plates as they were passed to him by Joseph. Historians Michael MacKay and Gerrit Dirkmaat summarize what happened:

> In the summer of 1830, after Joseph Smith was charged with disorderly conduct, Stowell was called by the defense and sworn in as a witness. He testified under oath that he saw the plates the day Joseph first brought them home. As Joseph passed them through the window, Stowell caught a glimpse of the plates as a portion of the linen was pulled back. Stowell gave the court the dimensions of the plates and explained that they consisted of gold leaves with characters written on each sheet. The printed transcript of the trial read: "witness saw a corner of it; it resembled a stone of a greenish caste." Because Stowell also mentioned in his statement that the record was made of plates of gold, it is difficult to know what he meant by this description. He may have seen the band that sealed two-thirds of the plates together, which may have been made of copper that had oxidized over the years and turned green. Alternatively, he may have seen the breastplate, which could have also been made of copper and appeared green from oxidation. In any case, the point Stowell made to the court was that the plates were real and that he had seen and felt them.[26]

Stowell thus becomes the first unintentional witness, having an experience somewhat like that of the formal Eight Witnesses later had as they were allowed to heft and see the plates.

Tangible as Oil Cloths

Others soon reported having tangible experiences with the plates or other relics Joseph had recovered from the Hill Cumorah. Some few days after bringing the plates home, Joseph's mother said that her son called her down from her upstairs work on some oil cloths. Lucy reported, "I finally concluded to go down, and see what he wanted, upon which he handed me the breast-plate spoken of in his history. It was wrapped in a thin muslin handkerchief, so thin that I could see the glistening metal, and ascertain its proportions without any difficulty." Lucy proceeded to describe the breastplate:

> It was concave on one side, and convex on the other, and extended from the neck downwards, as far as the centre of the stomach of a man of extraordinary size. It had four straps of the same material, for the purpose of fastening it to the breast, two of which ran back to go over the shoulders, and the other two were designed to fasten to the hips. They were just the width of two of my fingers, (for I measured them,) and they

> had holes in the end of them, to be convenient in fastening. After I had examined it, Joseph placed it in the chest with the Urim and Thummim.[27]

Lucy also reported that she saw the Urim and Thummim, or Nephite interpreters. According to her, on the evening Joseph obtained the plates he handed her the spectacles wrapped only in a thin silk handkerchief through which she could see and discern their shape. "I've got a key [the Nephite interpreters]," Joseph told his mother when he came back that evening, and she "took the article of which he spoke into [her] hands."[28] Upon her examination, she described the seer stones as two "three-cornered" stones set in "silver bows," connected with each other like "old fashioned spectacles." Lucy's experiences and accounts are yet another powerful witness to the tangible reality of Joseph's Book of Mormon origin story. Handling, feeling, measuring, and describing the breastplate and interpreters was not a supernatural experience, explained away by spiritual phenomena, but was as real and tactile as the very oil cloths she had painted only moments before she handled these relics.

Cooper's Shop, Hearth Stones, and Beans

Joseph was warned by the angel Moroni when he took charge of the plates that persons would seek to take them from him and that he would need to use all his efforts to preserve them. The Prophet's history relates:

> I soon found out the reason why I had received such strict charges to keep them safe and why it was that the messenger had said that when I had done what was required at my hand, he would call for them, for no sooner was it known that I had them than the most strenious exertions were used to get them from me. Every stratagem that could be invented was resorted to for that purpose. The persecution became more bitter and severe than before, and multitudes were on the alert continualy to get them from me if possible but by the wisdom of God they remained safe in my hands.[29]

Joseph's exertions to keep the plates safe are another example of the palpable reality of the objects obtained from the Hill Cumorah. Not long after bringing the plates home, Joseph was alerted through the Urim and Thummim of a company of men who were coming to find the plates. Joseph and others[30] pulled up the hearth stones from the family fireplace and dug a hole of sufficient size to bury the plates in, replacing the hearth stones to conceal what they had done just before the group of men arrived. According to Joseph Knight Sr., shortly after this, Samuel Lawrence and "a grate Rodsman" came to Joseph Smith Sr.'s home and tried to bargain with Joseph Smith "to go shares" with them on the plates. When Joseph refused, the rodsman (whom Brigham Young later described as a wicked man having "possessed as much talent as any man that walked on the American soil")[31] "took out his Rods and hild [held] them up and they pointed Dow[n] to the harth whare they ware hid." The rodsman proclaimed, "it is under that harth."[32] No record exists about what transpired next, but although the rodsman had correctly identified where they were concealed, Joseph obviously succeeded in keeping the plates safe from his hands.

On another occasion, Joseph was apprised of another attempt by a mob to come and take the plates. He took the record from the wooden box, wrapped the plates in some clothes, and hid them in some flax in the second-story loft of the cooper's shop across the road from his parents' home. In order to divert the mob, Joseph nailed shut the box that had housed the plates and buried it in the floorboards of the ground level of the shop. That evening, the mob (following instructions given by Sally Chase after looking through her green seer stone) came and searched around the entire Smith property, and at Chase's instructions searched the cooper's shop. The next morning they "found the floor of the cooper's shop torn up, and the box which was laid under it shivered in pieces,"[33] but the plates were safe in the loft.

Another concealment of and tangible interaction with the plates came a few months later, when, to escape the harassment they were experiencing at Joseph Smith Sr.'s home in Manchester, Joseph and Emma Smith took up Emma's father's offer to live with him on his farm in Harmony, Pennsylvania. Joseph and Emma would make the move to Harmony in December of 1827. Their plans to relocate became known to a growing mob, who threatened Joseph that "he should never leave until he had shown the plates."[34] Fearful of being accosted by the mob and having their property searched, thereby discovering the plates, Joseph nailed the plates up in a wooden box and hid them in a barrel of beans, filling it a third of the way, depositing the plates, and then covering them over by filling up the rest of the barrel. Interestingly,

Martin Harris, along with Joseph's brother-in-law Alva Hale, may have had a tangible interaction with the plates here, as Alva had come from Harmony to drive Joseph and Emma in his wagon. Although it is unknown for sure whether Alva hefted or handled the box containing the plates, Harris claimed he personally helped Joseph move the box into the barrel of beans.[35] Those who helped Joseph secrete the plates and protect them—removing hearth stones and covering a wrapped relic, as well as loading it into a barrel of beans—provide additional accounts and proofs of a tangible record that had actually, not mystically, been entrusted to Joseph Smith to protect and eventually translate.

Hefting the Plates

Some years prior to Joseph's having obtained the Book of Mormon plates, Joseph Smith Sr. had mentioned confidentially to Martin Harris that his son was seeking to obtain from God plates buried in the hill.[36] Although open to the idea, upon hearing that Joseph Smith had obtained a treasure from the Hill Cumorah, Martin Harris initially suggested that perhaps he merely had discovered an "old brass kettle,"[37] but not a divine record. After obtaining the plates, Joseph sent his mother to the Harrises' to elicit Martin's support in the translation. A few days later, Martin's wife, Lucy, came to the Smiths' home and questioned Joseph about the record, requesting to see the plates for which, if Joseph consented, she would lend him financial support. Joseph declined, telling Mrs. Harris that he couldn't show them to her, to which she responded, "Now, Joseph, are you not telling me a lie? Can you look full in my eye, and say before God, that you have in reality found a Record, as you pretend?"[38] Instead, Joseph later provided for Lucy Harris and her daughter a similar physical witness of the plates he offered to others: he let them lift the wooden box that contained the plates. Martin Harris recalled that his "daughter said, they were about as much as she could lift. . . . My wife said they were very heavy."[39]

Shortly after his wife's experience,[40] Martin Harris also received a tangible witness of the gold plates, hefting the box containing the plates at the Smiths' home. A few days after his wife's visit, Martin arrived at the Smith home and questioned various members of the family independently to verify the story of the plates. Later in the day, after Joseph had given Martin his account of finding the plates, Joseph allowed Martin the same experience he had given Martin's wife and daughter a few days earlier, giving him the box with the plates inside. Martin recalled, "While at Mr. Smith's I hefted the plates, and I knew from the heft that they were lead or gold, and I knew that Joseph had not credit enough to buy so much lead. I left Mr. Smith's about eleven o'clock and went home. I retired to my bedroom and prayed God to show me concerning these things, and I covenanted that if it was his work and he would show me so, I would put forth my best ability to bring it before the world. He then showed me that it was his work."[41] Harris stated in an 1859 interview that another man, apparently Alvah Beman, or "Old Mr. Beman" (who helped Joseph hide the plates and provided a box for them), also had the privilege of hefting the plates in the box, relating to Martin Harris that "he heard them jink, but he was not permitted to see them."[42] In that same interview, Harris stated that he "hefted the plates many times, and should think they weighed forty or fifty pounds."[43]

Thumbing and Feeling the Plates

Many members of Joseph Smith's immediate family recall also having physical contact and other sensory experiences with the Book of Mormon record. Joseph Smith's little sister Katherine reported that on the day Joseph brought the plates home he handed them to her.[44] On another occasion she said that when cleaning in the Smith home, she "saw a package on the table containing the gold plates," which she picked up to judge the weight, finding them "heavy like gold." However, Katherine's experience moved beyond those who hefted the plates in the box. She said that through the package of cloth she "rippled her fingers up the edge of the plates and felt that they were separate metal plates and heard the tinkle of sound that they made."[45] Her witness of tangible plates moved from simply lifting to the senses of physical touch and sound.

Additionally, Joseph's little brother William, who was a teenager at the time, also recounted having palpable interaction with the Book of Mormon plates. William later wrote that he "hefted the plates as they lay on the table wrapped in an old frock or jacket in which Joseph had brought them home." Almost identical to his sister Katherine's experience, William reported that he too had a tactile and auditory witness of the plates, recounting that he "had thumbed them through the cloth and ascertained that they were thin sheets of some kind of metal."[46]

Other than Joseph Smith, the person who had the most interaction with the tangible reality of the plates was the Prophet's wife, Emma Smith. She later recalled that after Joseph obtained the record, the plates "lay in a box under our bed for months but I never felt at liberty to look at them."[47] In a later interview with her son Joseph III, Emma recounted that when she and Joseph arrived in Harmony, Pennsylvania, she had given Joseph a small linen tablecloth to wrap the plates in. Emma explained that "the plates often lay on the table without any attempt at concealment," wrapped in this cloth.[48] She also recalled, "I once felt of the plates, as they thus lay on the table, tracing their outline and shape. They seemed to be pliable like thick paper, and would rustle with a metalic sound when the edges were moved by the thumb, as one does sometimes thumb the edges of a book."[49] Although some of Emma's answers on other topics in this interview are contrary to the historical record,[50] Emma's description of her tactile and auditory experience with the plates is remarkably consistent with William's and Katherine's descriptions.

Emma also moved the plates around in her Harmony home, as her son Joseph III remembered: "My mother told me that she . . . would lift and move [the plates] when she swept and dusted the room and furniture."[51] Although it would seem Emma naturally desired to view the plates (see D&C 25:4), her experiences were more than sufficient for her witness of their reality. She told her son: "I knew that he [Joseph] had them, and was not specially curious about them. . . . I did not attempt to handle the plates, other than I have told you, nor uncover them to look at them. I was satisfied that it was the work of God, and therefore did not feel it to be necessary to do so."[52]

Another tactile experience with the plates is described in the testimony of Joseph's father-in-law, Isaac Hale. Joseph and Isaac had a strained relationship due to Mr. Hale's disapproval of both Joseph's money-digging past and his marriage to Emma.[53] Upon returning to Harmony after eloping with Emma, according to Isaac Hale, Joseph had sworn to him that he had given up his treasure-searching past and that he intended "to work hard for a living."[54] A year into their marriage Joseph and Emma left Palmyra, New York, to live in a small home located on the Hale property in Harmony, Pennsylvania. Upon their arrival, Isaac Hale heard that Joseph had brought "a wonderful book of Plates down with them." Suspicious of Joseph because of his past claims, Isaac doubted the reality of Joseph's obtaining the Book of Mormon plates and confronted him about it. Joseph, under the sacred command given him of God through the angel Moroni to show the plates to nobody except whom God should command, but presumably wanting to allay his new father-in-law's suspicions and convince him that he indeed had an ancient record, offered to let Isaac Hale lift the wooden box containing the plates, just as he had let Lucy Harris, Martin Harris, and Alvah Beman do. Isaac Hale recounted: "I was allowed to feel the weight of the box, and they gave me to understand, that the book of plates was then in the box—into which, however, I was not allowed to look."[55]

Although this experience did not satisfy Isaac Hale as it had others,[56] it is nonetheless yet another example of someone who had a physical interaction with the tangible golden plates. Taking the collective experiences together of the many who did heft, handle, touch, feel, ripple, and hear the metallic rustle of the plates during the protection period—along with the eleven formal witnesses who later saw the open plates—one is led to logically deduce, as did one scholar, that *at minimum* "what emerges as alone indisputable is the fact that Joseph Smith [did] possess a set of metal plates."[57]

Conclusion

While none of the individual accounts related herein affirms single-handedly the certitude of Joseph's having obtained a sacred record (let alone of translating it correctly), the multiple independently recorded experiences suggest with convincing evidence the existence of the tangible Book of Mormon plates and relics. Descriptions and witnesses of stone boxes from the Hill Cumorah, multiple persons who hefted the plates as they lay inside assorted wooden containers, and those who felt, traced, and outlined the shape of the plates and breastplate or Urim and Thummim through various cloth coverings—never mind the visible and tangible witness of the plates that would come from the eleven formal eyewitnesses of the Book of Mormon—indicate indisputable physicality with respect to the sacred record's origin.

Moreover, Joseph Smith never explained the Book of Mormon as a purely spiritual production of a metaphorical people given to teach divine truths. Rather, he repeatedly and consistently declared that the Book of Mormon was an inspired translation done through the "gift, and power of God"[58] of a literal ancient record taken from a stone box from a nearby hill—actual plates created and recorded and preserved by historical prophets, physically entrusted to his care, that he really did hide, conceal, and protect, and that others really did have tangible experiences with.[59] The Lord has revealed that the translation of that record is true (see D&C 17:6). The experiences, records, and accounts of various persons who interacted tangibly with the relics of the Book of Mormon during the protection period of September–December 1827, taken collectively, confirm that the origin story of the Book of Mormon record is equally true.

Notes

1. Karen Lynn Davidson, David J. Whitaker, Mark Ashurst-McGee, and Richard L. Jensen, eds., *Histories, Volume 1: 1832–1844*, vol. 1 of the Histories series of *The Joseph Smith Papers*, ed. Dean C. Jessee, Ronald K. Esplin, and Richard Lyman Bushman (Salt Lake City: Church Historian's Press, 2012), 232 (hereafter *JSP*, H1).
2. See Terryl L. Givens, "'Devices of the Devil': The Book of Mormon as Cultural Product or Sacred Fiction," in *By the Hand of Mormon: The American Scripture That Launched a New World Religion* (New York: Oxford University Press, 2002), 155–84. See also, for example, sociologist Rodney Stark's comparison of Joseph Smith's unique production of modern scripture to Shakespeare's creation of literature and Mozart's musical compositions: "Suppose that someone with the literary gifts of William Shakespeare underwent a series of mental events he or she interpreted as contact with the supernatural. Would it not be likely that the revelations produced in this way would be messages of depth, beauty, and originality? . . . The case of Joseph Smith is remarkably similar." *The Rise of Mormonism* (New York: Columbia University Press, 2005), 40, 42.
3. As William E. McLellin, who served as a scribe for one of Joseph's revelations, described it: "The scribe seats himself at a desk or table, with pen, ink and paper. The subject of enquiry being understood, the Prophet and Revelator enquires of God. He spiritually sees, hears and feels, and then speaks as he is moved upon by the Holy Ghost, the 'thus saith the Lord,' sentence after sentence." Michael Hubbard MacKay, Gerrit J. Dirkmaat, Grant Underwood, Robert J. Woodford, and William G. Hartley, eds., "Volume 1 Introduction," *Documents, Volume 1: July 1828–June 1831*, vol. 1 of the Documents series of *The Joseph Smith Papers*, ed. Dean C. Jessee, Ronald K. Esplin, Richard Lyman Bushman, and Matthew J. Grow (Salt Lake City: Church Historian's Press, 2013), xxxiii.
4. Givens, *By the Hand of Mormon*, 178.
5. See Andrew H. Hedges, "'All My Endeavors to Preserve Them': Protecting the Plates in Palmyra, 22 September–December 1827," *Journal of Book of Mormon Studies* 8, no. 2 (1999): 14–23. This work has been foundational to the present study.

6. See Michael Hubbard MacKay and Gerrit J. Dirkmaat, *From Darkness unto Light* (Provo, UT: Religious Studies Center; Salt Lake City: Deseret Book, 2015). This work has been vital to the present study. I am particularly indebted to Michael MacKay for his generous help in providing me with source material from his research for many of the historical accounts related herein.
7. Lucy Smith, *Biographical Sketches of Joseph Smith the Prophet and His Progenitors for Many Generations* (Liverpool: S. W. Richards, 1853), 100.
8. Joseph Knight had apparently not given Joseph permission to take his wagon, as when he awoke the next morning and found his horse and wagon missing he was alarmed that it had been stolen, concluding "that a rogue had stolen them" according to Lucy Smith. *Biographical Sketches of Joseph Smith*, 101. See also Joseph Knight's Recollection that in the morning "my Horse and Carriage was gone" in Dean C. Jessee, "Joseph Knight's Recollection of Early Mormon History," *BYU Studies* 17, no. 1 (1976): 33.
9. *JSP*, H1:232.
10. Lucy Smith wrote, "he had deposited [the plates] in a cavity in a birch log 3 miles distant and he too covered it with the bark of the same." Lucy Smith, History, book 5, [11]; book 6, [2]; Joseph Smith, History, Vol. A-1, 8. See also Martin Harris's statement that the plates were originally concealed in a hollowed-out tree. Joel Tiffany, "Mormonism," *Tiffany's Monthly*, August 1859, 165.
11. See Hedges, "'All My Endeavors to Preserve Them,'" 14–23. Hedges summarizes multiple efforts of persons such as Samuel Lawrence, Willard Chase, and Sally Chase to take the plates because "Lawrence and perhaps others had learned of the plates' existence through 'revelation' from illegitimate sources" (p. 19).
12. Testimony of Willard Chase, Manchester, N.Y., 1833, as cited in Eber D. Howe, *History of Mormonism, or, A Faithful Account of that Singular Imposition and Delusion* (Painseville, OH: 1840), 243.
13. Jessee, "Joseph Knight's Recollection," 32.
14. *Kansas City Daily Journal*, June 5, 1881; reprinted in the *Deseret Evening News*, June 11, 1881; emphasis added.
15. "The Last Man," *Chicago Times*, October 17, 1881, as cited in George Reynolds, *The Myth of the "Manuscript Found"* (Salt Lake City: Juvenile Instructor Office, 1883), 82; emphasis added.
16. Ole A. Jensen, "Testimony of Martin Harris," MS 5569, folder 1, Church History Library, Salt Lake City.
17. Edward Stevenson, *Reminiscences of Joseph, the Prophet, and the Coming Forth of the Book of Mormon* (Salt Lake City: 1893), 10, 13.
18. Joseph Smith, History, Vol. A-1, 9.
19. Lucy Smith states that Joseph "went to bring the record which he had deposited in a cavity in a birch log 3 miles distant." Lucy Smith, History, book 5, [11].
20. Lucy Smith, *Biographical Sketches*, 102.
21. Lucy Smith, *Biographical Sketches*, 104. Lucy mentioned here that Joseph kept the Urim and Thummim "constantly about his person."
22. Herbert S. Salisbury, "Things the Prophet's Sister Told Me," July 2, 1945, Secure Stacks manuscript, MS 4122 2, folder 1, Church History Library, Salt Lake City.

23. Martha Campbell to Joseph Smith, December 19, 1843, Church History Library, Salt Lake City. Because both Lucy Smith and Josiah Stowell were present when Joseph handed the plates in at the window, perhaps they both helped or carried them simultaneously.
24. Tiffany, "Mormonism," 166.
25. Martha Campbell to Joseph Smith, December 19, 1843.
26. MacKay and Dirkmaat, *From Darkness unto Light*, 13.
27. Lucy Smith, *Biographical Sketches*, 107.
28. Lucy Smith, *Biographical Sketches*, 101.
29. Joseph Smith, History, Vol. A-1, 9.
30. Lucy Smith, *Biographical Sketches*, 108. Jessee, "Joseph Knight's Recollection," 33–34.
31. Brigham Young, in *Journal of Discourses*, 2:180.
32. Jessee, "Joseph Knight's Recollection," 34. There is confusion and conflicting accounts about who this great rodsman was. Joseph Knight Sr. identified him as "Beeman," perhaps confusing Alvah Beman, who had helped Joseph hide the plates under the fireplace, as the rodsman.
33. Lucy Smith, *Biographical Sketches*, 109.
34. Martin Harris, as quoted in Tiffany, "Mormonism," 170; see also Smith, *History of Joseph Smith*, 154.
35. Joseph Smith, History, Vol. A-1, 5; Tiffany, "Mormonism," 170.
36. See Hedges, "'All My Endeavors to Preserve Them,'" 18.
37. Tiffany, "Mormonism," 167.
38. Lucy Smith, *Biographical Sketches*, 111.
39. Tiffany, "Mormonism," 168.
40. It should be noted that Lucy Harris later denied having ever believed in the reality of the Book of Mormon record. She said the religion of Mormonism "was false" and called it a "delusion." E. D. Howe, *Mormonism Unvailed* (Painsville, OH: E. D. Howe, 1834), 256.
41. Tiffany, "Mormonism," 169–70.
42. Tiffany, "Mormonism," 167.
43. Tiffany, "Mormonism," 166.
44. Mary Salisbury Hancock, "The Three Sisters of Joseph Smith," *Saints' Herald*, January 11, 1954, 12.
45. "The Prophet's Sister Testifies She Lifted the B of M Plates," *The Messenger* (Berkeley, CA), October 1954, 1, 6. See also Dan Vogel, comp., *Early Mormon Documents* (Salt Lake City: Signature Books, 1996), 1:649.
46. Martha Campbell to Joseph Smith, December 19, 1843.
47. Nels Madsen and Parley P. Pratt, interview of Emma Smith Bidamon, 1877, Secure Stacks manuscript, MS 852, Church History Library, Salt Lake City.
48. "Last Testimony of Sister Emma," *Saints' Herald*, October 1, 1879, 290.
49. "Last Testimony of Sister Emma," 290.
50. For example, when asked in this same interview, "Did he [Joseph Smith] not have other wives than yourself?" Emma responded, "He had no other wife but me; nor did he to my knowledge ever have." This response is inconsistent with the

historical record. Brian C. Hales, "Emma and Hyrum Accept Plural Marriage," in *Joseph Smith's Polygamy* (Salt Lake City: Greg Kofford Books, 2013), 2:33–61.

51. Joseph Smith III to Mrs. E. Horton, March 7, 1900, Community of Christ Library–Archives, as cited in Vogel, *Early Mormon Documents*, 1:546–47.
52. "Last Testimony of Sister Emma," 290.
53. Isaac described Joseph at this time as a "careless young man" and "insolent to his father" and that he "followed a business [treasure searching through seer stones] I could not approve." Isaac Hale Statement, 1834, in Vogel, *Early Mormon Documents*, 4:284–85.
54. Isaac Hale Statement, 285.
55. Isaac Hale Statement, 286. See also Howe, *Mormonism Unvailed*, 257–58.
56. Isaac Hale said of the experience that he was "dissatisfied, and informed him [Joseph] that if there was any thing in my house of that description [the plates], which I could not be allowed to see, he must take it away; if he did not, I was determined to see it. After that, the Plates were said to be hid in the woods." Isaac Hale Statement, 286.
57. Givens, *By the Hand of Mormon*, 40. Although it is possible that Joseph Smith could have fabricated a set of metal plates as a "prop" to support his story, Martin Harris stated that he knew Joseph lacked sufficient money or credit to do so: "I knew that Joseph had not credit enough to buy so much lead" to fabricate the plates himself. Tiffany, "Mormonism," 169–70.
58. Joseph Smith, "Church History," in *JSP*, H1:495.
59. Read this detailed, physical description of the plates as an example: "I was also told [by the angel Moroni] where there was deposited some plates on which were engraven an abridgement of the records of the ancient prophets that had existed on this continent. . . .These record were engraven on plates which had the appearance of gold, each plate was six inches wide and eight inches long and not quite so thick as common tin. They were filled with engravings, in Egyptian characters and bound together in a volume, as the leaves of a book with three rings running through the whole. The volume was something near six inches in thickness, a part of which was sealed. . . . Through the medium of the Urim and Thummim I translated the record by the gift, and power of God." Joseph Smith, "Church History," in *JSP*, H1:495.

4

Firsthand Witness Accounts of the Translation Process

Michael Hubbard MacKay and Gerrit J. Dirkmaat

Michael Hubbard MacKay and Gerrit J. Dirkmaat are assistant professors of Church history and doctrine at Brigham Young University.

For decades, most Latter-day Saints have had little reason to examine the miraculous translation of the Book of Mormon beyond its most basic details. Recently, however, references to the translation on national television and the Internet have piqued the curiosity of many, and a much broader interest in the translation process has been the result, despite the fact that scholars have been addressing many of these questions for decades.[1] In 2014 the Church released a five-page statement on its website about the translation, one that reflected an understanding of the translation outlined in the introduction to *The Joseph Smith Papers: Documents, Volume 1.* This volume analyzed the documentary record surrounding the translation process and explained what witnesses said about the translation.[2] These two publications mark a concerted effort by the Church to help members understand the details of the translation process.

This chapter will help satisfy the rising interest in the translation of the Book of Mormon by analyzing what witnesses and close associates of Joseph Smith said about the manner in which Joseph Smith translated the gold plates.[3] Both believers and nonbelievers asked Joseph and his associates to explain the process numerous times, and Joseph Smith and his scribes left records of their responses.[4] We have gathered and evaluated these historical documents to help clarify how Joseph Smith and those close to him experienced the translation process. By analyzing the statements of those who witnessed the translation (primarily his scribes), we address what they said happened. Because they watched Joseph translate, their witness was primarily based upon what they saw or what Joseph explained to them about the process. The scribes explained a process that involved physical objects such as seer stones, a hat to block ambient light, and gold plates.

Latter-day Saints have always believed that the Book of Mormon came into the world as the result of a series of miraculous events, starting with the appearance of the angel Moroni and proceeding through the completion of a translation of an ancient record. As with any miracle, it is difficult to reconstruct or even understand what happened without having experienced the event firsthand. This limits our ability to understand the translation beyond what witnesses saw and described. As valuable as witness statements are, they do not offer a clear window into the consciousness of Joseph Smith. We will focus primarily upon the historical record and avoid theoretical models or approaches that attempt to identify Joseph's cognition or state of mind during the translation. What Joseph was thinking or experiencing as he translated the book is essentially beyond the realm of historical inquiry. Unless he spoke about it, one can only guess or speculate.

Joseph's Witness (By the Gift and Power of God)

Joseph Smith declared that he translated the Book of Mormon from an ancient language (reformed Egyptian) into English, but he spoke only one language. His parents provided him with only a limited education and though he did have a bright mind, he did not have the education necessary to translate one language into another. He later explained that he was taught to read and write, but that these skills "const[it]uted my whole literary acquirements."[5] His wife, Emma, and others emphasized this point to make the production of the Book of Mormon appear even more astounding than it already was. Emma wrote that he "could neither write nor dictate a coherent and well-worded letter, let alone dictat[e] a book like the Book of Mormon."[6] Joseph maintained that he did not possess the ability to write the Book of Mormon on his own. He occasionally referenced his gift to translate throughout his life. In each account he consistently gave God credit for the translation and never claimed that he produced the Book of Mormon from his own efforts or through independent volition.[7]

Unfortunately, Joseph left very little indication about how he translated. In the preface to the 1830 edition to the Book of Mormon, he wrote, "I would inform you that I translated, by the gift and power of God."[8] His friends and family provided further details about the process, but Joseph's public statements consistently described the translation in vague terms associated with the power of God. Yet there were parallels to Joseph's gift in the Book of Mormon. Ammon, for example, described King Mosiah as a person who also had the gift to translate. Ammon declared that "a gift which is greater can no man have, except he should possess the power of God, which no man can; yet a man may have great power given him from God" (Mosiah 8:16). Joseph and Ammon's statements say little about how God's power enabled them to translate ancient records, but both of them emphasized their callings as seers and prophets.

Some historical accounts claim Joseph explained the process further, but it is also clear that at times Joseph insisted on saying less. For example, in Orange, Ohio, during a conference in the fall of 1831, Joseph explained to the whole conference, "It was not intended to tell the world all the particulars of the coming forth of the book of Mormon."[9] Yet at another conference in Norton, Ohio, in 1834, Joseph apparently "gave a relation of obtaining and translating the Book of Mormon."[10] Nonetheless, Joseph continued to declare ambiguously that by "the gift and Power of God" he translated the Book of Mormon—a statement that by itself leaves readers to wonder about the mechanics of the translation itself. This vagueness has allowed many people to speculate about whether or not any of the produced text was the consequence of Joseph's own thought process and cognition or volition.

Even before Joseph wrote the preface to the Book of Mormon, his July 1828 revelation (D&C 3:9) provided some insight into how he was able to translate it. In the wording of the earliest manuscript, the revelation explains, "God had given thee sight <and power> to Translate." This suggests that Joseph's gift was his ability to *see* things that others could not.

Thus he was a seer. The concept of sight could possibly be a metaphor for a broader interpretation, but there is a parallel in the Book of Mormon that may help make sense of Joseph's revelation. The Book of Mormon explained that King Mosiah was a seer and that he could translate because "he has wherewith that he can *look*, and translate all records that are of ancient date; and it is a gift from God" (Mosiah 8:13). This parallel is even more germane to how Joseph translated because it appears that they both may have used the same device to translate ancient records.

Primary Scribes

The basic idea found within most of the historical accounts is that Joseph saw the translation of the Book of Mormon on seer stone interpreters, from which he dictated the text to a scribe who recorded the words. Nevertheless, the procedure appears to have differed slightly from scribe to scribe, as the accounts left by each person include unique elements. Joseph's scribes are extremely important witnesses, because they watched the process for hours at a time and though they apparently never witnessed the words appear on the seer stones, they conversed with Joseph about the translation for months during 1828 and 1829. They offer accounts of the process that are deeply personal and provide experiences that are second only to the experience of Joseph Smith. Therefore, it will be particularly helpful to observe the process through the eyes of Emma Smith, Martin Harris, and Oliver Cowdery—Joseph Smith's three primary scribes.

In December 1827, Joseph and Emma moved to a fourteen-acre farm in Harmony, Pennsylvania, where Joseph began translating the plates. Joseph's history states that in February 1828 he began peering into the interpreters, where he saw the words of the translation. Between that month and the spring of 1828, Joseph Smith may have dictated to Emma as much as two-thirds of a manuscript known as the Book of Lehi.[11]

During a private interview with her son Joseph Smith III in 1879, Emma responded to questions about the translation after a lifetime of thought and contemplation. Just months before her death, Emma told her son that she "frequently wrote day after day" at a small table in their house in Harmony. Joseph could not have concealed anything from Emma, as she sat "at the table close by him"—close enough to see exactly how the translation occurred. Believing that her husband could not have produced the text of the Book of Mormon on his own, Emma was as astonished by the translation as anyone. "Though I was an active participant in the scenes that transpired, and was present during the translation of the plates," she told one interviewer, as mentioned above, "it is marvelous to me, 'a marvel and a wonder,' as much so as to anyone else."[12]

By mid-April 1828, Martin Harris began recording the translation. He was much more outspoken about the translation of the Book of Mormon. Like Emma, Harris sat at the table near Joseph and wrote down the words as Joseph dictated. He likewise mentioned the plates lying on the table, wrapped in or covered with a small tablecloth. He left at least twenty-five statements about his involvement, declaring that "he was favored to write direct from the mouth of the Prophet Joseph Smith." Knowing that Joseph could not translate the ancient characters on the plates, he marveled at the complexity of the text and at how fluidly Joseph dictated the Book of Mormon to him.[13]

Oliver Cowdery began serving as Joseph Smith's scribe on April 7, 1829, in Harmony, Pennsylvania. From April until the end of May, the translation advanced at Joseph Smith's house in Harmony, and the remainder was finished in Fayette, New York, at Peter Whitmer Sr.'s house by the end of June. During that period, Cowdery recorded most of the original manuscript of the Book of Mormon, with some assistance from two other unidentified scribes (probably John Whitmer and possibly Christian Whitmer), who helped in June. Unlike Martin Harris and David Whitmer, who lived much longer and spoke often in their later years about their perception of the translation process, Oliver Cowdery died comparatively young, at age forty-three, so he left only a few statements.[14]

The Seer Stones

The scribes mentioned at least two types of seer stones: the spectacles, or interpreters, and one or more additional seer stones that Joseph had found.[15]

Spectacles, or Interpreters

Joseph explained that Moroni, "the same heavenly messenger" that delivered the plates, also gave him a device that held two stones, which Joseph referred to as "spectacles," and a breastplate to hold the spectacles.[16] (For more about this story, see chapter 2 herein.) Joseph's description of the stones as "spectacles" led to a misunderstanding of the way the stones actually functioned, according to witnesses.[17] The spectacles were simply two seer stones bound together like glasses without the earpieces, though they were not intended to sit on the bridge of a person's nose or wrap around the user's ears. The spectacles were larger than typical glasses.[18] Though most glasses are about six inches from one side to the other, Harris explained that the spectacles were about "eight inches" long.[19]

In the fall of 1830, Cowdery described the interpreters as "two transparent stones in the form of spectacles thro which the translator looked on the engraving & afterwards put his face into a hat & the interpretation then flowed into his mind."[20] In 1831 Cowdery testified under oath that Joseph Smith "found with the plates, from which he translated the book, two transparent stones, resembling glass, set in silver bows" and "that by looking at these, he was able to read in English, the reformed Egyptian characters, which were engraven on the plates."[21] One of Cowdery's earliest converts in Ohio wrote, "In the last part of October, 1830, four men appeared here . . . with a book, which they said contained what was engraven on gold plates found . . . about three years ago by a man named Joseph Smith Jr. who had translated it by looking into a stone or two stones, when put into a dark place, which stones he said were found in the box with the plates."[22] He explained that Cowdery had said, "While [Joseph] looked through the stone spectacles another sat by and wrote what he told them."[23] These statements can be compared with a newspaper article, not associated with Oliver Cowdery but published just a few weeks after the translation work was finished in June 1829. In this article, Jonathan Hadley, one of the printers Joseph Smith approached in Palmyra to print the Book of Mormon, claimed that the "very illiterate" Joseph told him the plates were found with a "huge pair of Spectacles," and that "By placing the Spectacles in a hat, and looking into it, Smith could (he said so, at least,) interpret these characters."[24]

Whether this report refers to Joseph's use of the Urim and Thummim in 1829 or to what was done in 1828 before Oliver's time is not certain, but it could refer to both. Drawing similarities between these stones and two stones that constituted the biblical Urim and Thummim, Joseph and others eventually called the Book of Mormon stones Urim and Thummim.[25] Though Oliver Cowdery later used the Book of Mormon term "interpreters," it is not found in many other accounts, and the term "spectacles" was later used interchangeably with Urim and Thummim.[26] William W. Phelps's article in the January 1833 issue of *The Evening and the Morning Star* exemplifies the use and confusion of these interchangeable terms. It claimed that the Book of Mormon "was translated by the gift and power of God, by an unlearned man, through the aid of a pair of Interpreters, or spectacles—(known, perhaps, in ancient days as Teraphim, or Urim and Thummim)."[27]

Other Seer Stones

Martin Harris saw Joseph Smith use the Urim and Thummim, but he also saw Joseph use a single stone. Harris explained that Joseph Smith "possessed a seer stone, by which he was enabled to translate as well as from the Urim and Thummim, and for convenience he then used the seer stone,"[28] which is understandable because the spectacles may have been somewhat awkward to use, making the long hours of translation more difficult.[29]

Harris claimed that he knew how Joseph was translating. He explained that by the "aid of the seer stone, sentences would appear and were read by the Prophet and written by [Martin], and when finished he would say, 'Written,' and if correctly written, that sentence would disappear and another appear in its place, but if not written correctly it remained until corrected." Harris was apparently an active participant in the translation, and his audible exchanges with Joseph made it apparent to him that words were appearing on the seer stone or stones in the hat. Harris believed that this process eliminated the possibility of any volition on the part of Joseph Smith. Joseph did not determine what was included in the text of the Book of Mormon; the translation apparently came directly from that which appeared on the seer stones.[30]

Emma Smith began transcribing again for Joseph Smith in the fall of 1828 and early 1829, but it is unknown what she wrote down for Joseph at this time. Emma wrote to Emma Pilgrim in 1870 that Joseph first "translated by the use of the Urim and Thummim [i.e., spectacles or interpreters], and that was the part that Martin Harris lost [the Book of Lehi], after that he [Joseph Smith] used a small stone, not exactly black, but rather a dark color."[31] Historical documents do not allow us to conclude whether Emma was speaking from actual knowledge or from supposition when she suggested that Joseph Smith carried out the remainder of the translation with this darker stone. She was not a scribe during the period from April to June 1829, but she was in the same house when the translation was taking place.

Because of Emma's statement about the dark stone, some historians have concluded that Joseph Smith used a single seer stone exclusively during this period of the Book of Mormon translation, but Joseph likely used another seer stone at that time as well. For example, interviews with Cowdery or speeches by him,[32] as well as one very early account close to the time when Oliver worked as Joseph's scribe, mention the interpreters or Urim and Thummim, which suggests their importance during the time Oliver scribed for Joseph.

Use of a Hat to Block Ambient Light

Significantly, the use of a hat appears in important witness statements relating to translation in Harmony (Emma Smith, Martin Harris),[33] as well as in Fayette (David Whitmer, Elizabeth Whitmer Cowdery).[34] In fact, before the printing of the Book of Mormon had even begun, in the earliest known account of the translation of the plates, the spectacles were described as being used in conjunction with a hat. The mention of the hat Joseph used often causes modern interpreters to relate the translation with magic. Yet the hat itself is as insignificant to the process as the table Oliver Cowdery used to write on during the translation. It was simply a tool that Joseph apparently used to block out all extraneous light.

According to several accounts, when Joseph used his hat, he began the process by placing the stone in the hat, in order to read the words that would appear on the stone. Joseph then dictated the words he saw to his scribe. Joseph Knight Sr., who provided financial support for Joseph Smith during the translation, recounted, "Now the way he translated was he put the urim and thummim into his hat and Darkned his Eyes" so that he could see the words a sentence at a time.[35] David Whitmer, one of the Three Witnesses of the Book of Mormon, gave many interviews about the translation between 1878 and 1888. Though he never claimed to have actually seen the words on the stone himself, his statements often spoke of the words appearing on something resembling parchment.[36] His statements typically testified with words to the effect that "Joseph Smith would put the seer stone into a hat, and put his face in the hat, drawing it closely around his face to exclude the light; and in the darkness the spiritual light would shine. Thus the Book of Mormon was translated by the gift and power of God, and not by any power of man."[37]

This process echoes the Book of Mormon account of a stone that "shall shine forth in darkness unto light" (Alma 37:23).[38] In addition, the placing of the seer stone and his face in the hat significantly suggests that Joseph was not reading from notes or a book.[39] In whatever way it happened, David Whitmer and some other commentators believed that the characters and the translation came into Joseph's fields of vision and understanding, and he was able to convey those emerging words to his scribes. This validates Joseph's lack of volition in the process and emphasizes Joseph's statements about the translation that it was by the "gift and power of God" that he translated the Book of Mormon. Emma explained that Joseph sat across from her "with his face buried in his hat, with the stone in it, and dictating hour after hour with nothing between us." Addressing criticisms that Joseph read from a prepared script or the Bible, Joseph III carefully inquired about her experience. Emma declared, "he had neither manuscript nor book to read from." In Emma's understanding, Joseph could not have read from anything that was not inside the hat, which was too small to encompass a large manuscript or a sizable Bible. "If he had had anything of the kind [books or manuscripts]," Emma declared, "he could not have concealed it from me." The seer stone in the hat was central to the translation; it was small enough to fit easily inside the hat, and according to Emma, the words appeared on the stones. Additionally, she explained that the plates "often lay on the table without any attempt at concealment, wrapped in a small linen table cloth."[40]

Witnesses testify that Joseph relied on divine assistance in carrying out the translation. As with the Liahona described in the Book of Mormon (see 1 Nephi 16:26–28), all these sacred objects required righteousness and diligence on Joseph's part in order to provide connectivity with divine inspiration. David Whitmer said that the seer stones worked only when Joseph was "humble and possessed the right feeling towards everyone."[41] Whitmer remembered a time in June 1829 when Joseph had a "stormy quarrel" with Emma. Still upset about their disagreement, Joseph went upstairs to resume the translation, only to find that "he could not translate a single syllable." The miraculous nature of the translation required Joseph Smith to be right before God and man; when this was not the case, his divine gift was temporarily withdrawn. Whitmer said Joseph went "out into the orchard and made supplication to Lord [and] was gone about an hour." He returned to the house, asked Emma for forgiveness, and returned to translating with Oliver Cowdery. The words again began to appear upon the stone.[42]

Controversy regarding Seer Stones

Despite their significance to the translation process, the seer stones have become a topic of mystery and even controversy. The most public and successful early attempt to denigrate Joseph Smith's use of the seer stones came with the publication of a book compiled by Eber D. Howe in 1834 called *Mormonism Unvailed.*

Motivated by the conversion of his sister and wife to Mormonism and funded by an anti-Mormon society in Kirtland, Ohio, Howe sent Doctor Philastus Hurlbut to New York in 1833 to gather evidence against Joseph Smith and the Book of Mormon. Howe attempted to prove to the public at large that Solomon Spaulding wrote a manuscript that Joseph Smith plagiarized in order to create the Book of Mormon. Howe claimed that, with Sidney Rigdon's help, Joseph plagiarized and appropriated Spaulding's text and manufactured the Book of Mormon.[43] In the process, he deliberately associated Smith's seer stone instrument with the culture of treasure seeking in New York. Instead of viewing the devices as instruments prepared by God for Joseph Smith, he associated them with mystical practices of using "peep stones" to find buried treasure. Howe stoked anti-Mormon sentiment and has continued to do so for almost two centuries by encouraging people to understand Joseph Smith's translation of the Book of Mormon as part of his agrarian folk practices. Though the more-educated classes often derided folk practices, the agrarian lower and middle classes, most of whom were presumably Christians, openly embraced them. In fact, these practices were often described through natural processes or "scientifically," but Howe attempted to reassociate Smith's seer stones as tools used for money digging.[44]

Folk practices like using a divining rod to find water can potentially represent the antithesis of our modern scientific worldview. Yet in Joseph's lifetime, using such stones to see lost or hidden objects was relatively normal, in much the same way that many people today believe that essential oils offer health benefits despite the skeptical response of the scientific community. Joseph occasionally joined with other local youth in attempts to use stones to find valuable objects. E. D. Howe and others negatively portrayed Joseph as a money digger because he knew about Joseph's treasure-seeking adventures with his friends.[45]

Modern historians have either seen Joseph's money digging as part of his religious radicalism or as a developmental period for his religious calling as a prophet. Either way, it has been difficult for historians to detach Joseph Smith's use of a seer stone from 1822 to 1826 from his use of seer stones after 1827 (when he began translating the Book of Mormon). Some historians have attempted to make his early experiences as a treasure digger insignificant, while others have described the same experiences as foundational for Smith's religious experiences as a translator.[46] These polarized views are supported by our knowledge of the culture at the time and by dozens of accounts taken from *Mormonism Unvailed* and other anti-Mormon sources produced decades later. Rectifying the differences of opinion will likely never happen, and firm conclusions about Joseph's interest in treasure digging may only be possible upon the discovery of new documents.[47]

Purpose of the Gold Plates

With Joseph looking into the hat at the seer stones, what need was there for Joseph to even have the plates in his possession? While most of the Book of Mormon translation accounts say little in this regard, the plates may well have served several purposes. Their mere existence may have instilled Joseph with confidence that the words that appeared on the stones were from an ancient record. In the face of persistent pestering, carrying and possessing the plates would have sustained his confidence that the translation process was authentic. His mission was to "translate the engravings which are on the plates" (D&C 10:41), and he spent some time scrutinizing and transcribing some of the characters on them. Yet the translation usually occurred while the plates lay covered on the table (although some accounts suggest that the plates were sometimes kept in a nearby box under the bed or even hidden in the Whitmers' barn during translation).[48] In addition, the plates encouraged belief in the minds of needed supporters, such as Emma, the Whitmer family, and the Three and the Eight Witnesses, each of whom spoke of having various experiences touching, hefting, feeling, and seeing the plates. The text of the Book of Mormon is abnormally self-aware of the plates; it focuses again and again on the provenance of and sources by which Mormon and Moroni compiled the gold plates. It essentially tracks the gold plates and their source material from person to person until the plates end up in the hands of Joseph Smith. The Book of Mormon even prophesies of Joseph's possession and translation of the record. Therefore, the physical plates fulfill thousands of years of preparation, and the witnesses provide authentication of the historicity of the plates. The plates were therefore indispensable for validating the ancient nature of the Book of Mormon.

Conclusion

Pulling together the accounts from witnesses and our understanding of the sacred instruments used for translation, we can now understand three components of Joseph Smith's translation process. He explained that he translated (1) by the gift and power of God (like Mosiah), (2) by way of an instrument (the seer stones), (3) which functioned through "sight" (as D&C 3 explained). Some of Joseph's close associates also elaborated upon what he revealed—most of whom spoke of Joseph's use of the term "Urim and Thummim" (either the spectacles or the seer stone),[49] while his scribes reference a single stone[50] placed in a hat used to shield his eyes from extraneous light. Given the different experiences of each of Joseph's scribes discussed above, it seems possible that Joseph Smith was not particular about using a single, consistent procedure. He seems to have alternated between one stone and two. In addition, as Joseph looked into his hat at the seer stones, he left the gold plates covered on the table or locked in a box.

Finally, though an examination of the translation relying on witness statements alone could be criticized as limited, it provides a historical foundation for others to expand upon. Literary theory, historical cognition studies, critical text work, and approaches from psychology will continue to produce interesting and thought-provoking theories and analyses, but the bedrock of their studies should be a well-documented religious experience given in the words of those who experienced it.

Notes

For a more complete discussion of this topic, see Michael Hubbard MacKay and Gerrit J. Dirkmaat, *From Darkness unto Light: Joseph Smith's Translation and Publication of the Book of Mormon* (Provo, UT: Religious Studies Center; Salt Lake City: Deseret Book, 2015).

1. For examples of apologetic scholarship that openly discusses the translation process, see the following works: Richard Lloyd Anderson, *Investigating the Book of Mormon Witnesses* (Salt Lake City: Deseret Book, 1981), 108; Hyrum Andrus, *Joseph Smith: The Man and the Seer* (American Fork, UT: Covenant Communications, 2005), 160–62; Leonard J. Arrington and Davis Bitton, *The Mormon Experience: A History of the Latter-day Saints* (New York: Vintage Books/Random House, 1979), 10–12; Milton V. Backman Jr., *Eyewitness Accounts of the Restoration* (Salt Lake City: Deseret Book, 1986), 84; LeGrand L. Baker, *Joseph and Moroni: The 7 Principles Moroni Taught Joseph Smith* (West Valley, UT: Eborn Books, 2007), 44; Susan Easton Black and Andrew Skinner, *Joseph: Exploring the Life and Ministry of the Prophet* (Salt Lake City: Deseret Book, 2005), 62–63, 266, 270; Steven C. Harper, *Joseph the Seer* (Provo, UT: Harper Publishing, 2005), 49, 62–63; Larry C. Porter and Susan Easton Black, *The Prophet Joseph: Essays on the Life and Mission of Joseph Smith* (Salt Lake City: Deseret Book, 1988), 13–14; John W. Welch, *Opening the Heavens: Accounts of Divine Manifestations, 1820–1844* (Provo, UT: Brigham Young University Press, 2005), 87; John W. Welch, *The Worlds of Joseph Smith: A Bicentennial Conference at the Library of Congress* (Provo, UT: Brigham Young University Press, 2006), 14–15.
2. LDS.org/Teachings/Gospel Topics/Book of Mormon Translation; Michael Hubbard MacKay, Gerrit J. Dirkmaat, Grant Underwood, Robert J. Woodford, and William G. Hartley, eds., *Documents, Volume 1: July 1828–June 1831*, vol. 1 of the Documents series of *The Joseph Smith Papers,* ed. Dean C. Jessee, Ronald K. Esplin, Richard Lyman Bushman, and Matthew J. Grow (Salt Lake City: Church Historian's Press, 2013), xxviii–xxxii (hereafter *JSP*, D1).
3. See Neal A. Maxwell, "By the Gift and Power of God," *Ensign*, January 1997, 26–41; Russell M. Nelson, "A Treasured Testament," *Ensign*, July 1993, 61.
4. The following are a few recent publications that try to address the extant sources: John W. Welch, "The Miraculous Translation of the Book of Mormon," in *Opening the Heavens: Accounts of Divine Manifestations, 1820–1844*, ed. John W. Welch and Erick B. Carlson (Provo, UT: Brigham Young University Press; Salt Lake City: Deseret Book, 2005), 82–98; Royal Skousen, "Translating the Book of Mormon: Evidence from the Original Manuscript," in *Book of Mormon Authorship Revisited: The Evidence for Ancient Origins*, ed. Noel B. Reynolds (Provo, UT: FARMS, 1997), 61–93. A hierarchy of sources is described in *JSP*, D1:xxviii–xxxii. For a recent speculative piece about the translation, see Brant A. Gardner, *The Gift and Power: Translating the Book of Mormon* (Salt Lake City: Greg Kofford Books, 2011).
5. Joseph Smith, History, ca. summer 1832, in Karen Lynn Davidson, David J. Whittaker, Mark Ashurst-McGee, and Richard L. Jensen, eds., *Histories, Volume 1: Joseph Smith Histories, 1832–1844*, vol. 1 of the Histories series of *The Joseph Smith Papers*, ed. Dean C. Jessee, Ronald K. Esplin, and Richard Lyman Bushman (Salt Lake City: Church Historian's Press, 2012), 11 (hereafter *JSP*, H1).

6. "Last Testimony of Sister Emma," *Saints' Herald*, October 1, 1879, 289–90. Emma declared "that the Book of Mormon is of divine authenticity—I have not the slightest doubt of it. I am satisfied that no man could have dictated the writing of the manuscripts unless he was inspired; for, when acting as his scribe, your father would dictate to me hour after hour; and when returning after meals, or after interruptions, he would at once begin where he had left off, without either seeing the manuscript of having any portion of it read to him. This was the usual for him to do. It would have been improbably that a learned man could do this; and, for one so ignorant and unlearned as he was, it was simply impossible." William Smith, Joseph's youngest brother, assessed Joseph's writing abilities by claiming that to say Joseph was illiterate was an exaggeration because he "wrote [with] a plain intelegable hand." William Smith, "Notes Written on 'Chambers' Life of Joseph Smith," ca. 1875, Church History Library.
7. As early as 1834, E. D. Howe in *Mormonism Unvailed* claimed that the text was taken from a manuscript by Solomon Spaulding and through the efforts of Sidney Rigdon. See Matthew P. Roper, "Myth, Memory, and 'Manuscript Found,'" *FARMS Review of Books* 21, no. 2 (2009): 179–223. Other, more-nuanced theories have emerged over the years, most of which included Joseph Smith having at least partial volition as he dictated the text. For examples, see Gardner, *The Gift and Power*, part 2; Brigham H. Roberts, *New Witnesses for God, Vol. 2* (Salt Lake City: Deseret Book, 1909); Skousen, "Translating the Book of Mormon," 61–93.
8. Book of Mormon (Palymra, NY: Grandin, 1830), iv. The statement specifically refers to the way Joseph Smith translated the Book of Lehi in the spring of 1828; Joseph used the same phrase in later years when referring to translation as a whole.
9. General Conference, Minutes, October 25, 1831, reproduced in Matthew C. Godfrey, Mark Ashurst-McGee, Grant Underwood, Robert J. Woodford, and William G. Hartley, eds., *Documents, Volume 2: July 1831–January 1833*, vol. 2 of the Documents series of *The Joseph Smith Papers*, ed. Dean C. Jessee, Ronald K. Esplin, Richard Lyman Bushman, and Matthew J. Grow (Salt Lake City: Church Historian's Press, 2013), 78–86. Perhaps his most detailed account came in an 1843 letter written to his friend James Arlington Bennet. The characters inscribed upon the gold plates, Joseph said, represented a language that "was lost to the world." Reflecting back upon the translation, "I stood alone, an unlearned youth, to combat the worldly wisdom and multiplied ignorance of eighteen centuries, with a new revelation." Even here, however, he does not describe the process beyond saying, "by the power of God I translated the Book of Mormon from hieroglyphics." Joseph Smith to James Arlington Bennet, November 13, 1843, Joseph Smith Collection, Church History Library.
10. See Minute Book 1, 43–47, Joseph Smith Collection, Church History Library. It was recorded at that meeting that Joseph "gave a relation of obtaining and translating the Book of Mormon."
11. *Saints' Herald*, May 24, 1884, 324. Anthony Metcalf claimed that Harris told him that he "wrote a great deal of the Book of Mormon . . . as Joseph Smith

translated or spelled the words out in English." Anthony Metcalf, *Ten Years before the Mast* (Malad City, ID: 1888), 70–71. In Joseph Smith's 1839 history he writes that Martin Harris "had written one hundred and sixteen <pages> of manuscript on foolscap paper." But, there is some doubt about this account since he edited the text to read: "we continued, until the 14th of June; having written. 216—pages of manuscript, on foolscap paper." *JSP*, H1:244–45.

12. Edmund C. Briggs, "A Visit to Nauvoo in 1856," *Journal of History* (October 1916): 454; Skousen, "Translating the Book of Mormon," 75–84.
13. Edward Stevenson, "One of the Three Witnesses: Incidents in the Life of Martin Harris," *Millennial Star* 44, nos. 5–6 (January 30 and February 6, 1882): 78–79, 86–87. See Welch, *Opening the Heavens*, 132–41.
14. Welch, "Miraculous Translation," 141–44; statements recorded by Ashbel Kitchell (1830), Josiah Jones (1841), Reuben Miller (1848), George Q. Cannon (1881), Edward Stevenson (1886), William Frampton (1901), Samuel W. Richards (1907), and Jacob F. Gates (1912).
15. Joseph Smith History, ca. summer 1832, 5. Joseph Smith seems to have used "spectacles" and "interpreters" interchangeably during the early years. Nancy Towle, an itinerant Methodist preacher, recounted Joseph Smith telling her about "a pair of 'interpreters,' (as he called them,) that resembled spectacles, by looking into which, he could *read* a writing engraven upon the plates, though to himself, in a tongue unknown." Nancy Towle, *Vicissitudes Illustrated in the Experience of Nancy Towle, in Europe and America* (Charleston: James L. Burges, 1832), 138–39.
16. Smith, History, vol. A-1, 7–8.
17. See "Golden Bible," *Palmyra Freeman*, August 11, 1829. See also Diedrich Willers to Reverend Brethren, June 18, 1830, reproduced in Welch, "Miraculous Translation," 173.
18. Martin Harris told Charles Anthon that the spectacles were "too large for the breadth of the human face." Charles Anthon to E. D. Howe, February 17, 1834, in *Mormonism Unvailed*, 270–71. One of Joseph Smith's neighbors, Parley Chase, who would not have seen them, improbably exaggerated the size by stating that "the glasses were as big as a breakfast plate." Parley Chase, April 3, 1879, in W. Wyl, *Joseph Smith the Prophet, His Family and His Friends* (Salt Lake City: 1886), 276. A late source more moderately claimed that Joseph had described them as "having very large round glasses, larger than a silver dollar." See Henry G. Tinsley, "Origin of Mormonism," *San Francisco Chronicle*, May 14, 1893, 12.
19. Tiffany, "Mormonism," *Tiffany's Monthly*, June 1859, 165–66. Speculating about this point, the size of the spectacles may have made it difficult for Joseph to focus on the text that appeared on its two stones and possibly forced him to focus on just one of its stones at a time to read the text.
20. Christian Goodwillie, "Shaker Richard McNemar: The Earliest Book of Mormon Reviewer," *Journal of Mormon History* 37, no. 2 (Spring 2001): 143.
21. A. W. Benton, "Mormonites," *Evangelical Magazine and Gospel Advocate* 2 (April 19, 1831).

22. Josiah Jones, "History of the Mormonites," *The Evangelist* 9 (June 1, 1841): 134–35.
23. Josiah Jones, "History of the Mormonites," *The Evangelist* 9 (June 1, 1841): 134–35.
24. "Gold Bible," *Palmyra Freeman*, August 11, 1829.
25. *JSP*, D1:xxx, xxxiii; Cornelis van Dam, *The Urim and Thummim: A Means of Revelation in Ancient Israel* (Winona Lake, IN: Eisenbrauns, 1997). Woodruff apparently saw one of Joseph's seer stones. Wilford Woodruff Journal, December 27, 1841; Richard Van Wagoner and Steven C. Walker, "Joseph Smith: 'The Gift of Seeing,'" *Dialogue: A Journal of Mormon Thought* 15 (Summer 1982): 58–59. See also Mark Ashurst-McGee, "A Pathway to Prophethood: Joseph Smith Junior as Rodsman, Village Seer, and Judeo-Christian Prophet" (master's thesis, Utah State University, 2000), 230–32, 247–48.
26. Exodus 28:30; Leviticus 8:8; Numbers 27:21; Deuteronomy 33:8; 1 Samuel 14:41–42; 28:6. On the biblical Urim and Thummim, see Cornelis van Dam, *The Urim and Thummim*. The "Urim and Thummim" mentioned in the Bible is apparently not the same object connected with the Book of Mormon in the Book of Ether. In D&C 17:1, the instrument is described as "the Urium and Thummim, which were given to the brother of Jared upon the mount."
27. "The Book of Mormon," *The Evening and the Morning Star*, January 1833, [2]. W. W. Phelps was editor of the paper.
28. Martin Harris, reported by Edward Stevenson to the editor, *Deseret Evening News*, December 13, 1881, 4. The interview occurred in 1870.
29. Each of the following sources describes the seer stones as large and even cumbersome. Joel Tiffany, "Mormonism," *Tiffany's Monthly*, June 1859, 165–66; *Deseret Evening News*, December 13, 1881, 4; W. Wyl, *Joseph Smith the Prophet, His Family and His Friends* (Salt Lake City: Tribune Print and Publishing, 1886), 276, footnote; Henry G. Tinsley, "Origin of Mormonism," *San Francisco Chronicle*, May 14, 1893, 12.
30. Stevenson, "One of the Three Witnesses," 78–79, 86–87. Regarding the spelling out of names or difficult English words, Joseph may have done this more often when Harris was the scribe than when Cowdery was the scribe. Although there is evidence in the Original Manuscript that Joseph sometimes spelled out proper names, the idea that he could not proceed without every word being spelled correctly is contradicted by a number of misspellings in the Original Manuscript, such as obediant, immagionations, treasurey, fateagued, and miricles (by Cowdery), inheretence, tortereth, covanants, and passified (by scribe 2), and treashury, diligent, desirus, and several others (by scribe 3), as shown in Skousen, "Translating the Book of Mormon," 65–66, 75–82. Many of these misspellings, written in the rush of dictation, were corrected by Cowdery when he copied the entire text over to make the Printer's Manuscript from which most of the Book of Mormon was typeset.
31. Emma S. Pilgrim to Emma Bidamon, March 27, 1870, Community of Christ Library-Archives.

32. When Cowdery returned to the Church in 1848, he declared that he "wrote with my own pen the intire book of mormon (Save a few pages) as it fell from the Lips of the prophet." Cowdery further explained, "As he translated it by the gift and power of god, By means of the urum and thummim, or as it is called by that book holy Interperters. I beheld with my eyes. And handled with my hands the gold plates from which it was translated. I also beheld the Interperters." Focusing upon his experiences while they translated, he emphatically stated, "That book [The Book of Mormon] is true." Reuben Miller, journal, October 21, 1848, Church History Library.
33. Smith, "Last Testimony of Sister Emma," 289–90; "The Three Witnesses to the Book of Mormon," 389–90; R. W. Alderman reminiscence, in *Naked Truths about Mormonism* 1 (January 1888): 3. In addition, Isaac Hale, Joseph Knight, and W. R. Hine also attested to use of the hat in translation that took place in Harmony. "Modern Superstition," *Visitor, or Monthly Instructor* (1841): 154–55; Joseph Knight Sr., History, 3–6; W. R. Hine statement, in *Naked Truths about Mormonism* 1 (January 1888): 2.
34. Traughber, "Testimony of David Whitmer," 341; Eri B. Mullin, Letter to the editor, *Saints' Herald*, March 1, 1880, 76; *Kansas City Daily Journal,* June 5, 1881; George Q. Cannon interview, February 27, 1884; Zenas H. Gurley, "Questions Asked of David Whitmer," Gurley Collection, CHL; "The Book of Mormon," *Chicago Tribune,* December 17, 1885, 3; *Richmond (Missouri) Democrat,* January 26, 1888; Nathan A. Tanner Jr. to Nathan A. Tanner, February 17, 1909, CHL; William E. McLellin to "My Dear Friends," February 1870, Community of Christ Library-Archives. In addition, William Smith also attested to use of the hat in translation that took place in Fayette. William Smith, *William Smith on Mormonism* (Lamoni, IA: Herald Steam Book, 1883), 80; "The Old Soldier's Testimony," *Saints' Herald*, October 4, 1884, 644; "Statement of J. W. Peterson Concerning William Smith," May 1, 1921, Community of Christ Library-Archives.
35. Joseph Knight Sr., History, reproduced in Dean Jessee, "Joseph Knight's Recollection of Early Mormon History," *BYU Studies* 17 (Autumn 1976): 35. Joseph Knight continues: "Then he [Joseph Smith] would take a sentance and it would apper in Brite Roman Letters. Then he would tell the writer and he would write it. Then that would go away the next sentence would Come and so on. But if it was not Spelt rite it would not go away till it was rite, so we see it was marvelous. Thus was the hol [whole] translated." Knight's belief that misspellings caused the sentence to remain on the stone until it was corrected allowing Joseph Smith to move on with translation has been refuted by the lack of such corrections in the original manuscript except in the case of a few proper names. Skousen, "Translating the Book of Mormon," 66–82.
36. David Whitmer, *David Whitmer Interviews: A Restoration Witness,* ed. Lyndon W. Cook (Provo, UT: Grandin Book, 1991). For example, in 1887 he said: "A piece of something resembling parchment would appear, and on that appeared the writing. One character at a time would appear, and under it was the interpretation in English. Brother Joseph would read off the English to

Oliver Cowdery, who was his principal scribe, and when it was written down and repeated to Brother Joseph to see if it was correct, then it would disappear, and another character with the interpretation would appear."

37. David Whitmer, *An Address to All Believers* (Richmond, MO: David Whitmer, 1887). David Whitmer repeated this description many times. While many of the details about the use of the seer stone in the hat are similar to Emma Smith's statements, the accounts of both Knight and Whitmer differ to some degree. According to Royal Skousen, leading scholar of the text of the Book of Mormon, the original manuscript supports the idea that Joseph saw and dictated multiple words or phrases, one cluster at a time, and that unusual names seem to have been sometimes spelled out and corrected if necessary, as David Whitmer indicated. The English text would not disappear from Joseph's view until he confirmed that what he heard from the scribe was correct. Edmund C. Briggs, "A Visit to Nauvoo in 1856," *Journal of History* (October 1916): 454; Royal Skousen, "How Joseph Smith Translated the Book of Mormon: Evidence from the Original Manuscript," *Journal of Book of Mormon Studies* 7, no. 1 (1998): 5.
38. David Whitmer explained that the hat would "exclude the external light. Then, a spiritual light would shine forth, and parchment would appear before Joseph." William Smith said that the hat, by blocking out the light, relieved Joseph's eyes from "strain" See Welch, "The Miraculous Translation," 146, 156, 165.
39. Thus Emma Smith, who mentioned the stone in the hat, could testify with assurance: "He [Joseph] had neither manuscript nor book to read from." Smith, "Last Testimony of Sister Emma," 289.
40. Smith, "Last Testimony of Sister Emma," 289–90.
41. Whitmer, *Address to All Believers*, 36.
42. Whitmer, *Address to All Believers*, 30; David Whitmer, interviews with William H. Kelly and G. A. Blakesless, January 15, 1882; and *Omaha Herald*, October 17, 1886, in Cook, ed., *David Whitmer Interviews: A Restoration Witness*, ed. Lyndon W. Cook (Provo, UT: Grandin Book, 1991), 86, 199.
43. Gerrit J. Dirkmaat, Brent M. Rogers, Grant Underwood, Robert J. Woodford, and William G. Hartley, eds., *Documents, Volume 3: February 1833–March 1834*, vol. 3 of the Documents series of *The Joseph Smith Papers*, ed. Ronald K. Esplin and Matthew J. Grow (Salt Lake City: Church Historian's Press, 2014), 116–20.
44. Keith Thomas, *Religion and the Decline of Magic: Studies in Popular Beliefs in Sixteenth and Seventeenth-Century England* (New York: Oxford University Press, 1971), 186, 215–18, 230, 242, 258, 410, 439, 635–36; David H. Hall, *Worlds of Wonder, Days of Judgment: Popular Religious Belief in Early New England* (Cambridge, MA: Harvard University Press, 1989); Jon Butler, *Awash in a Sea of Faith: Christianizing the American People* (Cambridge, MA: Harvard University Press, 1990), 225–88; Stephen A. Marini, *Radical Sects of Revolutionary New England* (Cambridge, MA: Harvard University Press, 1982); Ann Taves, *Fits, Trances, & Visions: Experiencing Religion and Explaining Experience from Wesley to James* (Princeton, NJ: Princeton University Press, 1999), part 1.

45. See Richard Lyman Bushman, *Joseph Smith and the Beginnings of Mormonism* (Urbana: University of Illinois Press, 1984), 64–76; Ronald W. Walker, "The Persisting Idea of American Treasure Hunting," *BYU Studies* 24, no. 4 (1984): 429–59; and Richard Lloyd Anderson, "The Mature Joseph Smith and Treasure Searching," *BYU Studies* 24, no. 4 (1984): 489–560.
46. Ashurst-McGee, "Pathway to Prophethood," 157–82; D. Michael Quinn, *Early Mormonism and the Magic World View*, rev. and enl. (Salt Lake City: Signature Books, 1998), 30–65; Ronald W. Walker, "Joseph Smith: The Palmyra Seer," *BYU Studies* 24, no. 4 (Fall 1984): 461–72; Alan Taylor, "The Early Republic's Supernatural Economy: Treasure Seeking in the American Northeast, 1780–1830," *American Quarterly* 38 (Spring 1986): 6–33.
47. For more, see the following document and its historical introduction: *JSP*, D1:345–52.
48. For "in the box," see Clark, *Gleanings by the Way*, 228, in Welch, "Miraculous Translation," 134; for "on the table," see "Last Testimony of Sister Emma," 51, in Welch, "Miraculous Translation," 130.
49. Joseph Smith, History A-1, in *JSP*, H1:222; "Mormonism—No. II," *Tiffany's Monthly*, May 1859, 163, 165–66; Josiah Jones, "History of the Mormonites," *Evangelist* 9 (June 1, 1841): 132–34; *New Hampshire Gazette*, October 25, 1831; John Corrill, *A Brief History of the Church of Christ of Latter Day Saints* (St. Louis: John Corrill, 1839), 7, 12.
50. It is possible that Joseph Smith detached one of the stones from the metal rims of the interpreters. In addition to the three accounts of Martin Harris and two accounts of David Whitmer that speak of him using first the Urim and Thummim and then a single stone, only the report by J. L. Traughber Jr. of a David Whitmer interview insisted that Joseph never used anything but the seer stone. According to Traughber, David Whitmer said that, in his presence, Joseph always used "a dark colored, opaque stone, called a 'seer-stone,'" and never the Urim and Thummim." J. L. Traughber Jr., "Testimony of David Whitmer," *Saints' Herald*, November 15, 1879, 341; reproduced in Welch, "Miraculous Translation," 145–46. David Whitmer, however, was speaking only of what he saw during the last stage of the translation in June 1829 in Fayette, for he never saw how the translation was conducted elsewhere. Furthermore, David objected that he was misquoted by Traughber. He clarified that he did not say that he "saw Joseph Smith translate," in the "immediate presence of the translator," but rather was simply "at the place and saw how the translation was conducted." David Whitmer to the editor, *Kansas City Journal*, June 19, 1881.

5

The Lost 116 Pages Story

What We Do Know, What We Don't Know, and What We Might Know

J. B. Haws

J. B. Haws is an assistant professor of Church history and doctrine at Brigham Young University.

From the outset, one thing we can say that we *do* know about the story of the lost 116 pages is that from the summer of 1828 until now, this episode has loomed large in the narrative history of The Church of Jesus Christ of Latter-day Saints.[1]

It would be difficult to imagine a more agonizing string of events in the life of Joseph Smith than what he experienced in June and July of 1828. Under pressure, he let Martin Harris take the hundred-plus manuscript pages of the Book of Mormon translation that Martin had scribed while Joseph had dictated.[2] The pages represented two months of work. The day after Joseph and his wife Emma bid farewell to Martin, Emma gave birth to their first child. The child was either stillborn or died soon after birth. Emma almost died in childbirth. After two weeks, and although Emma was still very much convalescing, Joseph and Emma's mutual anxiety about those manuscript pages prompted him to leave his wife in the care of her parents and make the long trip to Palmyra to find out why he had not heard anything yet from Martin.

Joseph had good reason to be uneasy as he made the trip. He reported that an angel had taken the interpreters from him even *before* he had discovered that the pages had been lost, taken "in consequence of [his] having wearied the Lord in asking for the privilege of letting Martin Harris take the writings."[3] This nagging anxiety so visibly affected Joseph that a fellow stagecoach passenger insisted that he accompany Joseph on the last leg of the trip to Joseph's parents' home in order to ensure that Joseph did not collapse under the weight of his worries.[4]

The sheer frequency with which the story of the pages' loss was retold in interviews and publications has something to say about the impact it made on all involved. So too does the emotion with which Martin Harris recounted this story to interviewers, by their account.[5] And as difficult as later setbacks and persecutions would undoubtedly be in the life of Joseph Smith, there is something uniquely piercing in the pain of self-recrimination. "It is I who have tempted the wrath of God. I should have been satisfied with the first answer which I received from the Lord," Lucy Mack Smith recalled her son crying out when he learned the pages were gone.[6]

This story has also been marked as a definitive moment in the prophetic career of Joseph Smith by two biographers who come at that career from completely different angles.[7] Such was the import of the events of the summer of 1828. This we do know.

What we do *not* know, of course, is what happened to those pages—or even if they are still extant.

Other than that, it seems that the most reasonable approach to be taken here is to discuss things that we *might* know, with varying degrees of substantiation and probability. Therefore, this chapter aims to survey current scholarship related to this formative moment in Mormon history, to draw on research from the Joseph Smith Papers Project and other documentary evidence to give a sense of the "state of the story," and to consider possible readings of early texts of revelations that grew out of what was both a pivotal point in Joseph Smith's life and ministry and a pivotal point in the development and makeup of the Book of Mormon.

Probabilities: Pages and Plots

The consensus of Joseph Smith's early critics and supporters alike seems to be that the 116 manuscript pages did, at one time, exist. That may seem like stating the obvious, but it is nevertheless worth stating. Even those who thought of Joseph Smith as a charlatan took it as a given that Martin Harris really did have a sheaf of handwritten pages from which he read to friends and family—and then subsequently lost. Joseph Smith and Martin Harris, over the course of the spring of 1828, really had produced *something*—and that something was apparently substantial enough, in Martin Harris's eyes, that he felt sure it would quell his family's doubts about the veracity of the work he was supporting. If anything, it was Martin's enthusiasm for the content of the pages that proved to be his undoing in this case. He had solemnly covenanted to show the pages to only a handful of family members; it was his disregard of this oath that was the transgression that precipitated the devastating loss. Later recollections had Martin not only breaking his promise, but also breaking the lock on his wife's bureau to do so, when the pages were apparently locked in that bureau for safekeeping and Martin wanted to get at them to show them to a visitor.[8]

The corroborating evidence of the pages' existence, then, even if that evidence is all in the form of human testimony, is strong on this point. Martin Harris, throughout his life, affirmed the basic details of the story; Joseph Smith recounted the story in the preface of the first edition of the Book of Mormon—and that preface was written just a year after the pages were lost. The fact that Joseph Smith made this story so public so early speaks to the common-knowledge status of the manuscript's disappearance.[9]

Just as telling, perhaps, is the absence of controverting testimony—the absence of claims, for example, that there never *was* a lost manuscript, or the absence of claims that the losing of the pages was a fabricated tale. This is especially significant when considering the principal actor in this drama—Lucy Harris—who had the most to gain, with regards to reputation, by disputing the *existence* of the pages if such were an open question. Lucy Harris was almost immediately implicated as the thief in question—and arguing that the pages never *existed* would have been a ready alibi to clear her name. But nothing in the historical record suggests that Lucy Harris (or anyone else, for that matter) attempted to dispute the pages' existence. It simply seems that such was not an open question.[10] Instead, as shall be seen, some acquaintances remembered her tacit corroboration of the pages' reality.

A more contested question is whether on not there was a plot to manipulate those pages. Joseph Smith said that he did not retranslate the lost manuscript because he had learned by revelation that a scheme existed to discredit him—and his detractors' manipulation of the 116 pages was central to that scheme. A tradition that has emerged in reminiscences, though, is that Lucy Harris burned the 116 pages immediately; one writer has recently concluded that this is "probably" what happened.[11] Hence, in that view, if Lucy Harris really burned the pages immediately, then Joseph Smith's fears (as outlined in the Book of Mormon preface) reflected a simple paranoia rather than well-founded (or divinely revealed) apprehensions about an actual conspiracy. But challenging Joseph Smith's credibility on that point seems much too hasty a conclusion, one that privileges some sources while downplaying others. This is because other early retellings of the 116 pages story suggest that a different report about the fate of the pages was still in circulation within only a few years of the pages' disappearance. For example, E. D. Howe, in his 1834 *Mormonism Unvailed*—a book that draws on affidavits collected by Doctor Philastus Hurlbut—wrote, "The facts respecting the lost manuscript, we have not been able to ascertain. They sometimes charge the wife of Harris with having burnt it; but this is denied by her."[12] In addition, John Clark, a former Palmyra pastor who had personal interactions with Martin Harris in 1827 and 1828, also assumed (in an 1840 publication) that Lucy did not immediately destroy the manuscript but instead planned to use the pages against Joseph Smith. Clark said that Lucy Harris "took the opportunity, when [Martin Harris] was out, to seize the manuscript and put it into the hands of one of her neighbors for safe keeping. When the manuscript was discovered to be missing," Clark continued, "suspicion immediately fastened upon Mrs. Harris, she however refused to give any information in relation to the matter, but she simply replied: 'If this be a divine communication, the same being who revealed it to you can easily replace it.'" The crux of the "plan" that "she had formed . . . to expose the deception," according to Clark, was to "keep the manuscript until the book [of Mormon] was published, and then put these one hundred and sixteen pages into the hands of some one who would publish them, and show how they varied from those published in the Book of Mormon"—because she "[took] it for granted" that the retranslated/reproduced portion "could not possibly" be "verbatim."[13]

John Clark may have, as one historian has read him, inferred the idea of a plot to sabotage Joseph Smith from the preface to the first edition of the Book of Mormon.[14] Yet not to be missed is the fact that the Lucy Harris plan that Clark describes is substantially different from the one that the preface describes, raising the possibility at least that Clark may have had other sources of information. It is difficult to ascertain precisely what Clark claimed as the basis of his familiarity with the story of the 116 pages. Clark said that he moved from Palmyra "very soon" after his 1828 conversation with Martin Harris but before the Book of Mormon was published in 1830. He also stated that he had "Harris' own account . . . to me" of the Book of Mormon translation process, including the use of a "thick curtain or blanket suspended between" Joseph Smith and Martin Harris during the translation. If what Clark was describing as "Harris' own account" referred to writing the Book of Mormon translation rather than just the so-called "Anthon transcript" of characters from the plates, then this suggests that at least one of Clark's 1828 interviews with Martin Harris might have come after Martin Harris had returned to Palmyra from Harmony after transcribing the 116 pages. If so, it is possible that Clark was still living in Palmyra when news about the loss of the 116 pages might have initially circulated. At the same time, Clark noted in 1840 that he was familiar with both the Book of Mormon preface and the revelation (now Doctrine and Covenants 10) to which the preface referred. In any case, that preface described the conspirators' plan to *alter* the text of the 116 pages so that this altered "original" would read differently than Joseph Smith's second attempt. However, Clark understood Lucy Harris's strategy to be simply holding onto the original and waiting to expose Joseph Smith when he published a second attempt that "could not possibly [be] verbatim." While it is true that Clark's proposal may have been his inference of the likeliest plot, based on his skepticism of Joseph Smith's work, it is also plausible that he remembered a Palmyra tradition that he picked up from conversations with his former neighbors.[15]

Regardless, there are enough examples of individuals who claimed knowledge about the pages' survival to complicate any easy conclusions about the fate of the pages. John Clark wrote in 1840 that Martin Harris "was indignant at his wife beyond measure—he raved most violently, and it is said [he] actually beat Mrs. H[arris] with a rod—but she remained firm, and would not give up the manuscript." William Hine of Colesville, New York, stated in 1885 that Lucy Harris gave the manuscript to one of his neighbors, a Dr. Seymour. Hine then remembered that Dr. Seymour "read most of it [the lost manuscript] to me when my daughter Irene was born; he read them to his patients about the country. It was a description of the mounds about the country and similar to the 'Book of Mormon.'" There are problems with the dates and places in Hine's record, but his principal assertion was that Lucy Harris had stolen the manuscript and "refused" to return it; "after I came to Kirtland," Hine asserted, "in conversation with Martin Harris, he has many times admitted to me that this statement about his wife and the one hundred sixteen pages as above stated, is true." Charles Comstock Richards remembered that he and his father, LDS Apostle Franklin D. Richards, met a man in 1880, Dr. J. R. Pratt, who "told my father that he could put his hand on the manuscript which Martin Harris lost, in an hour, if it was needed."[16]

Hine's and Richards's accounts are late reminiscences that should be treated critically as such, yet so are the recollections of those who claimed that Lucy burned the pages. In 1884, Lorenzo Saunders reported that Lucy Harris herself had told him that she had burned the pages. In fact, Saunders also claimed that Lucy Harris "never denied of burning the papers." As mentioned earlier, though, E. D. Howe reported in 1834 that Lucy Harris *did* deny burning the pages, and it is very conceivable that Howe based this denial on information he received from Philastus Hurlbut, who interviewed Lucy Harris in 1833.[17] Importantly, Howe's publication predated Saunders's reminiscence by fifty years. Of course, Lucy Harris's stealing the manuscript—with conspiratorial aims—on one hand, and Lucy Harris's burning of the manuscript on the other, are not mutually exclusive traditions; it is possible that both traditions reflect actual events. That is, it is possible that she (or others) *did* burn the pages *after* the preface of the Book of Mormon disclosed that Joseph Smith would not retranslate the Book of Lehi, thus thwarting any conspiracy.[18]

In the end, it seems that this question of the fate of the pages, and precisely what motivated their disappearance, cannot be answered with enough certainty to make definitive conclusions. But at the very least, it should be said that an attempt to use these reminiscences to dismiss Joseph Smith's fears or associated revelations as baseless does not do justice to the complexity of the evidence, especially the earliest evidence. To believers *and* to skeptics, Joseph Smith's claim that there existed a plan to discredit him did not seem either unreasonable or implausible.

Rather, there are a number of elements in this narrative that suggest the believability of the story that Joseph Smith and his associates repeatedly told. For example, two Latter-day Saint historians have described what they see as an independent "prophetic voice" evident in Doctrine and Covenants 3, the revelation that came right after the loss of the pages—and likely the first revelation that Joseph Smith committed to paper. Importantly, they see an authenticity in the independence of that voice—and almost surprisingly so, in the way that Joseph Smith is chastised. Richard Bushman wrote, "The speaker stands above and outside Joseph, sharply separated emotionally and intellectually. The rebuke of Joseph is as forthright as the denunciation of Martin Harris. There is no effort to conceal or rationalize, no sign of Joseph justifying himself to prospective followers. The words flow directly from the messenger to Joseph and have the single purpose of setting Joseph straight. . . . At twenty-two, Joseph was speaking prophetically."[19]

Also, in this authenticity vein, Jeffrey R. Holland asked some penetrating questions worth reconsidering: "If the loss of those 116 pages . . . was simply the disappearance of some thoughtful, wisdom literature and a few chapters of remarkably deft fiction, as opponents of the Book of Mormon would say, what's the big deal? Why then all that business about Joseph going through the depths of hell, worrying about whether he was going to get the manuscript back and fearing the rebuke of God. He's a quick study; he's a frontier talent. He can just write some more!" Then, after quoting Lucy Mack Smith's account of Joseph's despair and Martin's hopelessness when the pages were lost, Elder Holland said this:

> Well, my goodness, that's an elaborate little side story—which makes absolutely no sense at all unless, of course, there really were plates, and there really was a translation process going on, and there really had been a solemn covenant made with the Lord, and there really was an enemy who did not want that book to "come forth in this generation" (D&C 10:33). . . . Which is only to say what so many have said before: that if Joseph Smith—or anyone else, for that matter—created the Book of Mormon out of whole cloth, that, to me, is a *far* greater miracle than the proposition that he translated it from an ancient record by an endowment of divine power.[20]

Possibilities: Texts and Translation

"Reasonable" and "plausible" also seem good words to apply to two additional thought questions that arise in connection with the revelations Joseph Smith received and the translation work that he did after the loss of the 116 pages.[21] While these are tangential matters, they nevertheless offer some interesting possibilities about what we might learn about Joseph Smith's early prophetic ministry and education. The first such question deals with the contents of the 116 pages. The second question deals with the resolution of the lost pages story—a resolution that came through the translation of the plates of Nephi.[22]

First, Do we know any storyline details that were in the 116 pages but are not in the current Book of Mormon text? For a few years in the 1980s, we thought we knew more than we do now, thanks, unfortunately, to Mark Hofmann, a forger who sent shock waves through the LDS Church history community in the early 1980s, before his deceptions were discovered. In 1982, *BYU Studies* and the *Ensign* published the transcript of a purported January 1829 Lucy Mack Smith letter that a collector had purchased from Mark Hofmann. The letter was an incredible find—a window into the development of Mormonism, written as it appeared to be in the year before the Church was organized. In this letter to her sister, Lucy Smith purportedly described Joseph's loss of a portion of the manuscript this way: "On account of negligence the translation of the first part of the record was carried off by some unknown person but God is faithfull and the work is now about to proceed." Ten lines later in the letter, Lucy recounted to her sister some of the particulars of the Book of Mormon narrative, including the information that Lehi "fled from Jerusalem with his family and also his wife's brother's family a few days before Nebuchadnezzar besieged the City and layed it in ashes." Since that Sariah-Ishmael sibling connection is not explicit in the current text of the Book of Mormon, a reasonable inference was that Lucy had learned the detail from the 116 pages—and that's how the letter was presented in Church publications.[23]

But as is well known now, by 1985 the Lucy Mack Smith letter's provenance was called into serious question. It proved to be one of Mark Hofmann's far-reaching forgeries. His tangled web of deceit and murder unraveled before he could track down the two "finds" that he still sought after: the so-called William McLellin collection, and the 116 pages. At the very least, Hofmann's reported plan to forge the lost manuscript speaks to the prevalence—and believability—of reports that the 116 pages were *not* destroyed.[24]

Aside from this forged letter, there is, however, evidence for the possibility that another, authentic Lehi-Ishmael detail from the 116 pages did persist in Mormon tradition.[25] Nineteenth-century Apostle Erastus Snow mentioned in a sermon documented in the *Journal of Discourses* that

> the Prophet Joseph informed us that the record of Lehi, was contained on the 116 pages that were first translated and subsequently stolen, and of which an abridgement is given us in the first Book of Nephi, which is the record of Nephi individually, he himself being of the lineage of Manasseh; but that Ishmael was of the lineage of Ephraim, and that his sons married into Lehi's family, and Lehi's sons married Ishmael's daughters, thus fulfilling the words of Jacob upon Ephraim and Manasseh in the 48th chapter of Genesis, which says: "And let my name be named on them, and the name of my fathers Abraham and Isaac; and let them grow into a multitude in the midst of the land."

The current Book of Mormon text informs us that Lehi's sons married Ishmael's daughters, but there is no mention of Lehi's *daughters* having married Ishmael's *sons*, as Elder Snow described it. A careful reading of this Erastus Snow excerpt does not *require* that the 116 pages be the source of the information about Lehi's daughters and Ishmael's sons, but it seems a very likely inference.[26]

In a "things we might know" vein, then, details like these at least fall into the category of intriguing possibilities, and are simply further reminders of just how complex and layered the Book of Mormon narrative is.[27] That complexity and richness becomes especially evident as we think about the source plates of the Book of Mormon. It is on that topic that our final 116-pages-related question centers: *Could the reference to what seems like only one set of "plates of Nephi" in what is now Doctrine and Covenants 10—the revelation that informed Joseph Smith how to compensate for the loss of the 116 pages—be a subtle evidence of internal self-consistency in the Book of Mormon translation narrative?*

This question pivots on two hinges: the order of Book of Mormon translation; and what Joseph Smith would have understood—and when he understood it—by the phrase "plates of Nephi." What is suggested here, by way of response, is that the intricate link between the Book of Mormon translation work and the corresponding revelation in the Doctrine and Covenants (section 10) offers one more signal of Joseph Smith's narrative consistency and credibility in all of this.

There are enough persuasive bits of evidence to make a convincing case that Joseph Smith translated what we now know as 1 Nephi to Words of Mormon *after* he had translated Mosiah through Moroni. In other words, when Oliver Cowdery arrived in Harmony in April 1829, he likely began scribing as Joseph Smith translated Mosiah, where Joseph and Martin (and Emma and other possible fill-in scribes) had left off. One such piece of evidence that supports this is the appearance of the handwriting of John Whitmer as a scribe in the original Book of Mormon manuscript in the 1 Nephi–Words of Mormon section. It seems likely, then, that this section of the Book of Mormon was translated last because Joseph and Emma and Oliver did not arrive at the Whitmer farm until the first part of June 1829, after Joseph and Oliver had already been working on the translation consistently for two months. Another corroborating indicator is that the estimated pace of translation would have put Joseph and Oliver at 3 Nephi in mid-May 1829, right where Oliver said they were when they inquired about baptism, if they had started in April at the beginnings of Mosiah. This translation order seems like something that we can assert with a high degree of confidence.[28]

The order of translation is relevant to the story here because when Joseph Smith received the revelation that is now Doctrine and Covenants 10—the spring (probably April or May) 1829 revelation that instructed Joseph on what to do to resolve the lost manuscript dilemma—he had not yet translated the 1 Nephi–Words of Mormon portion, or that portion that we now commonly refer to as the "small plates of Nephi."[29] Because of that, it seems most likely that Joseph Smith would not yet have thought in terms of "small and large plates of Nephi"—more on that later. At stake, then, is how Joseph would have understood the Lord's words, and the Lord's intent, on that topic. Here is the earliest extant version of that revelation (now Doctrine and Covenants 10:38–42):

> And now, verily I say unto you, that an account of those things that you have written, which have gone out of your hands, are engraven upon the plates of Nephi; yea, and you remember, it was said in those writings, that a more particular account was given of these things upon the plates of Nephi. And now, because the account which is engraven upon the plates of Nephi, is more particular concerning the things, which in my wisdom I would bring to the knowledge of the people in this account: therefore, you shall translate the engravings which are on the plates of Nephi, down even till you come to the reign of king Benjamin, or until you come to that which you have translated, which you have retained; and behold, you shall publish it as the record of Nephi, and thus will I confound those who have altered my words.[30]

The passage just quoted seems to refer to only one set of plates: *the* plates of Nephi. However, today's readers of the Book of Mormon are accustomed to thinking in terms of two sets of "plates of Nephi"—a *large* set and a *small* set. Because of that common contemporary reading, it is not unexpected that a recent and important commentary on Doctrine and Covenants 10 suggested this about the passage just quoted: "The two references to 'the plates of Nephi' in this paragraph actually point to two different sets of plates."[31] But what if the repeated "plates of Nephi" phrases in Doctrine and Covenants 10:38–45 really only do refer to *one* set of "plates of Nephi," as they seem to do at first glance—and that is the set we know now as the "small plates"? This is the alternate (and perhaps more straightforward) reading suggested here. This reading would give the phrase more consistency because it fits the well-supported "small-plates-last" model of translation. Most important, in line with the theme here about narrative consistency and believability, this reading fits with what Joseph Smith likely would have known (and not known) about the composition of the gold plates *before* translating what is now 1 Nephi through Words of Mormon—remembering that he received Doctrine and Covenants 10 *before* translating 1 Nephi through Words of Mormon. This reading of Doctrine and Covenants 10:38–45 therefore avoids a possible anachronism and adds credence to Joseph Smith's account about the resolution of the lost 116 pages episode.

From everything we can glean about the plates that Joseph Smith possessed, only one section could accurately be called "the plates of Nephi," and that is the "small plates" section. All the other plates that Joseph translated from, based on internal descriptions from the Book of Mormon, consisted of Mormon and Moroni's abridgments and writings on plates of their own make. Therefore, contemporary students of the Book of Mormon understand the lost manuscript/Book of Lehi as comprising a significant portion of Mormon's *abridgment* of what we now know as "the large plates of Nephi" rather than a translation of the large plates of Nephi themselves. But it is doubtful that Joseph Smith and his scribes would have even thought yet in those terms. For one thing, the "large" and "small" descriptors do not come from Nephi or Mormon, but from Jacob's writings that were included on the small plates (see Jacob 1:1 and Jacob 3:13)—and Joseph had not yet translated the small plates at the time of the receipt of the revelation that is now Doctrine and Covenants 10.

How might Joseph have conceived of the source document for the 116 pages? In the preface to the first edition of the Book of Mormon, Joseph Smith described the contents of the 116 pages as "the Book of Lehi, which was an account abridged from the plates of Lehi"—*not* the plates of Nephi.[32] This characterization suggests a couple of key points. First, it is not unreasonable to infer that Joseph drew his understanding of this from Mormon's own characterization of, or introduction to, the opening portion of his abridgement. That is, since Lehi's story opened the record, it would have been natural for Mormon to designate that portion as the book or plates of Lehi; this fits, for example, the way Mormon introduced and grouped together books like Alma or Helaman, even though those books include abridged records of other custodial authors after Alma or Helaman. And Nephi himself wrote that he began his record (what we now call the "large plates") by documenting the account of his father, Lehi (see 1 Nephi 19:1). Second, up to this point in the Book of Mormon translation process—that is, up to the receipt of Doctrine and Covenants 10—Joseph and Martin had never translated directly from Nephi's writings (or Jacob's or Enos's) or from Nephi's plates, but rather from Mormon's abridgment of those writings—unless Mormon had included quoted passages or excerpts on his own plates from Nephi or Jacob or Enos, as he did with writings and sermons of, say, King Benjamin or Alma. But even those passages would not have come from what we know as "the small plates of Nephi," since before Benjamin's day, the "large plates of Nephi" were apparently kept by a different line of authors than were the small plates (see Jarom 3:14; Omni 1:25)—and Mormon reported that he did not even search out the small plates until he had *finished* abridging the account "down to the reign of this king Benjamin" (Words of Mormon 1:3).[33]

Therefore, if all of the references to the "plates of Nephi" in the revelation that is now section 10 of the Doctrine and Covenants refer to what modern Book of Mormon readers think of as the *small* plates of Nephi, the revelation reads very coherently. Here is a possible reading of the earliest extant copy of the revelation—chapter IX of the Book of Commandments—from that perspective, with suggested parenthetical interpretations: "And now, verily I say unto you, that an account of those things that you have written, which have gone out of your hands [the 116 pages], are engraven upon the plates of Nephi [small plates of Nephi]"—in other words, "The same basic story elements that you have already covered in translating the Book of Lehi ('an account of those things that you have written') are *also* narrated ('engraven') on the small plates of Nephi." The revelation continues:

> Yea, and you remember, it was said in those writings [the now-lost writings, or Mormon's abridgement of the Book of Lehi] that a more particular account was given of these things upon the plates of Nephi [the small plates]. And now, because the account which is engraven upon the plates of Nephi [the small plates] is more particular concerning these things, which in my wisdom I would bring to the knowledge of the people in this account: therefore, you shall translate the engravings which are on the plates of Nephi [the small plates], down even till you come to the reign of king Benjamin.

(The wording here is another indication that when Joseph recommenced translating after the loss of the 116 pages, he "apparently picked up where he and Harris had stopped, in the book of Mosiah," and then he translated the books of the "small plates" last, based on the instructions in this revelation.)[34]

As if to underscore the differences between the Book of Lehi and the plates of Nephi, the revelation makes this point: "Behold they [those who stole the Book of Lehi manuscript] have only got a part, or an abridgment of the *account* [notice: *not* plates] of Nephi. Behold there are many things engraven on the plates of Nephi [the small plates of Nephi] which do throw greater views upon my gospel."[35]

This suggested reading matters because the complexity of the relationship between the two sets of plates of Nephi likely only became clear to Joseph Smith *after* translating the small plates. Hence, it might very well have been anachronistic for a revelation in the spring of 1829 (Doctrine and Covenants 10) to refer to anything other than *one* set of the "plates of Nephi," since Joseph would not yet have been thinking in terms of having more than one record of Nephi, because Mormon only included in his compilation one set of records that appropriately bore the title "the plates of Nephi": the *small* plates. The phrasing of Doctrine and Covenants 10 thus fits with what Joseph Smith would have likely learned "line upon line" as he translated the plates, such that it also fits with a principle outlined in 2 Nephi and elsewhere: the Lord "speaketh unto men according to their language, unto their understanding" (2 Nephi 31:3; see also Doctrine and Covenants 1:24).[36]

In summary, the evidence for the order of translation, the dating of Doctrine and Covenants 10, and especially the "plates" phraseology of that revelation—all taken together—make for another example, subtle but noteworthy, of narrative consistency and authenticity in the way Joseph Smith and his associates related the "lost manuscript" chapter of the larger Book of Mormon translation story.

What is more significant, though, for modern readers of the Book of Mormon is the way Doctrine and Covenants 10 characterizes the addition of the small plates material: "Behold, there are many things engraven upon the plates of Nephi which do throw greater views upon my gospel" (D&C 10:45). It is this "greater views" aspect—this indication of providential foresight—that adds to the wonder of the inclusion of the small plates of Nephi, not only in our day but in Mormon's. President Boyd K. Packer has even proposed that Mormon's searching out and then reading of the small plates of Nephi, with their "things of [the] soul" (2 Nephi 4:15) orientation, "greatly influenced . . . the rest of his [Mormon's] abridgment."[37]

Conclusion: Misunderstandings and Miracles

In any event, thinking through the complex composition of the plates also defuses a criticism of Joseph Smith leveled by E. D. Howe, a criticism based wholly on a misunderstanding of the 116 pages episode. That misunderstanding, perhaps unexpectedly, offers an appropriate note on which to conclude this story. In his *Mormonism Unvailed*, Howe misread the Book of Mormon preface when it drew from the language of the revelation that is now Doctrine and Covenants 10. Howe did not realize that the translation of the "plates of Nephi" was to be a new, though parallel, account of the same time frame covered by the lost "Book of Lehi." Howe charged that the revelation's instruction to Joseph to "translate from the plates of Nephi until you come to that which ye have translated, which ye have retained, and . . . publish it as the record of Nephi" was simply giving the Book of *Lehi* a new title: "the record of Nephi." Thus, Howe accused, "the Lord, in order to counteract the works of the Devil, is represented by Smith as palming off on the world an acknowledged falsehood,—the records of Lehi must be published as the records of Nephi." Unfortunately, Howe incorrectly read the preface as nothing more than the Lord giving permission for some creative misdirection. What is also unfortunate is that Howe therefore missed what Latter-day Saints see as the miracle of God's foreknowledge in all of this. Howe wrote, "Again, an important record which had been made by a miracle, kept for ages by a miracle, dug from the ground by a miracle, and translated by a miracle, was *stolen* by some one, so that even a miracle could not restore it, and thus were the designs of the Lord counteracted by 'Satan putting it into their hearts to tempt the Lord.'"[38]

Latter-day Saints come to the precisely opposite conclusion. They see in the resolution of this lost manuscript episode—after all of the soul searching and heart wrenching it brought to Joseph Smith and Martin Harris—a miracle thousands of years in the making, beginning with Nephi's creation of a second record, and then Mormon's addition of that record to his abridgment (and both Nephi and Mormon wrote that they acted based on inspiration which they admitted they did not fully understand; see Words of Mormon 1:7; 1 Nephi 9:2, 5). Latter-day Saints see, in all of this, evidence that the Lord allows humans their agency, but neither human agency exercised in opposition to his will, nor "the cunning of the devil," can frustrate the works of God (D&C 10:43). They see in the 116 pages story a reassurance that "all things" really can "work together for good to them that love God" (Romans 8:28). For them, and for that reason, it is a story worth frequent retelling.

Notes

1. The story is summarized well in Grant Underwood, "The Book of Lehi," in *Joseph: Exploring the Life and Ministry of the Prophet*, ed. Susan Easton Black and Andrew C. Skinner (Salt Lake City: Deseret Book, 2005), 76–84; and in the "Historical Introduction" to "Revelation, July 1828 [D&C 3]," in Michael Hubbard MacKay, Gerrit J. Dirkmaat, Grant Underwood, Robert J. Woodford, and William G. Hartley, eds., *Documents, Volume 1: July 1828–June 1831*, vol. 1 of the Documents series of *The Joseph Smith Papers*, ed. Dean C. Jessee, Ronald K. Esplin, Richard Lyman Bushman, and Matthew J. Grow (Salt Lake City: Church Historian's Press, 2013), 6–7; hereafter *JSP*, D1.
2. A groundbreaking and important new book also discusses the 116 pages episode; see chapter 5 of Michael Hubbard MacKay and Gerrit J. Dirkmaat, *From Darkness unto Light: Joseph Smith's Translation and Publication of the Book of Mormon* (Provo, UT: Religious Studies Center; Salt Lake City: Deseret Book, 2015). One new claim the book makes—a claim about the scribing of the 116 pages—has bearing here. *From Darkness unto Light* proposes that "Emma had likely written the majority of the 'book of Lehi' before Harris ever arrived" (90). However, and without diminishing Emma's important work as a Book of Mormon scribe, other evidence suggests that this innovative new claim about Emma's primary role in the production of the 116 pages calls for further consideration. The bases for the claim seem problematic. For example, *From Darkness unto Light* has Martin Harris stating that "he wrote 'about one third of the first part of the translation of the plates as [Joseph] interpreted them by the Urim and Thummim'" (91). The quoted statement, though, is secondhand; it comes from an 1884 letter to the editor of the RLDS Church's *Saints' Herald*, in which the correspondent is reporting an interview he had had with Martin Harris in 1875. See Simon Smith's published letter in "Correspondence," *Saints' Herald*, May 24, 1884, 324. Significantly, that late reminiscence does not mention Emma at all, as scribe or otherwise; and in any case, Martin Harris's comment, if remembered accurately, could be read as his estimation that the lost 116 pages constituted about one-third of the eventual Book of Mormon manuscript. The same correspondent reported that Martin Harris told him, "I was Joseph's scribe, and wrote for him a *great deal*" (Simon Smith, "Correspondence," 324; emphasis added). *From Darkness unto Light* also quotes from Joseph Knight Sr. to imply that Emma was the earliest principal scribe in the Book of Mormon project: "Now when he [Joseph Smith] Began to translate he was poor and was put to it for provisions and had not one to write for him But his wife and his wifes Brother would sometime write a little for him through the winter" (85). But a closer examination of what follows this statement complicates that assumption. The "through the winter" time marker seems especially important, since the next line in Joseph Knight's account deals with *Oliver Cowdery's* arrival "the Next Spring," in April 1829—the year following Martin Harris's scribal work. Hence Joseph Knight's reminiscence seems to be pointing to Emma's work as scribe in the winter before Oliver Cowdery's arrival—that is, the winter of 1829 (which post-dated the loss

of the 116 pages), *not* the winter of 1828. To be sure, Joseph Knight's chronology of things is confused in this recollection. After relating that Oliver Cowdery "Came Down [to Harmony, Pennsylvania] and was soon Convinced of the truth of the work," Knight wrote, "The next Spring Came Martin Harris Down to pennsylvany to write for him and he wrote 116 pages of the first part of the Book of Mormon." While these questions of timing and narrative order make the Joseph Knight source a problematic one for establishing scribal order, what seems especially relevant in the full Joseph Knight account is that he specifically assigned the writing of the 116 pages to Martin Harris. See Dean Jessee, "Joseph Knight's Recollection of Early Mormon History," *BYU Studies* 17, no. 1 (1976): 35. Perhaps most significant in all of this is that locating Emma as a scribe in the interim *between* Martin Harris's work and Oliver Cowdery's arrival (the period "through the winter," in Joseph Knight's memory) also seems to fit with how Joseph Smith himself remembered this early translation work. In Joseph's earliest history, in 1832, *after* recounting the 116 pages story and in the context of discussing *Oliver Cowdery's* arrival, he stated "my wife had writen *some* for me to translate and also my Brothr Samuel H Smith." "History, Circa Summer 1832," in Karen Lynn Davidson, David J. Whittaker, Mark Ashurst-McGee, and Richard L. Jensen, eds., *Histories, Volume 1: Joseph Smith Histories, 1832–1844*, vol. 1 of the Histories series of *The Joseph Smith Papers*, ed. Dean C. Jessee, Ronald K. Esplin, Richard Lyman Bushman, and Matthew J. Grow (Salt Lake City: Church Historian's Press, 2012), 16; emphasis added; hereafter *JSP*, H1. In Joseph Smith's 1838/1839 history, he said that Martin Harris "returned again unto my house about the twelfth of April Eighteen hundred and twenty eight, and commenced writing for me while I translated from the plates, which we continued untill the fourteenth of June following, by which time he [Martin] had written one hundred and sixteen <pages> of manuscript on foolscap paper." "History Drafts, 1838–Circa 1841 [Draft 2]," *JSP*, H1:244. Thus Joseph Smith's histories seem to support the customary assertion that Martin Harris was the primary scribe for the 116 pages portion of the translation. It should also be noted that *From Darkness unto Light*, 100n33, acknowledges other evidence in support of this customary assertion.

3. *JSP*, H1:246.
4. See Lucy Mack Smith's account of this in Lavina Fielding Anderson, ed., *Lucy's Book: A Critical Edition of Lucy Mack Smith's Family Memoir* (Salt Lake City: Signature Books, 2001), 415–17.
5. See, for example, W. W. Blair's report of an 1860 interview with Martin Harris that was included in an 1880 RLDS printing of Lucy Mack Smith's *Biographical Sketches of Joseph Smith the Prophet, and His Progenitors for Many Generations*: "He seemed to be still conscience-smitten for permitting them to be stolen"; in Anderson, *Lucy's Book*, 422n179; also in Dan Vogel, ed., *Early Mormon Documents*, 5 vols. (Salt Lake City: Signature Books, 1996–2003), 2:311; hereafter *EMD*. See also "Interviews with William Pilkington, 1874–1875," in Vogel, *EMD*, 2:350–67.
6. Anderson, *Lucy's Book*, 418.

7. See Richard Lyman Bushman, *Joseph Smith: Rough Stone Rolling* (New York: Alfred A. Knopf, 2005), 69: "Eighteen twenty-eight was a turning point in Joseph Smith's development. It was the year when he found his prophetic voice." Compare Fawn Brodie, *No Man Knows My History: The Life of Joseph Smith, the Mormon Prophet*, 2nd ed., rev. and enl. (New York: Alfred A. Knopf, 1979), who saw in the 116 pages episode a point of no return in Joseph Smith's pious fraud: "A retreat from the fantasy he had created was impossible. . . . Although he may not have sensed their significance, these, Joseph's first revelations [after the loss of the 116 pages], marked a turning-point in his life. For they changed the Book of Mormon from what might have been merely an ingenious speculation into a genuinely religious book."
8. See Lucy Mack Smith's account of this in Anderson, *Lucy's Book*, 420–22. W. W. Blair remembered from his 1860 interview with Martin Harris that Martin claimed to have locked the manuscript in his bureau, which he then locked in the parlor, and to have put both keys in his pocket before going to bed—"after which he never saw them [the pages]." Anderson, *Lucy's Book*, 422n179; see also Vogel, *EMD*, 2:311.
9. Joseph Smith also briefly included the story of the 116 pages in his 1832 history; see *JSP*, H1:15–16. For a careful analysis of the timing of the writing of the Book of Mormon's preface—based on the typesetting of the first Book of Mormon signature—see Vogel, *EMD*, 3:480. See also *JSP*, D1:93n360. It is worth noting that it is in the preface to the Book of Mormon that Joseph first "specified the number of pages lost." The printing process, as the editors of *JSP*, D1, suggest, might thus also offer a clue to the source of the number "116": "This page count may be an approximation based on the page numbering found on the printer's manuscript of the Book of Mormon. The top of page 117 in that copy marks the beginning of the book of Mosiah, which corresponds to the end of the period covered in the pages lost by Harris." It is possible, though, that the numbering reflected what had been retained of the original pagination, since the editors of D1 note, "The process of preparing the printer's manuscript and providing portions to the typesetter suggests that the printer's manuscript may not have comprised 116 pages by the time JS wrote the preface." Historical Introduction to Preface to the Book of Mormon, circa August 1829, in *JSP*, D1:92–93. Compare Dan Vogel's analysis of the page numbering in Vogel, *EMD*, 3:480–81.
10. John Clark, a former Palmyra pastor who had personal interactions with Martin Harris in 1827 and 1828, reported that, from very early on, Lucy Harris was the chief suspect in this drama—yet Clark's account (published in 1840) only had Lucy "[refusing] to give any information in relation to the matter." As Clark portrayed it, Lucy did not deny anything; yet Clark, and others, still assumed Lucy Harris was the guilty party. See "Martin Harris Interviews with John A. Clark, 1827 & 1828," in Vogel, *EMD*, 2:269. In the affidavit Lucy Harris gave to Philastus Hurlbut in 1833, she spoke strongly against Joseph Smith's work and her husband's involvement—"the delusion of Mormonism," she called it—yet she did not mention the well-publicized 116 pages story. In Vogel, *EMD*, 2:36.

11. See Vogel, *EMD*, 2:270n26; and 3:480–81. See also Linda Sillitoe and Allen Roberts, *Salamander: The Story of the Mormon Forgery Murders*, 2nd ed. (Salt Lake City: Signature Books, 1989), 154–55, where they report that investigators in the Mark Hofmann forgery case met a descendant of Martin Harris who told investigators that her family tradition was that Lucy Harris burned the pages.
12. E. D. Howe, *Mormonism Unvailed* (Painesville, OH: E. D. Howe, 1834), 22. The preface to the first edition of the Book of Mormon is reprinted in "Preface to Book of Mormon, circa August 1829," in *JSP*, D1:93–94.
13. Vogel, *EMD*, 2:269–70.
14. For Dan Vogel's opinion that John Clark's account is based on an "inference taken from the Book of Mormon's preface, rather than any of the principals in the affair," see Vogel, *EMD*, 2:270n26.
15. Vogel, *EMD*, 2:268–69; see also Dan Vogel's analysis of John Clark's movements based on census records, in Vogel, *EMD*, 2:260. For a helpful analysis of statements by those who remembered a curtain/sheet hung between Joseph Smith and his scribe—and for an analysis of how that might affect questions of timing in the narrative of translation, see MacKay and Dirkmaat, *From Darkness unto Light*, 91, and 100n34–36.
16. John Clark, in Vogel, *EMD*, 2:270; William Hine, circa March 1885, in Vogel, *EMD*, 4:185–86; Charles Comstock Smith's account is reported in Vogel, *EMD*, 3:481. Recently, author Brant Gardner has also speculated that the "verbatim" issue might have been at the heart of the Lord's instruction not to retranslate the Book of Lehi, but Gardner comes at it from a different perspective, one based on what has been called a "loose" translation model: "Why didn't Joseph simply retranslate it? Ultimately, we have no answer other than the one Joseph gave, but there is another possibility. On some level, Joseph may have understood that he could not translate the same document twice in the same way, not because he lacked divine inspiration, but because the very nature of that inspiration produced a translation that was only a functional equivalent of the inspired meaning." Brant Gardner, *The Gift and Power: Translating the Book of Mormon* (Salt Lake City: Greg Kofford Books, 2011), 285. However, a number of Joseph Smith's associates remembered a Book of Mormon translation process where the verbiage revealed to Joseph Smith was more tightly controlled. See the extensive accounts compiled in John W. Welch, "The Miraculous Translation of the Book of Mormon," in *Opening the Heavens: Accounts of Divine Manifestations, 1820–1844*, ed. John W. Welch (Provo, UT: Brigham Young University Press; Salt Lake City: Deseret Book, 2005), 77–213.
17. Lorenzo Saunders interview, November 12, 1884, in Vogel, *EMD*, 2:149. On E. D. Howe and Doctor Philastus Hurlbut, see Dan Vogel's analysis in Vogel, *EMD*, 3:480. There is no mention in Lucy Harris's written affidavit of the 116 pages story, but that does not preclude the possibility that she and Hurlbut discussed the well-known story. See Vogel, *EMD*, 2:36.
18. This could be reflected in William Pilkington's accounts of his interviews with Martin Harris that show Martin considering both traditions concerning the fate of the pages. Pilkington remembered, in a 1934 affidavit, that Martin Harris

"believed his Wife burned it up," and then one paragraph later Pilkington reported that "[Harris's] Wife took the manuscript and he never saw it any more. So you see Willie, it was stolen from me." "Interviews with William Pilkington, 1874–1875," in Vogel, *EMD*, 2:354. It is worth noting that in an autobiography Pilkington composed four years later, he only recounted the theft thesis. Pilkington said, "She [Lucy Harris] took the manuscript from him and she was perusing them when someone jerked them from her, and then another got it, and Martin told me it disappeared, and he never saw it any more." "Interviews with William Pilkington, 1874–1875," in Vogel, *EMD*, 2:361–62. Lorenzo Saunders did not suggest the timing for the burning of the pages in his reminiscence, but James Reeves did in his 1872 account. Reeves suggested that Lucy Harris had burned the pages even before Martin Harris realized they were gone. However, Reeves's account is problematic (as are most of these late reminiscences) because it pictures Martin Harris "during the long winter evenings . . . [sitting] by the great open fire-place and [studying] his new text stopping now and then to pour a little inspiration into the ear of Aunt Dolly, who usually answered by telling him to 'shut up.'" Martin Harris, of course, had the pages during the summer of 1828. See "James H. Reeves Account, 1872," in Vogel, *EMD*, 2:342.

19. Bushman, *Rough Stone Rolling*, 69. See also Philip L. Barlow, *Mormons and the Bible: The Place of the Latter-day Saints in American Religion*, updated ed. (New York and Oxford: Oxford University Press, 2013), 22–25.
20. Jeffrey R. Holland, "A Standard unto My People," Eighteenth Annual Church Educational System Religious Educators Symposium, August 9, 1994, 5–6.
21. One possibility is that the mechanics of translation changed after the loss of the Book of Lehi manuscript. When Joseph resumed the translation, a curtain no longer was used to separate Joseph from his scribe; instead, the plates stayed on the table, covered by a cloth. And witnesses remembered him using a single seer stone more than the interpreters. See Bushman, *Rough Stone Rolling*, 71–72, for a summary of these recollections.
22. See Richard E. Bennett, "Joseph Smith and the First Principles of the Gospel, 1820–1829," in *Joseph Smith, the Prophet and Seer*, ed. Richard Neitzel Holzapfel and Kent P. Jackson (Provo, UT: Religious Studies Center; Salt Lake City: Deseret Book, 2010), 23–50, for insightful commentary on the lessons Joseph Smith learned during and after the 116 pages episode.
23. Dean C. Jessee, "Lucy Mack Smith's 1829 Letter to Mary Smith Pierce," *BYU Studies* 22, no. 4 (Fall 1982): 461; see also "1829 Lucy Mack Smith Letter Displayed," *Ensign*, October 1982, 70–73, which appeared under this descriptive heading: "Discusses information apparently from 'lost 116 pages'—including Ishmael as Sariah's brother."
24. See Richard E. Turley Jr., *Victims: The LDS Church and the Mark Hofmann Case* (Urbana and Chicago: University of Illinois Press, 1992), 58–67, 271, 318; Sillitoe and Roberts, *Salamander: The Story of the Mormon Forgery Murders*, 154–55, 534.

25. It is not unlikely that the Erastus Snow quote discussed in this paragraph served as the inspiration for the information Mark Hofmann included in his forged Lucy Mack Smith letter.
26. Erastus Snow, in *Journal of Discourses* (London: Latter-day Saints' Book Depot, 1883), 23:184.
27. Recently, historian Don Bradley has proposed that there may be lingering textual echoes of Book of Lehi content in the current Book of Mormon, as well. These include things like the identity of Aminadi, an ancestor of Amulek, whose appearance in the Book of Mormon is so brief as to imply that Mormon, as narrator, assumed readers would already know about Aminadi; or the story of how the Jaredite interpreters came into the hands of Nephite seers, something not spelled out in the current text of the Book of Mormon, but hinted at in the recollections of Fayette Lapham, who recounted a conversation on that topic with Joseph Smith Sr. See Don Bradley, "Piercing the Veil: Temple Worship in the Lost 116 Pages," paper presented at the 2012 FairMormon Conference, http://www.fairmormon.org/perspectives/fair-conferences/2012-fair-conference/2012-piercing-the-veil-temple-worship-in-the-lost-116-pages. Bradley has a forthcoming book on the 116 pages from Greg Kofford Books.
28. For a helpful summary of this, see Historical Introduction to "Book of Mormon Manuscript Excerpt, circa June 1829 [1 Nephi 2:2b–3:18a]," in *JSP*, D1:59–60. See also the translation order and dating analysis in Richard L. Bushman, *Joseph Smith and the Beginnings of Mormonism* (Urbana and Chicago: University of Illinois Press, 1984), 223n67.
29. For the dating of the revelation that is now Doctrine and Covenants 10—and the possibility that it is a composite revelation that was ultimately composed in April or May 1829—see Historical Introduction to Revelation, Spring 1829, in *JSP*, D1:38–39.
30. The revelation (the 1833 Book of Commandments version quoted here) is reproduced in Revelation, Spring 1829, in *JSP*, D1:40–42 [D&C 10].
31. The quote comes from *JSP*, D1:42n93. The reading proposed here is an alternate reading from that suggested in the D1 footnote.
32. Historical Introduction to Preface to the Book of Mormon, circa August 1829, in *JSP*, D1:93; emphasis added.
33. For a helpful discussion (and accompanying chart) of the custodians of Nephi's two sets of plates, see David Rolph Seely, "Plates of Nephi," in *Book of Mormon Reference Companion*, ed. Dennis L. Largey (Salt Lake City: Deseret Book, 2003), 645–47.
34. *JSP*, H1:38.
35. Revelation, Spring 1829, in *JSP*, D1:40–41 [D&C 10]. The passages quoted here correspond with Doctrine and Covenants 10:38–44. While the pages that contained most of what is now Doctrine and Covenants 10, in an earlier manuscript form, are missing from the "Book of Commandments and Revelations" ("Revelation Book 1" in the Joseph Smith Papers' designation), the manuscript page with the last part of the revelation (beginning with what corresponds now to Doctrine and Covenants 10:42) is extant in the manuscript Revelation Book

1. See Robin Scott Jensen, Robert J. Woodford, and Steven C. Harper, eds., *Revelations and Translations: Manuscript Revelation Books*, facsimile edition, *Joseph Smith Papers*, ed. Dean C. Jessee, Ronald K. Esplin, and Richard Lyman Bushman (Salt Lake City: Church Historian's Press, 2009), 13. It is worth noting that without knowing the contents of the 116 lost pages, it is impossible to know to what extent Mormon might have included information about Nephi's creation of a second set of plates. This part of the revelation (Doctrine and Covenants 10) suggests that the Book of Lehi at least alluded to the small plates of Nephi: "It was said in those writings that a more particular account was given of these things upon the plates of Nephi." Thus it is possible that this mention of the "more particular account" might have been the impetus behind Mormon's searching out the small plates of Nephi. But it is telling that the allusion is only to "*the* plates of Nephi" rather than a specific *set* of Nephi's plates.

36. It is also worth noting that Mormon does *not* refer to what we know as the "small plates" as the "plates of Nephi" in Words of Mormon; he calls them simply "these plates" (see Words of Mormon 1:3–5, 9, 10). Mormon seems to reserve the descriptor "plates of Nephi" for the "large plates." Thus the phrasing of Doctrine and Covenants 10 seems tailored to Joseph Smith's understanding, which was different than Mormon's understanding or terminology.

37. Boyd K. Packer, *Let Not Your Heart Be Troubled* (Salt Lake City: Bookcraft, 1991), 276.

38. Howe, *Mormonism Unvailed*, 22–23.

6

Martin Harris's 1828 Visit to Luther Bradish, Charles Anthon, and Samuel Mitchill

Richard E. Bennett

Richard E. Bennett is a professor of Church history and doctrine at Brigham Young University.

Few episodes in early Mormon history are as fascinating—and problematic—as the February 1828 visit of Martin Harris to Professor Charles Anthon of Columbia College in New York City. Scholars from both within and without the Church—those seeking corroboration for the translation of the Book of Mormon as well as those trying to debunk the authenticity of the whole story—continue to grapple with the details of this event and its implications. The purpose of this article is to shed light on this old story, to proffer new dimensions and interpretations on the trip's origin, to take a fresh look at Anthon's credentials and what he said to Harris, and to show whom Harris consulted with and what confirmation they provided. While there are details we do not fully know, it is clear that Harris returned from the East confirmed in his desire to assist in the translation and printing of the Book of Mormon, although perhaps for additional reasons than long supposed.[1]

The outlines of this story are well known in Mormon history. Working with the gold plates, Joseph Smith began the work of early translating in late

1827 from the "Reformed Egyptian" language found on Mormon's abridgment of the large plates of Nephi. Early on, he transcribed some of the characters from the plates as a sort of alphabet or reference guide.[2] His primary scribe was Martin Harris, a respected Palmyra farmer, an early and keen supporter of Smith's work who later became one of the Three Witnesses to the Book of Mormon. For a variety of reasons, Harris begged leave to take a transcription of the characters Smith had come across in his translation attempts to New York City, as historian B. H. Roberts writes, "to submit them to men of learning for their inspection."[3] Roberts says Harris submitted "two papers containing different transcripts, to Professors Anthon and Mitch[i]ll, of New York, one that was translated and one not translated."[4] According to Anthon's own accounts, Harris sought out Mitchill first, who then wrote a letter referring him to Anthon.[5] Harris later recounted that Anthon "stated that the translation was correct, more so than any he had before seen translated from the Egyptian," and after viewing the characters "said that they were Egyptian, Chaldaic, Assyriac, and Arabic, and he said that they were true characters and that the translation of such of them that had been translated was correct." He even wrote a note "certifying to the people of Palmyra that they were true characters." However, upon hearing Harris say in answer to his question that an angel of God had revealed such things and that part of the plates were sealed, Anthon promptly tore up his certificate. Denying the possibility of angels and of all such heavenly manifestations, he asked Harris to bring him the plates for him to translate. When Harris replied he could not do so and that parts of the plates were sealed, the man from Columbia brusquely responded, "I cannot read a sealed book." Harris then returned to Mitchill, "who sanctioned what Professor Anthon had said respecting both the characters and the translation" (Joseph Smith—History 1:65).

Unfortunately, Harris did not indicate how Mitchill would have been able to corroborate Anthon's response. Sometime later, perhaps after reporting back to Joseph Smith, this entire episode came to be interpreted as a fulfillment of Old Testament prophecy, that of "the words of a book that is sealed, which men deliver to one that is learned, saying, Read this, I pray thee: and he saith, I cannot; for it is sealed" (Isaiah 29:11).[6] Thus, "in spite of the limited ability of Anthon and Mitchell to pronounce judgment on the [Book of Mormon] transcription, and despite the ridicule from Anthon regarding the story of angels and the destruction of Anthon's certificate, Harris was sufficiently convinced to go into debt and devote his full time to the support of the young prophet."[7] Whatever Harris gleaned from these leading scholars, if he left Palmyra wondering and inquiring, he returned home supporting and defending the translation of the Book of Mormon.[8] Just who this Professor Mitchill was and what he actually said to Harris is no longer unknown, nor is it a mere footnote to this episode, and will constitute a major focus of this paper.

Many have presumed Harris went east primarily because he wanted scholarly validation or independent corroboration of the translation efforts of young Joseph Smith, who had very little formal education. Such a reason makes sense, particularly if he would be asked to help finance the publication of the final product. However, there may have been other reasons for Harris to seek insights from scholars. According to Joseph Smith's earliest 1832 history, Martin Harris had received his own independent, corroborative inspiration even before making the trip, as a result of his giving Joseph fifty dollars to move from Manchester, New York, to Harmony, Pennsylvania. "And because of his faith and this righteous deed, the Lord appeared unto him in a vision and showed unto him his marvelous work which he was about to do. And [he] immediately came to Susquehanna and said the Lord had shown him that he must go to New York City [with] some of the characters, so we proceeded to copy some of them and he took his journey to the eastern cities."[9] Perhaps, then, there was as much compliance as there was corroboration involved in Harris making the trip.

Furthermore, Lucy Mack Smith's account makes provision for precisely what kind of expertise Harris should seek after. "It was agreed that Martin Harris should follow him as soon as Joseph should have sufficient time to transcribe the Egyptian alphabet which Mr. Harris was to take to the east and through the country in every direction to all who were professed linguists to give them an opportunity of showing their talents."[10]

Much has been written about the so-called Anthon transcript which Harris took with him to New York, who authored it, what types of characters it represented, if it constituted an actual translation, and, if so, what it may have said.[11] Until recently, the prevailing notion was that this document (see fig. 1), now housed in the archives of the Community of Christ in

Independence, Missouri, was the actual piece of paper that Harris showed to Anthon and others in New York City in 1828.[12]

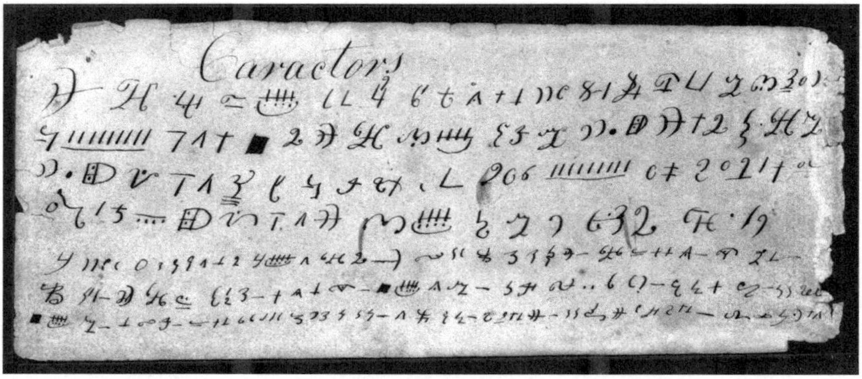

Figure 1. Anthon transcript. Photo courtesy of Community of Christ Library-Archives, Independence, Missouri.

B. H. Roberts has argued that at best the Community of Christ manuscript, containing only seven horizontal lines, was "a fragment" of what was submitted to Anthon and Mitchill and certainly not a translation manuscript in the true sense of the word.[13] Other accounts speak of parallel columns and a second transcription bearing the translation. According to Charles Anthon, the document which he saw showed letters in "perpendicular columns" in the "Chinese mode of writing" which indicates vertical, not horizontal, columns. He also remembered that "the whole ended in a rude representation of the Mexican zodiac."[14] Such is lacking in the Community of Christ copy. If Anthon's memory is correct, it is virtually impossible to argue with certainty that the Anthon transcript is the one he saw in 1828.[15]

Lucy Mack Smith says in her account that Harris was to seek out linguists "in every direction." Three of his contemporaries make it clear that he first stopped off at Albany, the capital city of the Empire State, before proceeding down the Hudson River Valley to New York. William W. Phelps said that Harris "went to New York City by way of Utica and Albany."[16] Pomeroy Tucker, who had sold the *Wayne Sentinel* newspaper and his printing operation to E. B. Grandin in 1827, remembered that Harris "sought . . . the interpretation and bibliographical scrutiny of such scholars as Hon. Luther Bradish, Dr. Mitchell, Prof. Anthon and others."[17] John H. Gilbert, Jr., typesetter of the Book of Mormon in E. B. Grandin's Palmyra print shop, remembered many years later that Harris "stopped at Albany and called on Lt. Gov. Bradish—with what success I do not know. He proceeded to New York, and called on Prof. C. Anthon."[18]

Why Harris chose to see Bradish is a topic of considerable interest.[19] Suffice it to say that the Bradish and Harris families had been well-established citizens of Palmyra for many years, that the two men therefore knew each other, that Bradish had become a very successful Wall Street lawyer and New York State assemblyman by this time, and that he was a man of means and influence and in a position to possibly assist in the costs of printing the Book of Mormon. Furthermore, Bradish had lived in Egypt as a special agent for the American government not many years before during the "War of the Consuls" between the British and French expeditions of the Upper Nile. Consequently he knew more than a little about zodiacs, manuscripts, Egyptian hieroglyphics, and the current state of research in Egypt. Any transcript purporting to show characters of reformed or ancient Egyptian would have been of interest to Harris's fellow Palmyran.

Furthermore, Bradish knew the printing business and an encouraging word from him could open doors in many places. For instance, we now know that Bradish not only knew the Grandin family well back in Palmyra;[20] but he was also a literary agent for James Fenimore Cooper, author of *Pioneer, Leather Stocking*, and other wilderness novels then coming into such rich popularity.[21] He also knew Washington Irving very well. Consequently Bradish knew Isaac Carey and Isaac Lea, well-known Philadelphia book publishers, and was in the ideal position to help Harris with the publication of any fine American manuscript, particularly one that might speak of Native American Indians. If Harris was looking for someone who could open doors for him in New York and Philadelphia, one who might help him either with financing the printing of the book or finding publishers for it, Bradish was the perfect man to see.

The two men likely met in Albany that February since the legislature was then in session. It is reasonable to conclude that they talked about Palmyra, Grandin, Joseph Smith and his work of translation, Egypt, and other topics. Very likely Harris showed him the characters which Joseph Smith had transcribed. The precise nature of their conversation awaits discovery, but there is no indication Bradish pledged any kind of financial support. An astute lawyer, politician, and businessman, Bradish had many friends in Palmyra and supporting Harris in a financially uncertain, highly debatable publishing enterprise might lose him credibility and support, especially when others in Palmyra were then also asking for his financial support.[22] Instead, Bradish likely recommended, since he knew the city well, that once in New York City Harris visit with the leading naturalist in the country: Professor Samuel L. Mitchill.

A Quaker from birth who was "rather short and inclining to corpulency," full-faced with a large double chin and "a pleasant open countenance," Mitchill in 1828 at age sixty-four was regarded by presidents and paupers, farmers and fishermen as one of America's greatest minds and scholars. A man of the many and a friend of every class, he possessed a voracious curiosity and "a taste for . . . new discoveries."[23] His door was always open for he delighted to learn from everyone, no matter what their station in life.

Mitchill also was well known for his "Mitchillian cabinet" of specimens of plants, seeds, and animals from all over the world.[24] His scientific interests knew no bounds. John Randolph called him "a chaos of knowledge," and Felix Pascali described him as "an umpire of all merits, inventions, discoveries, projects, arts [and] sciences."[25] He was known among his colleagues as the "nestor of American science," a "stalking library," and "the Delphic Oracle of New York," Even President Thomas Jefferson referred to him as "the Congressional Dictionary," greatly admiring him for his knowledge of the natural sciences.[26]

However, before offering his learned opinion on the written characters which Harris brought with him, Mitchill kindly referred him to his colleague, the young and upcoming scholar of linguistics, the thirty-one-year-old Professor Charles Anthon (1797–1867), AB, LLD. Born in New York City, Anthon began his study of Greek and Latin at Columbia when only fourteen years of age. At age twenty-three, he took up a position of professor of languages at Columbia. His famous edition of Lempriere's *Classical Dictionary*, first published in 1825, had already marked Anthon as a rising classical scholar. However, in 1828 he was but an adjunct professor of Greek and Latin, more an accomplished grammarian than a prestigious scholar. His first love was the classics, especially the works of Homer and Herodotus. While he knew Greek, Latin, German, and French superbly well, there is little indication he knew much about Egyptian, Hebrew, or any other Middle Eastern language. Because of his love of languages, he was probably aware of emerging research interests in Egyptian hieroglyphics and of the recent decodings of the ancient Egyptian writings on the Rosetta Stone by the magnificent French linguist Jean-François Champollion.[27] And, while it is reasonable to conclude that he may have been interested in ancient Near Eastern languages, Anthon was by no means a scholar of such. By force of his own brusque personality, he claimed to know more in this area than he really did.

When Anthon showed Harris the door, Mitchill welcomed him back and sanctioned what Harris showed him for at least two reasons. Like Anthon, Mitchill was a linguist having studied the Oriental languages, the classical languages of Greek and Latin, and was a student of many American Indian languages, hieroglyphs, and native dialects. He also knew of Champollion's great work.[28]

But, unlike his junior colleague, Mitchill had been studying the origins of the American Indian people for several years and had painstakingly developed his own "two races" theory of ancient America.[29] His interest in the history of the ancient American Indians was therefore at a peak when Harris showed him the transcripts.[30]

Professor Mitchill had, in fact, arrived at the conclusion that "three races of Malays, Tartars, and Scandinavians, contribute to make up the American population."[31] He believed that the Tartars (as he called the originating stock) were primarily from northeastern Russia and China.[32] He also had concluded that another great race of people had once coinhabited ancient America—a "more delicate race"—which he believed originated in the Polynesian Islands of the South Pacific. These people he called the Australasians or Malays. They were, however, eventually overtaken and exterminated by the more savage, warlike Tartars or Eastern Asiatics to the North—the ancestors of many of the North American Indians—and had long ago become extinct. Mitchill had come to the conclusion that they

> have probably been overcome by the more warlike and ferocious hordes that entered our hemisphere from the northeast of Asia. These Tartars of the higher latitudes have issued from the great hive of nations, and desolated, in the course of their migrations, the southern tribes of America, as they have done to those of Asia and Europe. The greater part of the North American natives are of the Tartar stock, the descendants of

> the hardy warriors who destroyed the weaker Malays that preceded them.[33]

Mitchill maintained that the "Iroguois" Indians were of "Tartar descent, who expelled or destroyed the former possessors of the fertile tracts reaching from Lake Ontario south westwardly to the River Ohio."[34] He went on to argue that the great last battles between these warring peoples had occurred in upstate New York, a few miles southeast of Rochester and not far from Palmyra, Harris' home.

It was probably for these and perhaps other reasons that Mitchill showed deep interest in the transcript of the characters Harris showed him. Whether or not he wrote anything to substantiate the veracity of the characters is yet unknown; however, we now know what the two men said to each other. According to the 1831 journal of New York newspaper reporter, Gordon Bennett, arguably the earliest account of Harris' visit to New York,

> He [Harris] carried the engravings from the plates to New York—shewed them to Professor Anthon who said that he did not know what language they were—Told him to carry them to Dr. Mitchell. Doctor Mitchell examined them and compared them with other hieroglyphs—thought them very curious—said they were the characters of a nation now extinct which he named.[35]

According to Bennett, the two men did not exchange any sort of a translation of the characters. If Harris had such in his possession, Mitchill never saw them. However, it is now clear that Harris showed the wise old sage of Columbia and "nestor of American science" the characters which he had brought with him from Palmyra. Mitchill, after carefully studying them and comparing them to the hieroglyphs in his possession, set them down as the language of an ancient American people.

Anthon's statement on not being able to read a "sealed book" gained traction and circulation among Mormon missionaries in the very early days of the Church. Furthermore, Church leaders and scholars have referred to Anthon's words many times since. Most notably, Le Grand Richards in his best-selling *A Marvelous Work and a Wonder*, a primer on the Restoration for millions of investigators to Mormonism, boldly declared that when Professor Anthon said "I cannot read a sealed book," he did not realize that he was literally fulfilling the prophecy of Isaiah found in the twenty-ninth chapter of Isaiah.[36]

In addition to the exchange with Anthon, those interested in the coming forth of the Book of Mormon should recognize that there was more to the story. It was likely Professor Mitchill, thanks to the recommendation of both Luther Bradish, Esq., and Charles Anthon himself, who gave the most scholarly corroboration Harris was looking for that winter of 1828. Returning home to Palmyra with the story of prophecy fulfilled on the one hand and, on the other, the sanctioning of all that Anthon may have said by America's foremost naturalist, Harris was ready to provide the financial means to publish the Book of Mormon.

Notes

1. Richard E. Bennett, "'Read This I Pray Thee': Martin Harris and the Three Wise Men of the East," *Journal of Mormon History* 36, no. 1 (Winter 2010): 178–216. See also Bennett "Martin Harris and Three Wise Men," in *Brigham Young University 2010–2011 Speeches* (Provo, UT: Brigham Young University, 2011): 77–92. An excellent earlier study on this topic is Stanley B. Kimball, "The Anthon Transcript: People; Primary Sources and Problems," *Brigham Young University Studies* 10, no. 3 (Spring 1970): 325–52. Kimball was the first to show that the Mitchell referred to in this episode was indeed Professor Samuel L. Mitchill.
2. Michael Hubbard MacKay, Gerrit J. Dirkmaat, and Robin Scott Jensen, "The 'Caractors' Document: New Light on an Early Transcription of the Book of Mormon Characters," *Mormon Historical Studies* 14, no. 1 (Spring 2014): 131–52.
3. B. H. Roberts, *A Comprehensive History of the Church of Jesus Christ of Latter-day Saints*, 6 vols. (1964; repr., Provo, UT: Brigham Young University Press, 1965), 1:99.
4. Roberts, *Comprehensive History*, 1:100. Where Roberts derived his information is subject to discussion. Sources other than the anti-Mormon 1834 publication *Mormonism Unvailed* include Joseph Smith's 1832 own history, in which he said Martin Harris "came to Susquehanna and said the Lord had shown him that he [Harris] must go to New York City with some of the characters so we proceeded to copy some of them and he took his journey to the Eastern cities and to the Learned [saying] read this I pray thee." Joseph Smith Letterbook 1, 1–6, Church History Library, cited in *The Papers of Joseph Smith: Autobiographical and Historical Writings*, ed. Dean C. Jessee (Salt Lake City: Deseret Book, 1989), 9. See also the account in the *Times and Seasons*, May 2, 1842, 772–73. Another possible source is Lucy Mack Smith, *Biographical Sketches of Joseph Smith the*

Prophet, and His Progenitors for Many Generations (Liverpool: S. W. Richards, 1853).

5. E. D. Howe, *Mormonism Unvailed* (Painesville, OH: published by the author, 1834) chapter 18, as quoted in Roberts, *Comprehensive History*, 104–5. See also Samuel M. Smucker, *The Religious, Social, and Political History of the Mormons, or Latter-Day Saints [microform]: from Their Origin to the Present Time; Containing Full Statements of Their Doctrines, Government and Condition, and Memoirs of Their Founder, Joseph Smith* (New York: Miller, Orton and Co., 1857), 37–39.
6. Joseph Knight, in his recollections of early Church History written "sometime" between 1833 and 1847, remembered the story this way: "[Joseph Smith] began to be anxious to git them translated. He therefore with his wife drew of[f] the Caricters exactley like the ancient and sent Martin Harris to see if he could git them Translated. He went to Albeny and to Philadelpha and to new york and he found men that Could Translate some of the Carictors in all those places. Mitchel [Samuel L. Mitchill] and Anthony [Charles Anthon] of New York were the most Larded [learned], But there were some Caricters they could not well understand. Therefore Anthony told him that he thot if he had the original he culd translate it. And he rote a very good piece to Joseph and said if he would send the original he would translate it. But at Last Martin Harris told him that he Could not have the original for it was Commanded not to be shone. And he was mad and said what Does this mean, and he tore the paper that he wrote all to pieces and stampid it under his feet and said Bring me the original or I will not translate it. Mr Harris, seeing he was in a passion, he said, "well, I will go home and see, and if they can be had I will wright to you immediately." So he Came home and told how it was and they went to him no more. Then was fulfild the 29th chapter of Isiah." Dean C. Jessee, "Joseph Knight's Recollection of Early Mormon History," *BYU Studies* 17, no. 1 (Autumn 1976): 34–35; original spelling retained.
7. Kimball, "The Anthon Transcript," 337. See also Vogel, *Joseph Smith—The Making of a Prophet*, 116.
8. *History of the Church of Jesus Christ of Latter-day Saints*, ed. B. H. Roberts, 2nd ed. rev. (Salt Lake City: Deseret Book, 1971), 1:20. See also *Times and Seasons*, May 2, 1842, 772–73.
9. Joseph Smith, History, circa summer 1832, in Karen Lynn Davidson, David J. Whittaker, Mark Ashurst-McGee, and Richard L. Jensen, eds., *Histories, Volume 1: Joseph Smith Histories, 1832–1844*, vol. 1 of the Histories series of *The Joseph Smith Papers*, ed. Dean C. Jessee, Ronald K. Esplin, and Richard Lyman Bushman (Salt Lake City: Church Historian's Press, 2012), 15.
10. *Lucy's Book: A Critical Edition of Lucy Mack Smith's Family Memoir* (Salt Lake City: Signature Books, 2001), 402.
11. See Howe, *Mormonism Unvailed*, 270–73, 352. See also John A. Clark, *Gleanings by the Way* (Philadelphia: W. J. and J. K. Simon; New York: Robert Carter, 1842), 232–38. Some have tried strenuously to debunk it as a hoax while others have made a painstaking comparison of the characters written on the one

transcript that has survived. Writing over sixty years ago, Ariel L. Crowley wrote a three-part series of articles in the Church-owned *Improvement Era* in which he offered a surprisingly candid and somewhat convincing argument, based on a careful comparison of the "caractors," that they showed strong parallels to the hieratic or demotic forms of a later Egyptian cursive language. See Ariel L. Crowley, "The Anthon Transcript: An Evidence for the Truth of the Prophet's Account of the Origin of the Book of Mormon," *Improvement Era*, January 1942, 14–15, 58–60; February 1942, 74–80, March 1942, 150–52, 182–83. Several Book of Mormon apologists since, in what critics have dismissed as "parallelomania," have tried to show similarities of the writings to "Merotic" and other forms of "Reformed Egyptian." Some have even compared them to Native American writings and have tried to translate them as part of the Jaredite exodus to the New World as recounted in the Book of Mormon. For a very careful, albeit sympathetic review of this topic, see David E. Sloan, *The Anthon Transcripts and the Translation of the Book of Mormon: Studying It Out in the Mind of Joseph Smith* (Provo, UT: FARMS, 1996), 57–81. For a negatively critical study, see William L. Moore, "The 1823 Detroit Manuscript: A Book of Mormon Prequel." See also Stan and Polly Johnson, *Translating the Anthon Transcript* (Parowan, UT: Ivory Books, 1999).

12. The Anthon transcript, a slip of paper 8 × 3¼ inches wide, passed into the hands of David Whitmer. After his death in 1888, the transcript remained in the custody of the Whitmer family, which eventually sold it to the Reorganized Church of Jesus Christ of Latter Day Saints in April 1902.
13. Roberts, *Comprehensive History*, 1:101.
14. Charles Anthon to Eber D. Howe, February 17, 1834, as cited in Eber D. Howe, *Mormonism Unvailed*, 271–72. See also Charles Anthon to Rev. T. W. Coit, April 3, 1841, as cited in John Clark, *Gleanings by the Way*, 232–38.
15. Recent research stemming from the Joseph Smith Papers Project convincingly shows that, based on handwriting analysis, the Anthon transcript described above was not written by Joseph Smith in 1828 but by John Whitmer in 1829 and therefore could not have been the one Harris displayed in New York City. In all likelihood it was a copy of an earlier facsimile, "likely derived from one of the documents that Joseph Smith created in the winter of 1827 and 1828." MacKay, Dirkmaat, and Jensen, "The 'Caractors' Document," 137.
16. William W. Phelps to E. D. Howe, January 15, 1831. I am indebted to my colleagues Susan Easton Black and Larry C. Porter for bringing this source to my attention. See their forthcoming biography tentatively entitled *Martin Harris: A Witness of the Book of Mormon*.
17. Pomeroy Tucker, *Origin, Rise and Progress of Mormonism* (New York: D. Appleton and Company, 1867), 41–42. Who the "others "may have been is still unknown.
18. Memorandum, made by John H. Gilbert Esq., Sept. 8th, 1892, Palmyra, NY: Palmyra King's Daughters Free Library, as cited in *Early Mormon Documents*, comp. Dan Vogel (Salt Lake City: Signature Books, 1998), 2:546–47. Fayette Lapham is reported to have had an interview with Joseph Smith Sr. in 1829,

but did not record it until 1870. According to his account, it was Joseph Smith himself who met with Luther Bradish in Franklin County, New York. Bradish could not read "the strange characters" shown him and advised Smith "to return home and go into other business." Fayette Lapham, "Interview with the Father of Joseph Smith, the Mormon Prophet, Forty Years Ago. His Account of the Finding of the Sacred Plates." *Historical Magazine* [2nd Series] 7 (May 1870): 305–9, as cited in *Early Mormon Documents*, 1:456–57. Considering the many inaccuracies of fact in this reminiscence, its lateness in writing and its spiteful, caustic tone, one must be careful about trusting this account implicitly. It was Harris, not Joseph Smith, who visited Bradish and it was in Albany, not Franklin County, where their meeting took place.

19. Bennett, "'Read This I Pray Thee': Martin Harris and the Three Wise Men of the East," *Journal of Mormon History* 36, no. 1 (Winter 2010): 178–216. See also his "A Very Particular Friend: Luther Bradish," in the forthcoming *Approaching Antiquity: The Ancient World in Joseph Smith's Mormonism*, ed. Lincoln H. Blumell, Matthew J. Grey, and Andrew H. Hedges (Provo, UT: Religious Studies Center; Salt Lake City: Deseret Book, 2015).
20. P[hilip] Grandin to Luther Bradish, April 18, 1829, Luther Bradish Papers, New York Historical Society. Philip Grandin was a brother of E. B. Grandin.
21. Cooper was a then a rising voice in American historical romantic novels of frontier and Indian life in early America. He had published his first novel, *Precaution*, in 1820. His much better and commercially more successful work, *The Spy*, came out the following year. After writing *The Pilot* and *Lionel Lincoln*, he published arguably his greatest work, *The Last of the Mohicans*, with Isaac Carey and Isaac Lea Publishers of Philadelphia.
22. Rev. Joseph Colt to Luther Bradish, October 30, 1827, Luther Bradish Papers, New York Historical Society. The fact is many others from all around the state were asking him for money. See, for instance, Martin Wilkins to Luther Bradish, June 14, 1829, Luther Bradish Papers, New York Historical Society.
23. Samuel Griscom Diary, May 24, 1824, New York Historical Society.
24. For example, see New York State Board of Agriculture, *An Examination into the Expediency of Establishing a Board of Agriculture in the State of New York* (Brooklyn: E. Worthington, 1819), 47–50. For his discovery of ancient mastadons, see *American Monthly* 1, no. 3 (July 1817): 195–96 and 2, no. 1 (November 1817): 46–47, 56–57.
25. Felix Pascali, MD, *Essay on the Life and Character of the Honorable Samuel Latham Mitchill, M. D. . . . October 15, 1831* (New York: American Argus Press, 1831), 22.
26. John W. Francis, *Reminiscences of Samuel Latham Mitchill* (New York: J. F. Trow, 1859), 26. "Dr. Mitchill's Letters from Washington: 1801–1813," *Harper's New Monthly Magazine* 58, no. 347 (April 1879): 740. Ronald E. Shaw, *Erie Water West: A History of the Erie Canal, 1792–1854* (Lexington; University of Kentucky Press, 1966), 94.
27. Among the better-known published works on Egyptian hieroglyphics available in 1828 were Jean-Pierre Rigord's longstanding *Memoire de Trevoux,* first

published in 1704, Georg Zoega's *Du Origine et Usu Obeliscorum* (1797), *Les Description d'Egypte*, (1809), Thomas Young's *Museum Criticum VI* (1815), and Jean-Francois Champollion's famous *Lettre a M. Dacier* (1822) and his follow-up work, *Precis du Systeme Hieroglyphique* (1824). The latter two works of Champollion not only gave facsimiles of hieroglyphs but code-breaking translations. How many of these works Anthon or Mitchill had in their possession or were aware of is impossible to determine. For a good study on this topic, see Maurice Pope, *The Story of Decipherment—From Egyptian Hieroglyphs to Maya Script*, rev. ed. (London: Thomas and Hudson, 1999), chapters 2 and 3.

28. Francis, "Reminiscences of Samuel Latham Mitchill," 16–18. At one time he gave a "profound exegetical disquisition upon Kennicott's Hebrew Bible in disproof of the interpretations of Gershom Seixas, the great Jewish rabbi of the age." Beverly Smith, *The Lantern*, College Papers.
29. Mitchill, "Discourse on Thomas Jefferson," 15.
30. Samuel L. Mitchill, *A Lecture on Some Parts of the Natural History of New Jersey. Delivered Before the Newark Mechanic Association . . . 3 June 1828* (New York: Elliott and Palmer, 1828).
31. Letter of Samuel L. Mitchill of New York to Samuel M. Burnside, Esq., Corresponding Secretary of the American Antiquarian Society, January 13, 1817, as published in *Archaeologia Americana: Transactions and Collections of the American Antiquarian Society* (1885; repr., Worchester, MA: Jonshon Reprint, 1971), 1:314–15.
32. E. Howitt, *Selections from Letters Written During a Tour of the United States, in the Summer and Autumn of 1819 Illustrative of the Character of the Native Indians, and Their Descent from the Lost Ten Tribes of Israel* (Nottingham, England: J. Dunn, 1819).
33. *Archaeologia Americana*, 324–25. Mitchill went on to write Clinton in 1816 that "the northern tribes were probably more hardy, ferocious, and warlike than those of the south" and that "the hordes dwelling in the higher latitudes have overpowered the more civilized, though feebler inhabitants of the countries situated towards the equator. . . . The surviving race in these terrible conflicts between the different nations of the ancient natives residents of North America, is evidently that of the Tartars." *Archaeologia Americana*, 326.
34. Samuel L. Mitchill to John W. Francis, September 13, 1816, Samuel L. Mitchill Collection, Rare Books Dept., Countway Library of Medicine, Harvard University Library, Boston.
35. From an original twenty-nine-page holograph journal of James Gordon Bennett, June 12–August 18, 1831. Bennett's holograph journal tells of his journey through upstate New York, part of the time in company with Martin Van Buren, Benjamin F. Butler, and Nathaniel S. Benton. Special Collections, New York Public Library, New York City.
36. LeGrand Richards, *A Marvelous Work and a Wonder* (1950; repr., Salt Lake City: Deseret Book, 1976), 49.

7

The Eleven Witnesses

Steven C. Harper

Steven C. Harper is a historian at the Church History Department, The Church of Jesus Christ of Latter-day Saints.

Throughout the spring of 1829, Joseph Smith translated and dictated the text of the Book of Mormon, pausing at times to preach to inquiring neighbors. By mid-June 1829, Joseph learned of the Lord's intent to provide three witnesses to the gold plates and apparently completed the translation through Moroni's words to his Lamanite brethren. Scribe Oliver Cowdery had penned what would become the book's beginning pages, listening to Nephi introduce himself, his family, and his various sets of plates (see D&C 5:11–15, 24–26, Ether 5:4).[1]

As the translation neared completion, Joseph learned more about the Lord's long-standing plan to show the plates to handpicked witnesses. "At that day when the book shall be delivered unto the man of whom I have spoken," Joseph said to his scribe, quoting Nephi, who was quoting the Lord's revelation to Isaiah, "the book shall be hid from the eyes of the world, that the eyes of none shall behold it save it be that three witnesses shall behold it, by the power of God, besides him to whom the book shall be delivered; and they shall testify to the truth of the book and the things therein." No one else would see it, the Lord continued, "save it be a few according to the will of God, to bear testimony of his word" (see 2 Nephi 27:12–13).

As the translation neared completion, Oliver Cowdery and David Whitmer, along with Martin Harris, who had come from Palmyra to the Whitmer's Fayette, New York, home to check the translation's progress, began begging to be the Three Witnesses. Joseph asked the Lord and looked in the stones, revealing a yes—if they relied on the Lord wholeheartedly and understood that they were committing themselves to testify, they could see.[2] For Martin, there was an added condition, the earlier revelation's requirement (see D&C 5:24). "You have got to humble yourself before your God this day," Joseph told him, "and obtain if possible a forgiveness of your sins."[3]

Joseph led the three men to the woods, where they knelt together and took turns asking God to show them the plates. But he didn't. Not the first time they prayed, nor the second. It wasn't until Martin stood up and confessed that he was the reason the heavens remained closed. He left the others to retreat further into the woods, and then the vision the men sought was opened. Joseph testified that an angel stood before them with the plates in his hands, turning the leaves one by one so they could see the engraved writing."[4] Oliver and David later declared, "An angel of God came down from Heaven & he brought & laid before our eyes that we beheld & saw the plates & the engravings thereon."[5]

Afterward, Joseph followed Martin's path and found him in prayer, contrite, complying with the instructions he had received. When Martin saw Joseph, he asked him to join his earnest prayer that he could have the same experience. Their prayer was only half uttered, Joseph said, when "the same vision was opened to our view" and he heard and saw the same angel with the engraved plates, while Martin began to cry joyfully, "Mine eyes have beheld, mine eyes have beheld."[6]

Joseph later showed the plates to his father, to his brothers Hyrum and Samuel, and to several of David's brothers: Christian, Jacob, Peter, and John, as well as to David's sister Catherine's husband, Hiram Page, each man handling the plates himself, each man later testifying that they saw the plates Joseph had, hefted them, and examined the engravings on them.[7] Then, when Joseph had finished translating, he returned the plates to the angel and gathered the witnesses and their families for an evening of testifying and celebration.[8] "I bless God in the sincerity of my soul," Martin said, "that he has condescended to make me, even me, a witness of the greatness of his work." Oliver and David added their amens.[9] (For other less-formal witnesses, see the chapter by Amy Easton-Flake and Rachel Cope herein.)

Evaluating the Book of Mormon Witnesses

The testimonies of the Three and Eight Witnesses printed in each copy of the Book of Mormon are some of the most compelling evidence in favor of its miraculous revelation and translation. It is remarkable to have depositions by eleven men of the gold plates' existence, including three who testified of an angelic visitation. The three saw and the eight "hefted" the plates. For believers, that approaches proof of Joseph Smith's miraculous claims. But some have questioned the nature of the witnesses' experiences, arguing that they were supernatural and visionary.[10] The witnesses, this argument asserts, did not see or touch ancient artifacts as we see or handle trees or chairs, but saw only through unreliably subjective "spiritual eyes," rendering their statements null and void.

Advocates of this thesis cite visionaries including Joseph Smith, who spoke of seeing with an "eye of faith" and distinguished between the kinds of seeing done with "spiritual" and "natural" eyes.[11] They claim Martin Harris saw only "with the spiritual eye" and rely on hearsay accounts that Harris disclaimed he saw the Book of Mormon artifacts with his natural eyes.[12] Skeptics also note reasons to suspect the testimony of the Eight Witnesses, citing Stephen Burnett's 1838 claim that Martin Harris said that "the eight witnesses never saw them."[13] The suggestion that the Eight Witnesses never actually saw or hefted the plates and that the Three Witnesses viewed them solely supernaturally leads some to wonder if the witnesses saw anything substantive at all, opening to question the plates' existence and the Book of Mormon's truthfulness.[14]

The evidence left by the Book of Mormon witnesses is rich, varied, and uneven, including the following: The earliest documented statement of the Three Witnesses—Oliver Cowdery, David Whitmer, and Martin Harris—is their statement in the handwriting of Oliver Cowdery subsequently published in the 1830 edition of the Book of Mormon. For the Eight Witnesses, it is their statement in the printer's manuscript of the Book of Mormon, also in the handwriting of Oliver Cowdery. The known historical record includes direct statements by two of the Three Witnesses and three of the

Eight Witnesses that affirm their original testimonies. In addition, there are statements from people who heard—or heard of—one or more witnesses describing their experiences.

This last kind of evidence is both the most plentiful and the most problematic because it is hearsay. It is not personal knowledge of a witness but filtered through someone else. These statements were heard, written, and sometimes published by persons with vested interests either in affirming the truthfulness of the Book of Mormon or undermining it. These statements are most valuable as evidence of how a variety of people have chosen to interpret and respond to the Book of Mormon witnesses. From a historical perspective, they are less valuable as evidence of what the witnesses experienced. The best evidence comes from the witnesses' direct statements.

To arrive at an independent judgment, seekers need to examine the evidence for themselves and draw their own conclusions about its meaning and importance. This chapter is designed to facilitate that process by providing the witnesses' own statements that are not in the Book of Mormon and then providing a sampling of the wide variety of hearsay accounts. Then, with particular attention to the assumption that seeing with spiritual eyes negates one's witness, I will analyze the statements as an historian who chooses to believe in the testimonies of the Book of Mormon witnesses and end with an invitation to my readers to join me in making that informed choice.

Joseph Smith's history is the primary historical source that tells how the Book of Mormon prophesied of witnesses, how he received a subsequent revelation inviting Oliver Cowdery, David Whitmer, and Martin Harris to become the Three Witnesses (see D&C 17) and how, after an angel showed them the plates, eight other men gathered to see and heft the plates themselves.[15] Joseph's mother's later memoir presents a later version of Joseph's earlier account.[16]

Beside Joseph's history and the statements of the Three and Eight Witnesses in the Book of Mormon, there are a few direct statements by witnesses themselves in which they affirmed their June 1829 experience seeing the plates. For example, Martin Harris wrote to Hannah Emerson in 1870: "Concerning the plates, I do say that the angel did show to me the plates containing the Book of Mormon. Further, the translation that I carried to Prof. Anthon was copied from these same plates; also, that the Professor did testify to it being a correct translation. I do firmly believe and do know that Joseph Smith was a prophet of God; for without I know he could not [have] had that gift; neither could he have translated the same. I can give if you require it one hundred witnesses to the proof of the Book of Mormon."[17]

David Whitmer wrote *An Address to All Believers in Christ* in 1881 in response to what he felt was a misrepresentation of his testimony by John Murphy. Echoing the statement of the Three Witnesses in the Book of Mormon, David wrote:

> A PROCLAMATION. Unto all Nations, Kindred Tongues and People, unto whom these presents shall come:
>
> It having been represented by one John Murphy, of Polo, Caldwell County, Mo., that I, in a conversation with him last summer, denied my testimony as one of the three witnesses to the "BOOK OF MORMON."
>
> To the end, therefore, that he may understand me now, if he did not then; and that the world may know the truth, I wish now, standing as it were, in the very sunset of life, and in the fear of God, once for all to make this public statement:
>
> That I have never at any time denied that testimony or any part thereof, which has so long since been published with that Book, as one of the three witnesses. Those who know me best, well know that I have always adhered to that testimony. And that no man may be misled or doubt my present views in regard to the same, I do again affirm the truth of all of my statements, as then made and published.
>
> "He that hath an ear to hear, let him hear;" it was no delusion! What is written is written, and he that readeth let him understand.[18]

As the last surviving of the Three Witnesses, David Whitmer spoke for all of them in 1887: "I will say once more to all mankind, that I have never at any time denied that testimony or any part thereof. I also testify to the world, that neither Oliver Cowdery or Martin Harris ever at any time denied their testimony. They both died reaffirming the truth of the divine authenticity of the Book of Mormon. I was present at the deathbed of Oliver Cowdery, and his last words were, *'Brother David, be true to your testimony of the Book of Mormon.'*"[19]

Besides their formal testimony in the Book of Mormon, three of the Eight Witnesses left known written accounts of their experience. Hiram Page was whipped in Jackson County, Missouri, in 1833 for his profession of Mormonism. He left activity in the Church in 1838 and in 1847 wrote to William McLellin. "As to the Book of Mormon," he affirmed,

> it would be doing injustice to myself and to the work of God of the last days, to say that I could know a thing to be true in 1830, and know the same thing to be false in 1847. To say my mind was so treacherous that I had forgotten what I saw. To say that a man of Joseph's ability, who at that time did not know how to pronounce the word Nephi, could write a book of six hundred pages, as correct as the Book of Mormon, without supernatural power. And to say that those holy angels who came and showed themselves to me as I was walking through the field, to confirm me in the work of the Lord of the last days—three of whom came to me afterwards and sang an hymn in their own pure language. Yea, it would be treating the God of heaven with contempt to deny these testimonies, with too many others to mention here.[20]

After escaping from jail in Liberty, Missouri, Hyrum Smith, another of the Eight Witnesses, wrote in 1839, "Having given my testimony to the world of the truth of the book of Mormon, the renewal of the everlasting covenant, and the establishment of the Kingdom of heaven, in these last days; and having been brought into great afflictions and distresses for the same, I thought that it might be strengthening to my beloved brethren, to give them a short account of my sufferings, for the truth's sake." As part of the subsequent narrative, Hyrum summed up what he had suffered and why. "I thank God that I felt a determination to die, rather than deny the things which my eyes had seen, which my hands had handled, and which I had borne testimony to, wherever my lot had been cast; and I can assure my beloved brethren that I was enabled to bear as strong a testimony, when nothing but death presented itself, as ever I did in my life."[21]

Joseph Smith's history mentions that John Whitmer, another of the Eight Witnesses, assisted much in scribing the Book of Mormon translation.[22] Writing subsequently as the Church's historian, John wrote in third person that his brother "David Whitmer, Oliver Cowdery, and Martin Harris, were the Three Witnesses, whose names are attached to the book of Mormon according to the prediction of the Book, who knew and saw, for a surety, into whose presence the angel of God came and showed them the plates, the ball, the directors, etc. And also other witnesses even eight viz:

Christian Whitmer, Jacob Whitmer, John Whitmer, and Peter Whitmer Jr., Hiram Page, Joseph Smith, Hyrum Smith, and Samuel H. Smith, are the men to whom Joseph Smith, Jr., showed the plates, these witnesses names go forth also of the truth of this work in the last days. To the convincing or condemning of this generation in the last days."[23]

In 1836 John wrote further: "To say that the Book of Mormon is a revelation from God, I have no hesitancy, but with all confidence have signed my name to it as such." This was John's last editorial in his role as editor of the Church's newspaper, and he asked his readers' indulgence in speaking freely on the subject. "I desire to testify," he wrote, "to all that will come to the knowledge of this address; that I have most assuredly seen the plates from whence the book of Mormon is translated, and that I have handled these plates, and know of a surety that Joseph Smith, jr. has translated the book of Mormon by the gift and power of God."[24] Three decades later, John and his brother David were the only two surviving Book of Mormon witnesses. At that point, just two years before his own death, John responded to an inquirer about their testimony. John replied, "I have never heard that any one of the three or eight witnesses ever denied the testimony that they have borne to the Book as published in the first edition of the Book of Mormon."[25]

These first-person statements by Book of Mormon witnesses are far outnumbered by hearsay statements of persons reporting what they heard about the testimonies. Hearsay is problematic evidence. It is, by nature, unverifiable. Furthermore, the hearsay accounts are inconsistent. What witnesses reportedly said in one account differs from the next. Historians value hearsay for what it reveals about how people and events were interpreted by others, but it is not reliable evidence for interpreting people and events in the first place. The secondary evidence is not reliable for reconstructing the experiences of the witnesses or for establishing what they actually said. Though much of the hearsay evidence unequivocally declares that the witnesses saw and or hefted the plates, some of it obfuscates that point. The hearsay accounts show that one's faith in the Book of Mormon witnesses or lack thereof is based not simply on hearing the witnesses' testimonies but on how one chooses to receive and understand their testimonies.

Believers in the Book of Mormon heard the witnesses declare that the plates were real and that the Book of Mormon was true. Sally Bradford Parker wrote of hearing Hyrum Smith: "He said he had but two hands and two eyes. He said he had seen the plates with his eyes and handled them with his hands."[26] Theodore Turley wrote of hearing John Whitmer say, "I now say I handled those plates. there was fine engravings on both sides. I handled them."[27] Joshua Davis heard John declare, "I, with my own eyes, saw the plates from which the Book of Mormon was translated."[28] Daniel Tyler heard Samuel Smith say that "he had handled them and seen the engravings thereon."[29] One remembered hearing Martin Harris say, "I know that Joseph Smith was a true prophet of God. . . . I know that the Book of Mormon was divinely translated. I saw the plates; I saw the angel; I heard the voice of God; I know that the Book of Mormon is true."[30]

A wide variety of nonbelievers in the Book of Mormon (including newspaper writers, Protestant missionaries, and Latter-day Saints who had lost their faith) claim they heard the witnesses declare something other than that the plates were real and that the Book of Mormon was true. In 1838, dissenting Church members Stephen Burnett and Warren Parrish wrote of hearing Martin Harris deny that he had seen the plates with his natural eyes or that the Eight Witnesses saw them at all or that Joseph ever had them.[31] Parrish wrote that Martin Harris "has come out at last, and says he never saw the plates, from which the book purports to have been translated, except in vision; and he further says that any man who says he has seen them in any other way is a liar, Joseph not excepted."[32] John Murphy wrote that he had interviewed David Whitmer, who acknowledged that his witness was nothing more than an impression.[33]

Book of Mormon witnesses responded to these hearings with corrections. When he learned how Burnett and Parrish were interpreting his statements, Martin Harris "arose & said he was sorry for any man who rejected the Book of Mormon for he knew it was true."[34] He maintained his faith and understood what he had said differently than Stephen Burnett and Warren Parrish did, as Burnett acknowledged. "No man ever heard me in any way deny . . . the administration of the angel that showed me the plates," Harris wrote later.[35] David Whitmer wrote and published a pamphlet in response to Murphy in 1881, in which he affirmed how literally he believed his testimony as stated in the Book of Mormon. That same year Whitmer wrote "A Few Corrections" to the editor of the *Kansas City Journal*, which had misrepresented him.[36]

As an early convert in Ohio, Stephen Burnett felt the Holy Spirit and a desire to take the gospel to his relatives. He led his parents into the church and responded successfully to revealed mission calls (see D&C 75:35; 80). He "was the first one that sounded the glad tidings of the everlasting gospel" in Dalton, New Hampshire.[37] But by 1838 Burnett felt completely disillusioned. He felt he had tried but failed to regain the Holy Spirit. Finally he "proclaimed all revelation lies" and left the church.[38] Burnett wrote candidly to Lyman Johnson, explaining his decisions. "My heart is sickened within me when I reflect upon the manner in which we with many of this Church have been led & the losses which we have sustained all by means of two men in whom we placed implicit confidence," Burnett wrote, referring to Joseph Smith and Sidney Rigdon. He felt that Joseph had used his influence for financial gain and had prophesied lies. He continued his compelling story:

> I have reflected long and deliberately upon the history of this church & weighed the evidence for & against it—lo[a]th to give it up—but when I came to hear Martin Harris state in ~~a~~ public ~~congregation~~ that he never saw the plates with his natural eyes only in vision or imagination, neither Oliver nor David & also that the eight witnesses never saw them & hesitated to sign that instrument for that reason, but were persuaded to do it, the last pedestal gave way, in my view our foundations was sapped & the entire superstructure fell [in] a heap of ruins, I therefore three week[s] since in the Stone Chapel gave a full history of the church since I became acquainted with it, the false preaching & prophecying of Joseph together with the reasons why I took the course which I was resolved to do, and renounced the Book of Mormon with the whole scene of lying and deception practiced by J. S & S. R in this church, believing as I verily do, that it is all a wicked deception palmed upon us unawares[.] I was followed by W. Par[r]ish Luke Johnson & John Boynton all of who concurred with me, after we were done speaking M. Harris arose & said he was sorry for any man who rejected the Book of Mormon for he knew it was true.[39]

Burnett gave us a rich metaphor by describing his faith as a building whose foundation had been shattered, leaving only a heap of ruins. Those who share his experience know what he means.

One strategy for coping with the devastating loss is to pull what remains from the heap of ruins and try to rebuild something sensible. Burnett and others since have dug into the pile of statements by and about the Book of Mormon witnesses and fashioned an alternative way to interpret the testimonies of the eleven eyewitnesses. Those with shattered faith in their own spiritual experiences doubt that the witnesses had authentic spiritual experiences either, and therefore seek alternative explanations for their testimonies. Acknowledging that "Harris and others . . . still believe the Book of Mormon," Burnett wrote, "I am well satisfied for myself that *if* the witnesses whose names are attached to the Book of Mormon never saw the plates as Martin admits that there can be nothing brought to prove that any such thing ever existed for it is said on the 171st page of the book of covenants [D&C 17:5] that the three should testify that they had seen the plates even as J[oseph] S[mith] Jr. & *if* they saw them spiritually or in vision with their eyes shut—J S Jr never saw them any other ~~light~~ way & *if* so the plates were only visionary."[40]

One is struck by the three instances of *if* in Burnett's statement. He built his interpretation of the witnesses on hypotheticals: *if* the witnesses never saw the plates as he believed Martin Harris had said, and *if* Joseph never saw them, then they were only visionary. After listening to Burnett expound that rationale, Martin Harris asserted unequivocally, in contrast, that the plates were real." Harris did not wish to be understood as Burnett understood him.[41]

The hearsay accounts like Burnett's have been useful to others for building a believable alternative to the straightforward statements of the witnesses. Grant Palmer wrote of his own youthful faith being undermined by later doubts. His chapter on the Book of Mormon witnesses expresses his doubts about the authenticity of accounts by the witnesses in the Book of Mormon and instead draws on the hearsay accounts, where he finds some threads that enable him to conclude that the witnesses thought they had experienced the plates but had not. This explanation is appealing to some because it does not completely dismiss the compelling testimonies of the Book of Mormon witnesses but it categorizes them as unreal.

Those who suspect their own spiritual eyes of playing tricks on them find it hard to believe that the witnesses saw anything with their spiritual eyes. To these souls, promises that the witnesses would see the plates with eyes of faith sound foreign, and are best regarded as artifacts of a bygone era when lots of people thought they could see things that were not real after all. They cannot trust the Book of Mormon witnesses. They literally find it easier to trust hearsay than direct statements. Grant Palmer and Dan Vogel repeatedly choose to privilege selected hearsay more than the direct statements of the witnesses.[42] Such choices led Palmer to conclude that the witnesses "*seem to have* seen the records with their *spiritual eyes* and inspected them in the context of a vision, *apparently* never having actually possessed or touched them" (emphasis added).[43] In their formal statements, their other direct statements, and in the hearsay accounts, the Book of Mormon witnesses did not speak that way. They did not say they had *apparently* seen or *seem* to have seen. Over and over, they testify that they saw. When their statements were misrepresented, being *interpreted* as visionary and therefore not real, they reasserted the authenticity of their experience. Some of them are on record expressing certainty in the reality of the plates and their divine translation. None of them is on record expressing doubt in those things. The skeptics selectively dismiss the earliest, most straightforward witness statements and favor accounts like Burnett's hypothetical alternative. They reject direct evidence and selectively accept some of the hearsay. They obfuscate.

The historical record describes a rich mix of what one scholar called the Book of Mormon's "artifactual reality" beheld with eyes of faith. Indeed, the statements of the Three and Eight Witnesses seem to purposefully mix and merge these ways of knowing and verifying. Regardless of how one decides to understand their words, the witnesses left us no evidence that they doubted the reality of what they experienced supernaturally as well as physically and tangibly. As Terryl L. Givens observed:

> One historian has written of Martin Harris's alleged equivocation about his vision, pointing out that he claimed to have seen the plates with his "spiritual eyes," rather than his natural ones, and thus that he "repeatedly admitted the internal, subjective nature of his visionary experience." It is not clear, however, that visionaries in any age have acquiesced to such facile dichotomies. . . . Paul himself referred to one of his own experiences as being "in the body, or out of the body, I cannot tell" (2 Cor. 12:3). He obviously considered such a distinction irrelevant to the validity of his experience and the reality of what he saw. It is hard to imagine a precedent more like Harris's own versions in which he emphatically asserts until the day of his death the actuality of the angel who "came down from heaven" and who "brought and laid [the plates] before our eyes, that we

> beheld and saw," while also reporting, *according to others,* that he "never claimed to have seen them with his natural eyes, only with spiritual vision."[44]

Givens clearly discerns the quality of direct versus hearsay evidence. Meanwhile, Vogel, who chooses to believe the hearsay more than the direct statements, acknowledges his need for "qualifying verbs and adverbs" because his "analysis is speculative or conjectural."[45]

When it comes to the Book of Mormon witnesses, the question is which historical documents is one willing to trust? Those whose faith has been deeply shaken sometimes find it easier to trust lesser evidence rather than the best sources or the overwhelming preponderance of the evidence. But that choice is not a foregone conclusion. It is neither inevitable nor irreversible. William McLellin believed the witnesses. He met three of them—David Whitmer, Martin Harris, and Hyrum Smith—when they passed his home in Illinois in August 1831. He walked several miles with them and "talked much" with them and other Saints for several days that summer. Of August 19, William wrote, "I took Hiram the brother of Joseph and we went into the woods and set down and talked together about 4 hours. I inquired into the particulars of the coming forth of the record, of the rise of the church and of its progress and upon the testimonies given to him." Of the next morning, McLellin wrote, "I rose early and betook myself to earnest prayr to God to direct me into truth; and from all the light that I could gain by examinations searches and researches I was bound as an honest man to acknowledge the truth and Validity of the book of Mormon." He asked Hyrum Smith to baptize him.

William McLellin later served several missions, some as an Apostle, before becoming deeply disaffected later in the 1830s. He spent half a century frustrated by what he simultaneously loved and hated about Mormonism before receiving a letter from a Salt Lake City anti-Mormon named James Cobb, who wrote assuming he would find an ally. McLellin wrote back: "When I thoroughly examine a subject and settle my mind, then higher evidence must be introduced before I change. I have set to my seal that the Book of Mormon is a true, divine record and it will require more evidence than I have ever seen to ever shake me relative to its purity I have read many 'Exposes.' I have seen all their arguments. But my evidences are above them all!" He explained further, "When a man goes at the Book of M. he touches the apple of my eye. He fights against truth—against purity—against light—against the purist, or one of the truest, purist books on earth. I have more confidence in the Book of Mormon than any book of this wide earth!" McLellin described his own repeated readings of the Book of Mormon before noting his personal experiences with some of the witnesses. "When I first joined the church in 1831," he wrote, "soon I became acquainted with all the Smith family and the Whitmer family, and I heard all their testimonies, which agreed in the main points; and I believed them then and I believe them yet. But I don't believe the many stories (contradictory) got up since, for I individually know many of them are false."[46]

It is hard to imagine someone better positioned to evaluate the testimonies of the Book of Mormon witnesses than William McLellin. He spent much of his life disaffected from The Church of Jesus Christ of Latter-day Saints and had no interest in sustaining it. Yet as he wrote of his 1831 experience with the Book and its witnesses, he was bound by the evidence to acknowledge its truth and validity. He not only knew the testimonies of the Book of Mormon witnesses, he knew some of the witnesses personally and interviewed them intimately. He was no fool, no dupe. And he was positioned to know whether the witnesses were fools, dupes, or conspirators. So well informed, McLellin chose to believe the testimonies of the witnesses were truthful.

Why not make the same satisfying choice? Why not opt to believe in the direct statements of the witnesses and their demonstrably lifelong commitments to the Book of Mormon? This choice asks us to have faith in the marvelous, the possibility of angels, spiritual eyes, miraculous translation, and gold plates, but it does not require us to discount the historical record or create hypothetical ways to reconcile the compelling Book of Mormon witnesses with our own skepticism.

Notes

This is an expanded version of an article published as "Evaluating the Book of Mormon Witnesses," *Religious Educator* 11, no. 2 (2010): 37–49.

1. Michael Hubbard MacKay, Gerrit J. Dirkmaat, Grant Underwood, Robert J. Woodford, and William G. Hartley, eds., *Documents, Volume 1: July 1828–June*

1831, vol. 1 of the Documents series of *The Joseph Smith Papers*, ed. Dean C. Jessee, Ronald K. Esplin, Richard Lyman Bushman, and Matthew J. Grow (Salt Lake City: Church Historian's Press, 2013), 58–60 (hereafter *JSP*, D1).

2. *JSP*, D1:82–85; Karen Lynn Davidson, David J. Whittaker, Mark Ashurst-McGee, and Richard L. Jensen, eds., *Histories, Volume 1: Joseph Smith Histories, 1832–1834*, vol. 1 of the Histories series of *The Joseph Smith Papers*, ed. Dean C. Jessee, Ronald K. Esplin, and Richard Lyman Bushman, 314n17 (hereafter *JSP*, H1).
3. Lucy Mack Smith, History, 1844–45, book 8, [11].
4. Joseph's testimony is in his History, 1838–1856, Vol. A-1, Church History Library, http://josephsmithpapers.org/paperSummary/history-circa-june-1839-circa-1841-draft-2?p=31&highlight=testimony%20of%20three%20witnesses.
5. Oliver Cowdery, David Whitmer, and Martin Harris, Testimony of Three Witnesses, Palmyra, New York, late June 1829, in Book of Mormon Printer's Manuscript, 463–64, handwriting of Oliver Cowdery, Community of Christ Library-Archives, Independence, Missouri, http://josephsmithpapers.org/paperSummary/testimony-of-three-witnesses-late-june-1829?p=1&highlight=testimony%20of%20three%20witnesses.
6. *JSP*, H1:317–21.
7. Christian Whitmer, Jacob Whitmer, Peter Whitmer Jr., John Whitmer, Hiram Page, Joseph Smith Sr., Hyrum Smith, and Samuel H. Smith, Testimony of Eight Witnesses, Palmyra, New York, late June 1829, in Book of Mormon Printer's Manuscript, page 464, Community of Christ Library-Archives, Independence, Missouri, http://josephsmithpapers.org/paperSummary/testimony-of-eight-witnesses-late-june-1829?p=1&highlight=testimony%20of%20eight%20witnesses.
8. Lucy Mack Smith, History, 1844–45, book 8, [11]–book 9, [2].
9. Lucy Mack Smith, History, 1844–45, book 9, [1].
10. Dan Vogel, "The Validity of the Witnesses' Testimonies," in *American Apocrypha: Essays on the Book of Mormon*, ed. Dan Vogel and Brent Lee Metcalfe (Salt Lake City: Signature Books, 2002), 79–80.
11. See Moses 1:11; Dan Vogel, *Early Mormon Documents* (Salt Lake City: Signature Books, 1996–2000, 2:256 (hereafter *EMD*). Emanuel Swedenborg described seeing visions "not seen with the eyes of my body, but with the eyes of my spirit." *Miscellaneous Theological Works of Emanuel Swedenborg* (New York: American Swedenborg, 1871), 391.
12. Pomeroy Tucker, *Origin, Rise and Progress of Mormonism* (1867), in *EMD*, 3:87–128. Several hearsay accounts declare that Harris testified to seeing the plates with spiritual eyes or eyes of faith. *EMD*, 2:255–56. Dissenters in 1838 cited Harris's declaration that he never saw the plates with his natural eyes. Stephen Burnett to Lyman E. Johnson, Orange Township, Geauga County, Ohio, April 15, 1838, MSS 155, box 2, folder 2, Letterbook 2, pages 64–66, Church History Library, The Church of Jesus Christ of Latter-day Saints, Salt Lake City.

13. Burnett to Johnson, April 15, 1838, 64–66.
14. *EMD*, 1:468–72. Grant Palmer follows this argument and reading of the evidence, leading him to the conclusion that "the witnesses seem to have seen the records with their *spiritual eyes* and inspected them in the context of a vision, apparently never having actually possessed or touched them." Palmer, *An Insider's View of Mormon Origins* (Salt Lake City: Signature Books, 2004), 207; emphasis added.
15. Joseph Smith's 1839 draft history and 1839 history are in *Papers of Joseph Smith: Autobiographical and Historical Writings*, ed. Dean C. Jessee (Salt Lake City: Deseret Book, 1989), 1:235–38, 294–98.
16. Lavina Fielding Anderson, ed., *Lucy's Book: A Critical Edition of Lucy Mack Smith's Family Memoir* (Salt Lake City: Signature Books, 2001), 453.
17. Martin Harris to Mr. Emerson, Sir, November 23, 1870, in *True Latter Day Saints' Herald*, 1875, 630.
18. David Whitmer, *An Address to All Believers in Christ* (Richmond, MO: David Whitmer, 1887), 8–9.
19. Whitmer, *Address to All Believers in Christ*, 8.
20. Hiram Page to William McLellin, May 30, 1847, in *Ensign of Liberty*, January 1848, 63.
21. Hyrum Smith, "Communications," *Times and Seasons*, November 1839, 21.
22. *Papers of Joseph Smith*, 1:234.
23. Book of John Whitmer, chapter 6, Community of Christ Library-Archives, Independence, Missouri, 25; spelling standardized.
24. *Messenger and Advocate*, March 1836, 286–87.
25. John Whitmer to Mark H. Forest [Forscutt], March 5, 1876, Community of Christ Archives, Independence, Missouri; quoted in Richard Lloyd Anderson, "Attempts to Redefine the Experience of the Eight Witnesses," *Journal of Book of Mormon Studies* 14, no. 1 (2005): 18–31.
26. Sally Bradford Parker to John Kempton, August 26, 1838, Doris Whittier Pierce Collection, Delaware County Historical Society, Delaware, Ohio, in Janiece Johnson, "The Scriptures Is a Fulfilling: Sally Parker's Weave," *BYU Studies* 44, no. 2 (2005): 115; spelling and punctuation standardized.
27. Theodore Turley's Memorandums, Church History Library.
28. "A Visit to John Whitmer," *Deseret Evening News*, April 12, 1875.
29. Daniel Tyler, "Incidents of Experience," *Scraps of Biography: Tenth Book in the Faith-Promoting Series* (Salt Lake City: Juvenile Instructor Office, 1883), 23.
30. William Harrison Homer, "The Passing of Martin Harris," *Improvement Era*, March 1926, 470.
31. Burnett to Johnson, 64–66.
32. *Evangelist* (Carthage, Ohio), October 1, 1838, 226.
33. "Murphy on Mormonism," *Hamiltonian*, January 21, 1881.
34. Burnett to Johnson, 64–66.
35. Martin Harris to H. B. Emerson, January 1871, in *Saints' Herald*, April 1, 1876, 198.

36. Lyndon W. Cook, ed., *David Whitmer Interviews* (Provo, UT: Grandin, 1991), 71–73.
37. Levi B. Wilder to the editor, February 15, 1835, in *Messenger and Advocate*, February 1835, 75.
38. Joseph Smith, editorial, *Elders' Journal*, August 1838, 57.
39. Burnett to Johnson, 64–66.
40. Burnett to Johnson, 64–66; emphasis added.
41. Burnett to Johnson, 64–66.
42. Vogel, "The Validity of the Witnesses' Testimonies," 79–121.
43. Palmer, *Insider's View*, 207, see also 175–76; emphasis added.
44. Terryl L. Givens, *By the Hand of Mormon: The American Scripture that Launched a New World Religion* (New York: Oxford University Press, 2003), 41–42, emphasis added; the two former quotations come from the Testimony of Three Witnesses in the front of the Book of Mormon, and the latter one is the statement of Reuben P. Harmon, made in about 1885, cited in Vogel, *EMD*, 2:255. Note how Givens, unlike Palmer, distinguishes between firsthand and hearsay accounts.
45. Dan Vogel, *Joseph Smith: The Making of a Prophet* (Salt Lake City: Signature Books, 2004, xvii.
46. William E. McLellin to James T. Cobb, Independence, Missouri, August 14, 1880, Manuscripts Collection, New York Public Library, in *The William E. McLellin Papers, 1854–1880*, ed. Stan Larson and Samuel J. Passey (Salt Lake City: Signature Books, 2007), 521–23.

8

A Multiplicity of Witnesses
Women and the Translation Process

Amy Easton-Flake and Rachel Cope

Amy Easton-Flake is an assistant professor of ancient scripture at Brigham Young University.

Rachel Cope is an assistant professor of Church history and doctrine at Brigham Young University.

Four women in early Church history—Mary Musselman Whitmer, Lucy Mack Smith, Lucy Harris, and Emma Hale Smith—played significant roles in the coming forth of the Book of Mormon and offered their own witnesses of the plates' reality. While their names and narratives are well known, scholars and members of the Church have largely overlooked their powerful and important contributions to the work of translation, since they were not a part of the official three or eight witnesses. This chapter addresses this gap in scholarship and historical memory by looking at a variety of sources (both those that are frequently cited and those that have been largely neglected) that recount these women's experiences with the plates. It considers the various ways in which they came to know of the plates' temporality and divinity and shows the multiplicity of witnesses that emerge when we privilege ways of knowing and seeing beyond the visual. Evaluating these women's memories of and interactions with the plates helps us to understand better the translation process and the truly communal effort it required.

Mary Musselman Whitmer

Mary Whitmer[1] has been referred to as the twelfth witness because her experience with the plates parallels most closely that of the official three and eight witnesses.[2] She is the only known woman to have physically seen the plates, and her experience with them and her role in the translation process aptly illustrate the familial and communal effort that enabled the translation of the Book of Mormon.

In June 1829, Mary and Peter Whitmer opened their home to Joseph Smith; his wife, Emma; and Oliver Cowdery to complete the translation when persecution in Harmony became too intense.[3] Here the translation process progressed rapidly as Joseph and Oliver devoted themselves fully to the work. The Whitmers' willingness to shoulder their temporal concerns for a time enabled Joseph and Oliver's single-minded focus; as the family matriarch, Mary, in particular, bore the brunt of this burden. As her son David reports, "My father and mother had a large family of their own, the addition to it therefore of Joseph, his wife Emma and Oliver very greatly increased the toil and anxiety of my mother. And although she had never complained she had sometimes felt that her labor was too much, or at least she was perhaps beginning to feel so."[4]

Life on an early nineteenth-century New York farm was laborious for anyone, but particularly taxing demands were placed on the farmer's wife, who, according to an 1862 US Department of Agriculture study "works harder, endures more, than any other on the place."[5] A farmer's wife oversaw the running of the household and was typically responsible for milking, butter churning, gathering eggs, and caring for livestock; planting, weeding, and harvesting the kitchen garden; shearing sheep, turning wool into yarn, and sewing garments; cooking, cleaning, laundry; and the list continues.[6] Much of the additional work of cooking, cleaning, and caring for the visitors invariably fell upon Mary, and those burdens must have taxed an already overworked woman. Encapsulated in David's statement, then, is a reminder of the labor and goods that Mary, along with others, had provided so that Joseph, a poor farmer dependent on the work of his own hands, might give his time and energy to the translation process. If not for the generosity of such individuals as the Whitmers, Martin and Lucy Harris, and Joseph Knight and his family, Joseph would not have had the resources to translate the plates. Consequently, their labor should be seen as crucial to the work of translation.

That God recognized and valued their sacrifice to aid the work of translation is perhaps most clearly suggested when Mary Whitmer was shown the plates. Her grandson, John C. Whitmer, summarized her experience as follows:

> One evening, when (after having done her usual day's work in the house) she went to the barn to milk the cows, she met a stranger carrying something on his back that looked like a knapsack. At first she was a little afraid of him, but when he spoke to her in a kind, friendly tone, and began to explain to her the nature of the work which was going on in her house, she was filled with inexpressible joy and satisfaction. He then untied his knapsack and showed her a bundle of plates, which in size and appearance corresponded with the description subsequently given by the witnesses to the Book of Mormon. This strange person turned the leaves of the book of plates over, leaf after leaf, and also showed her the engravings upon them; after which he told her to be patient and faithful in bearing her burden a little longer, promising that if she would do so, she should be blessed; and her reward would be sure, if she proved faithful to the end. The personage then suddenly vanished with the plates, and where he went, she could not tell.[7]

Her son David additionally reports the words the angel spoke to Mary: "You have been very faithful and diligent in your labors, but you are tried because of the increase of your toil, it is proper therefore that you should receive a witness that your faith may be strengthened."[8] In the angel's words, we seem to see God's recognition of Mary and her labor; he acknowledged what Mary was contributing to his work, he appreciated her efforts, and he blessed her for her faithfulness and bolstered her commitment. For Mary, as for the later witnesses, the witnessing experience she had was faith building. At the time, as her grandson reported, it "enabled [her] to perform her household duties with comparative ease, and she felt no more inclination to murmur because her lot was hard."[9]

When Mary was shown the plates, she became the first known individual to see them besides Joseph Smith. Within the month, all of the male members of her family, except for her husband, would join her in witnessing the physical reality of the plates; indeed, seven of the eleven official witnesses of the Book of Mormon were Whitmers by blood or marriage.[10] The entire Whitmer family enabled the translation work by providing for Joseph's, Emma's, and Oliver's temporal needs, and in turn many of them were privileged to become witnesses of the physical reality of the plates and the divinity of the translation process. Richard Lloyd Anderson has referred to the Whitmers as "a family that nourished the Church," and, as Mary's story demonstrates, this is certainly the case.[11] They provided the space for the organization of the Church and for the reception of many of the revelations during the New York period, they served missions, and they joined the Saints first in Kirtland and later in Missouri, where Mary's sons and sons-in-law served in many leadership positions. Sadly, in 1838, during a time of great hardship and apostasy, all of the living Whitmers left the Church following a falling out with Joseph Smith. Nevertheless, Mary, like all of her family and the other witnesses for the gold plates, never altered or denied her testimony of their reality, their divine origin, and the message contained in the book translated from them.[12] For the remainder of her life, she would continue to testify of the book—a book made possible through the collective efforts of Mary and the entire Whitmer family, as well as the Knight family, the Harris family, and the Smith family.

Lucy Mack Smith

As a memoirist and as a participant in the events surrounding the translation and publication of the Book of Mormon, Lucy Mack Smith introduces various ways of witnessing beyond the visual, including record keeping, sensory experiences, and spiritual impressions.[13] In her account, Lucy also broadens the traditional definition of witness to include the entire community of people who contributed to the coming forth of this text. As she sees it, her family and friends—female and male—played important roles within the context of a shared story.

During the winter of 1844–45, just months following the deaths of her sons Joseph, Hyrum, and Samuel, sixty-nine-year-old Lucy dictated her memoir to Martha Jane Knowlton Coray who hoped to preserve an important story. Lucy's memoir, recorded by a woman for a woman, includes the experiences and perspectives of many female witnesses. The memoir's purpose is captured in the original copyright description, which reads as follows:

"The History of Lucy Smith, Wife of Joseph Smith, the first patriarch of [the church of] Jesus Christ of Latter Day Saints, who was the father of Joseph Smith, Prophet, Seer, and Revelator; containing an account of the many persecutions, trials and afflictions which I and my family have endured in bringing forth the Book of Mormon and establishing the church of Jesus Christ of Latter Day Saints."[14] From Lucy's perspective, Joseph alone did not bring forth the Book of Mormon and establish the Church; rather, it was a family affair.

Lucy's memoir, which Leonard Arrington suggests "tells more about Mormon origins than any other single source,"[15] documents events surrounding the translation and publication of the Book of Mormon from the perspective of "an observer closely connected to the primary participants" in the Church's early history.[16] However, because the narrative framework of this text is so familiar to Church members, readers often overlook the texture that Lucy's account may add to our understanding of Church history. A closer and more careful read reveals a rich and complex narrative about dedicated, devoted, and flawed believers who willingly made sacrifices to enable the publication of this sacred text. The translation of the Book of Mormon, Lucy's narrative indicates, both required and created a community effort.[17]

The need for communal effort is evidenced from the beginning of Lucy's memoir, which recounts her family's religious heritage. She highlights, for example, the role of spiritual seeking in the lives of her progenitors, and she describes and interprets powerful dreams—both her own and those of her husband—that seem to have foreshadowed the Restoration.[18] She also discusses at length her own commitment to discovering the true gospel, and demonstrates how this quest impacted her children.[19] In sharing these stories, Lucy implicitly suggests that generations of the Smith and Mack family both were preparing themselves and were prepared by the Lord for the "marvelous work" they would perform.[20]

Although Joseph's calling to translate the Book of Mormon and to restore the gospel of Jesus Christ plays a central role in Lucy's memoir, she stresses her family's involvement in these events. Lucy notes that after Joseph learned about the gold plates from the angel Moroni, he often gathered his family together and shared his experiences with them. In so doing, she implicitly suggests that he made them active participants in the Restoration. For example, she recalls, "all seated round in a circle father Mother sons and

Daughters listening in breathless anxiety to the <religious> teachings of a boy 16 <19> yars of age who had never read the Bible through by course in his life."[21] Nonetheless, she continues: "Joseph would give us some of the most ammusing recitals which could be im magined he would de[s]cribe the ancient inhabitants of this continent their dress thier maner of traveling the animals which they rode The cities that were built by them the structure of their buildings with eve ry particular of their mode of warfare their religi ous worship as particularly as though he had Spent his life with them."[22] Remembering these powerful moments of instruction, William Smith simply explained, "The whole family were melted to tears, and believed all he said."[23] Although the Smiths lacked tangible evidence of the plates at this time, they experienced spiritual confirmation, and thus they anxiously awaited the day when Joseph would receive the important record he had described.[24] Together, the family became witnesses to the Book of Mormon, even prior to Joseph's acquiring of the plates.

After Joseph had obtained the plates, different forms of witnessing—more sensory in nature—opened up. While they did not physically see the plates, Lucy and other family members saw their outline through the cloth that covered them and even handled them on occasion, thus enabling them to become witnesses of the tangible nature of the object they encountered.[25] Shortly after Joseph and Emma had attained the plates, for example, Lucy handled the Urim and Thummim "with no covering but a silk handkerchief" while advising her son about getting a chest made in order to protect them.[26] Later, Lucy would see the box that held the plates, as well as the outline of the plates through their covering.[27] Lucy's daughter Katherine Smith also witnessed the plates' tangibility when she had the opportunity to "heft" the "package" containing the plates that her elder brother had brought home.[28] She "found them very heavy like gold and also rippled her fingers up the edge of the plates and felt that they were separate metal plates and heard the tinkle of sound that they made."[29] Due to her recollection of the physical and audible encounters she had with the plates, one individual referred to Katherine as "one of the choice, small circle given to bear firsthand witness to the truthfulness of the Prophet's assertions regarding possession of the gold plates."[30] Indeed, the range of experiences that individuals such as Lucy and Katherine Smith had with the plates broadens the definition of witnessing to include the senses of touch and sound as well as sight.

In addition to explaining individuals' tangible experiences with the plates, Lucy's history demonstrates that, as the family matriarch, she was involved with and aware of the various events surrounding the coming forth of the Book of Mormon. She is, for example, the only person who knew when Joseph and Emma went to receive the plates.[31] Of this event, she recalled, "I spent the night in prayer and at reasonable time for rising I went to preparing breakfast my heart fluttering at every footfall for I now expected Joseph & Emma every moment and was in dread of a second disappointment in his obtaining the plates When the male part of the family sat down to breakfast Mr. Smith [Joseph Smith Sr.] enquired for Joseph <for no one but myself knew where he was.>"[32] By preserving this story, Lucy reveals that both women and men in the family were intimately involved with the events surrounding the acquisition of the plates. As the translation process ensued, Lucy continued to be amongst the first and few to know about each aspect of the work. For instance, she, along with her husband and Mary Whitmer, were the first to learn that Oliver Cowdery, Martin Harris, and David Whitmer had been shown the plates by the angel Moroni.[33] And, as soon as the translation was completed, a messenger was sent from Fayette, New York, to share the good news with members of the Smith family.[34] In citing such stories, Lucy's memoir makes it clear that she served as a witness of an important work and recognized the value of preserving details only she knew.

Lucy also contributed to the translation process by making temporal sacrifices that enabled the important spiritual work her family had been called to do—"whilst we worked with our hands we endeavored to remmember the service of & the welfare of our souls," she recalled.[35] Indeed, she and her family sacrificed time, money, and goods in order to enable Joseph to work on this important project.[36] Like Mary Whitmer, Lucy allowed various individuals associated with the translation, including Joseph and Emma, Joseph Knight, and Lucy Harris and her daughter, to stay in her home; she, along with her daughters, inevitably had to assume additional housekeeping responsibilities on a regular basis.[37] Besides taking on extra household chores, Lucy helped protect the gold plates and prepare for the eventual publication of a new book of scripture. For example, she helped find hiding places for the plates' protection, remained astutely aware of their safety or lack thereof, and met with Martin and Lucy Harris to request financial assistance for the project.[38] In addition to engaging in temporal labors, Lucy willingly defended the translation work and spoke of the plates' reality. On one occasion, a group of men from a local church asked Lucy if they could see the gold plates. To them she declared, "We have not <got > any <no> gold bible and neither have we ever had any thing of the kind but we have a translation of some gold plates which was sent to the world to bring the plainess of the Gospel to the children of men and also to give a history of the people that used to inhabit this country."[39] When the men questioned her witness, Lucy continued, "even you should stick my body full of faggots and burn me at the stake I would declare that Jose[p]h has that record and that I know it to be true as long as God gave me breath."[40]

In many other cases, tangible aspects of Lucy's interaction with the Book of Mormon also took on a spiritual form. On one occasion, she agreed to help protect the manuscript pages of the Book of Mormon from the threat of a mob. After placing the manuscript in a trunk, she put it under her bed. While Peter Whitmer guarded her home, Lucy, now lying on the bed, began a reflective train of thought that captured her testimony about the work her family had engaged in. She recalled:

> this identicle work had not only been the object which we as a family had pursued so eagerly but that Prophets of ancient days and angels even the Gr[e]at God had <had> his eye upon it. and said I to myself Shall I fear what man can do will not the angels watch over the precious relict of the worthy dead and the hope of the living and ~~I~~ am I indeed the mother of a prophet of the God of Heaven—the honored instrument in performing so great work—I felt th[at] I was in the purview of angels and my bounded at the thought of the grat condescension of the A[l] mighty—thus I spent the night surrounded by enemies and yet in an extacy of happiness and truly I can say that my soul did magnify and my spirit rejoiced in God my savior.[41]

Here, Lucy shows how various aspects of witnessing combine: while protecting tangible manuscript pages, she bore a powerful spiritual witness—in the context of her memoir—about a sacred and divinely inspired work that multiple individuals had sacrificed for in order to make possible. Because Lucy never saw the plates, we do not refer to her as a Book of Mormon witness;

yet, as her memoir demonstrates, she was intimately involved in every event tied to the coming forth of the Book of Mormon.

Lucy Harris

Within the pages of her memoir, Lucy Mack Smith introduces her readers to Lucy Harris. Although Lucy Harris is typically remembered for her antagonism toward the Book of Mormon, in part because she claimed to have never actually believed in the gold plates following the manuscript's publication, it is important to recognize that Lucy Smith's history reveals another side of this complex figure.[42] Even though Lucy Mack Smith clearly disliked her neighbor, she still acknowledged Lucy Harris's initial interest in and support of the translation project. She also recalled that Harris had received a powerful spiritual witness of the plates, followed by an audible and tangible witness of them. As a result of these experiences, Smith intimated, Harris had willingly donated a significant amount of money in order to help enable the translation of the Book of Mormon.[43]

Shortly after Joseph and Emma had obtained the plates from the Hill Cumorah, Joseph asked Lucy Mack Smith if she would speak with a wealthy acquaintance, Martin Harris, about financing the project. She agreed to do so, but decided to first visit with his wife, Lucy, "in order to satisfy" Lucy Harris's curiosity.[44] According to Lucy Mack Smith's account, Lucy Harris was intrigued by the story Lucy Mack Smith shared with her and expressed an immediate interest in the plates, offering to donate a considerable sum of money from her own "private purse" for Joseph's translation efforts.[45] She then informed her visitor that she would come to the Smith home one evening in the following week so she could speak with Joseph. When Lucy Harris and her daughter paid a visit to the Smith home, she understandably hoped to see the plates before committing to provide financial support for the project. Although she pled with Joseph to let her see the gold plates, he insisted that he could not show them to her, explaining that the angel who had entrusted them into his care told him that he could only show them to those called as witnesses by God. Dissatisfied with this response, Harris declared, "Now Joseph . . . I will tell [you] what I will do If I can get a witness that you do speak the truth I will beleive it."[46] Harris, who was staying at the Smith home overnight, retired to bed following her conversation with Joseph.

The following morning, Lucy Harris shared "a very remarkable dream"—a common practice in the early nineteenth century—she had had that night with the Smith family.[47] In this dream, she reported, a personage had appeared to her and chastised her for importuning "the servant of the Lord."[48] The angel then showed her the plates. As a result of the powerful witness she received through this visionary dream, Lucy was able to describe the record in vivid detail, and she subsequently insisted on giving Joseph twenty-eight dollars (money she had received from her mother prior to her mother's death) to help with the project.[49] Fascinated by the witness Lucy Harris had borne and appreciative of her generosity, Joseph allowed her and her daughter to handle the wooden box containing the plates. Martin Harris remembered that his "daughter said, they were about as much as she could lift. . . . My wife said they were very heavy."[50] The experience of actually hefting the plates added a tangible and audible witness to the spiritual witness Lucy Harris had already received, according to Lucy Mack Smith's record.

Although Lucy Harris eventually became antagonistic to the work, in part because she never had the opportunity to see the plates despite her early support for the project, Lucy Smith implies that she continued to believe in their physical reality. On one occasion, for example, Lucy Harris traveled to the Joseph Smith Jr. home in Harmony, Pennsylvania, and insisted she would not leave until she saw the plates. She then ransacked "every nook & corner of the house chest cupboard trunk &c" to no avail.[51] The following day, Lucy searched the grounds surrounding the Smith home until early in the afternoon. She later reported that, upon discovering a location in which she thought the plates might be buried, a "tremendous great black snake stuck up its head before me and commenced hissing at me."[52] Feeling both frightened and frustrated, Lucy discontinued her search at that time. Nonetheless, she continued to believe in the plates' existence, and longed for evidence of the work Martin and Joseph were engaged in. Lucy's later opportunity to see the first 116 manuscript pages of the Book of Mormon appeased her for a time. Although she is often blamed for the disappearance of this manuscript, it is important to remember that she was intrigued by this visible witness and allowed Martin to protect the manuscript in her bureau.[53] When Martin later discovered that the translated pages were missing, Lucy "solemnly averred" that she had not taken them.[54] Even when Lucy Harris felt skeptical about the translation project, Smith's account suggests that she continued to believe in the plates' existence. Her early witnessing experiences seem to have convinced her that Joseph indeed had the physical object he claimed to have in his possession.

As remembered by Lucy Mack Smith, Lucy Harris's experiences demonstrate some of the varied ways in which multiple people witnessed the plates and aided Joseph throughout the translation process. Lucy Mack Smith reminds us that women and men—in this case, Lucy and Martin Harris—both offered to provide financial backing for the publication of the Book of Mormon—a manifestation, or witness, in and of itself, of their belief in and commitment to a vast and collective undertaking.[55] The fact that Lucy and Martin had doubts and struggles does not negate their early witnessing experiences, nor does it overshadow the sacrifices they made.

Emma Hale Smith

As the individual who was with Joseph from the beginning to the end of the translation process and who provided him with immeasurable assistance in various ways, Emma Smith was arguably more intimately involved in the coming forth of the Book of Mormon than any person besides Joseph. Therefore, by viewing the translation process through her own witness, we not only learn of the integral role she played in the work of translation and her own commitment to the coming forth of the Book of Mormon, but we also gain new knowledge about the translation process itself and about the plates' physicality. When the experience is seen through her eyes, as well as those of the other women, the work of translation becomes a familial and communal project, with many people contributing to the success of the endeavor.

Emma's involvement with the ancient Nephite record began when she accompanied Joseph to the Hill Cumorah to receive the long-anticipated plates. Early in his communication with the angel Moroni, Joseph was commanded to bring the right person with him to the hill. He believed that person to be Emma;[56] and thus at midnight on September 22, 1827, the two of them left the Smith's home, and, with the aid of Joseph Knight's horse and wagon, went to retrieve the plates.[57] After arriving at the Hill Cumorah, Joseph left Emma in the wagon and went alone to retrieve the plates. When he returned a few hours later, he carried a bundle wrapped in his coat. Joseph then left Emma again so he could deposit the plates in a hollowed-out birch log in the woods. For the next three years, Joseph and Emma's lives revolved around the protection and translation of the plates.

Persecution in Palmyra began immediately and required the entire Smith family to aid in the protection of the plates. Needing money to purchase a box to hold the plates, Joseph left a day or two after retrieving them for a well-digging job in Macedon, just west of Palmyra. In his absence, Joseph's father learned of a group of men who, with the aid of a conjurer, planned to find and steal the plates, which had been hidden in the woods. When Joseph Sr. reported what he had overheard to Emma, she directly mounted a horse and rode to warn Joseph. Together, they returned to Palmyra and Joseph retrieved the plates from their hiding place.[58] Three times he was assaulted on his way home. The persecution continued in the days that followed; once, mobs came to the Smith home and ransacked their cooper shop in search of the plates.[59] Joseph and Emma soon determined that they must leave Palmyra. Word was sent to Emma's brother, Alva Hale, asking him to come to Palmyra and take them back to Harmony.[60] Once settled in a home located on Emma's parents' property,[61] Joseph and Emma began the work of translation. Although the Hale's were antagonistic towards the work, they—like the Smith's—were vital to the translation process because of the space and protection they provided for Joseph and Emma.

Emma served as Joseph's first scribe, and some sources suggest that her work in this capacity may have been more significant and extensive than is commonly recognized. According to Joseph Knight, Emma assisted in "[drawing] of the Caricters" that Martin took to Charles Anthon.[62] She also possibly recorded the majority of Joseph's translation for the lost 116 pages, as Martin Harris remembered that he wrote "about one third of the first part of the translation of the plates as [Joseph] interpreted them by the Urim and Thummim."[63] While it is unknown precisely how long or how much Emma scribed for Joseph, Martin's statement raises the possibility that she recorded two-thirds of the lost 116 pages, which would make her Joseph's most prolific scribe besides Oliver Cowdery. Emma's own reminiscences of the translation work also indicate that her time scribing was extensive: "I frequently wrote day after day, often sitting at the table close by him . . . dictating hours after hour with nothing between us."[64]

Emma Smith's witness of this time also provides invaluable insight into the translation process, particularly as she scribed for Joseph both before and after the first 116 manuscript pages had been lost. From her we learn of "[Joseph] sitting with his face buried in his hat, with the stone in it. . . . He had neither manuscript nor book to read from."[65] She also informs us that when Joseph first began translating he used the Urim and Thummim, but later "he used a small stone, not exactly, black, but was rather a dark color."[66] Each of these details alter common perceptions of how Joseph translated. More specifically of the process, she reports:

> When my husband was translating the Book of Mormon, I wrote a part of it, as he dictated each sentence, word for word, and when he came to proper names he could not pronounce, or long words, he spelled them out, and while I was writing them, if I made any mistake in spelling, he could stop me and correct my spelling, although it was impossible for him to see how I was writing them down at the time. Even the word *Sarah* he could not pronounce at first, but had to spell it, and I would pronounce it for him. When he stopped for any purpose at any time he would, when he commenced again, begin where he left off without any hesitation, and one time while he was translating he stopped suddenly, pale as a sheet, and said, "Emma, did Jerusalem have walls around it?" When I answered, "Yes," he replied "Oh! I was afraid I had been deceived." He had such a limited knowledge of history at that time that he did not even know that Jerusalem was surrounded by walls.[67]

Scholars have used such information to argue for a tightly controlled translation process.[68] More important, though, Emma's witness also testifies repeatedly of the divinity of the work as Joseph corrected her spelling without seeing what she wrote, commenced where he left off "without either seeing the manuscript or having any portion of it read to him,"[69] and discovered things he did not know about, such as the walls around Jerusalem, as he translated.

Emma's experience as Joseph's scribe contributed to her lasting spiritual witness of the plates' divinity. Nearly fifty years later, she told her son:

> My belief is that the Book of Mormon is of divine authenticity. I have not the slightest doubt of it. I am satisfied that no man could have dictated the writing of the manuscript unless he were inspired. . . . Joseph Smith could neither write nor dictate a coherent and well worded letter, let alone dictating a book like the Book of Mormon. . . . And though I was an active

> participant in the scenes that transpired and was present during the translation of the plates, and had cognizance of things as they transpired, it is marvelous to me, "a marvel and a wonder," as much so as to any body else.[70]

From the individual who knew Joseph best, we learn of his capabilities at the time of translation and how far beyond those capabilities the Book of Mormon extended. The discrepancy between the two reaffirmed for Emma the divinity of the work—a spiritual witness that she would share repeatedly for the rest of her life.

Emma contributed to the work of translation not only through her scribal efforts but also through the support and care she provided Joseph as his wife. Emma was not able to be the full-time scribe that Joseph needed because, as Lucy Smith and Joseph Knight both report, most of her time was spent caring for their home and their temporal needs.[71] Maintaining a home was a full-time occupation in early nineteenth-century America, and Emma, without any hired help, fulfilled this necessary role for Joseph and herself, as well as at times for Martin Harris and Oliver Cowdery. Only with Emma caring for the home in Harmony, Joseph's brother Samuel tending the farm, and Joseph Knight providing food and paper could Joseph and Oliver devote themselves exclusively to the work of translation.[72] Notably, in her role as housekeeper Emma remained a close observer of the translation process as "Oliver Cowdery and [Joseph Smith] wrote in the room where [she] was at work."[73]

Emma, as an eyewitness of the translation process from the moment Joseph received the plates until the time when the Book of Mormon was published, also offered a temporal witness of the plates' physicality. In her role as housekeeper, "she would lift and move [the plates] when she swept and dusted the room and furniture."[74] At times the plates "lay under [their] bed for a few months."[75] Other times they sat in a sack or "wrapped in a small linen tablecloth"[76] on a "small table in their living room in their cabin."[77] Her witness of the plates' physicality takes on an added dimension when she describes "tracing their outline and shape."[78] She reports that the plates, "seemed to be pliable like thick paper, and would rustle with a metalic sound when the edges were moved by the thumb, as one does sometimes thumb the edges of a book."[79] Here Emma offers both auditory and tactile witnessing; nevertheless, many have questioned her lack of a visual witness.

Interestingly, though, she herself did not seem to; as she told her son, "I did not attempt to handle the plates, other than I have told you, nor uncover them to look at them. I was satisfied that it was the work of God, and therefore did not feel it to be necessary to do so."[80] Emma's complete assurance of the reality of the plates despite her never seeing them is a powerful statement about the validity of other ways of knowing and seeing beyond the visual.

The events surrounding the lost 116 pages illustrate well how the translation process was, in many respects, a truly joint effort for Joseph and Emma and how Emma, too, was deeply invested in the project. The day after Martin left with the 116 pages, Emma gave birth to their first son, who either was stillborn or lived for only a couple of hours.[81] Having undergone a long and extremely difficult labor, Emma's life was in danger for more than a couple of weeks. As her health improved, Joseph became increasingly anxious about the manuscript, "but he did not mention the subject to Emma for fear of agitating her mind to[o] much for the health of her body."[82] However, as Lucy Mack Smith reports, Emma—also concerned about the manuscript —told her husband, "I feel so uneasy . . . that I cannot rest and shall not be at ease untill I know something about what Mr Har ris is doing with it do you not think it would be ad visable for you to go and enquire into the reason of his not writing or sending any word back to you since he left us."[83] Emma's concern for the manuscript and insistence that Joseph leave her to inquire after it in the face of her own precarious health situation—and devastation over the loss of her first child—says much about her own commitment to the work.

Although many scholars have attributed Emma's professed concern for the plates to worry about Joseph's increasing despondency about the state of the manuscript,[84] consideration must also be given to Emma's own labor in scribing part of the 116 pages and the countless sacrifices she had made to assist in the translation work, as well as Lucy's statement about Emma's personal agitation over the manuscript. Additionally, Joseph's response to Martin when he learns Martin has lost the manuscript speaks to Emma's deep involvement in the project. "Then must I . . . return to my wife with such a tale as this I dare not do it least I should kill her at once."[85] Given Emma's fragile health, Joseph's words may not have been hyperbolic but rather may demonstrate his actual concern that her health may not have been able to withstand the additional loss of all that they had been working for together. A statement that Emma made at the end of her life, that "[she] was an active participant in the scenes that transpired and was present during the translation of the plates, and had cognizance of things as they transpired" is certainly accurate.[86] And through her witness we gain new knowledge of the translation process and the power in witnesses beyond the visual.

Conclusion

Each of these women—Mary Musselman Whitmer, Lucy Mack Smith, Lucy Harris, and Emma Hale Smith—aided the work of translation and offered their own witnesses of the plates' reality. By recognizing their contributions, we not only place women back into the narrative in which they were integral actors, but we also expand the scope of ways in which to witness and what it means to be a witness. Touch, sound, spiritual impressions, and visions may in fact produce, as these women illustrate, a more lasting and powerful experience than sight. In turn, through the witnesses of these women, we may see how the translation of the Book of Mormon both required and created community effort; males and females, people young and old, both family and friends all worked together on this important project. Almost two centuries later, the miracle of this great work may resonate more and build greater faith when we recognize how God used dedicated men and women to bring forth his great work of translation and restoration.

Notes

1. Mary Whitmer was born Mary Musselman in Germany on August 27, 1778. She immigrated to Pennsylvania and married Peter Whitmer, who was also of German descent. They moved to Fayette, New York, in 1809. Information taken from Mary Musselman Whitmer entry in the biographical directory in Karen Lynn Davidson, David J. Whittaker, Mark Ashurst-McGee, and Richard L. Jensen, eds., *Histories, Volume 1: 1832–1844,* vol. 1 of the Histories series of *The Joseph Smith Papers*, edited by Dean C. Jessee, Ronald K. Esplin, Richard Lyman Bushman (Salt Lake City: Church Historian's Press, 2012), 638 (hereafter *JSP*, H1). For more information, see Andrew Jenson, *Latter-day Saint Biographical Encyclopedia: A Compilation of Biographical Sketches of Prominent Men and Women in the Church of Jesus Christ of Latter-day Saints* (Salt Lake City: Andrew Jenson History Co., 1901), 1:283.
2. Dan Peterson, "Defending the Faith: Mary Whitmer, 12th Witness to the Book of Mormon," *Deseret News*, July 18, 2013.

3. Lucy Mack Smith, History, 1844–1845; handwriting of Martha Jane Knowlton Coray and Howard Coray; 240 pages, with miscellaneous inserted pages; Church History Library, book 8, 8–10; in citing book and page numbers, we follow the references available as part of the full text on *The Joseph Smith Papers*' website. See also interview of Joseph F. Smith and Orson Pratt with David Whitmer, as reported in *The Latter-day Saints' Millennial Star*, December 9, 1878, 772. For more information, see Richard Lloyd Anderson, *Investigating the Book of Mormon Witnesses* (Salt Lake City: Deseret Book, 1981), 67.
4. David Whitmer, *Deseret Evening News,* November 16, 1878, 1; as cited in Dan Vogel, comp., *Early Mormon Documents* (Salt Lake City: Signature Books, 1996–2003), 5:51–52.
5. As cited in Catherine Clinton and Christine A. Lunardini, eds., *The Columbia Guide to American Women in the Nineteenth Century* (New York: Columbia University Press, 2000), 35.
6. For more information, see Sally Ann McMurry, *Families and Farmhouses in Nineteenth-Century America: Vernacular Design and Social Change* (Cary, NC: Oxford University Press, 1988), 59–61; Clinton and Lunardini, 35–36; Nancy Grey Osterud, *Bonds of Community: The Lives of Farm Women in Nineteenth-Century New York* (Ithaca, NY: Cornell University Press, 1991), 156–58.
7. Statement of John C. Whitmer quoted in Andrew Jenson, *The Historical Record* 7, nos. 8–10 (October 1888): 621.
8. David Whitmer, *Deseret Evening News.*
9. Statement of John C. Whitmer.
10. Mary Whitmer raised seven children to adulthood. All five of her sons became witnesses for the gold plates, along with her sons-in-law, Hiram Page, who married Katherine in 1825, and Oliver Cowdery, who married Elizabeth in 1832.
11. Richard Lloyd Anderson, "The Whitmers: A Family That Nourished the Church," *Ensign*, August 1979, 35; Keith Perkins, "True to the Book of Mormon—The Whitmers," *Ensign*, February 1989, 34–42.
12. For more information on the Whitmers' role in the Church, later apostasy, and continual witness of the gold plates, see Anderson, "The Whitmers," 35; Keith Perkins, "True to the Book of Mormon," 34–42.
13. Lucy Mack Smith, History.
14. Copyright for Lucy Mack Smith, "The History of Lucy Smith," July 18, 1845, Robert Harris, Copyright Registry Records for Works Concerning the Mormons to 1870, Church History Library, Salt Lake City, UT.
15. Leonard J. Arrington, letter to the advisory editor of Arno Press, Edwin S. Gaustad, February 5, 1969. Quoted in Jan Shipps, *Mormonism: The Story of a New Religious Tradition* (Urbana: University of Illinois, 1987), 91.
16. Shipps, *Mormonism*, 92.
17. Lucy Mack Smith, History.
18. Lucy Mack Smith, History, book 6, 5; Miscellany, 9.
19. Lucy Mack Smith, History, book 2, 4–5; book 9, 5–6.
20. Asael Smith believed and declared that God intended to raise a branch of his family to be of great benefit to humankind. See Richard Lloyd Anderson, *Joseph*

Smith's New England Heritage: Influences of Grandfathers Solomon Mack and Asael Smith, 2nd ed. (Salt Lake City: Deseret Book; Provo, UT: Brigham Young University Press, 2003), 147–49, 286; and Joseph Smith, "Revelation, February 1829 [D&C 4]," in *The Joseph Smith Papers, Revelations and Translations, Manuscript Revelation Book*, ed. Robin Scott Jensen, Robert J. Woodford, Steven C. Harper (Salt Lake City: The Church Historian's Press, 2009), 1, http://josephsmithpapers.org/paperSummary/revelation-february-1829-dc-4?p=1.

21. Lucy Mack Smith, History, book 3, 12; and book 4, 1.
22. Lucy Mack Smith, History, book 4, 1–2.
23. From William Smith, *William Smith on Mormonism* (Lamoni, IA: Herald Steam Book and Job Office, 1883), 9. Quoted in Vogel, *Early Mormon Documents*, 1:620.
24. Smith, *William Smith on Mormonism,* 10.
25. Smith, *William Smith on Mormonism,* 11–12.
26. Lucy Mack Smith, History, book 5, 7.
27. Lucy Mack Smith, History, book 5, 7.
28. Quoted in Vogel, *Early Mormon Documents*, 1:524.
29. Vogel, *Early Mormon Documents*, 1:525.
30. Salisbury, "Things the Prophet's Sister Told Me," July 30, 1944 (San Rafael, CA), original typescript signed by the author, Church History Library, Salt Lake City, UT. Cited in Vogel, *Early Mormon Documents*, 1:524; "The Prophet's Sister Testifies She Lifted The B[ook] of M[ormon] Plates," *The Messenger*, October 1954, 1, 6, RLDS Church Library-Archives, Independence, MO. Quoted in Vogel, *Early Mormon Documents*, 1:649.
31. Lucy Mack Smith, History, book 5, 6.
32. Lucy Mack Smith, History, book 5, 6.
33. Lucy Mack Smith, History, book 8, 11.
34. Lucy Mack Smith, History, book 8, 10.
35. Lucy Mack Smith, History, book 3, 10.
36. Lucy Mack Smith, History, book 5, 6; book 5, 8; book 5, 12.
37. Lucy Mack Smith, History, book 5, 6; book 5, 4.
38. Lucy Mack Smith, History, book 6, 2–3; book 5, 6.
39. Lucy Mack Smith, History, book 9, 7.
40. Lucy Mack Smith, History, book 9, 8.
41. Lucy Mack Smith, History, book 9, 7.
42. E. D. Howe, *Mormonism Unvailed* (Painesville, OH: Printed and Published by the author, 1834), 254–57; 216–21. Lucy Harris may be disputed as a definitive witness, because she refuted the truth of Mormonism in an affidavit (see *Mormonism Unvailed*). Her behavior is not uncommon and may even be expected in one who becomes antagonistic towards the Church and suffers either indirectly or directly because of Church connections, as she attests she did via Martin. Consequently, Lucy Smith's account of Lucy Harris should be viewed as a credible recollection of events, particularly since Lucy Smith does not appear to like Harris or have any reason for placing these experiences upon her.
43. Lucy Mack Smith, History, book 6, 5–6.

44. Lucy Mack Smith, History, book 6, 4. Compare with Joel Tiffany, interview with Martin Harris, in "Mormonism—No. II," *Tiffany's Monthly*, August 1859, 168–70.
45. Lucy Mack Smith, History, book 6, 3–5.
46. Lucy Mack Smith, History, book 6, 4–5.
47. Lucy Mack Smith, History, book 6, 5. See also Mechal Sobel, *Teach Me Dreams: The Search for Self in the Revolutionary Era* (Princeton: Princeton University Press, 2002); and Phyllis Mack, "Agency and the Unconscious: The Methodist Culture of Dreaming," in *Heart Religion in the British Enlightenment: Gender and Emotion in Early Methodism* (New York: Cambridge University Press, 2008), 219–60. Oliver Cowdery had a similar experience before becoming one of the Book of Mormon scribes. The Lord "appeared unto a young man by the name of Oliver Cowdery and showed unto him the plates in a vision, and also the truth of the work, and what the Lord was about to do through me, his unworthy servant. Therefore, he was desirous to come and write for me to translate." Spelling and punctuation modernized. See Dean C. Jessee, ed., *Personal Writings of Joseph Smith*, rev. ed. (Salt Lake City: Deseret Book, 2002), 14, 20.
48. Lucy Mack Smith, History, book 6, 5.
49. Lucy Mack Smith, History, book 6, 5.
50. Tiffany, interview with Martin Harris, 168.
51. Lucy Mack Smith, History, book 6, 9; book 6, 8–10.
52. Lucy Mack Smith, History, book 6, 9.
53. As described in Lucy Mack Smith, History, book 7, 7–8.
54. Lucy Mack Smith, History, book 7, 8.
55. Although Lucy Harris initially offered financial assistance, she later refused to sign the $3,000 mortgage agreement that was to be used to satisfy the printer, E. B. Grandin.
56. According to Joseph Knight, Joseph Smith was first told by the angel Moroni that he must bring his oldest brother Alvin with him. After Alvin's death he was subsequently shown that he was to bring Emma Hale. Joseph Knight Sr., "Joseph Knight's Recollection of Early Mormon History," ed. Dean C. Jessee, *BYU Studies* 17, no. 1 (Autumn 1976): 31.
57. Lucy Mack Smith, History, book 5, 6. Joseph Knight refers in his recollections to a horse and carriage rather than the horse and wagon that Lucy referenced in her memoir. See "Knight's Recollection," 32.
58. Lucy Mack Smith, History, book 5, 9–10.
59. Lucy Mack Smith, History, book 5, 11–12; book 6, 1–3; Richard Lyman Bushman, *Joseph Smith: Rough Stone Rolling* (New York: Alfred A. Knopf, 2005), 60–61.
60. Lucy Mack Smith, History, book 6, 6.
61. Joseph had an agreement that he was to purchase the home and thirteen acres from Isaac Hale for $200. He made the last payment in August 1830. Bushman, *Rough Stone Rolling*, 63.
62. "Knight's Recollection," 34.

63. Simon Smith, letters to the editor, *Saints' Herald*, April 30, 1884; May 24, 1884, 324. Sources originally cited and assertion originally made that Emma wrote the translation for the majority of the lost 116 pages in Michael Hubbard MacKay and Gerrit J. Dirkmaat, *From Darkness unto Light: Joseph Smith's Translation & Publication of the Book of Mormon* (Provo, UT: Religious Studies Center; Salt Lake City: Deseret Book, 2015), 90–91. Possibly contradicting this point, Anthony Metcalf claimed that Harris told him that he "wrote a great deal of the Book of Mormon . . . as Joseph Smith translated or spelled the words out in English." See *Ten Years before the Mast* (Malad City, ID: publisher not identified, 1888), 70–71. The assertion that Emma wrote two-thirds of the lost 116 pages is also in conflict with Joseph's own statement that "he [M Harris] had written one hundred and sixteen <pages> of manuscript on foolscap paper." (*JSP*, H1:244). However, this statement by Joseph about the 116 pages does not account for Joseph's other statement in which he wrote that "my wife had written some for me to translate and also my Brothr Samuel H. Smith" (*JSP*, H1:16).
64. Emma Smith Bidamon, interview with Joseph Smith III, February 1879, Miscellany, RLDS Church Library-Archives, Independence, MO. Reproduced in Vogel, *Early Mormon Documents*, 1:539.
65. Emma Smith Bidamon interview, February 1879, reproduced in Vogel, *Early Mormon Documents*, 1:539.
66. Emma Smith Bidamon to Emma Pilgrim, March 27, 1870, Emma Smith Papers, RLDS Church Library-Archives, Independence, MO. Also published in *The Return*, July 15, 1895, 2. Reproduced in Vogel, *Early Mormon Documents*, 1:532.
67. From Edmund C. Briggs, "A Visit to Nauvoo in 1856," *Journal of History* 9 (January 1916): 454, reproduced in Vogel, *Early Mormon Documents*, 1:530–31.
68. Royal Skousen, "How Joseph Translated the Book of Mormon: Evidence from the Original Manuscript," *Journal of Book of Mormon Studies* 7, no. 1 (1998): 24–25.
69. Emma Smith Bidamon interview, February 1879, reproduced in Vogel, *Early Mormon Documents*, 1:538.
70. Emma Smith Bidamon interview, February 1879, reproduced in Vogel, *Early Mormon Documents*, 1:538–40.
71. Lucy Mack Smith, History, book 8, 4; "Knight's Recollection," 35.
72. For more information on Samuel Smith's role, see Lucy Mack Smith, History, book 8, 1–4; Linda King Newell and Valeen Tippets Avery, *Mormon Enigma: Emma Hale Smith*, 2nd ed. (Champaign, IL: University of Illinois Press, 1994), 28–29; Kyle R. Walker, *United by Faith: The Joseph Sr. and Lucy Mack Smith Family* (American Fork, UT: Covenant Communications, 2005), 207–9. For more information on Joseph Knight providing food and supplies, see "Knight's Recollection," 36.
73. Emma Smith Bidamon interview, February 1879, reproduced in Vogel, *Early Mormon Documents*, 1:539.
74. Joseph Smith III to Mrs. E. Horton, March 7, 1900. Miscellany, RLDS Church Library-Archives, Independence, MO. See also Emma Smith Bidamon, interview, reproduced in Vogel, 1:546–47.

75. Nels Madson, "Visit to Mrs. Emma Smith Bidamon," 1877 signed statement, Church History Library, Salt Lake City, reproduced in Vogel, *Early Mormon Documents*, 1:546.
76. Emma Smith Bidamon interview, February 1879, reproduced in Vogel, *Early Mormon Documents*, 1:539.
77. Joseph Smith III to Mrs. E. Horton, March 7, 1900; see also Emma Smith Bidamon, February 1879, reproduced in Vogel, *Early Mormon Documents*, 1:546.
78. Emma Smith Bidamon interview, February 1879, reproduced in Vogel, *Early Mormon Documents*, 1:539.
79. Emma Smith Bidamon interview, February 1879, reproduced in Vogel, *Early Mormon Documents*, 1:539.
80. Emma Smith Bidamon interview, February 1879, reproduced in Vogel, *Early Mormon Documents*, 1:540.
81. For more information, see Linda King Newell and Valeen Tippets Avery, *Mormon Enigma: Emma Hale Smith*, 2nd ed. (Champaign, IL: University of Illinois Press, 1994), 27.
82. Lucy Mack Smith, History, book 7, 2.
83. Lucy Mack Smith, History, book 7, 2.
84. See Newell and Avery, *Mormon Enigma*, 28; Gracia N. Jones, *Emma and Joseph: Their Divine Mission* (American Fork, UT: Covenant Communications, 1999), 27; Bushman, *Rough Stone Rolling*, 67.
85. Lucy Mack Smith, History, book 7, 6.
86. Emma Smith Bidamon interview, February 1879, reproduced in Vogel, *Early Mormon Documents*, 1:540.

9

Joseph Smith's Negotiations to Publish the Book of Mormon

Gerrit J. Dirkmaat and Michael Hubbard MacKay

Gerrit J. Dirkmaat and Michael Hubbard MacKay are assistant professors of Church history and doctrine at Brigham Young University.

In the summer of 1829, Joseph Smith's years-long odyssey to obtain and translate the gold plates into English as the Book of Mormon was finally nearing an end. Almost six years had passed since Joseph had experienced his first startling visitation from an angel calling himself Moroni. During that time he had experienced numerous setbacks and disappointments, both personal and spiritual.

He had failed to obtain the plates immediately after that first night of angelic visitations in 1823, later explaining that he had not been able to get them at first because he had "saught the Plates to obtain riches and kept not the commandment that I should have an eye single to the Glory of God."[1] After four more years of repentance, preparation, and heavenly instruction, Joseph finally obtained the plates in 1827. Rebuffed by worldly scholars who averred that they could not translate the characters copied from the plates, Joseph had proceeded to use specially prepared seer stones to miraculously render the characters into English words that he dictated to various scribes including his wife Emma and Martin Harris. But triple tragedy struck the

Smith home in the spring and summer of 1828, starting with Joseph's loss of the gold plates and the seer stones, often referred to as spectacles, which he found with the plates.

After Joseph repeatedly requested permission to allow Martin Harris to take the translated pages constituting the Book of Lehi to show his family, the angel returned and confiscated the plates and the spectacles. Shortly thereafter, Emma delivered the couple's first child, but the male baby was either stillborn or died immediately after birth, dealing a shattering blow to their young family. Worse still, Emma nearly died as a result of the difficult delivery and Joseph spent weeks nursing her back to health. As Emma began to recover, Joseph set out for Palmyra to learn why Harris had not yet returned with the manuscript pages he had taken, only to learn that Harris had lost them; nearly all of the translation work that had been accomplished over the previous months was now gone. Devastated by the loss of the pages, in mourning for the loss of his son, and in dire economic straits, Joseph "cried unto the Lord that he would provide for me to accomplish the work whereunto he had commanded me."[2]

At this time of desperation and demoralization, Oliver Cowdery fortuitously appeared on the scene. Unbeknownst to Joseph and Emma, Cowdery had been boarding at Joseph Smith Sr.'s home in Manchester. Though Joseph Sr. had initially been hesitant to share many details on his son's visions and mission, he had finally opened up to Cowdery about the gold plates and the visitation of angels, likely the result of a revelation Joseph Jr. had given his father (D&C 4) which instructed Joseph Sr. to share the gospel. As he contemplated and prayed about the astonishing things Joseph Sr. had told him, Cowdery had his own remarkable vision in which the Lord appeared and showed "unto him the plates in a vision and also the truth of the work and what the Lord was about to do."[3] The two men, though hampered at times with insufficient means to buy paper or even food, quickly recommenced the translation work with a vigor.

Through a spring and summer that brought more than a dozen new revelations, more angelic visitations, and an increase in the number of people that followed the new teachings revealed by Joseph, the project of translation was finally nearing completion. But producing the hundreds of pages of translated manuscript was only part of the difficulty in bringing forth the Book of Mormon. Now Joseph and his friends were faced with perhaps an even more daunting prospect: finding a willing publisher and paying the staggering sum it would cost to get the Book of Mormon printed.

The men first went to the largest print shop in town, owned by a friend of Martin Harris, Egbert B. Grandin. Grandin was the publisher of the *Wayne Sentinel*, a local newspaper, and had a business agreement with Luther Howard to bind books printed on his press. It is not certain when the initial negotiations began, but in the June 16, 1829, issue of Grandin's paper, the newspaperman published the title page of the forthcoming Book of Mormon, one of the requirements Joseph Smith needed to fulfill in order to secure a copyright for the book.[4] At this early point, though, Grandin seemed completely disdainful of the entire project. Alongside the published title page of the forthcoming Book of Mormon, Grandin added his own derisive commentary that it was "pretended that it will be published as soon as the translation is completed."[5]

It is not surprising then that Grandin rejected the initial offer of Joseph Smith and Martin Harris to publish the book. Grandin had his reputation as an editor and community leader to think of, and he knew only too well concerning the translation of the gold plates that "most people entertain an idea that the whole matter is the result of a gross imposition, and a grosser superstition."[6] Moreover, at least according to some accounts, Grandin was apparently concerned about the welfare of Martin Harris and his family. While many printers were content to publish books and then share the proceeds of the expected sales with the author, this arrangement was predicated upon the printer's belief that the book would sell well enough to recoup the costs of production. Grandin was adamant that the Book of Mormon would not sell, and refused to consider such an arrangement. When Harris proposed to sell his farm in order to pay for the publication himself, Grandin "at once advised them against the supposed folly of the enterprise" and was indefatigable in his opposition to the entire plan. Grandin apparently even tried to rally community support against the proposed publication. He went to Harris's prominent friends and enlisted their aid to try to talk Harris into abandoning his support of Joseph Smith and to "desist and withdraw" his pledge to pay for the book. Harris doggedly "resisted with determination" the entreaties of Grandin and his other friends, remaining determined to pay for the publication of the Book of Mormon. But Grandin would not be budged either. Although Joseph Smith and Martin Harris reportedly met with Grandin multiple times attempting to negotiate a deal, Grandin flatly refused "to give it further consideration."[7]

Having failed to secure Grandin's press for the publication, Joseph Smith and Martin Harris next turned to another printer in Palmyra, Jonathan A. Hadley. Hadley was the editor and proprietor of the *Palmyra Freeman*, an anti-Masonic newspaper that had since 1828 sent repeated salvos of blistering rhetorical attack crashing against the breastworks of freemasonry's image in the public mind. Hadley was a fiery young man, only twenty years old, but already had risen in the print ranks from an apprentice to become the editor of his own publication. Like Thurlow Weed, the master printer he had apprenticed under in Rochester, Hadley published a paper that concentrated on political news with a biting editorial sarcasm that never wasted a moment to demonize the institution of freemasonry. For instance, when another paper reported the proposed idea to form an "Anti-eating-too-much-society," Hadley sardonically scoffed, "It ought to be an Anti-use-too-little-exercise-society. . . . We suspect there are few cases known of laboring men eating too copiously." In a parting shot to the masons he opined, "We should prefer an anti-murder-and-treason-not-excepted-society, to either of the above."[8]

Hadley had repeatedly advertised his printing abilities in his paper, claiming he could perform "all kinds of Job Printing . . . as expediciously and reasonable as at any office . . . west of the Capital."[9] As the immense cost of publishing the Book of Mormon had been at the heart of Grandin's refusal to print the book, Joseph may have hoped that he could find a more willing associate in Grandin's competitor, and perhaps one willing to perform the work more inexpensively. While it is difficult to determine what their negotiations and interactions were like, Hadley later claimed that Martin Harris had often talked to him about the gold plates and tried to convince him to embrace Joseph Smith's visions. At some point in the summer of 1829, at least Martin Harris, if not Joseph as well, approached Hadley about publishing the Book of Mormon. In an account written years later and at the height of national anti-Mormon agitation Hadley claimed, "I was so sceptical as to utterly refuse to have any 'part or lot' in the imposition, telling him at the same time, that if he proceeded with the publication, I should feel it my duty, as the conductor of a faithful public journal, to expose him and the whole Mormon gang."[10]

Despite this later claim to have rejected the Book of Mormon out of disgust for its contents, Hadley apparently refused to publish the book for practical rather than moral reasons. Although "Harris owned a good farm in that town, and offered to mortgage it to secure the expense of printing," Hadley did not have the means to undertake a project so large as the publication of five thousand copies of a nearly six-hundred-page book.[11] The actions of Joseph Smith and Martin Harris after their interview with Hadley do not bespeak an outright rejection at Hadley's hand. Instead, the pair journeyed the nearly twenty-five miles to the city of Rochester, forgoing much closer towns such as Canandaigua which had several printing establishments at least the size of Grandin's. Why did they then travel to Rochester, at least a good day's journey away? The most logical explanation for such a journey is that while Hadley did not have the facilities to publish the Book of Mormon himself, he referred them to the master printer he had apprenticed under in Rochester, Thurlow Weed.

Thurlow Weed was already renowned throughout western New York, but not for his book printing prowess. Rather, the fiery writer was known for the militant position he had staked out in opposition to freemasonry. Having previously served in the New York State legislature, Weed used his newspaper, the *Anti-Masonic Enquirer,* and his political connections to foment a statewide revolt against the power and positions of freemasons in American society. He led the charge to form a new political organization of anti-Masons throughout the state.[12] His political acumen would later make him one of the leading organizers of the Whig and then Republican Parties.

It is difficult to determine just how Weed reacted to Joseph Smith's initial visit and explanation of both the Book of Mormon and his desire for Weed to publish it. The only accounts of their negotiations are late reminiscences of Thurlow Weed himself, and in each case Weed publishes his story about negotiating with Joseph Smith during a time of heightened anti-Mormon furor in the nation. As a savvy newspaperman and politician, he was careful to portray his involvement in the foundation of the Mormon faith as antagonistically and derisively as possible.

In addition, by the time Weed published his accounts, he was clearly influenced by other antagonists' claims against Joseph Smith and the Book of Mormon; for instance, Weed appropriated the arguments made by Doctor Philastus Hurlbut and Eber D. Howe and told his readers that before the Book of Mormon was ever produced, Smith "went a vagabonding off into Western Pennsylvania, where, nobody knows how, he got possession of the manuscript of a half-deranged Clergyman, with which he returned to Palmyra." After espousing Howe's claim that the Book of Mormon originated from a manuscript written by Solomon Spaulding, Weed further claimed that Joseph Smith attempted to deceive people by claiming to have found a stone that produced the words of the book. He told readers that Joseph had reportedly obtained a stone and it was from this stone or "inspired 'slate,' which he used to place in his hat, [that] he read to the 'gaping few' new and strange revelations; and finally, he produced the 'Book of Mormon,' as the creed and faith of a People of whom he was designed by Providence to be the Prophet and Ruler." After dutifully slandering and distorting the origins of the faith, Weed proceeded to explain his role in the Book of Mormon negotiations: "The Prophet and his Convert [Smith and Harris] came to Rochester and offered us the honor of being their Printer . . . but as we were only in the newspaper line, we contented ourselves with reading a chapter of what seemed such wretched and incoherent stupidity, that we wondered how 'Joe' had contrived to make the first fool with it."[13] To Weed in 1845, belief in Mormonism was a "mental [disease]."

Nearly a decade later, following an article that decried Mormonism and its attendant polygamous marriage practices, Weed again portrayed the negotiations in a negative light:

> Twenty-eight years ago, "JOE SMITH," the founder of this sect, and "HARRIS," his first convert, applied to the senior editor of The Journal, then residing at Rochester, to print his "Book of Mormon," then just transcribed from the "Golden Bible" which Jo. had found in the cleft of a rock to which he had been guided by a vision. We attempted to read the first chapter, but it seemed such unintelligible jargon that it was thrown aside. Jo. was a tavern-idler in the village of Palmyra. Harris, who offered to pay for the printing, was a substantial farmer. Disgusted with what we deemed a "weak invention" of an impostor, and not caring to strip Harris of his hard earnings, the proposition was declined. The manuscript was then taken to another Printing-office across the street, whence, in due time, the original "Mormon Bible" made its advent.[14]

Playing to the anti-Mormon mood of his readers, Weed argued that his decision to reject the manuscript was one of moral and civic duty, laced with an altruism that prevented him from accepting the job because Harris would have been financially ruined. Gone was his earliest explanation that his office was simply not set up to publish books at that time.

As Weed's political fortunes continued to rise throughout the 1850s along with his ally William Seward's, he once again published an article that addressed his early negotiations with Joseph Smith. This 1858 article, however, was written in a climate in which President James Buchanan had ordered the US army out to Utah Territory after declaring it to be in a state of rebellion and promising that the inhabitants should "expect no further lenity, but look to be rigorously dealt with."[15] Though Weed lamented how "mortifying" it was that "Mormonism seeks and finds Believers among those who have enjoyed the advantages of civilization, and by whom the Truths of Revelation have been rejected," his purpose in writing was to decry the anticipated violence that was to be directed at the so-called rebellious Mormons in Utah. Weed urged the government to "RESCUE rather than DESTROY" the deluded Mormons in Utah, as he hoped the army would "achieve a moral conquest over Mormons, far more humane and enduring than Victories won by bullets and baptized in blood."[16]

Perhaps in an effort to burnish his bona fides in a discussion about the way the government should deal with the present Mormon situation, Weed once again recounted the 1829 visit from Joseph Smith and Martin Harris. Weed explained how Smith came to his office "with the manuscript of his Mormon Bible, to be printed . . . but after reading a few chapters, it seemed such a jumble of unintelligible absurdities, that we refused the work, advising Harris not to mortgage his Farm and beggar his family."[17]

Although Weed often made his negotiations with Joseph Smith seem as if they were just a brief, single encounter, his final explanation of the episode in his autobiography described a multiday interview, and this account includes details missing from all of his previous renditions. In this account, Weed describes Joseph Smith coming to his office in Rochester alone. Joseph Smith told Weed that "he wanted a book printed, and added that he had been directed in a vision to a place in the woods near Palmyra, where he resided, and that he found a 'golden Bible,' from which he was directed to copy the book which he wanted published." Weed's reaction must have been so skeptical that Joseph Smith attempted to prove the divine nature of the book to him in (if Weed's account is true) an unprecedented display of Joseph's power to translate. Weed recounted that Smith placed a stone in his hat "from which he read a chapter of the 'Book of Mormon.'" This display of the divine origin of the book failed to convince Weed, however, and Joseph left that day without an agreement with him. Nevertheless, Joseph returned the next day, this time with Martin Harris. That Joseph returned with Martin the next day suggests that despite Weed's self-serving protestations to the contrary, he had not rejected the work out of hand because of his own moral compass; rather, economics drove his decision. Harris insisted to Weed that if the latter would print the book he would "become security for the expense of printing." Weed was either not convinced that Harris could raise the funds or, as he claimed much later, the words of the Book of Mormon "seemed so senseless that I thought the man [Joseph Smith] either crazed or a very shallow imposter, and therefore declined to become a publisher."[18]

Met with this disappointment, and having already traveled the substantial distance to Rochester, Joseph and Martin turned elsewhere, this time to one of Weed's ardent critics and competitors, Elihu F. Marshall, the editor of the *Rochester Album*. An accomplished printer, Marshall had written and published a spelling book in 1819 that received accolades from the likes of Supreme Court Chief Justice John Marshall. This very successful book was still being sold in Palmyra in 1829 and was likely one used by Oliver Cowdery in his own teaching.[19] By June of 1829, Marshall had expanded operations and was actively seeking books to publish and sell in his Rochester shop.[20]

It is not known whether Joseph Smith went to negotiate with Elihu Marshall by chance, as a result of Marshall's advertisements, because Weed suggested him, or because some of Marshall's public statements impressed him.[21] Only a few months before Joseph Smith and Martin Harris called upon Marshall in his shop to solicit his aid in publishing the Book of Mormon, Marshall had himself been involved in a very public religious dispute. Ostracized from the main body of the Religious Society of Friends (Quakers) for accepting the teachings of radical Quaker theologian Elias Hicks[22] Marshall had coauthored a pamphlet that delivered a stinging rebuke not only to the Quakers but to any religious group that did not allow for "private judgment." Instead, Marshall argued, God accepted individual men based upon the life they lived, the Protestant obsession with creeds and confessionals notwithstanding. Adherence to "speculative religion or abstract theology," Marshall argued, was not a legitimate reason to reject someone that was trying to live the gospel of Christ.[23]

If Joseph Smith were aware of Marshall's religious sentiments, these public pronouncements in support of religious tolerance would have been a welcome reprieve from the incessant attacks he withstood on the subject of his own perceived heresy. Joseph later recorded that he and Oliver Cowdery had been visited in Fayette by many people who had attacked their beliefs and had asked them many "hard questions, trying to confound" them. Among those seeking to refute Smith's claims to revelation were "several learned priests who generally came for the purpose of disputation."[24] Joseph Smith's own willingness later in life to defend the religious beliefs of others was something that was often recognized by others. For instance, in 1843, English utopian John Finch visited Nauvoo and was astonished at the lack of religious pretention emanating from Joseph Smith. Not only had Joseph Smith invited him to address the people in Nauvoo on two separate occasions, the astonished Finch explained how general this practice seemed. He wrote, "Joe Smith was in the practice of inviting strangers, who visited Nauvoo, of every shade of politics or religion, to lecture to his people. A Unitarian minister, from Boston, was to lecture them the following Sunday. He said that he allowed liberty of conscience to all, and was not afraid of any party drawing his people away from him."[25]

Whether actuated by common sentiments of tolerance or not, Elihu Marshall was the first publisher to meet with Joseph Smith and give him a positive response. Unfortunately, no records of their negotiations exist, so the terms agreed upon cannot be known. What is known is that Joseph Smith and Martin Harris still preferred to publish the Book of Mormon in Palmyra if at all possible. Likely fearing another disaster such as the debacle that ensued when Harris had the manuscript portion known as the 116 pages taken from him, Joseph intended to do two things to protect the text. First, he instructed Oliver Cowdery to make a copy of the manuscript. The intention was to take these copied pages to the print shop rather than the original manuscript itself. Second, instead of taking the entirety of the manuscript to the printer at once, Joseph intended to have only a few pages brought at a time, thus mitigating the possibility that the text could be lost or misappropriated and eliminating the possibility that the entire text could be stolen. While these safeguards were judicious given the previous loss of the Book of Lehi manuscript, they also required a much more hands-on approach to the publication process than was generally the case. Oliver Cowdery, Martin Harris, and Hyrum Smith would all need to be in close proximity to the printing work, a fact that made a Rochester rather than Palmyra print shop present a whole host of expensive, logistical challenges. Were the book to be published in Rochester, these men would need to secure room and board for months in an unfamiliar city. If there were any problems with the printing that required Joseph's intervention, Rochester was another day further away from his home in Harmony, Pennsylvania.

Returning to Palmyra with Marshall's agreement already assured, Joseph Smith and Martin Harris once again sought an audience with Egbert Grandin, the publisher of the *Wayne Sentinel*, who had so thoroughly rebuffed them in the first place. Explaining to Grandin that if he continued to refuse to perform the work "that the printing was to be done at any rate," Grandin finally relented and "entered into a contract for the desired printing and binding."[26]

Although Grandin had reportedly hesitated to accept the job out of deference for Harris, not wanting to deprive Harris of his fortune to pay for the book, by the time the two returned to Grandin's shop from Rochester, Grandin's altruism had entirely faded. Rather than grant liberal terms in order to soften the blow upon Harris's property, Grandin, likely sensing the profit to be made from the seemingly desperate men, imposed harsh terms for his services indeed. First, Grandin demanded that the payment for the printing be made entirely up front. No halfway measures or partial payments would suffice. Second, he placed the cost of publishing the five thousand copies of the Book of Mormon at three thousand dollars, an exorbitant sum that seemed to greatly eclipse the usual profit margin made by printers during that time period.[27]

Despite the cost, Smith and Harris struck the deal with Grandin and agreed to the demanded price. The weeks-long effort to find a willing publisher had finally come to an end. The men had met disappointment on numerous occasions, faced harsh ridicule and incredulity, but through perseverance finally obtained their original objective: persuading Egbert Grandin to publish the Book of Mormon in Palmyra. While it is uncertain precisely when this agreement was reached, it apparently occurred sometime before August 11, 1829.[28]

While Joseph Smith must have been elated that their search for a publisher had ultimately ended in Palmyra, Jonathan Hadley, the publisher of the *Palmyra Freeman* that had sent the pair to Rochester, was thoroughly outraged. Not only was Smith not going to publish the book with his ally and mentor, Thurlow Weed, he was planning to have Hadley's political and economic in-town rival, Grandin, publish it. Hadley's anger resulted in his printing of a detailed diatribe against the anticipated publication of the Book of Mormon, providing the earliest known published account of the visitation of an angel to Joseph Smith, the finding of the plates and the seer stones, and the mechanics by which Joseph translated the plates.

Hadley's philippic inveighed against the entirety of Joseph Smith's claims to divine revelation. Calling the "Gold Bible" the "greatest piece of superstition that has ever come within the sphere of our knowledge," Hadley proceeded to relate the details surrounding the discovery and translation of the gold plates that he had received from Joseph Smith and Martin Harris during their publication negotiations earlier in the summer. Though Hadley was certainly an antagonist, like several other early opponents of Mormonism Hadley seemed to relay the claims of Joseph Smith with relative accuracy. He claimed that Smith's claims to angelic visitations, miraculous translations, and gold plates containing the writings of ancient prophets were so unbelievable that there was no need to attack Smith personally or provide alternate explanations for the creation of the Book of Mormon text. Hadley concluded that the claims of Joseph Smith would be viewed as fantastical and farcical by his readers that he did not have to take the effort to refute the story categorically.

He wrote of the "Gold Bible":

> Its proselytes give the following account of it: In the fall of 1827, a person by the name of *Joseph Smith*, of Manchester, Ontario County, reported that he had been visited in a dream by the spirit of the Almighty, and informed that in a certain hill in that town, was deposited this Golden Bible, contains an ancient record of divine nature and origin. After having been thrice thus visited, as he states, he proceeded to the spot, and . . . the Bible was found, together with a huge pair of Spectacles!"

After mocking the fact that Joseph Smith had been told not to show the plates to anyone, Hadley proceeded to provide details that were simply unavailable to anyone that had not had a direct conversation with Joseph Smith. He told his readers that "It was said that the *leaves* of the Bible were *plates* of gold, about eight inches long, six wide, and one eighth of an inch thick, on which were engraved characters or hieroglyphics. By placing the Spectacles in a hat, and looking into it, Smith could (he said so, at least,) interpret these characters."[29] This description of the dimensions of the plates was the same that would be repeated in Joseph Smith's famous Wentworth letter well over a decade later.[30] That Joseph Smith performed the translation by placing the seer stones into a hat to block out the ambient light was later attested to by close associates and scribes such as David Whitmer, Joseph Knight, and even Emma Smith herself.

Hadley's skeptical and critical accounting of the events did not stop with the discovery and translation of the plates. Rather, Hadley began to inform his readers in detail that while the story "was almost invariably treated as it should have been— with *contempt*"—Martin Harris, "an honest and industrious farmer of this town," had come to wholeheartedly believe. In fact, "So blindly enthusiastic was Harris, that he took some of the characters interpreted by Smith, and went in search of some one, besides the interpreter, who was learned enough to *English* them; but all to whom he applied (among the number was Professor Mitchell, of New-York,) happened not to be possessed of sufficient knowledge to give satisfaction! Harris returned, and set Smith to work at interpreting the Bible." Then, informing Palmyra residents that their name would soon be forever attached to the Book of Mormon, Hadley wrote with a mixture of emotion and incredulity, "The work is soon to be put to press in this village!!"[31]

Hadley's accurate but dismissive account of the plates and the translation no doubt served to further antagonize a Palmyra public that had already rejected Joseph Smith's claims to miraculous experiences. Yet the rising tide of public sentiment against the Book of Mormon was not Joseph Smith's immediate problem at the time Hadley published his scathing criticism. Instead, Joseph fought an unexpected headwind from a storm he neither anticipated nor knew how to react to.

Having struck the deal with Grandin, the sheer magnitude of the financial resources necessary to publish the book came into full view. Three thousand dollars was not just a great sum of money, the cost to publish the book was fifteen times more expensive than the fourteen-acre farm Joseph owned in Harmony, and that included a small house. Digging wells or serving as a day laborer, Joseph could have hoped to earn little more than one dollar per day. Even if he had no living expenses or mortgage to pay or family considerations, it would have taken Joseph Smith nearly a decade to earn enough money to pay Grandin to publish the book. The fate of the publication did not rest with the nearly penniless and debt-ridden Joseph, or his equally indigent and impoverished family. All hopes for publication were pinned, where they always had been, squarely on the chest of Martin Harris.

Martin Harris had professed many times that he would be the means of paying for the Book of Mormon. As early as his 1828 visit to Charles Anthon, Harris had reportedly "intended selling his farm and handing over the amount received to those who wished to publish the plates."[32] Harris had offered to pay for the printing during their initial negotiations with Grandin; he had again asserted he would pay the entire cost of printing to the skeptical Thurlow Weed. He likely had made the same selfless offer to Jonathan Hadley. But now, having finally struck the deal with Grandin to print the book, Harris apparently balked at the required sum. As Weed and Grandin had told him, the cost of printing the book would financially ruin Harris. Charles Anthon reported that Harris had initially believed that copies of the Book of Mormon would sell well because the book "would produce an entire change in the world and save it from ruin."[33] But learned professors, friends and family members, and experts in the printing and bookselling trade had with unanimity maintained that such a book would not sell at all, and certainly not five thousand copies. Men like Weed and Grandin and Anthon called upon their worldly experience to deliver the matter-of-fact news to Harris that he was facing certain financial ruin if he indeed paid for the book.

The enormous cost of the endeavor combined with the unmitigated negativity with which the project was received by experts apparently gave Harris pause. Though they had struck the deal with Grandin to print the books likely in late July or early August, weeks went by without Grandin beginning the undertaking. Paying for the entire printing up front would require nearly all of Harris's substantial assets. As Grandin's son-in-law later recalled, "Harris became for a time in some degree staggered in his confidence; but nothing could be done in the way of printing without his aid."[34] And so the days and then weeks began to pass by without the printing work commencing as Grandin, who had despised the project from the outset, utterly refused to set the first line of type before he received his payment up front.[35]

This time a frustrated Joseph Smith was presented with a supernatural rather than temporal solution to his dilemma. Sometime during the impasse with Martin Harris over the payment of the printing during the summer of 1829, Joseph Smith received one of his most well-known revelations, directed at the suddenly recalcitrant Harris. The text of the revelation spoke to Harris in the voice of Jesus Christ: "Wherefore, I command you by my name, and by my Almighty power, that you repent: repent, lest I smite you by the rod of my mouth, and by my wrath, and by my anger, and your sufferings be sore: How sore you know not! How exquisite you know not! Yea, how hard to bear you know not!"[36]

After calling Harris to repent and vividly describing the abject suffering of Christ during his Atonement for the sins of the world, the revelation then declared, "I command you, that thou shalt not covet thine own property but impart it freely to the printing of the book of Mormon which contains . . . the word of God." Not only did the revelation command Harris to impart his property to pay for the printing, the revelation then proceeded to explain to Harris precisely what such an imparting meant: "Impart a portion of thy property; yea, even a part of thy lands and all save the support of thy family. Pay the Printers debt. Release thyself from bondage." The lines just preceding those instructions reminded Harris that "misery thou shalt receive, if thou wilt slight these councils; Yea, even destruction of thyself and property."[37]

Despite his obvious reservations and the growing cacophony of voices that derided such a decision, Harris heeded the words of the revelation and took the courageous step of fronting the entire cost of the publication of the Book of Mormon. As the revelation had directed him, he mortgaged most of his property to Egbert Grandin for the promised three thousand dollars on August 25, 1829, placing himself in peril of almost total financial ruin.[38] His profits ensured, Grandin immediately set out for New York City to purchase the needed type and commence work on the project.

With Harris's mortgage, Joseph Smith's difficult odyssey to find a willing printer of the book had finally come to an end. Although Joseph apparently anticipated that the book would be finished by February 1, 1830, it was not until late March that copies were finally available for sale. And while the secular prognosticators were right in asserting that the general public would eschew the book and there would be no brisk sales, they were wrong in asserting that there would be no sales at all. Over the course of the next decade, the stockpile of five thousand copies of the original printing was eventually exhausted, and plans to reprint the Book of Mormon were already under way as early as 1833. And though cynics like Weed and Grandin were certain Harris would lose everything and Harris did indeed lose most of his Palmyra property as a result of his difficult decision to follow through on his commitment and pay for the publication, Harris was eventually repaid as the books were sold. He later told an interviewer, "I never lost one cent. Mr. Smith . . . paid me all that I advanced, and more too.[39]

Ultimately Joseph Smith and Martin Harris made great sacrifices to translate and publish the Book of Mormon because they believed what detractors scoffed at, that the work derived from "an ancient record of divine nature and origin" and that it would indeed, as Charles Anthon so blithely dismissed, "produce an entire change in the world and save it from ruin."[40]

Notes

1. Joseph Smith, 1832 History, in Joseph Smith Letterbook, MS 155, box 2, folder 2, 5, Church History Library, Salt Lake City. The full text of this account can also be found in Karen Lynn Davidson, David J. Whittaker, Mark Ashurst-McGee, and Richard L. Jensen, eds., *Joseph Smith Histories 1832–1844*, vol. 1 of the Histories series of *The Joseph Smith Papers*, ed. Dean C. Jessee, Ronald K. Esplin, and Richard Lyman Bushman (Salt Lake City: Church Historian's Press, 2012), 14, and at www.josephsmithpapers.org.
2. Joseph Smith, 1832 History, 16.
3. Joseph Smith, 1832 History, 16.
4. For more information on the efforts to obtain a copyright to the Book of Mormon, see Michael Hubbard MacKay, Gerrit J. Dirkmaat, Grant Underwood, Robert J. Woodford, and William G. Hartley, eds., *Documents, Volume 1: July 1828–June 1831,* vol. 1 of the Documents series of *The Joseph Smith Papers,* ed. Dean C. Jessee, Ronald K. Esplin, Richard Lyman Bushman, and Matthew J. Grow (Salt Lake City: Church Historian's Press, 2013), 76–80.

5. *Wayne Sentinel* (Palmyra, NY), June 26, 1829.
6. *Wayne Sentinel*, June 26, 1829.
7. "Mormonism and Joe Smith—The Book of Mormon or Golden Bible," *Wayne Democratic Press* (Lyons, NY), May 26, 1858.
8. "New Societies," *Palmyra Freeman* (Palmyra, NY), July 28, 1829.
9. "Job Printing," *Palmyra Freeman*, July 14, 1829.
10. Jonathan Hadley to the *Lowell Journal* (Lowell, MA), July 14, 1842, published under the heading "Origin of Mormonism," in the *Wayne County Whig* (Lyons, NY), 14 September 1842.
11. Jonathan Hadley to the *Lowell Journal*, July 14, 1842.
12. "Morgan," *Pennsylvania Gazette* (Philadelphia), October 27, 1827; "Morgan, Morgan, Morgan," *Olive Branch* (New York), September 15, 1827; "Highly Important," *Republican Compiler* (Gettysburg, PA), October 27, 1827; *Louisville Public Advertiser* (Louisville, KY), October 11, 1828, reprinted from the *New York American*; Thurlow Weed and Harriet Weed, *Life of Thurlow Weed, Including His Autobiography and A Memoir* (Boston: Houghton Mifflin, 1883), 341–42.
13. "A Letter From Joe Smith's Widow," *Albany Evening Journal* (Albany, NY), December 10, 1845.
14. "Recent Progress of the Mormons," *Albany Evening Journal*, July 31, 1854.
15. House Executive Document 2, 35th Congress, 2nd Session 72.
16. "Prospect of Peace With Utah," *Albany Evening Journal*, May 19, 1858.
17. "Prospect of Peace With Utah."
18. Thurlow Weed and Harriet Weed, *Life of Thurlow Weed*, 358–59. In one final account published in *Scribner's Monthly*, Weed made many of the same claims from his autobiography, but reaffirmed as he had in his earliest account: that while he considered the Book of Mormon to be "incomprehensible jargon" the primary reason he gave Joseph Smith for his refusal to publish the book was Weed "was only publishing a newspaper, and that he would have to go to a book publisher." Ellen E. Dickinson, Affidavit of Thurlow Weed in "The Book of Mormon," *Scribner's Monthly* (New York), August 1880, 614.
19. "Marshall's and Webster's Spelling Books," *Palmyra Freeman*, August 18, 1829.
20. *Directory for the Village of Rochester: Containing the Names, Residence and Occupations of All Male Inhabitants over Fifteen Years of Age, in Said Village, on the First of January, 1827. To Which Is Added, A Sketch of the History of the Village, from 1812 to 1827* (Rochester, NY: Elisha Ely, 1827), 96; "Book and Job Printing," *Craftsman* (Rochester, NY), March 3, 1829.
21. In the affidavit published in 1880 by Ellen Dickinson, Weed alleged that after he told Joseph Smith that he was not a book publisher he had suggested "a friend who was in that business." It is doubtful that Weed would have suggested Marshall, however, as the anti-Masonic Weed regularly clashed with pro-Masonic editors such as Marshall. Ellen E. Dickinson, Affidavit of Thurlow Weed.
22. Thomas D. Hamm, *The Quakers in America* (New York: Columbia University Press, 2003), 40.

23. Elihu Marshall, *The Inquisition and Orthodoxy: Contrasted with Christianity and Religious Liberty* (Lockport, NY: L. A. Spalding and Others, 1829), 3–4.
24. Joseph Smith History, vol. A-1, 20, Church History Library.
25. "Notes of Travel in the United States," *New Moral World and the Gazette of the Rational Society* (London), October 5, 1844.
26. Pomeroy Tucker, "Mormonism and Joe Smith," *Wayne Democratic Press*, May 26, 1858.
27. For an analysis of the costs likely incurred to print the Book of Mormon and profit margin Grandin likely enjoyed, see Michael Hubbard MacKay and Gerrit J. Dirkmaat, *From Darkness unto Light: Joseph Smith's Translation and Publication of the Book of Mormon* (Provo, UT: Religious Studies Center; Salt Lake City: Deseret Book, 2015), 175.
28. Jonathan Hadley's paper, the *Palmyra Freeman*, reported on August 11, 1829, that the book was soon to be put to press in Palmyra, rather than Rochester.
29. "Golden Bible," *Palmyra Freeman*, August 11, 1829.
30. The 1842 letter to John Wentworth gives this description of the plates: "These records were engraven on plates which had the appearance of gold, each plate was six inches wide and eight inches long and not quite so thick as common tin." Joseph Smith, "Church History," *Times and Seasons*, March 1, 1842.
31. "Golden Bible," *Palmyra Freeman*, August 11, 1829.
32. Charles Anthon to Eber D. Howe, February 17, 1834, published in Howe's *Mormonism Unvailed*, 271.
33. Charles Anthon to Eber D. Howe, 271.
34. Pomeroy Tucker, *Origin, Rise, and Progress of Mormonism*, 51.
35. John Gilbert, the typesetter employed by Grandin to print the Book of Mormon, later explained that "before the work was commenced" Martin Harris "had given security for the full amount agreed upon for printing." Kate B. Carter, comp., *Our Pioneer Heritage* (Salt Lake City: Daughters of Utah Pioneers, 1967), 10:294.
36. *A Book of Commandments for the Government of the Church of Christ* (Zion, MO: W. W. Phelps & Co., 1833), 40.
37. *Book of Commandments*.
38. Martin Harris to Egbert B. Grandin, Indenture, August 25, 1829, Wayne Co., NY, Mortgage Records, 3:325–26, Family History Library.
39. David B. Dille, "Additional Testimony of Martin Harris," *Millennial Star*, August 20, 1859, 545.
40. Charles Anthon to Eber D. Howe, 271.

10

The Early Reception of the Book of Mormon in Nineteenth-Century America

Jeremy J. Chatelain

Jeremy J. Chatelain is a teacher at the Fremont Seminary in Ogden and a field curriculum writer for Seminaries and Institutes. He is a PhD candidate at the University of Utah.

Not long after the Book of Mormon was first printed, it came into the hands of a man who hesitatingly declared, "Hold on. . . . Wait a little while; what is the doctrine of the book, and of the revelations the Lord has given? Let me apply my heart to them." Finally, after examining "the matter studiously for two years," he made up his mind to "receive that book." Who was this careful, contemplative man who "wished time sufficient to prove all things" for himself? He was none other than Brigham Young, who later said, "I knew it was true, as well as I knew that I could see with my eyes, or feel by the touch of my fingers, or be sensible of the demonstration of any sense."[1]

About the same time, however, the New York newspapers the *Rochester Daily Advertiser* and the *Rochester Republican* printed: "BLASPHEMY—'BOOK OF MORMON,' alias THE GOLDEN BIBLE. The 'Book of Mormon' has been placed in our hands. A viler imposition was never practised. It is an evidence of fraud, blasphemy and credulity, shocking to the Christian and moralist."[2] At least ten more newspapers in Massachusetts,

Rhode Island, New York, Maryland, and Vermont reprinted this article during April and May 1830. Moreover, by the time these articles were printed, no fewer than forty-one articles on the Book of Mormon and Joseph Smith had already been published in the previous year. The arrival of the famous and infamous book would irreversibly influence the course of humankind.

The reception of the Book of Mormon in the first half of the nineteenth century reveals a fascinating dichotomy of ridicule and dismissal, and quiet, deep discernment of the word of God. Newspaper editors, philanthropists, and religionists were stridently critical of the new scripture for a variety of reasons: from exasperation about the revivalism of the Second Great Awakening to the fear of losing members of their own flock to Mormonism. On the other hand, those seeking the restoration of Christ's Church often felt the import of the book without even having met the Prophet Joseph.

This chapter will consider the reaction to the Book of Mormon in its first three years: from its publication beginning in 1829 to the end of 1831. The Book of Mormon was more heavily addressed in newspapers in these three years than in the next nine years combined. The primary sources used for the study are from a newly assembled collection of over 10,000 articles on Mormonism in more than 660 newspapers from 1829 to 1844.[3] Among these sources are at least 583 articles that mention the Book of Mormon by name. More than two-thirds of those articles were written in the first three years. The attitudes toward and perceptions of the Book of Mormon found in these newspapers will be reviewed for content and development over time, and juxtaposed with accounts by those like Brigham Young, who had the sincere intent and faith to obtain the promised witness that the book is true, some even before the book was bound.

Since its tenuous start, the Book of Mormon has been printed in over 100 languages, surpassed 150 million copies, was recognized as one of the most influential books in American history, and is now carried throughout the world in the hands of more than 83,000 missionaries.[4] The coming forth of the Book of Mormon is a marvelous work and a wonder.

The Book of Mormon Goes to Print, 1829

Unlike Joseph's religious contemporaries whose ministries began with a feeling to preach, Joseph's arrival on the religious scene began with a book. For the Smith family, the book was "the source of so much secret gratification,"[5] but because of the book, they would be excoriated and vilified on thousands of newspaper pages. No fewer than twenty-four articles mentioning some aspect of the Book of Mormon appeared in newspapers from June to December 1829, before the Book of Mormon was even available for sale. This time frame included, among other things, completing the translation, searching for a printer in Palmyra and Rochester, obtaining the copyright, making formal arrangements with E. B. Grandin, having the eleven witnesses see the plates, receiving the revelation directing Martin Harris to not covet his property and to pay the printer's debt,[6] beginning the printer's manuscript, receiving the first printer's proofs, and starting the typesetting and printing. One of the first-known references to the Book of Mormon in the newspapers is found in E. B. Grandin's June 26, 1829, newspaper from Palmyra, New York, called the *Wayne Sentinel*:

> Just about in this particular region, for some time past, much speculation has existed, concerning a pretended discovery, through superhuman means, of an ancient record, of a religious and divine nature and origin, written in ancient characters, impossible to be interpreted by any to whom the special gift has not been imparted by inspiration. It is generally known and spoken of as the *"Golden Bible."* Most people entertain an idea that the whole matter is the result of a gross imposition, and a grosser superstition. It is pretended that it will be published as soon as the translation is completed. Meanwhile we have been furnished with the following, which is represented to us as intended for the title page of the work—we give it as a curiosity.[7]

Grandin had initially turned down Joseph's request to print the book. His reluctance is evident in his passive reference to the publication of the work and his distanced statement that "most people entertain an idea that the whole matter is the result of a gross imposition, and a grosser superstition." Nevertheless, the copyright request for the Book of Mormon was filed in the office of Richard R. Lansing, clerk of the Northern District Court in Utica, New York, on June 11, 1829,[8] and Grandin agreed to print five thousand copies for three thousand dollars.[9]

Local newspapers from July and August 1829 included some vague allusions to the Book of Mormon,[10] but it was the *Palmyra Freeman* of August 11, 1829, that would perpetuate the next significant reactions and rumors. The article contains a variety of details of how Joseph obtained the plates, including three divine visits, the discovery of the buried plates "together with a huge pair of spectacles," the dimensions of the plates, the warning not to show them to others, and a description of placing the spectacles in a hat during the process of translation. The article also tells of Martin Harris's visit to Professor Mitchell, "who was learned enough to English them," but "happened not to be possessed of sufficient knowledge to give satisfaction!"[11] (For more about this visit, see chapter 6 by Richard E. Bennett herein.) The writer's disbelieving commentary was striking and contagious. The article entered the nineteenth-century American "newspaper exchange"[12] and spread quickly. At least six additional newspapers reprinted the article, or variations of it, from August 1829 to January 1830, repeating such caustic barbs as "the greatest piece of superstition," "the subject [the Book of Mormon] was almost invariably treated as it should have been—with *contempt*," and "It is certainly a '*new thing*' in the history of superstition, bigotry, inconsistency, and foolishness. It should, and doubtless will, be treated with the neglect it merits. The public should not be imposed upon by this work."[13]

To what degree such articles shaped the reception of the Book of Mormon in the minds of Americans is difficult to assess. Yet print historians have recognized the power of the "national print culture" that took shape in the early nineteenth century, and one such scholar declared, "An expanding press was a visible force for change in the new nation, its impact registered in every area of American life."[14] Regarding the barrage of bad press directed at Joseph and the Book of Mormon, historian Richard L. Bushman wrote, "The [news]papers elevated Joseph from an obscure money-digger of local fame to full-blown religious imposter."[15]

By September 1829, another local editor named Abner Cole began manipulating the reception of the still-printing Book of Mormon. Cole, writing under the pseudonym Obadiah Dogberry, printed his Palmyra newspaper, the *Reflector*, in the evenings and on Sundays on the same press engaged in printing the Book of Mormon. Setting the type for his newspaper while surrounded by drying, unbound sheets of the Book of Mormon, Cole was, no doubt, aware of the stories and rumors in the small village about the plates and about the young, pretentious "Jo Smith," and Cole was not impressed.[16] But his proximity to the printing of the controversial scripture gave him unprecedented firsthand knowledge and access. The fact that Cole was perusing the text of the Book of Mormon in Grandin's offices is apparent in his tongue-in-cheek reference to the noticeable frequency of the phrase "and it came to pass" in the Book of Mormon. He printed, "The Book of Mormon is expected to be ready for delivery in the course of one year.—Great and marvellous things will 'come to pass' about those days."[17] "The Gold Bible," he wrote, "by Joseph Smith Junior, author and proprietor, is now in press and will shortly appear. Priestcraft is short lived!"[18] This was Cole's first mention of the book, and the only time he honored Joseph by using a formal version of his name. Ironically, Cole accused the editor of the aforementioned *Palmyra Freeman* of examining "the hidden mysteries" of the unfinished Book of Mormon—something he himself was doing.[19] Cole, the first prolific writer on Joseph and early Mormonism, wrote other harmless banter in September 1829. "We understand," he printed with feigned concern, "that the Anti-Masons have declared war against the Gold Bible.—Oh! how impious."[20]

While Abner Cole was dismissing the possibility that God had again spoken on earth, Solomon Chamberlain was inquiring "through the country . . . if there was any strange work of God, such as had not been on the earth since the days of Christ." Being guided by the Spirit to Palmyra, a town with which he was unfamiliar, he was asked if he had heard of the Gold Bible. "When they said 'Gold Bible,'" he wrote, "there was a power like electricity [that] went from the top of my head to the end of my toes." He soon arrived at the home of the Smith family, where he recalled, "The Lord revealed to me by the gift and power of the Holy Ghost that this was the work I had been looking for." Solomon accompanied Hyrum Smith to the printing office where, "as soon as they had printed 64 pages," Solomon "took [the pages] with their leave" and journeyed to Canada to preach the Book of Mormon. Solomon was present the next spring when the Book of Mormon went on sale; he purchased "8 or 10 of them" and quickly resumed his mission.[21]

Thomas B. Marsh had a similar experience. Being unable to make his Methodist faith "correspond" with the Bible, he wrote that he "kept aloof from sectarians"[22] until one day a "lady enquired if [he] had heard of the Golden Book found by a youth named Joseph Smith." Being "very anxious to know concerning the matter," Thomas traveled to Palmyra and discovered

Martin Harris at the printing office, where the proof sheets of the first sixteen pages had just been struck. After learning of Joseph's experiences, he took the proof sheet home to his wife, who "was well pleased, believing it to be the work of God."[23]

By October 1829, on the other hand, Abner Cole's sarcasm had increased, along with his familiarity with the Book of Mormon. "The 'New-Jerusalem Reflector' states that the building of the TEMPLE OF NEPHI is to be commenced about the beginning of the first year of the millennium. Thousands are already flocking to the standard of Joseph the Prophet. The Book of Mormon is expected to astonish the natives!!"[24] Cole's approach intensified in December when he offered a tantalizing glimpse of the controversial book, perhaps seizing the opportunity to increase his readership and try to defame Joseph. Citing the "much curiosity" in the area regarding the Book of Mormon and the "solicitation of many of [his] readers," Cole promised in the December 9 issue to "commence publishing *extracts* from it" in January 1830.[25] True to his word, the entire front page of the January 2, 1830, issue of the *Reflector* contained pilfered text from 1 Nephi 1:1 through 2:3 and concluded with the assurance that it was "To be Continued."[26]

President Ezra Taft Benson deftly described in 1988 what was already beginning on the pages of newspapers and in the hearts of men and women in 1829. "I have noted," he proclaimed, "a difference in discernment, insight, conviction, and spirit between those who know and love the Book of Mormon and those who do not. That book is a great sifter."[27] Those like Cole who wagged their heads in derision would never experience what those like Solomon Chamberlain gained from bowing theirs.

The Book of Mormon in Print, 1830

Historians have questioned Cole's motives for copying from the Book of Mormon and have written on his cantankerous personality.[28] Most recently, scholars have found evidence that Cole was a freethinker, part of the American Freethought movement from 1825 to 1850.[29] Not disposed to orthodoxy or angelic ministrations, Cole instead gloried in his brash attempts at "lifting the veil, tearing off the mantle, and stripping the cloak from the vain pretender, and hold[ing] him up to public ridicule for the finger of scorn to point at."[30] His intractable nature led to the well-known confrontations with Hyrum, Oliver, and Joseph over his unauthorized printing of

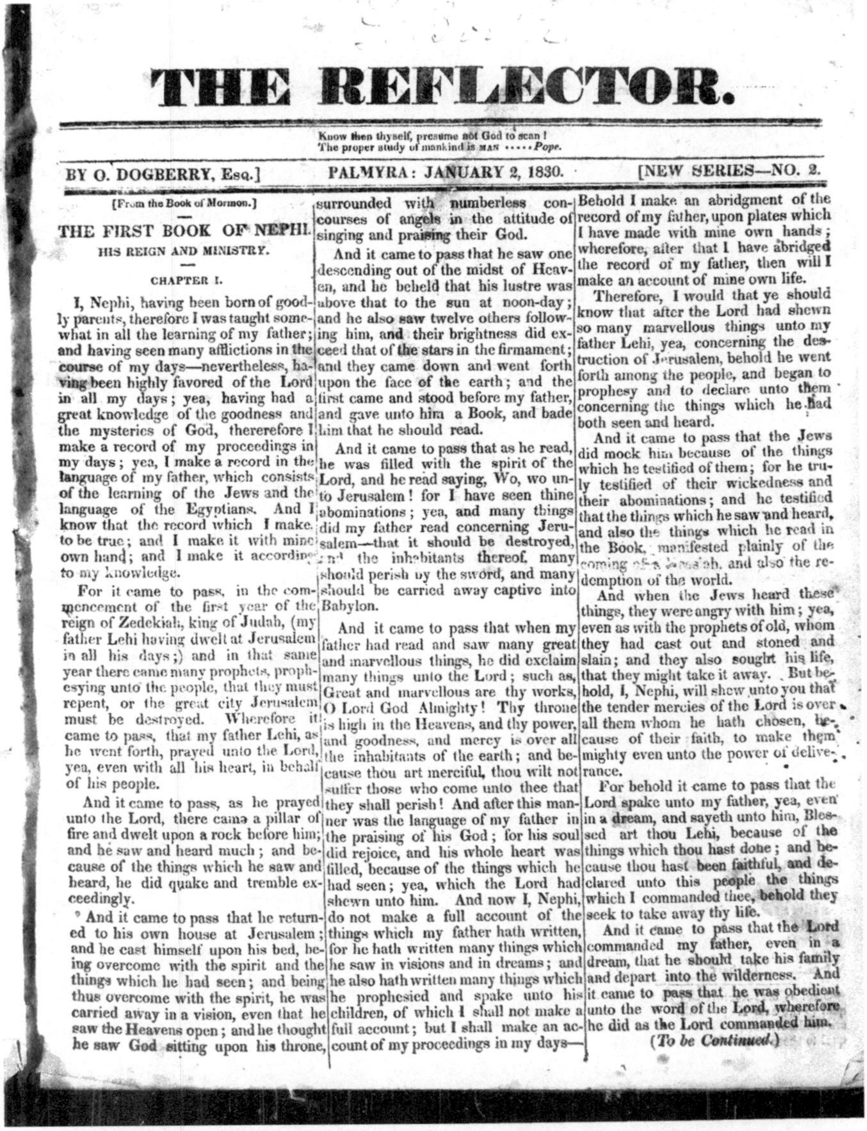

THE REFLECTOR.

Know then thyself, presume not God to scan!
The proper study of mankind is MAN ·····*Pope.*

BY O. DOGBERRY, Esq.] PALMYRA: JANUARY 2, 1830. [NEW SERIES—NO. 2.

[From the Book of Mormon.]

THE FIRST BOOK OF NEPHI.

HIS REIGN AND MINISTRY.

CHAPTER I.

I, Nephi, having been born of goodly parents, therefore I was taught somewhat in all the learning of my father; and having seen many afflictions in the course of my days—nevertheless, having been highly favored of the Lord in all my days; yea, having had a great knowledge of the goodness and the mysteries of God, thererefore I make a record of my proceedings in my days; yea, I make a record in the language of my father, which consists of the learning of the Jews and the language of the Egyptians. And I know that the record which I make, to be true; and I make it with mine own hand; and I make it according to my knowledge.

For it came to pass, in the commencement of the first year of the reign of Zedekiah, king of Judah, (my father Lehi having dwelt at Jerusalem in all his days;) and in that same year there came many prophets, prophesying unto the people, that they must repent, or the great city Jerusalem must be destroyed. Wherefore it came to pass, that my father Lehi, as he went forth, prayed unto the Lord, yea, even with all his heart, in behalf of his people.

And it came to pass, as he prayed unto the Lord, there came a pillar of fire and dwelt upon a rock before him; and he saw and heard much; and because of the things which he saw and heard, he did quake and tremble exceedingly.

And it came to pass that he returned to his own house at Jerusalem; and he cast himself upon his bed, being overcome with the spirit and the things which he had seen; and being thus overcome with the spirit, he was carried away in a vision, even that he saw the Heavens open; and he thought he saw God sitting upon his throne, surrounded with numberless concourses of angels in the attitude of singing and praising their God.

And it came to pass that he saw one descending out of the midst of Heaven, and he beheld that his lustre was above that to the sun at noon-day; and he also saw twelve others following him, and their brightness did exceed that of the stars in the firmament; and they came down and went forth upon the face of the earth; and the first came and stood before my father, and gave unto him a Book, and bade him that he should read.

And it came to pass that as he read, he was filled with the spirit of the Lord, and he read saying, Wo, wo unto Jerusalem! for I have seen thine abominations; yea, and many things did my father read concerning Jerusalem—that it should be destroyed, and the inhabitants thereof, many should perish by the sword, and many should be carried away captive into Babylon.

And it came to pass that when my father had read and saw many great and marvellous things, he did exclaim many things unto the Lord; such as, Great and marvellous are thy works, O Lord God Almighty! Thy throne is high in the Heavens, and thy power, and goodness, and mercy is over all the inhabitants of the earth; and because thou art merciful, thou wilt not suffer those who come unto thee that they shall perish! And after this manner was the language of my father in the praising of his God; for his soul did rejoice, and his whole heart was filled, because of the things which he had seen; yea, which the Lord had shewn unto him. And now I, Nephi, do not make a full account of the things which my father hath written, for he hath written many things which he saw in visions and in dreams; and he also hath written many things which he prophesied and spake unto his children, of which I shall not make a full account; but I shall make an account of my proceedings in my days—Behold I make an abridgment of the record of my father, upon plates which I have made with mine own hands; wherefore, after that I have abridged the record of my father, then will I make an account of mine own life.

Therefore, I would that ye should know that after the Lord had shewn so many marvellous things unto my father Lehi, yea, concerning the destruction of Jerusalem, behold he went forth among the people, and began to prophesy and to declare unto them concerning the things which he had both seen and heard.

And it came to pass that the Jews did mock him because of the things which he testified of them; for he truly testified of their wickedness and their abominations; and he testified that the things which he saw and heard, and also the things which he read in the Book, manifested plainly of the coming of a Messiah, and also the redemption of the world.

And when the Jews heard these things, they were angry with him; yea, even as with the prophets of old, whom they had cast out and stoned and slain; and they also sought his life, that they might take it away. But behold, I, Nephi, will shew unto you that the tender mercies of the Lord is over all them whom he hath chosen, because of their faith, to make them mighty even unto the power of deliverance.

For behold it came to pass that the Lord spake unto my father, yea, even in a dream, and sayeth unto him, Blessed art thou Lehi, because of the things which thou hast done; and because thou hast been faithful, and declared unto this people the things which I commanded thee, behold they seek to take away thy life.

And it came to pass that the Lord commanded my father, even in a dream, that he should take his family and depart into the wilderness. And it came to pass that he was obedient unto the word of the Lord, wherefore he did as the Lord commanded him.

(*To be Continued.*)

The front page of the January 2, 1830, issue of Abner Cole's *Reflector* (Palmyra, NY).

the Book of Mormon. According to Lucy Mack Smith's later recollection,[31] Hyrum, acting on an uneasy feeling, took Oliver into Palmyra one Sunday afternoon to discover Cole hard at work on his newspaper and belligerently denying the illegality of his actions. Joseph, who then lived in Harmony, Pennsylvania, was sent for. He went into town to confront the irascible Cole. The older editor hoped for a fistfight, but "Joseph could not help smiling at [Cole's] grotesque appearance" and ridiculous behavior.[32] The copyright infringement was instead settled through arbitration,[33] but not before Cole printed excerpts in two more January issues of his newspaper.[34]

The arbitration may have had softening, or, at the least, legally mandated, effects on Cole. Assuming an uncharacteristically objective position regarding the Book of Mormon, Cole included in the same issue as the First Book of Nephi an opinion that he did not intend to "discuss the merits or demerits of this work." He claimed to be "astonished" that certain citizens should be so uneasy about "the Book [which] must stand or fall, according to the whims and fancies of its readers." Although he had not "as yet examined many of its pages" (which is doubtful), he was prepared to state that he could not "discover anything *treasonable*, or which will have a tendency to subvert our liberties." Then, more characteristically ironic, he declared: "As to its religious character, we have as yet no means of determining, and if we had, we should be quite loath to meddle with the *tender* consciences of our neighbors."[35]

Eleven days later, Cole published a front-page continuation of First Nephi and, once again, also donned an atypical professionalism towards Joseph and the book: "We inadvertently neglected in our remarks last week, respecting this *wonderful* work, to accompany them with the *explanations* requisite to a correct understanding of it." He then clarified that the "appellation of 'Gold Bible'" was an improper form of the proper name, "The Book of Mormon," which was a compilation of books in ancient hieroglyphics written on plates of gold by one named Mormon.[36] Cole gave no indications as to what inspired his change in temperament. Nevertheless, one can still see his irrepressible disdain embedded in the text. His third installment, an extract from Alma 27, appeared in the *Reflector* without commentary.[37]

Unhappy about the legal restraints, Cole turned to satire over the next couple months. His "Book of Pukei" mocked the "prophet Jo," his "book, and his rusty sword, and his magic stone."[38] By June 1830, Cole had shed any restraint and resumed his outright castigation: "No prophet . . . has performed half so many wonders as have been attributed to that *spindle shanked* ignoramus **Jo Smith** [who] appears to possess the *quint essence* of impudence."[39] The first serious agitator in print, Cole addressed some aspect of the Book of Mormon and Joseph Smith in no fewer than fifty-three articles from 1829 to the *Reflector*'s conclusion in 1831.

Meanwhile, the March 19, 1830, *Wayne Sentinel* announced the upcoming availability of the Book of Mormon.[40] At least thirty-six articles had been printed in the nine months since the *Sentinel's* first cautious recognition of the Book of Mormon. One week later, March 26, 1830, with a surprising lack of fanfare considering what had been printed to this point about the book, the *Sentinel* reprinted the title page of the Book of Mormon and this addition: "The above work, containing about 600 pages, large Duodecimo, is now for sale, wholesale and retail, at the Palmyra Bookstore, by HOWARD & GRANDIN."[41]

The quietness with which the Book of Mormon went on sale was shattered less than one week later. The *Rochester Daily Advertiser* of April 2, 1830, printed an article that surpassed the earlier rebuke of the *Palmyra Freeman* in the number of exchange-newspaper reprints, geographical coverage, and derision. At least eleven newspapers, with a small degree of variation, gave the aforementioned shout: "**Blasphemy—. . .** The 'Book of Mormon' has been placed in our hands. A viler imposition was never practised. It is an evidence of fraud, blasphemy and credulity, shocking to the Christian and moralist." The editors were aghast that "a fellow" named Joseph Smith Jr. had, "by some hocus pocus, acquired such an influence over a wealthy farmer of Wayne county [Martin Harris], that the latter mortgaged his farm for $3,000 which he paid for printing and binding 5000 copies of this blasphemous work." The editors then included a surprisingly accurate, brief description of the books of the Book of Mormon, and reproduced, without

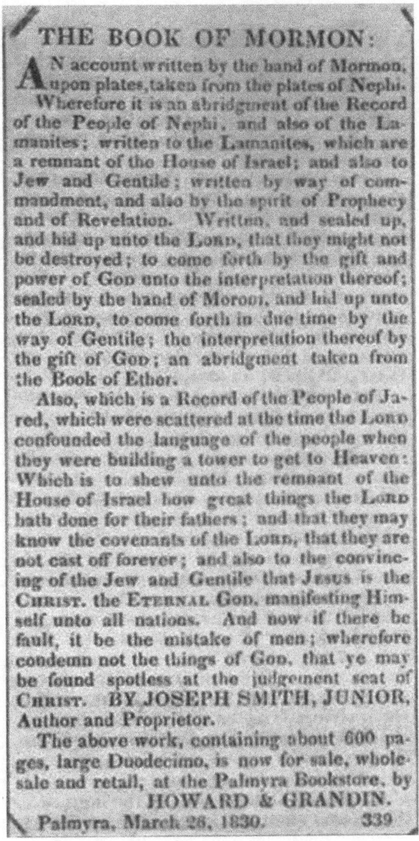
THE BOOK OF MORMON:
AN account written by the hand of Mormon, upon plates, taken from the plates of Nephi. Wherefore it is an abridgment of the Record of the People of Nephi, and also of the Lamanites; written to the Lamanites, which are a remnant of the House of Israel; and also to Jew and Gentile; written by way of commandment, and also by the spirit of Prophecy and of Revelation. Written, and sealed up, and hid up unto the Lord, that they might not be destroyed; to come forth by the gift and power of God unto the interpretation thereof; sealed by the hand of Moroni, and hid up unto the Lord, to come forth in due time by the way of Gentile; the interpretation thereof by the gift of God; an abridgment taken from the Book of Ether.

Also, which is a Record of the People of Jared, which were scattered at the time the Lord confounded the language of the people when they were building a tower to get to Heaven: Which is to shew unto the remnant of the House of Israel how great things the Lord hath done for their fathers; and that they may know the covenants of the Lord, that they are not cast off forever; and also to the convincing of the Jew and Gentile that Jesus is the Christ, the Eternal God, manifesting Himself unto all nations. And now if there be fault, it be the mistake of men; wherefore condemn not the things of God, that ye may be found spotless at the judgement seat of Christ. BY JOSEPH SMITH, JUNIOR, Author and Proprietor.

The above work, containing about 600 pages, large Duodecimo, is now for sale, wholesale and retail, at the Palmyra Bookstore, by HOWARD & GRANDIN.

Palmyra, March 26, 1830. 339

Figure 2. Egbert B. Grandin's announcement that the Book of Mormon was now for sale in the Friday, March 26, 1830, *Wayne Sentinel*. Courtesy of the Church History Museum.

alteration, the preface regarding the 116 stolen pages and the "testimonials" of the three and eight witnesses.[42]

The 1830 preface,[43] prepared by Joseph approximately eight months earlier in August 1829, revealed the nefarious scheme of those who stole the 116 pages of the Book of Lehi in the summer of 1828:

> As many false reports have been circulated respecting the following work, and also many unlawful measures taken by evil designing persons to destroy me, and also the work, I would inform you that . . . some person or persons have stolen and kept from me [one hundred and sixteen pages], . . . for Satan has put it into their hearts to tempt the Lord their God, by altering the words, that they did read contrary from that which I translated and caused to be written.[44]

Joseph had been directed in a revelation currently published as Doctrine and Covenants 10 to keep this knowledge to himself, to "hold [his] peace until [the Lord] shall see fit to make all things known unto the world concerning the matter."[45] Thus, those who had calculated to discredit Joseph and the Book of Mormon by attempting to reveal contradictory versions of the book were frustrated in their designs.[46] It is not entirely clear why the editors of these newspapers would have followed their brash denunciation of "credulity, . . . knavery, . . . [and] Blasphemy" eight months later with an almost sympathetic reprint of the lawlessness perpetrated against Joseph and the bold testimonies of eleven witnesses.[47] Regardless of the reason, Joseph learned the Lord's omniscience was conclusive: "I will not suffer that they shall destroy my work; yea, I will show unto them that my wisdom is greater than the cunning of the devil."[48] Perhaps the devil had not learned that even in the 1830s, bad press is still press.

Five more newspapers simultaneously reproduced from April to June 1830 a fairly objective summary of the Book of Mormon that recognized the "viler imposition" article but focused instead on the letters of the "eleven individuals, setting forth the excellence of the work and the existence of the original 'plates,' of gold, on which the contents of the volume were engraved, in a language which the translator was taught by inspiration." The harshest words were these: "We subjoin, with some hesitancy, one of the certificates [testimony of the three witnesses], which smacks pretty strongly of what would once have been called blasphemy."[49] Whether the aforementioned editors' intents were positive or negative, they aided the responsibility of the witnesses "to witness unto the world that which [they had] seen"[50] by reprinting the testimony in at least twenty-four newspaper articles, across seven states, and in nineteen cities.

Those Who Believed

Samuel H. Smith, Joseph's younger brother, enthusiastically departed for his opportunity to declare the truthfulness of the Book of Mormon in the summer of 1830. However, Samuel struggled, according to Lucy Mack Smith's later reminiscences, to find a sincere listener. Dejected, he placed a copy with Methodist preacher John P. Greene, who dismissed it as a "nonsensical fable." His wife, Rhoda Young Greene, on the other hand, believed it and "burst into tears" when Samuel came to collect it. Samuel was touched by her emotion and felt impressed to leave it with her as a present. Not knowing the future of the book, Samuel returned "sick at heart" to Joseph after his mission, claiming he had failed. Meanwhile, Rhoda eventually convinced her husband to read it seriously, and then passed it along to her brothers, Phineas, Lorenzo, Brigham, and Joseph Young.[51] The book continued its circuitous course and landed in the hands of Heber C. Kimball's mother-in-law. "Thus was this book," wrote Lucy, observing the Lord's hand in the matter, "the means of convincing this whole family, and bringing them into the Church, where they have continued faithful members from the commencement of their career until now. And, through their faithfulness and zeal, some of them have become as great and honorable men as ever stood upon the earth."[52]

Very few neutral or positive commentaries on the Book of Mormon can be found in the newspapers during 1829 and 1830. One must generally turn to personal, autobiographical accounts to find the life-changing power of the book.[53] Parley P. Pratt was moved in August 1830 to stop in an unfamiliar region of New York for reasons he did not know but which were "plainly manifest by the Spirit." After visiting with "an old Baptist deacon," he was told "of a *book*, a strange book, a VERY STRANGE BOOK!" Parley remarked, "I felt a strange interest in the book. . . . Next morning I called at his house, where, for the first time, my eyes beheld the 'BOOK OF MORMON,'—that book of books . . . which was the principal means, in the hands of God, of directing the entire course of my future life."[54] Parley continued:

> I opened it with eagerness, and read its title page. I then read the testimony of the several witnesses in relation to the manner of its being found and translated. After this I commenced its contents by course. I read all day; eating was a burden, I had no desire for food; sleep was a burden when the night came, for I preferred reading to sleep.
>
> As I read, the spirit of the Lord was upon me, and I knew and comprehended that the book was true, as plainly and manifestly as a man comprehends and knows that he exists. My joy was now full, as it were, and I rejoiced sufficiently to more than pay me for all the sorrows, sacrifices and toils of my life.[55]

Parley determined to find Joseph Smith but, finding Joseph absent from his home, spent the night conversing with Hyrum. Parley left the next morning to fill a preaching commitment with a copy of the Book of Mormon in hand. As he walked, he considered the joy that filled his soul and enlarged his heart to be of more value than "all the beautiful farms, houses, villages and property," he mused, "which passed in review before me on my journey." The book had changed him. "After duly weighing the whole matter in my mind I saw clearly that these things were true," he wrote in his autobiography.[56] Little did he know the extent the book would "[direct] the entire course of [his] future life"—Parley died a martyr at the age of fifty while on a mission bearing testimony of the Book of Mormon.[57]

Likewise, in the fall of 1830, amid the printed insults and derision, a bridge- and mill-builder named Ezra Thayre physically felt the power of the Book of Mormon. Ezra was initially "filled with wrath" about the Book of Mormon—so much so that he offered to loan "a pair of horses [to take Joseph Smith] to prison." However, upon hearing Hyrum speak, Ezra recalled, "Every word touched me to the inmost soul. . . . The tears rolled down my cheeks. . . . When Hyrum got through, he picked up a book and said, 'here is the Book of Mormon.' I said, let me see it. I then opened the book, and I received a shock with such exquisite joy that no pen can write and no tongue can express. . . . I opened it again, and I felt a double portion of the Spirit, that I did not know whether I was in the world or not. I felt as though I was truly in heaven." Ezra saw the Prophet Joseph the next

Sunday and related his experience to him. Joseph asked him what hindered him "from going into the water [to be baptized. Ezra] said, I am ready and willing at any time."[58]

Ezra told his brother, who also believed the Book of Mormon, that "when God shows a man such a thing by the power of the Holy Ghost he knows it is true. He cannot doubt it."[59] Ezra rejoiced when the Lord called him to sound a trump of the truthfulness of the Book of Mormon "unto a crooked and a perverse generation."[60]

Other sincere seekers such as John and Julia Murdock and William W. Phelps had equally compelling encounters with the Book of Mormon. The power and spirit of the Book of Mormon influenced some of the early Saints so profoundly that even the critical newspapers took note. Early Mormon missionaries declared the marvelous work and wonder with as much enthusiasm as editors denounced it. Like Solomon Chamberlain, these irrepressible missionaries frequently carried printer's proof sheets because they could not wait for the finished, bound copies before preaching the Restoration.[61] Such zeal showed up in the papers. One concerned citizen wrote, "Mr. Editor—Please advise *hyrum* smith, and some of his ill-bred associates, not to be quite so impertinent, when *decent* folks denounce the imposition of the '**Gold-Bible.**' The anathemas of such ignorant wretches, although not feared, are not quite so well relished by some people—Apostles should keep cool."[62] Apparently, the Lord's imposed waiting period for Hyrum a year earlier to "obtain [the Lord's] word" before preaching was satisfied. Hyrum now had the Lord's "Spirit, and [His] word: Yea, the power of God unto the convincing of men,"[63] insomuch that citizens wrote to the newspapers about it.

The first year of the published Book of Mormon concluded with a few objective descriptions, reports of missionaries preaching, additional criticisms, and Abner Cole gnashing, "It is time the wretch [Joseph Smith] was unmasked and his hideous form exhibited."[64] Whatever its reception so far, the Book of Mormon could not be recalled.

The Copious Commentary of 1831

The year 1831 included more than 115 articles on the Book of Mormon, outnumbering the sum of the previous two years, as well as the combined number of the next six years. The articles became more refined and more vitriolic and were reprinted more frequently in the exchange than previously. The year began, not surprisingly, with Abner Cole applying his "censorial lash."[65] On January 1, 1831, he quipped, "We have been informed, that one of Jo Smith's Gold bibles was lately burnt at the stake in the village of Newark, Wayne county."[66] Nevertheless, the humor would be short-lived. In the final three months before his newspaper failed in March 1831, Cole wrote a series of haphazard editorials on the Gold Bible. "It is our intention," he declared in his introduction, to give "a plain and unvarnished statement of facts . . . [connected] with the origin, rise, and progress of the book in question; so that our readers may . . . judge . . . matters for themselves."[67] Six articles of considerable length were printed somewhat biweekly over three months. The content of the articles wandered across a fanciful history of the Smith family, Mohammed and the Koran, Joanna Southcott,[68] and a criticism of the alleged variations in the historical details of the testimonies of the Book of Mormon witnesses. Two Ohio newspapers, the *Ashtabula Journal* and the *Painesville Telegraph*,[69] reprinted three of the series, perhaps as a result of Joseph and the New York Saints arriving in nearby Kirtland, Ohio, in early 1831.

More profound in its ability to shape the reception of the Book of Mormon than Cole's Gold Bible series was the reaction of the *Ashtabula Journal* to its new neighbors. "The believers in the sacred authenticity of this miserable production," it denounced, "are known by the name of 'Mormonites'" and are led by "additional revelation from the prolifick [*sic*] prophet, Smith." The article reported the Mormon population in the adjoining counties at four hundred. The article then recounted a revelation to a young man "written in heaven by the finger of God . . . [in] letters of gold," but as soon as he attempted to copy the ethereal call to the ministry, the letters entirely vanished. Then followed a description of a "man of colour, a chief man," said to fancy he could fly and, "sometimes seized with strange vagaries, and conceits," jumped off a cliff of twenty-five feet but fell unharmed into a tree.[70] The article was swept up in the exchange, and variations were reprinted fourteen times from February to June 1831. It made its way back to the *Wayne Sentinel* in Palmyra, and, for the first time, more than nine hundred miles away to Little Rock, Arkansas Territory.

February 1831 saw the first comprehensive, methodical excoriations of the Book of Mormon. The first anti-Mormon pamphlet was also the first formal anti–Book of Mormon pamphlet. Written by reformist clergyman

Alexander Campbell, *Delusions* contained a surprisingly succinct summary of the 590-page Book of Mormon. Campbell's most well-known criticism was that Joseph endeavored to answer in the Book of Mormon "every error and almost every truth discussed in New York for the last ten years. He decides all the great controversies;—infant baptism, . . . the trinity, . . . the fall of man, the atonement, transubstantiation, . . . the general resurrection, eternal punishment, . . . the question of free masonary [*sic*], republican government, and the rights of man."[71] *Delusions* was first printed in Campbell's highly recognized *Millennial Harbinger* (Bethany, VA) on February 7, 1831. Newspapers such as the *Painesville Telegraph* and the *Cleveland Herald* anticipated the opportunity to reprint the review "from the able pen of Alexander Campbell [which] unequivocally and triumphantly sets the question of the divine authenticity of the 'Book' forever at rest, to every *rational* mind."[72] *Delusions* was still circulating in the newspaper exchange at least eighteen months later and one newspaper, the *Essex Gazette* from Haverhill, Massachusetts, even printed it twice, consuming the entire front page for two consecutive weeks.[73]

Campbell had not taken lightly the defection of Sidney Rigdon to Mormonism,[74] and the source of Rigdon's conversion, the Book of Mormon, would bear the brunt of his attack. The bitterness between the factions became sufficiently noteworthy to surface in the papers. An article printed on March 22, 1831, in the *Vermont Telegraph* (Brandon, VT) reprinted a letter written to the Utica, New York, *Baptist Register* on the subject: "'Campbellism with us,' wrote the author, 'is on the decline. Many of its votaries have embraced Mormonism, or the new revelation. The war has changed its appearance, and seems now to be between Campbellites and Mormonites.'"[75] Joseph Smith and the Book of Mormon had aroused the ire of one of the most recognized religionists of the time. When Joseph lamented in his 1838 history that his "circumstances in life [were] such as to make a boy of no consequence in the world, Yet men of high standing would take notice sufficient to excite the public mind against [him] and create a hot [bitter] persecution,"[76] he may well have had in mind such persons as Alexander Campbell.

Campbell was not the only writer to systematically analyze the Book of Mormon. The editors of the Hudson, Ohio, *Observer and Telegraph* conceded to "clear up [the] doubts" of a reader "solicitous to know the truth" concerning the "volume of silly impostures," and they presented a five-point discourse defining why new revelation was impossible.[77] Those who are familiar with the Book of Mormon can readily recognize in the argument Nephi's prophecy of the latter days wherein "many of the Gentiles [would] say, A Bible, a Bible, we have got a Bible, and there cannot be any more Bible."[78] A portion of the article was reprinted in the *Connecticut Observer* (Hartford) two weeks later.[79]

The reception of the Book of Mormon in its first three years was continually shaped by descriptions of the Saints themselves. A letter sent to an Ohio newspaper "signed by ten individuals of the first respectability," declared the followers of the "gold bible [to be] few and generally of the dregs of community, and the most unlettered people that can be found anywhere."[80] The Saints were continually classified by and identified in the pages of newspapers with small jabs at their belief in the Book of Mormon.[81]

Believers in the Book of Mormon were not spared being called names either. Articles since 1829 included a flurry of epithets using the word "Mormon." Religious devotees of Joseph's time were, like Book of Mormon peoples, frequently termed "-ites" of their leader. Followers of Joseph were referred to as "Smithites" in at least one article.[82] Interest in and skepticism of the name Mormon by 1831 led to the regular use of the appellation *Mormonites*, which was later shortened to *Mormons*. It was, nevertheless, not used in kindness. The New York–based *Brockport Free Press* of April 6, 1831, helped spread a contortion of the unfamiliar name: "We hear much these days about the Mormonites, the Mormon Bible, the Book of Mormon, and people are very desirous to know what *Mormon* signifies. . . . The word Mormon comes from the Greek word *mormoo* [and signifies,] '*bugbear, hobgoblin, raw head and bloody bones*.'" The editors claimed the definition came from an English dictionary "of quite ancient date," and, conveniently for them, only "very few copies are now extant"—and only in London. The editors reassured their readers, though, that they had seen a copy of the dictionary and verified the definition. They then surmised that Joseph's choice of the word *Mormon* "was no doubt done for the purpose of carrying out his experiment on human credulity to the greatest extent—even to give the book a name, in addition to its contents, which would carry on the very face of it the nature of its true character—a fiction of hobgoblins and bugbears."[83]

This definition stayed in the newspaper exchange over the years and eventually resurfaced thirteen years later in the *New Hampshire Patriot and State Gazette* (Concord, NH). However, the editor claimed to increase the "credibility" of the definition by citing ancient Greek texts and added to the end of the definition the phrase, "a hideous spectre, a frightful mask, something to frighten children."[84] Even Joseph's clarification in the *Times and Seasons* (Nauvoo, IL) that Mormon's name literally means "more good"[85] was trivialized by the editor when he claimed that Joseph "ignorantly [pretended] that Mormon was a sacred Jewish name . . . and [has] attempted to clothe the word Mormon with a sacred meaning."[86]

The months of May, June, and July in 1831 presented what must have been an especially painful surprise when Joseph and Emma (and John Murdock) opened their papers. "The wife of a Mr. Murdock . . . and a believer in Mormonism," it rapaciously reported, "died among them in child-bed [birth], for want of professional assistance. The wife of the prophet Smith hardly escaped the same fate; she was in labor three days, during which time they tried their spells in vain, at last they called an accoucheur,[87] and she was delivered of the dead bodies of two fine boys. The mother barely survived."[88] The editor was careful not to miss the fact that Mormons claimed the gift of healing and added this flippant, poignant example to regularly printed examples of failed Mormon miracles. What new wounds did it cause, particularly for Emma, as it was reprinted in at least four different exchange newspapers in four different states (Ohio, New York, Pennsylvania, and Massachusetts)?[89]

Occasionally, editors exhibited a rare degree of professionalism and objectivity in reporting about the Book of Mormon. Controversial freethinker and social reformer Francis (Fanny) Wright published a high-profile New York City newspaper named the *Free Enquirer*. The editor, Robert Dale Owen, printed on September 10, 1831, a nearly full-page "comparison between the Book of Mormon and the Scriptures of the Old and New Testaments, or the Golden Bible vs. the Holy Bible" written by his brother. He, "after a pretty careful perusal," wrote that "the Golden Bible will bear a very good comparison with the holy Bible. I find nothing in the former inconsistent with the doctrines or opposed to a belief in the latter; on the contrary, the one seems to corroborate the other; and I can discover no good reason why the generality of Christians should scoff, as I have generally found them do, and hoot at the idea of believing in such a monstrously absurd book."[90] These conclusions are surprising, considering how many editors were reprinting opposite claims that Joseph had cobbled together the Book of Mormon by plagiarizing the Bible.[91]

The year 1831 ended with an unexpected, counterintuitive boon. Apostate Ezra Booth wrote nine derogatory letters on Mormonism that were published in the *Ohio Star* (Ravenna, OH) from October 13 to December 8, 1831, centered on his dissatisfaction with the dedicatory trip to Zion in June and July 1831. His second letter denounced the alleged idea that the Book of Mormon was the "test by which every man's fate is to be tried"—that those who reject it "are threatened with eternal damnation," and shall be "swept off as with the besom of destruction."[92] It reemphasized the oft-published claim that Mormons considered the Book of Mormon far superior to the Bible, an incriminating accusation in the Bible-loving America. The letters initially had a dire effect. Ambrose Palmer, a Church member, wrote letters to Oliver Cowdery in which he described Booth's letters as giving the Book of Mormon such a coloring and appearance of falsehood that observers worried Mormonism would be overthrown by them.[93] Booth's letters were reprinted in the exchange primarily, it appears, by three newspapers in Ohio, but as far as one hundred miles from Kirtland. The letters would make another appearance in the first formal anti-Mormon book, *Mormonism Unvailed*, written by *Painesville Telegraph* newspaper editor Eber D. Howe two years later.

The effect of the letters was potent enough that on December 1, 1831, the Lord called Joseph and Sidney (and others) to leave their work of translating the Bible to go on "a mission for a season." They were to "confound [their] enemies . . . both in public and in private" and were promised that although the detractors may "bring forth their strong reasons against the Lord," they "shall be confounded."[94] Sidney Rigdon challenged Ezra Booth and Symonds Rider "in public" on pages of the same *Ohio Star* newspaper to a written or oral debate in December 1831 and January 1832. Booth and Rider declined, and the missions proved effective in defeating the rumors and spreading the truth.[95] Once again, the devil's attempt to thwart the work instead propelled it forward. After about six weeks, Joseph declared, "We did much towards allaying the excited feelings which were growing out of the scandalous letters."[96]

As for Ezra Booth, Joseph did not mince words. Booth's letters, "by their coloring, falsity, and vain calculations to overthrow the work of the Lord," railed Joseph, "exposed his weakness, wickedness and folly, and left him a monument of his own shame for the world to wonder at."[97] Historian Richard L. Bushman observed, "Booth then dropped from sight. Only his letters . . . remained to mark his trail across Joseph's life."[98]

The year concluded with an unintended reaffirmation of the unstoppable spread of the marvelous, wonderful work. The *Philadelphia Album and Ladies' Literary Gazette* of December 18, 1831, marked the swelling deluge: "The book which these men have pretended to translate from these sheets of gold has been printed, and they are now busily engaged in scattering copies of it throughout the country."[99]

Conclusion

The first three years of the publication of the Book of Mormon included more than 208 articles mentioning the Book of Mormon in 88 newspapers identified thus far. The Book of Mormon was more frequently addressed in newspapers from 1829 to 1831 than in the next nine years combined. The attitudes toward and perceptions of the Book of Mormon found in these newspapers were overwhelmingly negative. Nevertheless, truthful, diligent seekers ignored the pointing fingers from the great and spacious building (see 1 Nephi 8:26–27, 33) and felt both spiritual and physical power as they prayerfully pondered its pages. From the first announcement in the *Wayne Sentinel* that the Book of Mormon was for sale, the Book of Mormon continued to trickle into villages, hamlets, and townships all through the country—and to the edges of the ever-expanding frontier.

How much of the destiny of this book written upon gold plates and deposited in nearby Cumorah could Joseph have fathomed the night Moroni first mentioned it? The unearthing of this book that whispered from the dust (see Isaiah 29:4; 2 Nephi 3:19–20; 33:13) was a turbulent sifting process for nineteenth-century America. Nevertheless, the backwash of negative newspaper reception could never stem the tide stirred by the Book of Mormon. The worst that nineteenth-century tongue, quill, or printing press screeched could not halt the coming forth of the marvelous work called the Book of Mormon.

Notes

1. Brigham Young, in *Journal of Discourses* (Liverpool: Orson Pratt, 1856), 3:91.
2. "Blasphemy," *Rochester Daily Advertiser*, April 2, 1830; "Blasphemy," *Rochester Republican*, April 6, 1830; emphases and spelling in original. It is interesting to note that on the same date the *Rochester Republican* printed the article, the Church was being formally organized in Fayette, New York. See Doctrine and Covenants 21.
3. These sources have been collected by the author for his PhD at the University of Utah. The dissertation, which has a journalism history emphasis, is an examination of the influence of the printing press on the development of the Church in its formative years. It is expected to be completed in late 2015. The numerical descriptions given in this essay are expected to increase as additional newspapers are digitized and chronicled.
4. See "Book of Mormon Reaches 150 Million Copies," *Church News*, April 20, 2011; "20 Books That Changed America," *ABC News*, January 7, 2006; Statistical Report, 2013, in Conference Report (Salt Lake City: The Church of Jesus Christ of Latter-day Saints, April 2014).
5. Lucy Mack Smith, History, 1845, [132], in *The Joseph Smith Papers*.
6. The date of Martin's revelation, now section 19, has been changed from the previously thought spring of 1830 to the earlier summer of 1829, based on new evidence discovered by scholars of the Joseph Smith Papers Project. For more information, see Michael Hubbard MacKay, Gerrit J. Dirkmaat, Grant Underwood, Robert J. Woodford, and William G. Hartley, eds., *Documents, Volume 1: July 1828–June 1831*, vol. 1 of the Documents series of *The Joseph Smith Papers*, ed. Dean C. Jessee, Ronald K. Esplin, Richard Lyman Bushman, and Matthew J. Grow (Salt Lake City: Church Historian's Press, 2013), 85–92 (hereafter *JSP*, D1).
7. *Wayne Sentinel*, June 26, 1829; emphasis in original.
8. "Copyright for Book of Mormon, 11 June 1829," in *JSP*, D1:76–81. It is unknown if it was Joseph Smith or someone acting on his behalf that completed the copyright registration. See the "Historical Introduction" on page 77 of the same volume.
9. See Joseph Smith Jr., "History, 1838–1856, Volume A-1 [23 December 1805–30 August 1834]," n.d., 34, in *The Joseph Smith Papers*.
10. See, for example, "From the Golden Bible," *Paul Pry's Weekly Bulletin*, July 25, 1829; "From the Golden Bible," *Paul Pry's Weekly Bulletin*, August 1, 1829; "From the Golden Bible," *Paul Pry's Weekly Bulletin*, August 8, 1829. From the titles, the connection may seem obvious; however, the editor was writing a satire using biblical references, not addressing the Book of Mormon directly.
11. "Golden Bible," *Palmyra Freeman*, August 11, 1829; emphases in original.
12. Antebellum newspaper editors exchanged their papers with each other for little or no cost, through the US postal service—courtesy of the Post Office Act of 1792. This system allowed national news to be disseminated throughout the new Republic and for noteworthy local news to spread beyond its hometown

origin. See Richard A. Schwarzlose, *The Nation's Newsbrokers* (Evanston, IL: Northwestern University Press, 1989), 1:4–7; Daniel Walker Howe, *What Hath God Wrought: The Transformation of America, 1815–1848* (New York: Oxford University Press, 2007), 226–27.

13. "Golden Bible," *Palmyra Freeman*, August 11, 1829; emphases in original.
14. Robert A. Gross, "Editor's Introduction," in *A History of the Book in America: An Extensive Republic, Print, Culture, and Society in the New Nation, 1790–1840*, ed. Robert A. Gross and Mary Kelley (Chapel Hill: The University of North Carolina Press, 2010), 2:4; emphasis removed for clarity.
15. Richard L. Bushman, *Joseph Smith: Rough Stone Rolling* (New York: Vintage Books, 2007), 82.
16. See Abner Cole, "Selected Items," *Reflector*, September 23, 1829, 2.
17. Abner Cole, *Reflector*, September 16, 1829, 2; emphases and spelling in original. Joseph endured frequent ridicule for his "overuse" of the English iteration of the Hebrew literary connecting thought, *wayehi*. Mark Twain, decades later, called the phrase "Joseph's 'pet.'" "If he had left that out," Twain continued, "his Bible would have been only a pamphlet." Samuel L. Clemens, *Roughing It* (Hartford, CT: American Publishing Company, 1873), 127–28. Joseph removed a number of redundant instances of the phrase when reviewing the 1830 edition for the 1837 printing.
18. Abner Cole, *Reflector*, September 2, 1829, 2.
19. Abner Cole, "Beware of Secret Associations," *Reflector*, September 30, 1829, 1.
20. Cole, "Selected Items," 2.
21. As reproduced in Larry C. Porter, "Solomon Chamberlain—Early Missionary," *BYU Studies* 12, no. 33 (1972): 1–3. A holograph of Chamberlain's autobiography can be found in the "Book of Abraham Project" associated with the BYU Harold B. Lee Library, at http://www.boap.org/LDS/Early-Saints/SChamberlain.html.
22. Thomas B. Marsh, "History of Thomas Baldwin Marsh," *Latter-Day Saints' Millennial Star*, June 4, 1864, 360.
23. Thomas B. Marsh, "History of Thomas Baldwin Marsh," *Millennial Star*, June 11, 1864, 375.
24. Abner Cole, *Reflector*, October 7, 1829, 2; emphasis in original. It is unclear if Cole's reference to "the natives" meant the Palmyra citizens, or the Native Americans, regarding which Mormonism would later be sharply criticized, but which had not surfaced significantly in the papers yet. If Cole's remark was about the Native Americans, it is evidence of his deeper reading of the Book of Mormon.
25. Abner Cole, "Gold Bible," *Reflector*, December 9, 1829, 1; emphasis in original.
26. Abner Cole, "The First Book of Nephi," *Reflector*, January 2, 1830, 1. Despite his growing antagonism, Cole's reprinted text is largely without error or intentional corruption.
27. Ezra Taft Benson, "Jesus Christ—Gifts and Expectations," *Ensign*, December 1988, 4. President Benson was speaking of the difference in members of the Church who had and had not developed an abiding love for the Book of Mormon.

28. See, for example, Andrew H. Hedges, "The Refractory Abner Cole," in *Revelation, Reason, and Faith: Essays in Honor of Truman G. Madsen*, ed. Truman G. Madsen et al. (Provo, UT: FARMS, 2002).
29. For an examination of Cole's Freethought philosophies and an alternate theory about his reasons and methods of writing, see Kimberley Mangun and Jeremy J. Chatelain, "For 'the Cause of Civil and Religious Liberty': Abner Cole and the Palmyra, New York, Reflector," *American Journalism* 32, no. 1 (2015): forthcoming.
30. Abner Cole, "To the Public," *Reflector*, September 2, 1829, 1.
31. Lucy Mack Smith's history was recorded with the assistance of Martha Jane Coray approximately fifteen years after the events with Abner Cole took place, and when she was 70 years old, which makes it prone to errors in accuracy. See "Historical Introduction" for Lucy Mack Smith, History, 1845, in *The Joseph Smith Papers*. To date, no account of this interaction has been discovered in the histories of Joseph Smith, Oliver Cowdery, or Hyrum Smith to corroborate the details.
32. Lucy Mack Smith, History, 1845, in *The Joseph Smith Papers*, [165–68].
33. See Nathaniel Hinckley Wadsworth, "Copyright Laws and the 1830 Book of Mormon," *BYU Studies* 45, no. 3 (2006): 77–99.
34. See Abner Cole, "The First Book of Nephi (Continued from Our Last.)," *Reflector*, January 13, 1830, 1; Abner Cole, "Book of Mormon," *Reflector*, January 22, 1830, 3.
35. Abner Cole, "GOLD BIBLE," *Reflector*, January 2, 1830, 5; emphases in original; spelling has been modernized for readability.
36. Abner Cole, "Gold Bible," *Reflector*, January 13, 1830, 4; emphases in original.
37. See Cole, "Book of Mormon," 3–4.
38. Abner Cole, "The Book of Pukei," *Reflector*, June 12, 1830; see also Abner Cole, "The Book of Pukei Chapter 2," *Reflector*, July 7, 1830.
39. Abner Cole, *Reflector*, June 30, 1830; emphases in original.
40. See *Wayne Sentinel*, March 19, 1830.
41. See "The Book of Mormon," *Wayne Sentinel*, March 26, 1830. Similarly, the bookbinder, Luther Howard, also advertised the availability of the Book of Mormon in his Palmyra newspaper, buried amid titles of other books for sale. See, for example, Luther Howard, "Miscellaneous Books," *Western Spectator and Public Advertiser*, April 5, 1831. "Duodecimo" refers to a book size of about 5 × 7.5 inches (13 × 19 cm), determined by printing on sheets folded to form twelve leaves or twenty-four pages.
42. "Blasphemy," *Ithaca Journal and General Advertiser*, April 28, 1830; emphasis and spelling in original.
43. This preface was discontinued in the next version of the Book of Mormon in 1837.
44. Preface, The Book of Mormon (Palmyra, NY: E. B. Grandin, 1830), 1, iv.
45. *Book of Commandments* (Independence, MO: W. W. Phelps & Co., 1833), chap. IX:8; see also D&C 10:37.

46. The manuscript was stolen from Martin Harris in the summer of 1828; the Book of Mormon went on sale March 26, 1830. If the conspirators were waiting until all five thousand copies were finished and the $3,000 had been spent so as to maximize the damage, the cunning plan of the devil would have required nearly two years of patience on the part of his workers. Lucy Harris, Martin's wife, did not escape implication. Her role in the plot also made it into the exchange and was printed in various newspapers at least in New York, Ohio, and Pennsylvania. "She it was," the articles state, "who purloined several pages of the first revelation, and which, by the direction of the angel, have never been supplied." "The Progress of Mormonism," *Philadelphia Album*, May 28, 1831, 173.
47. Some editors may have hoped that revealing some of the "style of the work [the Book of Mormon]" would expose weaknesses. B. F. Hallett, *Rhode Island American*, April 16, 1830, 4. Indeed, many people found fault with the close relationships of the witnesses. Mark Twain sarcastically wrote that he would not have been any more convinced of the truthfulness of the Book of Mormon had the entire Whitmer family witnessed of it. See Clemens, *Roughing It*, 130.
48. *Book of Commandments*, chap. IX:10; See also D&C 10:43.
49. *United States Gazette*, April 13, 1830, 4.
50. "Testimony of Eight Witnesses," in Book of Mormon (1830), 590. The witness testimonies are found at the end of the 1830 edition as opposed to the front, as is more common today.
51. An alternate account of Brigham Young's introduction to the Book of Mormon is recounted in the autobiography of the aforementioned Solomon Chamberlain. Solomon recalled the story twenty-nine years later, saying that he used the proof sheets printed in 1829 on his Canadian mission to preach to a group of reformed Methodist preachers. "[They] abused me very bad," he wrote. He claimed that Brigham Young and his brother, Phineas, were attending the conference. "They did not oppose me," he explained, "but used me well." "Autobiography of Solomon Chamberlain," as reproduced in Porter, "Solomon Chamberlain—Early Missionary," 3. This is an instance of later recollections becoming convoluted. Brigham's account on the first page of this essay was given in a conference in 1852, some twenty-two years later, and he states he received the Book of Mormon from a man two or three weeks after it was printed. Whereas Solomon only had proof sheets at the Canadian conference, he would not have been able to leave a copy of the Book of Mormon with Brigham at that time, which was prior to March 1830 anyway. Lucy does not state that when Rhoda Young gave her copy of the book to her brothers that they hadn't already heard of it, but seems to indicate it was that specific copy that converted the Youngs and the Kimballs. Brigham doesn't mention either Solomon or his sister in his 1852 account when he relates his Book of Mormon conversion story.
52. Lucy Mack Smith, History, 1845, in *The Joseph Smith Papers*, [169–71], [186–88]. Lucy does not clarify which family she meant by "this whole family."
53. Such autobiographical accounts are essential when weaving a historical narrative. Nevertheless, they were most commonly written decades later, when the writer had been seasoned by events that took place afterwards. For example, although

the following account of Parley P. Pratt occurred when these articles were being printed, it was not written contemporaneously to the events described.

54. Parley P. Pratt, *The Autobiography of Parley Parker Pratt, One of the Twelve Apostles of the Church of Jesus Christ of Latter-Day Saints* (New York: Russell Brothers, 1874), 36–38; emphases in original.
55. Pratt, *Autobiography of Parley Parker Pratt*, 38.
56. Pratt, *Autobiography of Parley Parker Pratt*, 39–40; punctuation modernized for readability.
57. Pratt, *Autobiography of Parley Parker Pratt*, appendix, i–ii.
58. Ezra Thayre, "Testimony of Brother E. Thayre," *The True Latter Day Saints' Herald*, October 1862, 79–83. As with the account of Parley P. Pratt, it is worth noting that this account was recorded thirty-two years after the fact.
59. Thayre, "Testimony," 80.
60. *Book of Commandments*, chap. XXXV:2; D&C 33:2; see also Steven C. Harper, *Making Sense of the Doctrine & Covenants* (Salt Lake City: Deseret Book, 2008), 110–12.
61. See Terryl L. Givens, *By the Hand of Mormon: The American Scripture That Launched a New World Religion* (New York: Oxford University Press, 2003), 55–61; see also Paul C. Gutjahr, *The Book of Mormon: A Biography* (Princeton, NJ: Princeton University Press, 2012), 114.
62. Abner Cole, *Reflector*, April 19, 1830, 6; emphases in original.
63. *Book of Commandments*, chap. X:10. See also D&C 11:21–22.
64. Abner Cole, "The Marion Monk," *Reflector*, September 13, 1830, 4.
65. "Information Wanted," *Reflector*, January 2, 1830, 6.
66. Abner Cole, "AUTO DA FE," *Reflector*, January 1, 1831, 5; spelling in original.
67. Abner Cole, "Gold Bible," *Reflector*, January 6, 1831, 4.
68. Nineteenth-century writer John Hayward, known for his gazetteers and descriptive book of religions, described the "prophetess" Joanna Southcott (1750–1814) as one "who made considerable noise in England." Southcott became famous for her prophecies regarding Christ, Satan, and events described in the book of Revelation. See John Hayward, *The Book of Religions*, 2nd ed. (Boston: John Hayward, 1842), 255–58. In the same book, Hayward published a favorable twelve-page description of the Mormons based on a lengthy letter from Joseph Smith in 1842. Joseph was generous in his praise for the untainted reprinting of his letter.
69. Eber D. Howe established the Ohio-based *Painesville Telegraph* in 1822 and regularly published anti-Mormon articles from 1831 until 1835 before selling the paper to his brother. Some of the vitriol in his editorials may have been a result of his sister joining the Mormons in 1831 and his wife having been baptized by 1834.
70. "The Golden Bible, or The Book of Mormon," *Ashtabula Journal*, February 5, 1831, 3; spelling in original.
71. Alexander Campbell, "Delusions," *Millennial Harbinger*, February 7, 1831, 93.
72. *Painesville Telegraph*, March 1, 1831, 3; emphasis in original; see also "Summary," *Cleveland Herald*, March 10, 1831, 3.

73. See "Delusions. An Analysis of the Book of Mormon," *Essex Gazette*, September 8, 1832, 1–2; "Delusions. An Analysis of the Book of Mormon," *Essex Gazette*, September 15, 1832, 1–2.
74. Richard L. Bushman observed that Campbell took the Book of Mormon "seriously." For his comments on Campbell and Rigdon, see Bushman, *Joseph Smith: Rough Stone Rolling* (New York: Alfred A. Knopf, 2005), 89–90.
75. "Mormonites," *Vermont Telegraph*, March 22, 1831, 103.
76. "History, 1838–1856, Volume A-1 [23 December 1805–30 August 1834]," in Karen Lynn Davidson, David J. Whittaker, Mark Ashurst-McGee, and Richard L. Jensen, eds., *Histories, Volume 1: Joseph Smith Histories, 1832–1844*, vol. 1 of the Histories series of *The Joseph Smith Papers*, ed. Dean C. Jessee, Ronald K. Esplin, and Richard Lyman Bushman (Salt Lake City: Church Historian's Press, 2012), 76 (hereafter *JSP*, H1); Joseph Smith—History 1:22. Although Joseph was speaking of his adolescence, as many as eighteen years had passed, and his feelings had been seasoned with encounters with those such as Campbell.
77. "The Golden Bible," *Observer and Telegraph*, February 10, 1831.
78. 2 Nephi 29:6.
79. See "The Golden Bible," *Connecticut Observer*, February 28, 1831, 36.
80. *Painesville Telegraph*, March 22, 1831; spelling modernized for readability; see also "From the Painesville Telegraph," *Huron Reflector*, May 16, 1831, 1.
81. For example, a group of Saints migrating from New York to Ohio were called "a company of 'Golden Bible Pilgrims'" in April 1831. *Ithaca Journal and General Advertiser*, April 27, 1831, 3. Another paper referred to the group as "followers of Jo Smith's Bible speculation." "Mormon Emigration," *Erie Gazette*, May 19, 1831, 3.
82. See, for example, "Correspondence of the Baltimore Sun," *Sun*, September 20, 1842, 4.
83. "Mormon Bible," *Brockport Free Press*, April 6, 1831, 1; italics in original.
84. "Mormon," *New Hampshire Patriot and State Gazette*, February 29, 1844, 4.
85. Joseph Smith Jr., "Correspondence," *Times and Seasons*, May 15, 1843, 2; see also Gordon B. Hinckley, "Mormon Should Mean 'More Good,'" *Ensign*, November 1990.
86. "Mormon," *New Hampshire Patriot and State Gazette*, 4.
87. A man who assists women in childbirth. Noah Webster, "Accoucheur," in *American Dictionary of the English Language* (n.p.: n.p., 1828), http://websters dictionary1828.com/.
88. "The Mormon Fanaticism," *Salem Gazette*, June 24, 1831, 2.
89. It is not inconceivable that Emma's family, only approximately 128 miles away, would have read a similar article. Although strong feelings existed, a family member hoping to keep abreast of the distrusted sect would not have found it difficult to find information in the papers. Articles in the newspaper exchange traveled hundreds of miles and even as far as Hawaii in the 1830s and 1840s. As for Emma's feelings, Joseph left for Missouri to dedicate Zion in June 1831 and was probably unaware of the article's frequency and duration.
90. William Owen, "Communications," *Free Enquirer*, September 10, 1831, 3.

91. Though beyond the scope of this essay, one of the most highly organized attacks on the Book of Mormon, including a comprehensive list of alleged plagiarisms, is found in "Mormonism," *Zion's Watchman*, February 3, 1838, 2. The editorial is approximately 7,860 words long, the equivalent of about twenty double-spaced pages on 8.5" × 11" paper.
92. Ezra Booth, "Mormonism—No. II," *Ohio Star*, October 20, 1831.
93. See Ambrose Palmer, "Brother O. Cowdery," *Latter Day Saints' Messenger and Advocate*, January 1835, 61–62. For more on Ezra Booth's letters, see Dennis Rowley, "The Ezra Booth Letters," *Dialogue: A Journal of Mormon Thought* 16, no. 3 (Autumn 1983): 133–37; Bushman, *Joseph Smith: Rough Stone Rolling*, 177–78.
94. "Revelation, 1 December 1831," in *Revelation Book 2* (Kirtland, OH: n.p., n.d.), 11–12.
95. See Harper, *Making Sense of the Doctrine & Covenants*, 247–49.
96. Smith, "History, 1838–1856, Volume A-1 [23 December 1805–30 August 1834]," 179.
97. Smith, "History, 1838–1856, Volume A-1 [23 December 1805–30 August 1834]," 154.
98. Bushman, *Joseph Smith: Rough Stone Rolling*, 177.
99. "The Book of Gold," *Philadelphia Album*, December 18, 1831, 405. The article, nevertheless, was not kind in its appraisal of Joseph, the plates, and the Book of Mormon, and the statement appears to have been given in alarm at the wide dispersion of the book.

11

The Book of Mormon among the Saints

Evolving Use of the Keystone Scripture

Casey Paul Griffiths

Casey Paul Griffiths is a visiting assistant professor of Church history and doctrine at Brigham Young University.

As the keystone of our religion, the Book of Mormon has always played an important role in the culture and thought of Latter-day Saints,[1] but the ways the Saints use the Book of Mormon have evolved throughout the history of the Church. While the story of the coming forth of the Book of Mormon became a central narrative of the Restoration during the first few decades of the Church's history, the contents of the Book of Mormon have been used in varying ways. Those converted to the restored gospel have long defended and cherished the book as proof of the divinity of Joseph Smith's prophetic calling. The story of the coming forth of the Book of Mormon was often, and still is, cited as the primary miraculous proof of Joseph Smith's divine calling. In one address, Elder Jeffrey R. Holland declared, "Either the Book of Mormon is what the Prophet Joseph said it is or this Church and its founder are false, fraudulent, a deception from the first instance onward. Not everything in life is so black or white, but it seems the authenticity of the Book of Mormon and its keystone role in our belief is exactly that."[2] While the Book of Mormon has always held a special place in our witness of the Restoration, one of the vital aspects of the coming forth of the Book of Mormon is the story of how it grew to become appreciated not just as an artifact, but as a fully utilized tool in teaching the pure gospel of Jesus Christ.

As the twentieth century progressed, the Book of Mormon truly came into its own as a doctrinal, literary, and spiritual guide for the Saints. The influence of the Book of Mormon in the wider world is steadily increasing, with the Book of Mormon even listed among the *New York Times* list of most influential books.[3] In the last few years alone, the Book of Mormon has inspired songs, films, and even a Broadway musical.

This study will primarily focus on the life story of the Book of Mormon among the members of the Church and attempt to track its influence, its usage, and the general awareness of the Church regarding this sacred text. It is a story in which millions have played a part, though the experiences of only a few can be treated here. Most important, it is a story without an end, for the coming forth of the Book of Mormon among the Saints is a continual and vital part of the work of the Lord in the latter days.

This paper builds upon the excellent work of a number of other scholars, chiefly Noel B. Reynolds and his 1999 study "The Coming Forth of the Book of Mormon in the Twentieth Century." Reynolds's work was pioneering in the way it analyzed Book of Mormon usage among members of the Church. I am in debt to Reynolds for providing the framework and a large amount of excellent research for this study. His general conclusion was that "the Book of Mormon was underutilized by most Latter-day Saints until interest in it surged during the second half of the twentieth century."[4] It is clear that the way the Book of Mormon has been used has changed over time. From its beginning as an item of objective evidence of Joseph Smith's prophetic calling, the Book of Mormon grew to become more utilized as a doctrinal, theological, and literary tool among the Saints.

A secondary aim of this study is to highlight some of the individuals who played a role in moving forward our approach to the Book of Mormon. The earlier study of Noel Reynolds built upon statistical analyses of scholars such as Grant Underwood and Alton Merrill,[5] who sampled Church literature to examine the usage of the Book of Mormon. Behind these statistics are stories that illustrate the power of the Book of Mormon in the conversion process; this study will also provide a look at a few such stories.

Early Use of the Book of Mormon

Even before its publication, the Book of Mormon was important in rallying the support of Joseph Smith's friends and family to his aid. As related in his history, the young prophet first enlisted his father in the cause by relating to him the instructions given by the angel Moroni to locate the plates in the nearby Hill Cumorah.[6] As Joseph continued his prophetic tutelage under the direction of Moroni, he told others in the family of his experiences with the work. One of the most poignant memories to emerge from the Smiths during these years is found in the death of Alvin Smith, the Prophet's older brother. On his deathbed, Alvin counseled his younger brother to "do everything that lies in your power to obtain the Record."[7] Lucy Mack Smith later commented that Alvin Smith "ever manifested a greater zeal and anxiety if it were possible than any of the rest with regard to the record which had been shown to Joseph."[8] Even before the record fully came forth, it possessed a power to draw people to it: first, the Prophet's family, and later, a small band of followers who formed the nucleus of the new religion. When Samuel H. Smith, the first official missionary of the Church, set out on his mission, he carried with him a knapsack full of copies of the new scripture, touting it as "a history of the origin of the Indians." He was met mostly with rejection, but did manage to place the book with John P. Greene, the brother-in-law of Brigham Young—possibly assisting in the conversion of the second President of the Church.[9]

When the Book of Mormon was published and the Church was organized, the Articles and Covenants of the Church (now D&C 20) declared that the book was "a record of a fallen people, and also the fullness of the gospel of Jesus Christ to the Gentiles and also to the Jews, proving to them that the holy scriptures be true, and also that God doth inspire men and call them to his holy work in these last days, as well as in days of old, that he may be the same God forever."[10]

In the months following the organization of the Church, the Book of Mormon produced a dramatic impact on the converts it reached. Among the most dramatic and most quoted of those touched by the Book of Mormon was Parley P. Pratt. Introduced to the book by an acquaintance, Pratt memorably wrote, "He began to tell of *a book*, a STRANGE BOOK, A VERY STRANGE BOOK!" He continues, "The next morning I called at his house, where, for the first time, my eyes beheld the 'BOOK OF MORMON'—that book of books—that record which reveals the antiquities of the new world." Describing his eagerness to learn more, Pratt wrote, "I read all day; eating was a burden, I had no desire for food; sleep was a burden when the night came, for I preferred reading to sleep."[11]

Parley P. Pratt was just one among dozens who were deeply moved by their encounter with the book. Thomas B. Marsh, later the first President of the Quorum of the Twelve Apostles, heard rumors of a "Golden Book found by a youth named Joseph Smith" and was eventually led to the printing office in Palmyra from which he took home the first sixteen pages of the book. Within a year he moved to Palmyra to find fellowship with other members of his new faith.[12] Stories similar to this multiplied in the early days of the Restoration. Brigham Young, who obtained a copy of the Book of Mormon just a few weeks after the first printing, later recalled saying to himself, "Wait a little while; what is the doctrine of the book, and of the revelations the Lord has given? Let me apply my heart to them." After "studiously" examining the book for two years, he concluded, "I knew it was true, as well as I knew that I could see with my eyes, or feel by the touch of my fingers, or be sensible of the demonstration of any sense."[13]

The Book of Mormon soon became a key tool in the work of spreading the gospel. Information on *how* the Book of Mormon was used in proselytizing is fragmentary yet frequently mentioned during the early years of the Church. William McLellin wrote in his journal about Parley P. Pratt rebuking a Methodist preacher who rejected the book because of its "provintialisms [*sic*] or Yankeeisms" by reading part of Moroni's discourse that "the Gentiles will mock at these things, because of our weakness in writing," most likely adding the powerful warning: "fools mock, but they shall mourn" (Ether 12:23, 26).[14] On another occasion, Elder McLellin reported Pratt reading several pages on "the personal ministry of Christ" on the American continent, as set forth in the Book of Mormon.[15]

Not all missionaries appeared to have taught the Book of Mormon with such enthusiasm. With a tone of slight annoyance, McLellin noted the sermon of a different companion, writing, "It was a fine discourse but he never mentioned the book of mormon once."[16] The Lord likewise expressed his dismay with the elders' use of the book, chastising them in a revelation given on September 22–23, 1832 (D&C 84). The Lord warned the elders, "Your minds in times past have been darkened because of unbelief, and because you have treated lightly the things you have received—which vanity and unbelief have brought the whole church under condemnation. And this condemnation resteth upon the children of Zion, even all. And they shall remain under this condemnation until they repent and remember the new covenant, even the Book of Mormon and the former commandments which I have given them, not only to say but to do according that which I have given."[17]

The Book of Mormon in Early Church Publications

Was the Book of Mormon underutilized? While the story of the Book of Mormon remained a central part of the message of Mormonism, studies reveal that in some ways the book was underused. An extensive review of Church periodicals printed before 1846 reveal that there were 1,489 citations to the Bible and 77 to the Book of Mormon, or a 19:1 ratio.[18] This is understandable given the newness of the Book of Mormon and the population of the Church, who were almost all converts, with no training or teaching in how to use the Book of Mormon as a text. While there are numerous examples in the minutes of Church meetings with members bearing testimony of the truthfulness of the Book of Mormon, most of the early Saints felt more comfortable sharing doctrine pulled from biblical passages.[19]

At the same time, Church periodicals played a vital role in bringing the new scripture to members and potential converts alike. *The Evening and the Morning Star*, a Church newspaper printed in Independence, Missouri, published a number of passages from the Book of Mormon, announcing to its readers, "There are not a few honest enquiring persons who wish to learn the truth of the book of Mormon. To put them in possession of such testimony as may lead to truth is our duty."[20] Later issues of the *Star* printed excerpts from the books of 1 Nephi, Jacob, Ether, and Moroni.[21] W. W. Phelps, the editor of the *Star*, quoted liberally from the Book of Mormon, declaring that the book "opened a flood of light and might justly be called a wonderful volume."[22] The proprietors of the *Star* originally intended to publish the entire book in the newspaper, but instead declared their intention to publish the work anew as its own volume.[23]

In a theological context, the Book of Mormon passages often quoted by the early Saints differ greatly from those frequently utilized today. The most commonly cited set of verses from early Mormon literature was Ether 13:4–8, which contained a prophecy "that a New Jerusalem should be built up upon this land, unto the remnant of the seed of Joseph."[24] This emphasis highlights the concern felt by the early Saints for the building up of the city of Zion, a frequent topic in the revelations given to Joseph Smith.[25] Another frequently cited excerpt was 3 Nephi 21, with a close focus on verses 1–7, including the Savior's dramatic prophecy of "a sign, that ye may know the time when these things shall be about to take place—that I shall gather in, from their long dispersion, my people, O house of Israel, and shall establish again among them my Zion" (3 Nephi 21:1).[26] The sign given by the Savior was the coming forth of the Book of Mormon itself. The frequent citation of these passages demonstrates the millennial mindset of the Saints, and their hope for the coming city of Zion. To them, the Book of Mormon was more than a scriptural text; it was a literal sign from heaven of the coming of the Savior.

Even the Prophet Joseph Smith, the instrument used in bringing forth the book, showed a tendency to favor biblical passages in his teachings. A study of the Nauvoo discourses of Joseph Smith revealed allusions to 451 different biblical passages compared to 22 references to the Book of Mormon, or a ratio of 21:1.[27] This should not imply in the least any insecurity on the part of the Prophet regarding the truthfulness of the Book of Mormon. During this same period, Wilford Woodruff recorded in his journal, "Joseph said the Book of Mormon was the most correct of any Book on Earth & the key stone of our religion & a man would get nearer to God by abiding its precepts than any other Book."[28] Joseph's marked propensity toward using the Bible was likely the product of his upbringing and his desire to build on the common beliefs already held by most new converts. The discovery of the Book of Mormon as a doctrinal gem was still in the process during the first generation of the Church, the Prophet included.

At the same time, Joseph Smith recognized the power of the Book of Mormon as a witness of the Restoration. Parley P. Pratt witnessed one of the most dramatic illustrations of Joseph Smith's convictions concerning the book during a meeting held in Philadelphia with about three thousand people in attendance. Pratt records, "Brother [Sidney] Rigdon spoke first, and dwelt on the Gospel, illustrating his doctrine by the Bible. When he was through, brother Joseph arose like a lion about to roar; and being full of the Holy Ghost, spoke in great power, bearing testimony of the visions he had seen, the ministering of angels which he had enjoyed, and how he had found the plates of the Book of Mormon, and translated them by the gift and power of God." According to Pratt, Joseph commenced his discourse with a mild rebuke for Rigdon's timidity. Pratt recorded, "If nobody else had the courage to testify of so glorious a message from Heaven, and the finding of so glorious a record, he felt to do it justice to the people, and leave the event with God."[29]

Further evidence of Joseph's convictions concerning the Book of Mormon came in the final days before his martyrdom, when he and his close friends read and marked Ether 12:36–38, which reads in part, "And now I . . . bid farewell unto the Gentiles, yea, and also unto my brethren whom I love, until we shall meet before the judgment seat of Christ, where all men shall know that my garments are not spotted with your blood." Elder Jeffrey R. Holland pointed out the conviction of the truth of the Book of Mormon demonstrated by the Prophet and his associates in Carthage Jail, saying, "I ask you: would these men blaspheme before God by continuing to fix their lives, their honor, and their own search for eternal salvation on a book (and by implication a church and a ministry) they had fictitiously created out of whole cloth?"[30]

From the Nineteenth to the Twentieth Century

After Joseph Smith's martyrdom, the pattern of using the Book of Mormon chiefly as a miraculous witness of Joseph Smith's prophetic calling continued. One study of Latter-day Saint literature from 1830 to 1855 found 232 references to the Book of Mormon. A close look at these references shows twenty-six different instances where just the translation of the plates was referenced, a number nearly equal to the thirty-two times from this period Church leaders referred to doctrine taught in the book.[31]

Although the Book of Mormon was not widely used as a theological tool in the early days of the Church, it is important to note the centrality of the book to the new faith. It is not an overstatement to say that for the early

Saints the coming forth of the book transcended theology; its existence was a testimony of the existence of God and proof of new revelation in modern times. The events of the early Restoration created a new fusion of history and theology, where the historic incidents, such as the First Vision and the inspired translation of the Book of Mormon, became an ingrained part of the belief of the Saints. It was just as important to tell the story of how the book came into the hands of Joseph Smith as it was to examine what the book taught. The book was new revelation, and the story of the book itself was as compelling as any found in sacred literature.

At the same time, part of the reason why the doctrinal teachings of this new revelation received less attention stemmed from its role as a defender of older revelation. In filling its role of "proving unto them that the holy scriptures be true,"[32] the Book of Mormon was often used by the early Saints as proof of the veracity of the Bible. In so doing, many Church leaders emphasized the similarity of Book of Mormon doctrines to those found in the Bible. In an 1870 discourse, Brigham Young taught, "We do believe in the Old and New Testaments, and we have also another book, called the Book of Mormon. What are the doctrines of the Book of Mormon? The same as those of the Bible. . . . 'What good does it do you, Latter-day Saints?' It proves that the Bible is true, . . . and the two prove each other true."[33]

During the latter part of the nineteenth century, the Church leader who taught most often from the Book of Mormon was Orson Pratt. He spoke with greater frequency and emphasis on the Book of Mormon than the majority of his contemporaries, but he followed their lead in using the book as a second witness for the doctrines of the Bible, rather than as a primary source. In an 1859 discourse, Elder Pratt challenged his listeners to "try its [the Book of Mormon's] doctrine and you will find that the gospel taught in ancient America 1800 years ago is like that taught in ancient Judea and the regions round about. . . . The ancient Apostles organized the church with miracles and gifts, with power to heal the sick, to cast out devils, to work miracles and with power over the elements. The Book of Mormon tells us that the Israelites on ancient America organized one after the same pattern."[34] Elder Pratt authored a series of pamphlets collected under the title *Divine Authenticity of the Book of Mormon*. Leaving no doubt as to his stance regarding the book, Elder Pratt declared, "The nature of the Book of Mormon is such, that if true, no one can possibly be saved and reject it;

if false, no one can possibly be saved and receive it. Therefore, every soul in all the world is equally interested in ascertaining its truth or falsity."[35] He then proceeded to argue, almost exclusively from biblical sources, of the authenticity of the Book of Mormon. Near the end of his life, Elder Pratt made perhaps his most valuable contribution towards advancing Book of Mormon studies when he divided the book into chapters and verses, and added footnotes with scriptural commentary. Prior to this time, the Book of Mormon existed in a chapter-and-paragraph format similar to a novel, heightening the difficulty in finding and utilizing doctrinal passages.[36]

During the latter half of the nineteenth century, the Church experienced severe persecutions due to the practice of plural marriage, and paranoia grew throughout American society concerning Latter-day Saint beliefs and practices. Ironically, these anti-Mormon crusades stimulated some of the first serious scholarship focused on the Book of Mormon. While locked in the Nebraska State Penitentiary for unlawful cohabitation, Elder George Reynolds filled his time conducting and writing a series of studies on the Book of Mormon. His articles included such titles as "Proper Names of the Nephites" and "Science and Literature among the Nephites." He also wrote a series of thirteen biographical sketches of Book of Mormon personalities, and other articles focusing on Book of Mormon history. After producing approximately eighty articles one day out of sheer "psychological desperation," he struck on the idea of writing the first complete concordance of the Book of Mormon. He spent the next several months in an intensive study of the book, sometimes copying out as many as 350 references per day. By the end of his labors, he had produced a manuscript with nearly 25,000 entries from the Book of Mormon text.[37]

After he was freed from prison, Reynolds continued his analysis of the book, becoming an enthusiastic proponent of its study. He went on to write *The Story of the Book of Mormon*, featuring a simplified version of the story, complete with some of the earliest illustrations of the book. *The Story of the Book of Mormon* contained some of the earliest attempts to visually capture the content of the book, with illustrations depicting Nephi's vision of the virgin Mary, Moroni raising the title of liberty, and others depicting ancient Mesoamerican culture.[38]

Later, with the assistance of Janne M. Sjodahl, Reynolds authored a seven-volume commentary, the first extended study of the Book of

Mormon.[39] Reynolds's work began moving the public consciousness toward seeing the Book of Mormon as an independent work of literature and doctrine, able to stand on its own merits. In the introduction to his commentary, Reynolds wrote, "Every book has, or should have an objective. It may not be to impart knowledge of religion, of history, of pedigree, or whatnot; it may be to edify by mediation and essays; or it may be to instruct with poetry and by parable. The Book of Mormon, indeed, includes all these objectives and more, but its principal purpose, throughout, is similar to that of the Bible—to bring God and man together through the one great Mediator, Jesus Christ."[40]

With the help of Reynolds and other supporters within the Church, the Book of Mormon slowly moved toward becoming a more recognized source of teaching and inspiration within Mormonism, but this journey was just beginning. In his 1999 study Noel Reynolds maintained that in Sunday School curriculum, the Book of Mormon did not become "a major element until the 1970s."[41] Perhaps it was not a "major element," but analysis of curriculum produced by the Church does show a slow yet growing recognition in the early twentieth century. For instance, the 1889–90 lessons produced for Sunday School on the life of Christ featured thirty lessons from the New Testament and one from the Book of Mormon. Several years later, the Book of Mormon gained its own class with five lessons. By 1901, the Sunday School was producing a full course, with fifty-one lessons focusing just on the Book of Mormon.[42]

Around this same time, there began to appear hints of a growing sophistication in the approach taken toward the Book of Mormon. Rather than just as a token of Joseph Smith's prophetic calling, the book began to be studied as a significant doctrinal work in its own right. Around the turn of the twentieth century, the Church operated a network of academies throughout the Intermountain West. A sampling of the courses taught at these schools reveals a rigorous course offered in the Book of Mormon, focusing on the "history of its coming forth" and "external evidence of its divine authenticity," but also promising that "the doctrinal aspects of its teachings will be especially dwelt upon."[43]

Book of Mormon teachings at the Church academies inadvertently led to the establishment of another unique form of Latter-day Saint education—the seminary program. In 1912, Joseph F. Merrill, a newly called counselor in the presidency of the Granite Stake in the Salt Lake Valley, sat in a family home evening meeting listening to his wife, Laura, tell their children stories from the Bible and the Book of Mormon. Afterwards, Merrill asked his wife where she learned all the stories. She told him the stories came from her experiences in the religion classes taught by James E. Talmage at the Salt Lake Stake Academy.[44]

Concerned over the steadily increasing population of students in his stake who were attending the growing number of public schools in Utah, Merrill struck upon the idea of building a theological seminary nearby, where students could attend religion classes on a released-time basis during the school day.[45] Working in tandem with Thomas Yates, a member of the Granite Stake selected to be the first teacher, Merrill worked out a curriculum for the first class based on the study of the Bible, the Book of Mormon, and Church history.[46] Merrill negotiated with the Utah State School Board and managed to secure high school credit for Old and New Testament studies, a boon for the fledgling institution. Most early seminary programs combined the study of Church history and the Book of Mormon into one non-credit class taken by students their senior year. Unfortunately, this tended to de-emphasize the Book of Mormon. Textbooks in early seminary classes focused on the story of the coming forth of the Book of Mormon, but it was less utilized as a doctrinal text. One seminary textbook from the early twentieth century devoted only six out of one hundred chapters to the Book of Mormon. Of these six chapters, one covered the story of the book, one dealt with its doctrinal message, and the remaining four focused entirely on the translation, publication, and witnesses of the book.[47]

The missionary tracts used in the early twentieth century devoted themselves primarily to biblical arguments for the Restoration. "A Friendly Discussion," the tract used most frequently in missions during the first decades of the century, consisted of a fictional dialogue between several men on a veranda. The Book of Mormon is only mentioned peripherally, in relation to Joseph Smith and the Restoration.[48] One notable exception during this time is found with German E. Ellsworth, the president of the Northern States Mission. In a general conference address, Ellsworth shared a spiritual experience that impressed on his mind the importance of the Book of Mormon in missionary work: "I remember while standing on the Hill Cumorah, of hearing these words, 'Push the distribution of the record that was taken from this hill, for it will help bring the world to Christ.'" Invigorated by this experience, Ellsworth arranged to launch a new effort to distribute the Book of Mormon, eventually placing 130,000 copies throughout the northern United States during his mission.[49] However, when Ellsworth departed as mission president, the use of the Book of Mormon in missionary work was considerably reduced, as missionaries returned to more traditional methods of proselytizing.[50]

One of the more prominent General Authorities who lamented the state of Book of Mormon scholarship in the early twentieth century was the eminent Latter-day Saint historian B. H. Roberts. Within the first decade of the century, he produced *New Witnesses for God*, a short defense of the Book of Mormon and its origins. Later, in a move still surrounded by controversy today, Roberts undertook a study concerning difficult issues in regards to the Book of Mormon. He later presented the study to the First Presidency and Quorum of the Twelve. Roberts unflinchingly confronted alternate-origin theories of the book. He analyzed literary and historical speculations common in the nineteenth century and asked if Joseph Smith could have absorbed them, reproducing them later in the Book of Mormon.[51] Roberts was acting as devil's advocate in presenting these arguments, but while he never doubted the divine authenticity of the book, he was concerned with the lack of serious study performed on it. In a letter to Church President Heber J. Grant, he urgently wrote, "It is not necessary for me to suggest that maintenance of the truth of the Book of Mormon is absolutely essential to the integrity of the whole Mormon movement, for it is inconceivable that the Book of Mormon should be untrue in its origin or character and the Church of Jesus Christ of Latter-day Saints be a true Church."[52] In another letter he wrote, "I am most thoroughly convinced of the necessity of all the brethren . . . becoming familiar with these Book of Mormon problems, and finding the answer for them, as it is a matter that will concern the faith of the Youth of the Church now as also in the future."[53]

Beginnings of the Second Coming Forth of the Book of Mormon

Roberts voiced legitimate concerns in regards to the use of the Book of Mormon in the Church. Neglect of the book was not deliberate, just a gradual drift away from one of the foundational documents of the Restoration. It is also likely the drift came about as an unintended side effect of the transitional period following the end of the practice of plural marriage in 1890, and the gradual transition of the Church into more direct contact with mainstream American culture. In public settings, particularly educational programs, leaders may have been less likely to mention something as alien to the general public as the Book of Mormon. The discussions sparked by Roberts among the hierarchy of the Church tend to indicate not a lack of faith in the book itself, but anxiety about how to defend and utilize the book, particularly in scholarly circles.

However, around the same time that Roberts lamented the state of scholarship on the book, a renaissance in Book of Mormon scholarship and teaching began to emerge. It started gradually, moving from a trickle to a steady flow, eventually becoming a downpour. While it is impossible to name every individual responsible for this rise in the use of the Book of Mormon, there are several key individuals who merit special attention.

Sidney B. Sperry was a recently returned missionary from the southern states when he was invited by the head of Church schools, Adam S. Bennion, to teach seminary in 1922. Sperry's work as a seminary teacher allowed him to devote his time to gospel study, and he soon became concerned over the state of scriptural scholarship in the Church. At his own volition and expense, he enrolled in the divinity school at the University of Chicago, receiving his master's degree in 1926.[54] When he returned, he was asked to teach the entire corps of seminary teachers during their summer trainings. Impressed by his scholarship, Church leaders asked Sperry and a number of teachers to travel to the University of Chicago to obtain training in religious studies.[55] Methods of higher biblical criticism had been introduced into Church teaching at BYU in 1911, resulting in a controversy ending in the dismissal of several professors,[56] but Sperry was determined to put the tools of scholarship to use in defense of the Restoration. While at the university, he engaged in vigorous debates with his fellow divinity students. He later commented, "As a 'Mormon' . . . I either made enthusiastic friends or enthusiastic enemies."[57] But Sperry was delighted at the prospect of finding solutions to critical issues in Restoration scripture, writing to one colleague, "You and I are going to have a lot of pleasure doing Book of Mormon and Pearl of Great Price problems."[58]

After his arrival at the newly formed Religion Department at Brigham Young University in 1932,[59] Sperry soon launched a remarkably fruitful career applying scholarly techniques to Restoration scripture. *Our Book of Mormon* (1947), his first major book on the topic, began a rigorous exploration of the Book of Mormon as a historical, literary, and doctrinal work. His writings not only dealt with the origins of the book, but also included an in-depth study of its teachings. His research demonstrated thorough treatments of key doctrines in the book, including "The Church among the Book of Mormon Prophets," "The Concept of God in the Book of Mormon," and "The Teaching Concerning Death and the Hereafter in the Book of Mormon." He also tackled long-standing issues used by critics to attack the book, including the Book of Mormon's use of biblical passages such as Isaiah and 1 Corinthians 12 and 13. Beginning in his preface, Sperry declared, "In sending forth this volume, I do so with a strong conviction that the Book of Mormon is a translation of a document of Semitic provenience. . . . The Nephite scripture needs no defense; its message is one of which every Latter-day Saint may be proud."[60]

Sperry's work is even more compelling considering it took place in an era when even some scholars within the Church neglected or even felt open disdain for the book. As the number of students clamoring to take classes in Book of Mormon studies increased, one institute teacher lamented to a colleague, "I find too that Book of Mormon is in much greater demand than 'Bible.' We do succeed admirably in displacing real volumes."[61]

Faced with doubts presented by other scholars, Sperry remained firm in his convictions. One of Sperry's students recalled being in his office when a skeptical visitor came in. Learning that Sperry was currently writing on the Book of Mormon, the skeptic cynically asked, "Oh, Sid, you don't believe that stuff about the Book of Mormon, do you?" "Dr. Sperry," his student recalled, "in a courteous and respectful manner, but in firm and unmistakable terms, bore a resolute testimony concerning the Book of Mormon."[62] When another colleague wrote a book about the Old Testament but failed to include any commentary or connections to the Book of Mormon, Sperry wrote to him, "Inasmuch as the Book of Mormon is one of the foundation stones of the Church I cannot see how a man who professes to be a Latter-day

Saint can fail to use it as a source, when it has so many valuable points to give us with respect to the Old Testament."[63]

Sidney Sperry's work was emblematic of a growing wave of Book of Mormon scholarship in the 1930s and '40s. In 1938, the first Book of Mormon course for institute appeared, promising as one of its objectives to "acquaint the student with the Gospel plan presented in the book and its outstanding evidences that Jesus is the Christ."[64] The Sunday School manual for adult courses produced by the Church in 1947 was authored by Sperry and focused entirely on a sequential study of the Book of Mormon.[65]

The first seminary class devoted solely to the Book of Mormon appeared as a happy accident. In the Salt Lake City school district, the practice of releasing students for religious studies was not allowed, so LDS students took classes in the morning instead. At West High School, a volunteer teacher, Marion D. Hanks, began teaching a course using the Book of Mormon. The class became so popular it came to the attention of the Church Commissioner of Education, Franklin L. West. Hanks's recollection of Commissioner West's interrogation concerning the class highlights what a pleasant surprise the growing eagerness to study the Book of Mormon was. He recalled, "'How many come?' asked [Commissioner] West. 'Sixty,' said Brother Hanks. 'What do you teach them?' asked West. 'Book of Mormon,' Brother Hanks said. 'How do you teach it?' West asked. 'I just open up the book, we read and discuss what we read.' 'How many come each day?' asked West. 'All of them,' Brother Hanks said."[66]

In missionary work too, the Book of Mormon began to move back to the forefront. While serving as president of the European Mission, Apostle Joseph F. Merrill, the former Church Commissioner of Education, counseled mission presidents to use the Book of Mormon to a greater extent in their labors. "The coming forth of the Book of Mormon is for the latter-day Church analogous to the resurrection of Christ for the primitive Church," Merrill wrote. He continued, "We stand or fall with the authenticity of the Book of Mormon. We must use it more than we have been doing."[67] Merrill was so concerned over the lack of Book of Mormon materials, he dispatched a young returning missionary, Gordon B. Hinckley, to meet with the First Presidency to begin the development of slideshows and other media to more effectively tell the story of the Book of Mormon.[68]

Accelerating Awareness

The spark lit by Sidney Sperry and his contemporaries grew into a flame because of the work of Hugh Nibley and a new generation of scholars. Nibley arrived at BYU in 1946 and immediately began publishing a series of groundbreaking works on the Book of Mormon. Nibley was interested in the Book of Mormon during his youth. While serving in the army in World War II, he wrote home to his mother, "When I can snatch a moment or two off it is devoted to a single engrossing item: at this late date I have discovered the Book of Mormon and live in a state of perpetual excitement—that marvelous production throws everything done in our age completely into the shadows."[69] Nibley's work refocused LDS apologetics away from their traditional approaches on the coming forth of the book and archaeological searches, instead focusing on the internal evidences within the book itself. His first study, "The Book of Mormon: A Mirror of the East," appeared in the *Improvement Era* in April 1948, noting similarities between the Book of Mormon and early Middle Eastern cultures.[70] He followed up this work with a series of articles entitled "Lehi in the Desert," focusing on the Middle Eastern parallels found in the journey of Lehi's family in 1 Nephi. He followed up with a second series, "The World of the Jaredites," comparing the book of Ether with other early Asiatic cultures.[71]

Nibley's work soon caught the attention of Church President David O. McKay, who suggested a series of lessons on the Book of Mormon for the 1957 Melchizedek Priesthood manual. The manual almost didn't make it to print, because members of the review committee felt that Nibley's intellectual approach was too sophisticated for lay audiences. However, President McKay intervened, and the manual was published to wide praise. Nibley himself commented, "The evidences for the Book of Mormon are simply overwhelming; they leave me breathless."[72] Nibley's studies generated excitement and raised the bar for scholarship on the Book of Mormon. Commenting on the accelerating pace of Book of Mormon scholarship, Nibley said, "This is the very beginning of Book of Mormon research, not the end. . . . On to the fray!"[73]

Nibley's work took place in the midst of a steadily growing wave of enthusiasm for the Book of Mormon in the Church. In Brigham City, Utah, another young seminary teacher named Boyd K. Packer began teaching an early-morning class just for senior students with the Book of Mormon as the text. Packer later described his approach toward using the Book of Mormon as a doctrinal text: "I announced to begin with that if they wanted to know about the wars and rumors of wars and the migration of peoples and the cities and the narrow neck of land and all else about the Book of Mormon, this wasn't the class they should be in. I told them that we'd approach the subject on the basis, 'Who is speaking through this book and what is it He wants to say?'"[74] Within a few years Packer became one of the supervisors over the seminary program, integrating the Book of Mormon into seminary curriculum. In 1961, the Church Board of Education approved a new policy that "all students at both seminary and institute levels must take a full year of Book of Mormon in order to graduate."[75] A similar movement took place around the same time at Brigham Young University to make the Book of Mormon a required course for freshman students. In his third decade of teaching by this time, Sperry helped bring about this change. One of the teachers from the time remembered of Sperry, "He was a total believer in the Book of Mormon, and he encouraged us more than anybody else to go ahead."[76]

During this same time, the Book of Mormon became more central to the missionary work of the Church. When the first Churchwide missionary discussions appeared in 1952, they featured seven sequential topics, with the fourth focusing entirely on the Book of Mormon. A decade later, a further revision of the missionary lessons moved the Book of Mormon to the place of the second discussion.[77]

Among the leadership of the Church, the Book of Mormon was used with a rising frequency as well. In 1949, Elder Marion G. Romney gave a key address in general conference, beginning by quoting the Lord's warning concerning the Book of Mormon in the Doctrine and Covenants, and adding, "I recommend that every person within the sound of my voice read the Book of Mormon. . . . It will enrich the life of every person who will read it, unless he is in rebellion against the truth; and in that event it will advise him of his awful fate unless he changes his ways."[78] Talks focusing on the doctrine of the Book of Mormon began appearing with greater regularity in general conference with Elders Milton R. Hunter, Mark E. Petersen, Gordon B. Hinckley, and Bruce R. McConkie all delivering addresses focusing on the Book of Mormon throughout the 1950s and '60s.[79] The Book of Mormon was also quoted with greater emphasis as not just a witness of Joseph Smith's calling, but as a source of testimony in Jesus Christ. In a 1961 conference address, Elder McConkie said, "The Book of Mormon is a new, living, modern witness of the divine Sonship of Christ. It testifies of him and of the doctrines of the gospel."[80]

In the early 1970s, another key event occurred when Church auxiliaries began to emphasize the scriptures as the direct source for gospel teaching. Truman G. Madsen, a member of the general board of the Sunday School, recalled, "We were determined, in the early 1970s . . . to put the scriptures at the center of the Gospel Doctrine curriculum and to rewrite manuals so they enhanced rather than replaced the scriptures. . . . We kept hammering the point in conferences and publications, 'The manuals are the scriptures themselves.'"[81] Scholarship in all of the standard works benefitted from this move.

President Benson's Emphasis of the Book of Mormon

The growing surge of interest in the Book of Mormon reached new heights due in large measure to the influence of Elder Ezra Taft Benson. Well known outside of the Church because of his service as the secretary of agriculture under US president Dwight D. Eisenhower, Elder Benson was never shy about his convictions concerning the Book of Mormon, and he was not afraid to mix the secular and religious. A letter from President Eisenhower sent to Elder Benson read, "Thank you for drawing on your wide knowledge of the Book of Mormon to send me certain prophecies and revelations. The quotations I have read with the greatest of interest, with special application to the growth and problems of America."[82] One of Elder Benson's sons later recalled a business acquaintance telling him how many different copies of the Book of Mormon he had received from Elder Benson on multiple occasions.[83]

In 1975, Benson, then the President of the Quorum of the Twelve, delivered a seminal address in general conference entitled "The Book of Mormon is the Word of God." In the talk he re-emphasized the Lord's condemnation to the Church given in section 84 of the Doctrine and Covenants (vv. 54–57) and added his own voice of warning: "Now, we have not been using the Book of Mormon as we should." President Benson saw the book as an effective tool to "combat the false educational, political, religious, and philosophical concepts of our time."[84]

President Benson also emphasized the Book of Mormon as a tool to bring people to Christ. He taught that the book "contains the words of Christ, and its great mission is to bring men to Christ and all other things are secondary. The golden question of the Book of Mormon is 'Do you want to learn more of Christ?'"[85] He also stated that "Our homes are not as strong unless we are using it to bring our children to Christ." When new editions of the scriptures were published in 1979 and 1981, they came with an extensive system of footnotes connecting the Book of Mormon with the other standard works. In addition, the Book of Mormon received a new subtitle, "Another Testament of Jesus Christ."[86]

When Ezra Taft Benson became President of the Church in 1985, he immediately reiterated his counsel concerning the Book of Mormon, this time with prophetic authority. For the first few years of Benson's presidency, nearly every general conference featured an address on the Book of Mormon from President Benson.[87] Even as his health declined, President Benson continued to push the distribution and study of the Book of Mormon. He published a collection of Book of Mormon messages, *A Witness and a Warning*, and arranged with publishers to put his royalties toward the distribution costs so that the work could sell at the lowest possible price.[88] In addition, he developed the Family-to-Family Book of Mormon program, where Church members gave copies of the Book of Mormon with personalized messages inside for use in the mission field.[89]

In one of his final addresses, President Benson spoke of his struggle to bring forth the Book of Mormon: "Moses never entered the promised land. Joseph Smith never saw Zion redeemed. Some of us may not live long enough when the Lord lifts His condemnation (D&C 84:54–58). But, God willing, I intend to spend all my remaining days in that glorious effort."[90]

Ezra Taft Benson's presidency was the culmination of a long journey to bring the Book of Mormon from obscurity to primacy in Church doctrine and teaching. Partially as a result of his urgings, there was an explosion in the use of the Book of Mormon within the Church. Noel Reynolds's 1999 study showed the skyrocketing use of the Book of Mormon by exploring three categories: first, before Ezra Taft Benson's presidency, the number of scriptures from the Book of Mormon used in conference hovered consistently around 12 percent. After President Benson's first challenge in 1986, the number shot to 40 percent, then it gradually leveled off to 25 percent. Other statistics—measuring not just the references to scriptures but the topics of the talks themselves—also showed a peak in Book of Mormon topics during 1986–89, when President Benson sparked the new emphasis on the Book of Mormon.[91] Even before President Benson's tenure, the number of publications, both in favor and polemical, experienced a dramatic increase during the latter part of the 1980s.[92]

Among the missionary materials of the Church, the Book of Mormon reemerged as the primary tool for conversion. The Book of Mormon was made part of the first discussion with investigators in 1973. When a new series of lessons was introduced in 1986, the Book of Mormon, along with a challenge for investigators to begin reading it, was the first lesson given by the missionaries. The Book of Mormon was used as an integral part of all interactions, as missionaries were instructed to follow up and encourage their investigators to continue a study of the book.[93]

President Benson's successors continued to emphasize the Book of Mormon, most notably in August 2005, when President Gordon B. Hinckley issued "a challenge to members of the Church throughout the world and to our friends everywhere to reread the Book of Mormon." He added, "If you will read a bit more than one and one-half chapters a day, you will be able to finish the book before the end of this year."[94] The challenge again produced remarkable results. One BYU professor surveyed students on campus and found that 62 percent of students completed the entire book before the end of the year, and 36 percent completed a partial reading. While many did not complete the Book of Mormon before the deadline, the same survey found that only 12 out of the 1,303 students surveyed failed to read any of the Book of Mormon. A similar survey among adults in a nearby congregation produced encouraging results, with 41 percent completing the book and 56 percent carrying out a partial reading.[95]

The Book of Mormon reached another milestone during President Hinckley's administration when the hundred millionth copy of the book rolled off the presses in February of 2000.[96] The same year, the Book of Mormon was printed in its hundredth language. Out of the hundred million copies, the majority were printed in English, though a significant number of copies in other languages were produced. By the end of the twentieth century, Book of Mormon translations existed in every major European language. It was also found in a multitude of other languages such as Arabic; Hindi; African dialects, including Efik, Lingala, Shona, and Urdu; and even in languages only found in Mexico and Central America, like Tzotzil, Mam, and Kekchi.[97]

More recently, a change in eligibility age for both men and women to serve full-time missions, announced by President Thomas S. Monson in 2012, resulted in a significant surge in the missionary population of the Church. The growing missionary force, along with the continued emphasis on the Book of Mormon as the primary proselytizing tool, offers the promise of an ever-increasing number of young people steeped in the knowledge of the book. Additionally, in 2014 a new set of required courses for religious education in Church colleges and institutes of religion was presented. The new curriculum proposed the replacement of the two Book of Mormon courses then taught (still available as electives) with one class focusing on the doctrinal teachings of the Book of Mormon (rather than a sequential study of the text). The discussions surrounding the change demonstrated how central the Book of Mormon has become within the minds of the religious educators of the Church. Only a generation earlier, battles were fought to include the Book of Mormon in the curriculum of Church colleges; now a concerned number of teachers asked if the move meant a step back from emphasizing the Book of Mormon. With these concerns in mind, discussions surrounding the new course of study centered on charting the best way to promote a greater understanding of the doctrine contained in the Book of Mormon. According to one participant, "The guiding principle in all the curriculum discussions was, 'What will elevate Book of Mormon scholarship and understanding?'"[98]

Chad Webb, the administrator of seminaries and institutes, felt the teaching of the Book of Mormon within the Church has progressed to the point where college students could dive directly into the doctrinal teachings of the Book of Mormon. "We wanted to build on what they already have. . . . They have had seminary, been on missions, and studied the scriptures in Church and by themselves. Their previous experiences have brought them to a point where we can say, 'Let's go directly to the sermons of Lehi and his children, and really study the doctrines in the Book of Mormon.'"[99] Brent L.

Top, dean of Religious Education at Brigham Young University, added that the intent of this change was to help students understand the Book of Mormon text "on a deeper level," deeper "than we ever have before."[100] The increasing literacy in the Book of Mormon among the young people of the Church, combined with different approaches toward its study, offers the possibility of an ever-greater emphasis on the book in the future.

The Future Challenge of the Book of Mormon

The use of the Book of Mormon throughout the history of the Church in many ways mirrors the way an individual might approach the book over the course of a lifetime. A first reading of the book reveals a dramatic world of heroes and villains, exciting battles and grand adventures. Over time and through repeated study, the reader comes to appreciate not only the vivid history of the Book of Mormon but also the sublime doctrinal and philosophical teachings contained in its covers. When I was a young man, I thrilled over the heroic exploits of Captain Moroni. Now the reasoning of Jacob, the philosophy of Alma the Younger, and the hopeful discourse of Mormon are just as moving. Likewise, as a people, the Saints have matured in the understanding of the Book of Mormon. Our early writings and teachings focused on the high drama of the book's narrative. As time went on, we began to discover the Book of Mormon as a fully alive book of philosophy, literature, and theology.

At the same time, it must be noted that no prophetic leader of the Church has yet received revelation indicating that the condemnation issued by the Lord early in the Restoration has lifted. While this study highlights some of the more dramatic events in the life of the Book of Mormon among the Saints, the backstory is a steady increase in awareness and use of the book and its teachings. However, it took generations for the Saints to truly realize the value of the Book of Mormon as a source for inspiration, doctrine, and a witness that "Jesus is the Christ, the Eternal God, manifesting himself unto all nations" (Book of Mormon title page).

Yet what does the coming forth of the Book of Mormon truly mean? One of the prophecies in the Book of Mormon favored by the early members of the Church was found in 3 Nephi 21. The Savior told the Nephites,

"I will give unto you for a sign—for verily I say unto you that when these things which I declare unto you . . . shall be made known unto the Gentiles . . . it shall be a sign unto them, that they may know that the work of the Father hath already commenced unto the fulfilling of the covenant which he hath made unto the people who are of the house of Israel" (3 Nephi 21:2, 7). In the same vein, the condemnation issued by the Lord in 1832 and reiterated by President Benson exhorted the Saints "not only to say, but to *do* according to that which I have written" (D&C 84:57; emphasis added). For all the possible metrics to consider in measuring the coming forth of the Book of Mormon, the most significant change is one impossible to measure: the number of individuals changed, converted, and moved to action by the Book of Mormon. Millions of stories about how the Book of Mormon has changed lives have already been told, and there are millions more to come. The miracle of the coming forth of the Book of Mormon happens one individual at a time, when men and women accept the timeless invitation issued by the book to "come unto Christ, and be perfected in him" (Moroni 10:32).

Notes

1. I am heavily indebted to Noel B. Reynolds for the generous use of portions of his research in this study. In addition to consulting with me and offering suggestions, Dr. Reynolds provided a wealth of analysis and research to augment this study. This study also draws from previous work performed by Grant Underwood, Allison Clark, Alton D. Merrill, Jan Shipps, John W. Welch, and many others. Dr. Reynolds's seminal article "The Coming Forth of the Book of Mormon in the Twentieth Century," *BYU Studies* 38, no. 2 (1999), provided a rich cache of data for scholars to draw from contained in the Noel B. Reynolds Book of Mormon research collection in the Harold B. Lee Library at BYU.
2. Jeffrey R. Holland, "A Standard unto My People," CES symposium on the Book of Mormon, August 9, 1994, 1.
3. Esther B. Fein, "Book Notes," *New York Times* on the Web, November 20, 1991.
4. Reynolds, "Coming Forth of the Book of Mormon," 7.
5. Grant Underwood, "Book of Mormon Usage in Early LDS Theology," *Dialogue* 17, no. 3 (Autumn 1984); Alton D. Merrill, "An Analysis of the Papers and Speeches of Those Who Have Written or Spoken about the Book of Mormon, Published during the Years of 1830 to 1855 and 1915 to 1940, to Ascertain the Shift in Emphasis" (master's thesis, Brigham Young University, 1940).
6. Karen Lynn Davidson, David J. Whitaker, Mark Ashurst-McGee, and Richard L. Jensen, eds., *Histories, Volume 1: 1832–1844*, vol. 1 of the Histories series

of *The Joseph Smith Papers*, ed. Dean C. Jessee, Ronald K. Esplin, and Richard Lyman Bushman (Salt Lake City: Church Historian's Press, 2012), 233.

7. Lavina Fielding Anderson, ed., *Lucy's Book: A Critical Edition of Lucy Mack Smith's Family Memoir* (Salt Lake City: Signature Books, 2001), 352.
8. Anderson, *Lucy's Book*, 356.
9. Lucy Mack Smith, *Biographical Sketches of Joseph Smith the Prophet, and His Progenitors for Many Generations* (Liverpool: S. W. Richards, 1853), excerpt in *Early Mormon Documents*, ed. Dan Vogel, 5 vols. (Salt Lake City: Signature Books, 1996), 1:418–19. An alternative account of Brigham Young's introduction to the Book of Mormon—one that doesn't include Samuel Smith—is found in Larry C. Porter, "Solomon Chamberlain—Early Missionary," *BYU Studies* 12, no. 33 (1972): 3.
10. Michael Hubbard MacKay, Gerrit J. Dirkmaat, Grant Underwood, Robert J. Woodford, and William G. Hartley, eds., *Documents, Volume 1: July 1828–June 1831*, vol. 1 of the Documents series of *The Joseph Smith Papers*, ed. Dean C. Jessee, Ronald K. Esplin, Richard Lyman Bushman, and Matthew J. Grow (Salt Lake City: Church Historian's Press, 2013), 121 (hereafter *JSP*, D1); original spelling and punctuation preserved.
11. Parley P. Pratt, *Autobiography of Parley P. Pratt*, revised and enhanced edition, ed. Scot Facer Proctor and Maurine Jensen Proctor (Salt Lake City: Deseret Book, 2000), 30–32; emphasis in original.
12. Thomas B. Marsh, "History of Thomas Baldwin Marsh," *Millennial Star*, June 4, 1864, 359, 375.
13. Brigham Young, Discourse in the Salt Lake Tabernacle, August 8, 1852, Deseret News, in *The Complete Discourses of Brigham Young*, ed. Richard S. Van Wagoner (Salt Lake City: Smith-Pettit Foundation, 2009), 558.
14. Jan Shipps and John W. Welch, eds., *The Journals of William E. McLellin, 1831–1836* (Provo, UT: BYU Studies; Urbana and Chicago: University of Illinois Press, 1994), 103; original spelling and grammar preserved.
15. Shipps and Welch, *Journals of William E. McLellin*, 110.
16. Shipps and Welch, *Journals of William E. McLellin*, 148; original punctuation preserved.
17. Matthew C. Godfrey, Mark Ashurst-McGee, Grant Underwood, Robert J. Woodford, and William G. Hartley, eds., *Documents, Volume 2: July 1831–January 1833*, vol. 2 of the Documents series of *The Joseph Smith Papers*, ed. Dean C. Jessee, Ronald K. Esplin, Richard Lyman Bushman, and Matthew J. Grow (Salt Lake City: Church Historian's Press, 2013), 298 (hereafter *JSP*, D2); original spelling and punctuation preserved.
18. Underwood, "Book of Mormon Usage," 53. Underwood's research examined the scriptural citations in *The Evening and the Morning Star* (1832–34), the *Messenger and Advocate* (1834–37), the *Elders' Journal* (1837–38), and Parley P. Pratt's *Voice of Warning* (1837).
19. Minutes from *Far West Record: Minutes of The Church of Jesus Christ of Latter-day Saints, 1830–1844*, ed. Donald Q. Cannon and Lyndon W. Cook (Salt Lake City: Deseret Book, 1983), 22–23; and *Kirtland Council Minute Book*, ed.

Fred C. Collier and William S. Harwell (Salt Lake City: Collier's Publishing, 1996, 2002), 37, 128.

20. "The Book of Mormon," *The Evening and the Morning Star*, June 1832, 8; original spelling and punctuation preserved.
21. See *The Evening and the Morning Star*, June 1833, 196; August 1832, 40; April 1833, 174; October 1832, 75. See also Kenneth W. Godfrey, "Book of Mormon, Condemnation for Treating Lightly," in *Book of Mormon Reference Companion*, ed. Dennis L. Largey (Salt Lake City: Deseret Book, 2003), 106–8.
22. "The Book of Mormon," *The Evening and the Morning Star*, January 1833, 1.
23. "The Book of Mormon," *The Evening and the Morning Star*, July 1833, 224.
24. Grant Underwood, *The Millenarian World of Early Mormonism* (Urbana: University of Illinois, 1999), 78–79.
25. Only a small sampling of the early revelations concerning the building of the city of Zion includes Revelation, 7 December 1830 [D&C 35:24], in *JSP*, D1:223; Letter from Oliver Cowdery, 8 April 1831, in *JSP*, D1:291; Revelation, 10 March 1831 [D&C 48:6], in *JSP*, D1:288; Revelation, September 1830 [D&C 28:9], in *JSP*, D1:185–86; Revelation, 20 July 1831 [D&C 57:1–2], in *JSP*, D2:7–8; and Revelation, 22–23 September 1832 [D&C 84:2], in *JSP*, D2:223.
26. Underwood, *Millenarian World of Early Mormonism*, 78.
27. Andrew F. Ehat and Lyndon W. Cook, eds., *The Words of Joseph Smith: The Contemporary Accounts of the Nauvoo Discourses of the Prophet Joseph* (Provo, UT: Religious Studies Center, 1980), 421–25.
28. Wilford Woodruff journal, November 28, 1841, in *Waiting for the World's End: The Diaries of Wilford Woodruff*, ed. Susan Staker (Salt Lake City: Signature Books, 1993), 49; original spelling and punctuation preserved.
29. Pratt, *Autobiography*, 362.
30. Jeffrey R. Holland, "Safety for the Soul," *Ensign*, November 2009.
31. Merrill, "Analysis of Papers and Speeches," 16. For this study Merrill reviewed over 1,950 articles, drawing his sources from the *Millennial Star*, *Deseret News*, the *Seer*, *Times and Seasons*, and Conference Reports.
32. Articles and Covenants, circa April 1830 [D&C 20:11], in *JSP*, D1:121.
33. Brigham Young Discourse, May 29, 1870, *Deseret News*.
34. Orson Pratt Discourse, January 2, 1859, *Deseret News*, January 12, 1859, 1.
35. Orson Pratt, *A Series of Pamphlets on the Doctrines of the Gospel* (Salt Lake City: George Q. Cannon & Sons, 1891), 125.
36. Royal Jon Skousen, "Book of Mormon, Editions of," in *Book of Mormon Reference Companion*, 113.
37. Bruce A. Van Orden, *Prisoner for Conscience' Sake: The Life of George Reynolds* (Salt Lake City: Deseret Book, 1992), 96, 107–8.
38. George Reynolds, *The Story of the Book of Mormon* (Chicago: Hillison & Etten, 1888), 31, 36, 43, 151, 357.
39. See George Reynolds and Janne M. Sjodahl, *Commentary on the Book of Mormon*, ed. Philip C. Reynolds, 7 vols. (Salt Lake City: Deseret Press, 1955).
40. Reynolds and Sjodahl, *Commentary*, 1:v.
41. Reynolds, "Coming Forth of the Book of Mormon," 18.

42. Allison Clark, "Analysis of Book of Mormon Usage in Church Manuals," 4, Noel B. Reynolds Book of Mormon Research Collection, box 1, folder 2, L. Tom Perry Special Collections, Harold B. Lee Library, Brigham Young University, Provo, UT.
43. Beaver Branch of the Brigham Young Academy, Circular, 1903–1904, Beaver Branch of the Brigham Young University Collection, L. Tom Perry Special Collections, 9.
44. See Joseph F. Merrill, "A New Institution in Religious Education," *Improvement Era*, January 1938, 12.
45. A. Theodore Tuttle, "Released Time Religious Education Program of The Church of Jesus Christ of Latter-day Saints" (master's thesis, Stanford University, 1949), 56–57.
46. Thomas J. Yates and Nancy Burrows Wright, *Autobiography and Biography of Thomas Jarvis Yates* (unpublished document, ca. 1949), Church History Library, Salt Lake City, 80.
47. See John Henry Evans, *The Heart of Mormonism*, 2nd ed. (Salt Lake City: Church Department of Education, 1931), 39–72.
48. "FARMS Preliminary Report on the Development of Missionary Plans," 1, Reynolds Collection, L. Tom Perry Special Collections.
49. German E. Ellsworth, in Conference Report, June 1919, 95–96.
50. "FARMS Preliminary Report," 2.
51. See Truman G. Madsen, "B. H. Roberts and the Book of Mormon," *BYU Studies* 19, no. 4 (1979): 440.
52. B. H. Roberts to Heber J. Grant, March 15, 1923, in B. H. Roberts, *Studies of the Book of Mormon*, ed. Brigham D. Madsen (Urbana: University of Illinois Press, 1985), 57–58.
53. B. H. Roberts to Heber J. Grant and Counsellors, the Quorum of the Twelve Apostles, and the First Council of the Seventy, December 29, 1921, in Roberts, *Studies of the Book of Mormon*, 46–47.
54. See Sidney B. Sperry, "Biographical Sketch," in *They Gladly Taught: Ten BYU Professors*, 3 vols. (Provo, UT: Brigham Young University and the Emeritus Club, 1986), 1:159–60.
55. See Casey Paul Griffiths, "The Chicago Experiment: Finding a Voice and Charting the Course of Religious Education within the Church," *BYU Studies* 49, no. 4 (2010).
56. See Phillip L. Barlow, *Mormons and the Bible: The Place of the Latter-day Saints in American Religion* (New York: Oxford University Press, 1991), 129–34; Gary James Bergera, "The 1911 Evolution Controversy at Brigham Young University," in *The Search for Harmony*, ed. Gene A. Sessions and Craig J. Oberg (Salt Lake City: Signature Books, 1993), 23–41; and Boyd K. Packer, "The Snow-White Birds," BYU devotional, August 29, 1995.
57. Sidney B. Sperry to Russel B. Swensen, November 20, 1930, Russel B. Swensen Collection, L. Tom Perry Special Collections.
58. Sperry to Swensen.

59. See Richard O. Cowan, *Teaching the Word: Religious Education at Brigham Young University* (Provo, UT: Religious Studies Center, 2008), 10.
60. Sidney B. Sperry, *Our Book of Mormon* (Salt Lake City: Stevens & Wallis, 1947), vi–viii.
61. Heber C. Snell to Sterling McMurrin, September 14, 1947, Logan, Utah, Sterling McMurrin Papers, box 68, folder 8, J. Willard Marriot Library, University of Utah, Salt Lake City.
62. David H. Yarn Jr., "Sidney B. Sperry: A Reminiscence," in *They Gladly Taught*, 1:169. I am indebted to Noel Reynolds for bringing this story to my attention. See also Reynolds, "Coming Forth of the Book of Mormon," 25.
63. Sidney B. Sperry to Sterling McMurrin, August 31, 1949, McMurrin Papers, box 68, folder 12, University of Utah.
64. William E. Berrett, Milton R. Hunter, Roy A. Welker, and Heber A. Fitzgerald, *A Guide to the Study of the Book of Mormon* (Salt Lake City: The Church of Jesus Christ of Latter-day Saints, 1938), foreword.
65. Sidney B. Sperry, *Book of Mormon Studies* (Salt Lake City: Deseret Book, 1947).
66. Kenneth W. Godfrey, as quoted in David B. Rimington, *Vistas on Visions: A Golden Anniversary History of Church Education in Southern California* (Anaheim, CA: Shumway Family History Services, 1988), 22.
67. "Report of the Conference of the Presidents of the European Missions Held at Berling, Germany, June 11th to 15th (inclusive), 1936," 21, Joseph F. Merrill Papers, box 22, folder 2, L. Tom Perry Special Collections.
68. Gordon B. Hinckley to Joseph F. Merrill, August 21, 1935, Merrill Papers, box 20, folder 4, L. Tom Perry Special Collections. See also Rob Taber, "The Church Enters the Media Age: Joseph F. Merrill and Gordon B. Hinckley," *Journal of Mormon History* 35, no. 4 (Fall 2009): 218–33.
69. Hugh Nibley, letter to Agnes Sloan Nibley, April 8, 1944, as quoted in Boyd Jay Peterson, *Hugh Nibley: A Consecrated Life* (Salt Lake City: Greg Kofford Books, 2002), 247.
70. Hugh Nibley, "The Book of Mormon as a Mirror of the East," *Improvement Era*, April 1948, 202–4, 249–51.
71. See Hugh Nibley, *Lehi in the Desert & the World of the Jaredites* (Salt Lake City: Bookcraft, 1952).
72. Hugh Nibley to Henry D. Moyle, March 2, 1956, quoted in *A Consecrated Life*, 250.
73. Hugh Nibley to Spencer W. Kimball, November 1, 1957, quoted in *A Consecrated Life*, 252.
74. Boyd K. Packer, interview with Gordon Irving, December 10, 2004, James Moyle Oral History Program, Church History Library, Salt Lake City, 9–10.
75. Executive Committee Minutes, June 1, 1960, 6–7, as quoted in Leland Gentry, "Variation on a Theme: Seminaries and Institutes, 1962–1970, More Course Corrections and Status Reports," in *A History of Religious Education and the Central Office* (unpublished document), copy in author's possession, 3.
76. Allison D. Clark, interview with Glenn L. Pearson, 6, Reynolds Collection, box 1, folder 10, L. Tom Perry Special Collections.

77. "FARMS Preliminary Report," 14, Reynolds Collection, box 1, folder 5, L. Tom Perry Special Collections.
78. Marion G. Romney, in Conference Report, April 1949, 35–41.
79. Allison D. Clark, "Analysis of General Conference Talks, 1950–1995," 6, Reynolds Collection, box 1, folder 7, L. Tom Perry Special Collections.
80. Bruce R. McConkie, in Conference Report, April 1961, 38–40.
81. Truman G. Madsen, interview, March 12, 1996, 6, Reynolds Collection, box 1, folder 12, L. Tom Perry Special Collections.
82. Dwight D. Eisenhower to Ezra Taft Benson, December 4, 1957. A copy of this letter may be found in the Ezra Taft Benson Building at Brigham Young University.
83. Allison D. Clark, interview with Reed Benson, April 4, 1996, 6, Reynolds Collection, box 1, folder 12, L. Tom Perry Special Collections.
84. Ezra Taft Benson, in Conference Report, April 1975, 63–66.
85. Benson, in Conference Report, April 1975, 63–66.
86. Boyd K. Packer, in Conference Report, October 1982, 73–77.
87. President Benson's key addresses on the Book of Mormon include "The Power of the Word," in Conference Report, April 1986, 79; "The Book of Mormon—The Keystone of Our Religion," in Conference Report, October 1986, 4; "The Savior's Visit to America," in Conference Report, April 1987, 4; "The Book of Mormon and the Doctrine and Covenants," in Conference Report, April 1987, 83; and "Flooding the Earth with the Book of Mormon," in Conference Report, October 1988, 4.
88. Clark, interview with Benson, April 4, 1996.
89. "The Family-to-Family Book of Mormon Program," *Ensign*, May 1987.
90. Ezra Taft Benson, in Conference Report, October 1988, 4–6.
91. Reynolds, "Coming Forth of the Book of Mormon," 10–11.
92. Reynolds, "Coming Forth of the Book of Mormon," 16–17.
93. "FARMS Preliminary Report," 15.
94. Gordon B. Hinckley, "A Testimony Vibrant and True," *Ensign*, August 2005.
95. Sarah Jane Weaver, "BYU Students Meet Challenge in Large Numbers," *Church News*, February 25, 2006.
96. "100 Million Copies of the Book of Mormon," *Ensign,* May 2000, 112.
97. "Book of Mormon Milestone: 100 Million Copies Printed and Sent around the World," *Church News*, April 22, 2000, 6, 10.
98. Brent L. Top, email to Casey Paul Griffiths, February 25, 2015; copy in author's possession.
99. Chad H. Webb, interview with Casey Paul Griffiths, February 24, 2015; notes in author's possession.
100. Brent L. Top, interview with Casey Paul Griffiths, February 25, 2015; notes in author's possession.

12

"To Every Nation, Kindred, Tongue, and People"

Po Nien (Felipe) Chou and Petra Chou

Po Nien (Felipe) Chou is a religious educator and manager of the Office of Research for the Seminaries and Institutes (S&I) of The Church of Jesus Christ of Latter-day Saints.

Petra Chou is a homemaker and teaches in the Chinese Immersion program for the Alpine School District.

The Book of Mormon was first translated into the English language by the Prophet Joseph Smith in 1829. The goal is now to make it available "to every nation, kindred, tongue, and people" (Mosiah 15:28). This chapter explores the efforts of The Church of Jesus Christ of Latter-day Saints to bring forth the Book of Mormon in other languages and to make it accessible to all the world. Although it will not provide an exhaustive review of all 110 translations (87 full book and 23 selections)[1] distributed by the Church by spring 2015, it will examine a number of translations, versions, and editions, along with the efforts to bring forth this sacred volume to "all nations, kindreds, tongues and people" (D&C 42:58).

Ancient prophets declared that in the latter days the Lord would "commence his work among all nations, kindreds, tongues, and people, to bring about the restoration of his people upon the earth" (2 Nephi 30:8). The Book of Mormon was to "be kept and preserved" so that the knowledge of the Savior and his gospel would go forth and be taught unto "every nation, kindred, tongue, and people" in preparation for the Second Coming of the

Lord (see 1 Nephi 13:40; Mosiah 3:20; Alma 37:4; D&C 42:48; D&C 133:37). John the Revelator saw in a vision that an angel would "fly in the midst of heaven, having the everlasting gospel to preach unto them that dwell on the earth, and to every nation, and every kindred, and tongue, and people" (Revelation 14:6; D&C 88:103). After Joseph Smith translated the Book of Mormon into the English language in 1829, the Church would call upon numerous other translators to assist in fulfilling the scripture mandate to carry this latter-day scripture to all the nations of the world with their numerous tongues and languages.

English Editions of the Book of Mormon

It is important to first consider the various English editions of the Book of Mormon in order to explore the translation of the book into other languages. Translators generally utilize Joseph Smith's English translation of the book as their original source document.[2] In general, the most recent English edition available is consulted by translators.

Prior to the death of the Prophet Joseph Smith, four English editions of the Book of Mormon were published. The 1830 edition by E. B. Grandin in Palmyra, New York, was generally taken from the printer's manuscript, the copy that Oliver Cowdery made from the original manuscript that he (and a few others) had scribed. The 1830 edition included a preface by the Prophet Joseph Smith and the Testimony of the Three and the Eight Witnesses. Grandin's typesetter John H. Gilbert paragraphed and punctuated the manuscript, and he also made changes to fix what he considered grammatical errors. The 1837 edition was published by Parley P. Pratt and John Goodson in Kirtland, Ohio, and it provided grammatical changes after comparing the 1830 edition with the printer's manuscript. The 1840 edition published for Ebenezer Robinson and Don Carlos Smith in Nauvoo, Illinois (by Shepard and Sterns in Cincinnati, Ohio), corrected errors found between the printer's and the original manuscript. Finally, the 1841 edition published for Brigham Young, Heber C. Kimball, and Parley P. Pratt (by J. Tompkins in Liverpool, England), was basically a reprint of the 1837 edition with British spelling. This was the first European edition. Additional British editions came in 1849 and 1852, edited by Orson Pratt and Franklin D. Richards, respectively (Richards also added paragraph numbers).[3]

Subsequent editions received minor editing but incorporated major format changes. Orson Pratt, in editing the 1879 edition, divided long chapters and added scriptural reference footnotes. The 1920 edition, edited by James E. Talmage, saw new introductory material, double columns, chapter summaries, and new footnotes (minor editing from the 1905 and 1911 editions was also included). The 1981 edition, edited by a committee headed by members of the Quorum of the Twelve, came with updated introductory material, chapter summaries, and footnotes. Editors of this edition also corrected textual errors that they discovered when comparing the printer's manuscript with the 1840 edition and original manuscript.[4]

In addition to these print editions, various formats of the Book of Mormon have come over the years. Audio and video versions have been produced in videocassettes, DVDs, CDs, mp3 audio format, and so forth.[5] Braille came in 1936 (revised in 1994), followed by American Sign Language (ASL) on videotape in 2001, on DVD in 2006, and online in 2011.[6] The Church has released audio recordings, internet editions, and scripture applications for mobile devices in English and select languages, with more people than ever before using the online edition of the scriptures in multiple digital formats.[7] The Doubleday Publishing Company in New York provided a commercial version of the Book of Mormon in 2004, and the Book of Mormon appeared as a Penguin Classic in 2008.[8] In 2013 the Church published an updated English edition of the scriptures in digital (and then print) format, with new photos, updated study aids, maps, and chapter and section headings.[9] President Thomas S. Monson said that "the Lord brought forth the Book of Mormon at a period of time [that] would enhance its distribution far and wide,"[10] and, as President Ezra Taft Benson said, all of these platforms for accessing the scriptures "in this age of electronic media and mass distribution of the printed word" are making it possible to "move the Book of Mormon in a monumental way."[11]

Language Translations Followed Missionary Work

The Prophet Joseph Smith said, "I . . . should be pleased to hear, that [the Book of Mormon] was printed in all the different languages of the earth."[12] In general, the language translations of the Book of Mormon have followed the missionary work of the Church. As missionaries went forth to preach the gospel to the various nations and people of the world, they needed translated materials, especially the Book of Mormon.[13] These efforts began in Europe and the Pacific in the 1800s, the most fertile international missions at the time.[14]

Danish, the First Non-English Translation

In August 1850, Elder Erastus Snow from the Quorum of the Twelve Apostles and Peter Olsen Hansen arrived in Copenhagen, Denmark, and immediately began efforts to translate the Book of Mormon. Brother Hansen was a native of Denmark but struggled to work on the translation because his Danish was rusty. Elder Snow began to learn Danish and traveled to England to explore publication options, but was unsuccessful in finding someone to assist with the translation even after interviewing several professors.

Shortly afterward, the missionaries found an unnamed Danish sister who was fluent in English, French, and German to assist. A proofreader reviewed the manuscript three times followed by a personal review by Elder Snow himself, who at this time felt he had mastered the basics of the Danish language. In his July 10, 1851, letter to Brigham Young, Elder Snow wrote that "through the blessing of God after eight months . . . [we] have succeeded in the translation and publication of the Book of Mormon, in the Danish language. . . . I feel that I have done the best I could under the circumstances, and that the Lord has accepted it and will add his blessing." In 1851 this Danish edition became the first non-English-language translation of the Book of Mormon.[15]

Other European Languages

Elder John Taylor of the Quorum of the Twelve arrived to open and preside over the French Mission in Paris in June 1850. He appointed Curtis E. Bolton, a fellow missionary and counselor in the mission presidency, to begin the French translation of the Book of Mormon. Bolton was assisted by two new converts who joined the Church in December 1850, Louis A. Bertrand and a Mr. Wilhelm. Lazare Auge, a nonmember, was hired by Bertrand to replace Wilhelm, who left the Church in February 1851. Bolton became the mission president when Elder Taylor left France due to the political unrest.

Shortly after, on January 22, 1852, the first French translation of the Book of Mormon became available.[16]

Elder Taylor also assembled a team of translators to work on the German translation of the Book of Mormon. Elder Taylor arrived in Hamburg, Germany, in September 1851 to meet George P. Dykes, a Scandinavian missionary who knew German, and George Viett, a German school teacher who was baptized in France. They later baptized John Miller, who was added to the translation team. Daniel Carn was a German convert living in the US who was sent to Germany as a mission president at the time Elder Taylor fled Germany to avoid being arrested. Carn himself was arrested several times, but worked with Dykes, Viett, and Miller to complete the German translation in May 1852.[17]

In March 1851, Elder Lorenzo Snow enlisted an unnamed scholar from England to work on the translation of the Book of Mormon into Italian. The translation was finished in October 1851, and printing by William Bowden in London was accomplished the following April.[18]

In 1845, Dan Jones, a new missionary in Wales, began printing Welsh translations of Church pamphlets at his brother's press. John S. Davis, who worked at the press, joined the Church and later translated the Doctrine and Covenants into Welsh in 1850. He sold subscriptions to his periodical which would print parts of the Welsh Book of Mormon each week to raise funds for the translation efforts. On April 17, 1852, the thirty-first and final signature was published, completing the translation of the entire Book of Mormon in Welsh.[19]

Other translations into European languages followed: Swedish in 1878, Dutch in 1890, Czech in 1933, Western Armenian in 1937, Norwegian in 1950, Finnish in 1954, Greek in 1979, Icelandic in 1981, and so forth. Additional translations of the Book of Mormon followed for Central and Eastern Europe, including Croatian in 1979, Hungarian in 1979, Bulgarian in 1980, Polish in 1981, Romanian in 1981, Russian in 1981, Ukrainian in 1997, Albanian in 1999, Estonian in 2000, Latvian in 2000, Eastern Armenian in 2000, Lithuanian in 2000, Slovenian in 2002, Serbian in 2008, and Slovak in 2013.

Three examples from Europe illustrate the efforts of new converts called upon to translate the Book of Mormon into their native languages. Sister Sveinbjörg Gudmundsdóttir was baptized in 1976 in Iceland and soon after became a translator for the Church. She said, "My first assignment was to translate the Book of Mormon . . . I knew I wasn't qualified . . . I knew I could not do it without the help of the Lord." Like other translators, she prayed for help and was guided by the Spirit in the translation process. Her efforts resulted in the publication of the Book of Mormon for the people of Iceland in 1981.[20]

Another example of the efforts in Europe was the experience of Sister Ledia Kita. The Church was still young in Albania when Paul Kern, then an area translation manager in Europe, traveled to Albania in search of a member who was fluent in English and Albanian. Kerns found Kita and taught her how to use a computer. Kita would translate Church materials in "the early morning hours for about 30 minutes before the lights and the power left." She was instrumental in the translation of the Albanian Book of Mormon, released in 1999.[21] Likewise, the efforts of Maria Krolikowska allowed for the publication of a Polish Book of Mormon. Born and raised in Poland, Krolikowska joined the Church in England in 1966. Her prior job as a translator and her subsequent mission prepared her to translate the Polish Book of Mormon, published in 1981.[22]

To the Isles of the Pacific

As a young twenty-three-year-old missionary, Elder George Q. Cannon was called by Brigham Young to serve in the Sandwich (Hawaiian) Islands in 1850. He spent part of his mission translating the Book of Mormon into Hawaiian and noted that the "Spirit of translation rested upon [him]."[23] Others, including William Farrer and Jonatana H. Napela, worked with Cannon on the Hawaiian translation of the Book of Mormon.[24] After Cannon returned from his first mission, Brigham Young called him on a second mission to travel to California to publish the Book of Mormon in Hawaiian, complete in 1855.[25]

The 1889 translation into the Maori language came as a result of the growth of the Church in New Zealand. As a young missionary, Elder Matthew Cowley assisted with the revised translation of the Book of Mormon into the Maori language in 1917.[26] He would return as a mission president in New Zealand, and was later called into the Quorum of the Twelve. Elder Cowley recognized the importance of both the culture and language among the Saints in the Pacific in the miracle of the translation process. He said, "I've learned a lot from [the people of the Pacific islands]. . . . They have some kind of power. . . . They accept miracles as a matter of course."[27] Daniel T. Miller received permission from the First Presidency to have the Book of Mormon translated into Tahitian (1904) because the Catholics were "mistranslating" parts of it to mislead the people.[28] Missionaries who participated in these translation efforts recognized the importance of having a correct translation to teach the truths of the gospel. The Book of Mormon then appeared in Samoan in 1903 and Tongan in 1946.[29]

The Diverse Languages in the Far East

The Church expanded its missionary reach to Japan in the early 1900s, although these initial missionary efforts were stymied by significant obstacles due to cultural and religious differences. Translating the Book of Mormon into Japanese (and then later into the diverse languages of the Far East) presented a new set of challenges. Unlike most European languages and their familiar alphabet and grammar, Asian languages presented a remarkable diversity of scripts, syntax, and structure that were foreign to those from the West. The presence of LDS military personnel after World War II helped to reinstate missionary work in Asia.[30]

Elder Alma O. Taylor was a nineteen-year-old farm boy and one of the first four missionaries sent to Japan in 1901 along with Elder Heber J. Grant of the Quorum of Twelve, who would dedicate Japan for the preaching of the gospel. Learning Japanese was very difficult for Taylor. But during a testimony meeting, Elder Grant prophesied that Taylor would be the Lord's main instrument in translating the Book of Mormon into Japanese. Taylor's service as a young missionary and as a mission president would be accompanied by his diligence to learn the language as well as the Japanese customs.[31] In July 1904, Taylor was assigned to direct the translation of the Japanese Book of Mormon. Taylor said this "was the direct answer to the earnest desire of my heart."[32] Besides the challenge of providing a translation that was true to the original text, there were additional complications from the differences in the spoken and written Japanese language.[33] For example, following the translation into Japanese using Romanized characters, translators would need to convert it into *kanji,* the Chinese-style characters.[34]

Taylor had to decide between translating the book into the more colloquial or spoken style understood by the populace, or the classical literary style characteristic of sacred texts understood by few. Taylor opted for the spoken style, but the native speakers who reviewed the translation, Zenshiro Noguchi and Genta Suzuki, returned with revisions aligned with the classical style used in the language of the Bible. The modern classical style was adopted, and Taylor worked with Hiroharu Ikuta, who was contracted to revise Taylor's translation. In October 1909 the first Japanese Book of Mormon was published. In the mid-1950s in Japan a contemporary writing style was gaining traction to unify the spoken and written language, but it wasn't until 1995 that a full colloquial style of the Japanese Book of Mormon became available.[35]

The translation of the Book of Mormon into Chinese and Korean came in 1965 and 1967, respectively, followed by Thai in 1976 and Indonesian in 1977. Other Southeast Asian languages came in the 1980s, including Vietnamese in 1980, Cambodian and Lao in 1982, and Hmong in 1983. Cultural differences, the lack of language proficiency by American missionaries, and limited gospel knowledge in local new converts created translation challenges. For example, challenges existed in the effort to provide one Chinese translation of the scriptures for Cantonese in Hong Kong and Mandarin speakers in Taiwan respectively.[36] However, missionaries like Elder Vernon Poulter would be guided to find future translators like Hu Wei-I.[37] Elder Gordon B. Hinckley, then a member of the Quorum of the Twelve, called and set apart Larry Browning, a former missionary, and Hu Wei-I to help with the Chinese translation of the Book of Mormon.[38] Misunderstanding and cultural differences accentuated the challenges involved in bringing forth the Chinese translation. Browning wanted more flexibility and was willing to consider some literary liberties to help convey the meaning, whereas Hu desired a more literal translation, which prevailed in the end.[39] Despite these challenges, the first Chinese edition of the Book of Mormon (traditional characters) was finally published in 1965.

The first Korean translation of the Book of Mormon was completed with the help of Elder Han In Sang, who was baptized in 1957 and became the first native Korean missionary to serve in the Korean Mission in 1964.[40] While ill with hepatitis, his mission president assigned him to translate the Book of Mormon into the Korean language. Elder Han noted this was a difficult assignment during his illness, but he relied upon the Lord to fulfill this great privilege and blessing.[41] At the age of 26, Elder Han completed the translation of the Book of Mormon and by 1967, the first edition of the Korean Book of Mormon was published. Besides being the first Korean to serve a full-time mission, he would also be the first Korean to serve as a mission president, regional representative, and General Authority when he was called to the Second Quorum of the Seventy in 1991.[42] Han was also hired as the head of the Translation Services Department created in Korea in 1967.[43] As the "first" Korean in so many aspects of Church service, his achievements highlight a life of faith and dedication.

Sister Srilaksanaa "Sri" Suntarahut was born in Bangkok, Thailand, in 1924. Her father was a doctor to the Thai royal family, and the queen requested permission from him to raise the six-year-old Sri. Sri was raised by the queen in the royal palace in Thailand, developing language skills as she studied with European nuns and later as she served as the financial secretary for high-level government officials.[44] Elder Larry R. White recorded the following regarding the conversion of Sister Sri:

> [Sister Sri] was waiting to go out with some of her friends when she noticed the Book of Mormon on the shelf. Because she had paid ten baht (about 50 cents) for it, she felt that that she should at least read a little. She casually took the book off of the shelf and opened it at random. As soon as her eyes fell upon the first passage, she began to shake, and she felt something which she had never felt before. Immediately, she knew the book was true.[45]

Joining the Church came at a great personal sacrifice to Sri. She lost, for example, her association with Thailand's royalty and social elite. Nevertheless, after receiving her testimony of the Book of Mormon, Sri was blessed as its lead translator for the people of Thailand. Sri said, "I love my Heavenly Father so much for pouring upon me this gift of tongues and language." The Thai Book of Mormon was published in 1976, and a revision came in 2010.[46]

In Vietnam, Sister Cong Ton Nu Tuong Vy, a direct descendant from the imperial family and a former university professor, was baptized after translating the *Joseph Smith's Testimony* pamphlet.[47] In 1970 she was set apart by President W. Brent Hardy, the mission president, to serve as head translator of the newly established local translation committee.[48] She helped to bring forth the Vietnamese translation of the Book of Mormon.[49] Her life illustrates the sacrifice of many early converts who were called to the work of translation. She recorded the following:

> In 1970 or 1971, I was extended a calling to translate the Book of Mormon. . . . I prayed, "How can I translate this book and still earn a living?" Soon after, my son . . . came to me early one morning. To my great surprise, he gave me a gift of 400,000 piasters that he had just won in a government contest. When I got the money . . . I found a quiet place . . . [and] built a cottage and planted a garden. . . . It took me two years to finish [the Vietnamese Book of Mormon translation]. . . . The North Vietnamese took over Saigon in April 1975 . . . [and] they confiscated my property. They also wanted to put me in jail because of my past contact with Americans. . . . I took all my scriptures, translations, and books and buried them in the beach. . . . The police put me in prison.[50]

Vy attempted to flee Vietnam several times unsuccessfully and was jailed many times. Eventually, she spent her life in hiding as a hermit in a cave or "Tiger's Den," shaving her head to disguise herself as a poor Buddhist nun for many years. Ten years after losing contact with the Church, she was able to re-establish contact with members of the Church and through the Veterans Assisting Saints Abroad Association (VASAA) she was able to leave Vietnam. In 1988, she finally visited Salt Lake City and noted that "the first time I saw Temple Square I could not help but weep for my blessings. In the Tiger's Den, it had been my greatest wish to see the temple. At last, I was able to receive my endowment in the Lord's house."[51] Her life highlights the faith and sacrifice of early converts and translators who helped to bring forth the translation of the Book of Mormon to "every nation, kindred, tongue, and people" (D&C 133:37).

New Frontiers and Milestones

Translation of the Book of Mormon into the languages of Africa and the Middle East began with Afrikaans in 1972.[52] The Church employed a scholar, not a Latter-day Saint, at the University of Pretoria in South Africa to translate the Book of Mormon into Afrikaans, and professors at the University of Utah worked on translating it into Arabic in 1980.[53] A Swahili translation (spoken in Southeast Africa) came in 1982, Malagasy in 1986 (Madagascar), Zulu in 1987 (South Africa), Lingala in 1988 (Democratic Republic of the Congo and Republic of Congo), Amharic in 2000 (Ethiopia), Xhosa in 2000 (South Africa and Zimbabwe), Igbo in 2000 (Nigeria), Setswana or Tswana in 2003 (South Africa), Twi in 2005 (Ghana), and Yoruba in 2007 (Nigeria).

Although English, French, and Portuguese were also used in many African countries, African Saints observed that translation of the Book of Mormon into their native languages deepened their gospel knowledge and expanded local missionary efforts. Gemechu Wariyo Goja of the Addis Ababa Branch in Ethiopia said: "Today I became the first Ethiopian member to receive the Book of Mormon in Amharic, and I am very, very happy. . . . When I distributed the first copies of members who I worked with in translating the book, everyone cheered and jumped up and down. I just brought my own copy home, and . . . [we are] reading it to each other in Amharic. It is wonderful."[54]

Several important milestones of the Book of Mormon should be noted (see appendix A). In 1982, the First Presidency and the Quorum of the Twelve Apostles approved the decision to add a subtitle, "Another Testament of Jesus Christ."[55] This further emphasized the central message of the Book of Mormon to the world. Other important milestones included the hundredth language translation of the Book of Mormon in 2000, coinciding with the dedication of the hundredth operating temple of the Church.[56] In addition, the printing of its 50 millionth copy in 1990, 100 million in 2000, and 150 million in 2011 were significant milestones to "flood the earth with the Book of Mormon."

In 2000, the Church reported that the over 99 percent of Church members and 87 percent of the people of the world could read or listen to the Book of Mormon or selections in their own language.[57] *Book* magazine named it one of the "20 Books That Changed America" in 2003.[58] Audio, digital, and mobile formats of the Book of Mormon in various languages continue to be added online, increasing access for more people around the world. The language of the Spirit transcends customs, cultures, and languages; however, a thorough consideration and appreciation for the Book of Mormon can be enhanced by its study in one's native language.

Translating the Book of Mormon

The translation of the Book of Mormon into the numerous languages of the world is an effort to fulfill the scriptural mandate that in the last days "it shall come to pass . . . that every man shall hear the fulness of the gospel in his own tongue, and in his own language" (D&C 90:11). President James E. Faust, then Second Counselor in the First Presidency, said, "The multiplicity of languages and cultures is both an opportunity and a challenge for members of the Church. Having everyone hear the gospel in their own tongue requires great effort and resources."[59] For this reason, the process of translation is carefully regulated.

Directed by the First Presidency and the Quorum of the Twelve

Approval to provide a new or revised translation is directed by the First Presidency and the Quorum of the Twelve.[60] As one *Ensign* article explains,

> The Council of the First Presidency and Quorum of the Twelve Apostles considers recommendations from Area Presidencies for new translations of the Book of Mormon. Before the Book of Mormon is translated, Gospel Fundamentals and other basic doctrinal items such as the Articles of Faith are translated (if they haven't been already) in order to establish standard terminology. Translation work for the Book of Mormon is carried out by worthy, qualified members who are assigned specifically to the task.
>
> From the beginning of the translation process to the end, great care is taken to ensure that the translation is accurate. The manuscript goes through many reviews before it is approved and printed. Once the books are available on distribution center shelves, a letter from the First Presidency is sent to wards and branches in the language area announcing the new book.[61]

As new translations or revised translations become available, Church leaders "encourage members to obtain their own copies of the scriptures and to use them in regular personal, and family study, and in Church meetings and assignments." Letters from the First Presidency announcing newly translated scriptures also note that as individuals "prayerfully learn and teach from the scriptures, their testimonies will grow, their knowledge will increase, their love of family and others will expand, their ability to serve others will enlarge, and they will receive greater strength to resist temptation and defend truth and righteousness."[62]

While serving as the chairman of the Church's Scripture Committee, Elder M. Russell Ballard of the Quorum of the Twelve Apostles said that "all that we do is meant to help bring our Father's children to Jesus Christ. The projects we undertake are chosen and planned after prayerful consideration in the highest priesthood councils of the Church. Under this priesthood direction, much has been accomplished, but there is more yet to do, and the work will go on."[63]

From Their Second Languages to Their Native Tongue

In some areas, when there were no translated materials in the native or first language, missionaries would begin with a copy of the Book of Mormon translated in a second language spoken in a particular area. As noted earlier, Saints in Africa had the Book of Mormon in English, French, and Portuguese before it was translated into their various native African languages. "Before the Book of Mormon was translated into Mongolian, for example, many members in Mongolia studied the Russian edition."[64] Before the Book of Mormon was translated into Bahasa Indonesian in 1977 through the efforts of Brother Budi Darmawan in Indonesia and Arne Hallam in Salt Lake City, the Indonesian Saints used the Dutch, Chinese, and English editions of the Book of Mormon.[65] The Bahasa Indonesian translation was important as it was the spoken language of 70 percent of the people in Indonesia. In India, missionaries started with English copies of the Book of Mormon, even though there were 16 official languages in India. Eventually the Book of Mormon was translated into some of the other official languages in India including Hindi, Telugu, and Tamil in 1982, Bengali in 1985, and Urdu in 1988.[66]

Missionaries in the Philippines began with copies of the Book of Mormon in English and many assumed that English was sufficient for those in the Philippines. English was practical and useful in the rapid growth of the Church in the Philippines. However, it also alienated millions in the Philippines who didn't know English. Church leaders soon recognized the need to provide the scriptures and other Church materials in local languages to take the gospel to every nation, kindred, tongue, and people (see D&C 42:58).[67] Members of the Church in the Philippines incorrectly assumed that they needed to read and speak English to serve in the Church. But eventually that notion disappeared as other translations came for some of 14 major languages spoken by the Filipinos.[68] These included Tagalog in 1987, Ilokano in 1991, Cebuano in 1992, Hiligaynon in 1994, Pampango in 1994, Waray in 1996, Pangasinan in 1998, and Bikolano in 1998. Elder John H. Groberg noted that "Our prime role . . . is not to teach people English. . . . Gospel standards and the message of the Atonement and the Restoration don't vary from language to language. . . . We believe there is value in teaching the gospel in the languages of the earth, because your mother tongue is the language of your heart."[69]

An example from Slovenia illustrates the difference between having the Book of Mormon in one's second language rather than one's native or first language. Missionaries in Slovenia had limited success using the Croatian or English Book of Mormon. But when the Slovenian Book of Mormon was available in 2002, the missionaries found increased success sharing the gospel.[70]

> Before the Book of Mormon was available in Slovenian . . . the work was difficult. . . . The missionaries carried copies of the Book of Mormon in Serbo-Croatian and English, which most young people had studied in school. But more often than not, people declined the book. . . . [Months later] the first shipment of copies of the Slovenian Book of Mormon arrived. . . . With the Slovenian Book of Mormon in hand, not only did the missionaries have more success approaching people, but they also had a way to reinvigorate the testimonies of less-active members who hadn't been to church in years.[71]

Sister Mojca Zheleznikar was baptized in Slovenia after gaining a testimony of the Church. She studied the Book of Mormon in Croatian and English before it was available in Slovenian. But once it was available in her native language and she was able to read it, she said: "I felt the truth expand before me in clear simplicity and profound purity. . . . The voice of my Creator [spoke] to me in my own language, the language that my mother spoke to me."[72]

Evolution of the Scripture Translation Process

The scripture translation process today has evolved since the early days of the Church. In those days the work of translation was typically accomplished by a single person or a small group of individuals. Depending on the circumstances, missionaries, new converts, and even those who were not members of the Church were called upon to assist with the translation of the scriptures. In some instances, missionaries may have not been as versed in the language they were translating into, or new members may have had only limited gospel knowledge as they prepared translated manuscripts. Nevertheless, many determined missionaries and members of the Church contributed greatly to the work of translation in those early days of the Church. As the Church matured and membership increased in various parts of the world, committees of faithful, worthy, and qualified members, rather than a single individual, accomplished the work of translation. Church members who are both worthy and competent are called upon by the Church to serve as translators today. Their work is reviewed by local leaders who are mature in the gospel, and coordinated with the Church's Publishing Services Department.[73]

Translators generally use as their source text the English version of the Book of Mormon translated by the Prophet Joseph Smith.[74] Various scholars have provided in-depth discussion of the various English editions, which will not be described in detail here. However, it was typical for translators of the various languages to use the most current English edition of the Book of Mormon available to them at the time they began the work of translation, as it provided the most "correct" updates. A translator in South Africa noted that to resolve translation issues, he would consult the English version because it "was an inspired translation from the original."[75]

Translation tools and aids have become available. Elder Robert K. Dellenbach of the Second Quorum of the Seventy wrote, "Unlike Joseph's day . . . many of our modern translators utilize computers and word processors, lexicons and encyclopedias to help and guide them in their sacred assignment. The modern work is extensive, and each step must be critically analyzed by Church translation experts."[76] For example, a keyword list for each language has been established to ensure consistency in the terminology being used during the translation process for words such as *priesthood*, *temple*, *First Vision*, *Brigham Young*, *Oliver Cowdery*, *Kirtland*, *Nauvoo*, and so forth. These aids help to reduce discrepancies, such as in the case of the Chinese character for *Kimball*, being previously translated differently in Heber C. Kimball's name and that of Spencer W. Kimball. These translation aids include the LDS International Glossary for official translation and definition of Church terminology, an LDS Translation Index of previously translated materials, the LDS Church History Word List (with events, names, and places of Church history), and the Scripture Comparison List. When applicable, the same terminology is used to translate Bible phrases found in the Book of Mormon. In addition, the use of computer-assisted translation continues to develop to facilitate the translation process.[77] Computers have helped to reduce the total time required to produce a translation of the Book of Mormon.[78] In addition to these modern aids, various translators throughout different periods of time have noted the heavenly help received. These translators have sought for the gift of translation and the help of the Holy Ghost in their work of translation. After completing the Chinese Book of Mormon, Hu Wei-I said that "the translation was done through much prayer and fasting . . . through the Holy Ghost and power from on high."[79] Srilaksana "Sri" Suntarahut, who translated the Thai Book of Mormon, said she learned to translate "by the gift of the language, by the Holy Ghost, by the Lord."[80] Elder Boyd K. Packer, then a member of the Quorum of the Twelve Apostles, noted that "there is that universal language, the language of the Spirit."[81]

Linguistic and Cultural Considerations

There are unique linguistic and cultural issues that translators must consider and adjust to. In most languages of the Pacific, for example, they do not have a word to distinguish between hills and mountains, nor do they have a word for snow, so a substitute word must be created.[82] In some cultures, there is no word for "brother" and the translator must decide to translate it as either "older brother" or "younger brother." The Chinese translation for the brother of Jared, for example, is translated as "older brother."[83] Besides translating the words, translators also consider the "many nuances with language . . . making sure you have all the meaning, all the emotions, all the culture, and everything else that affects how we say things."[84] Consider the task of translating the Spanish Book of Mormon for the various Spanish-speaking countries and cultures in Spain or Latin America, or translating the Chinese scriptures for Cantonese speakers in Hong Kong and Mandarin speakers in Taiwan.[85] Translators work to find words that would make sense to the various countries and cultures that share the same language.[86]

In some instances when a word did not exist, translators have sought for inspiration to create a new word. This is particularly true for many languages in Asia, where Christian concepts were not yet introduced. For instance, the Thai translation for the word *Savior* did not exist and ended up being translated as "the Holy One who helps." While translating the Book of Mormon into Thai, Sister Srilaksana "Sri" Suntarahut struggled with the word *priesthood.* After much fasting and praying she had a vision and saw the word *thana purohit*, or "in the air on the ceiling." This word would become the official word for *priesthood* for the Church in Thailand.[87]

Another example is the Bahasa Indonesian word for *consecration*. This one word means ordaining someone, giving everything to the Lord, setting someone apart, and so forth. "There is no single Bahasa Indonesia word that means all these things—and for some of these meanings there is no word at all! Figures of speech such as 'harrowing up' also cause this type of problem."[88] Despite these challenges, a number of translators reported help from the unseen world. Sister Cong Ton Nu Tuong Vy, from Vietnam, who translated *The Testimony of the Prophet Joseph Smith* pamphlet before translating the Book of Mormon, wrote the following:

> As I read, something strange happened to me. It was as if someone unseen was helping me understand. The first translator translated word for word; but as I finally understood part of the testimony [of Joseph Smith], I put it aside and wrote the translation in my own words. I translated according to the thoughts and feelings that were impressed upon me. I did not know it at the time, but I was translating by the Spirit. . . . I secluded myself and studied extensively. I read many books on the life of the Savior, and, because my French was better than my English, I studied a French Book of Mormon. I read the English Book of Mormon many times. . . . When trying to translate the difficult parts, I pondered and prayed. I would often dream about them and see where I could find help in my library. . . . And as I translated, I pondered. I forgot myself. It was almost as if someone else was helping me write. . . . I don't know how I was able to translate the book, but Heavenly Father helped me. The translation is a good one—many have studied it and said so. It took me two years to finish.[89]

Translators must also consider the level of the language and balance between a formal or informal language.[90] A translation that results in common street slang is inappropriate, but translating the scriptures into something that is too formal and only understood by highly educated scholars could render the translation inaccessible to the people.[91] This is how the Church's *Handbook 2* approaches this:

> When a sacred text is translated into another language or rewritten into more familiar language, there are substantial risks that this process may introduce doctrinal errors or obscure evidence of its ancient origin. To guard against these risks, the First Presidency and Council of the Twelve give close personal supervision to the translation of scriptures from English into other languages and have not authorized efforts to express the doctrinal content of the Book of Mormon in familiar or modern English. (These concerns do not pertain to publications by the Church for children.)[92]

Maria Krolikowska, who translated the Book of Mormon into Polish, spoke about striking the right balance:

> As a translator I believe that the language used should be familiar and comfortable for people to read, so that it can speak to their hearts. . . . When we translate scriptures we try to be very strict. The translation must be literal, but it also must allow for the people to understand the spirit of the scripture and thus recognize and accept the truthfulness of it. While translating the scriptures, I learned a lot more about understanding the gospel, about understanding the Book of Mormon. I came to know what it means to know with all my heart that it is the word of God. My greatest satisfaction and reward is that my people will be able to understand this book of scripture and say, "It is true."[93]

Revision and Selections

The labor and sacrifice of those who helped with the first translations of the Book of Mormon will be forever honored and revered. However, there are no perfect translations. In some instances, there has been a need to provide a revised translation of earlier publications, as in the cases mentioned above when first translations were made by nonmembers, new members, or missionaries not yet fluent in the language.

Over the years, revisions have been made in various languages to provide a better or improved translation. Members of the Church are encouraged to use the most recent edition of the scriptures in their language.[94] Updated translations are found in the newest editions providing a scriptural text which is better aligned with the spirit and intent of the translation given to us by the Prophet Joseph Smith.[95] Although corrections and changes typically accompany new translated editions, in most cases these changes are generally corrections to the translation rather than doctrinal changes. For example, Robert J. Morris noted the following in regards to the Chinese translation of the Book of Mormon.

> The [Chinese] Book of Mormon was first issued in Hong Kong in January 1966, and each succeeding edition has seen many corrections in wording and concept, "clarifying the wordings in some instances," as translator Hu Wei-I told me in an interview. He calls them purely translation changes, not doctrine changes.[96]

In some languages, only selections from the Book of Mormon rather than the full text were translated initially. This practice, now discontinued, occurred with a number of languages beginning with Spanish in 1875 and several other languages between 1977 and 1998.[97] Selections were approved by the Quorum of Twelve Apostles and provided translation for key passages from the Book of Mormon in languages that only a small number of Church members speak. The translation and the printing of selections provided basic scripture passages quickly, whereas a full translation of the Book of Mormon might take years to complete.[98] As one article celebrating the translation of the Book of Mormon into new languages explained, "In some of the languages . . . translators as well as members are few, making the translation process a rather difficult and lengthy one. . . . Selections can be produced much more readily and allow for feedback and revisions more easily than the full book. . . . The approved selections make it possible for new members and investigators to gain access to the Book of Mormon's basic teachings of the gospel."[99]

Taking India as an example, the full text of the Book of Mormon was translated in Hindi, the primary local language, whereas only selections were made for Telugu and Tamil. A member of the Church, Daniel K. Shanthakumar, helped to translate the selections in Tamil. However, the translations into Telugu and Hindi were accomplished by nonmembers,

Reverend P. Sreenivasam and Vijendra Sharma respectively. Sreenivasam learned of the Book of Mormon after his daughter Elsie and her husband, Dharmaraju Edwin, joined the Church in Western Samoa. Sreenivasam translated the Telugu selections, and the Edwins typed and delivered the 700-page manuscript to the Church. They noted that this was their "greatest, single humble contribution to The Church of Jesus Christ of Latter-day Saints in India."[100]

Many years earlier, the Book of Mormon was translated into Spanish, first in selections and then as a full text. Daniel Webster Jones, a new convert, was sent to Mexico on a mission by Brigham Young to learn Spanish and to translate extracts from the Book of Mormon into the same.[101] Melitón Trejo was born in Spain, graduated from a military academy, and received his doctorate from the University of Bordeaux. After hearing about a group of "saints" led by a prophet in the Rocky Mountains, he had an intense desire to meet these people. Trejo traveled far to visit Brigham Young, and related his desire to help translate the Book of Mormon into Spanish in order to take it to his people. Jones and Trejo worked together on *Selected Portions from the Book of Mormon* in 1875. Then Trejo and James Z. Stewart helped complete the full Spanish translation in 1886. Changes in spellings led to a revised edition by Rey L. Pratt in the 1920s with the assistance of Eduardo Balderas, the latter becoming the chief Spanish translator for future editions.[102] Balderas would be instrumental in reviewing and updating the Spanish translation of the Book of Mormon. President Gordon B. Hinckley, then Second Counselor in the First Presidency, noted the following about Balderas: "I soon came to appreciate his great skill as a translator, as well as his integrity as a man and his faithfulness as a member of the Church."[103]

Perhaps the greatest example of the usefulness of the selections is illustrated by the various Filipino languages. The English Book of Mormon was first used in the Philippines until Church leaders recognized the need to provide the scriptures in the numerous local languages. In 1995, the Church reported that of the fifty languages in which selections were available, 84.1 percent of those purchased were of local Filipino languages.[104] Elder Ruben G. Gapiz, then a regional representative who was assigned to lead a committee for the translation of selections from the Book of Mormon into Tagalog ("Mga Piniling Bahagi Mula sa Aklat ni Mormon"), said, "Our intention was to have a selection that is comprehensive and understandable to all levels without sacrificing its scriptural context."[105]

In 1998, the Church discontinued the practice of translating selections and announced it would instead make every new translation a full text edition.[106] Thus the work of translation continues onward, including the expansion of selections in some languages into full text translations of the Book of Mormon, as well as revised editions with improved translations.[107]

Unto "Every Kindred, Tongue, and People"

The prophet Moroni said that the Book of Mormon "shall shine forth out of darkness, and come unto the knowledge of the people" (Mormon 8:16). Members throughout the world rejoice when the Book of Mormon is made available in their languages. Brother Zoltán Horváth of the Dunaújváros Branch in Budapest said, "Moroni 10:3–5 . . . penetrated my heart as if these sentences were written to me personally. I prayed and knew through the Holy Spirit that the Book of Mormon was true." Sister Hwei Chi Hsu of the Taipei Second Ward in Taiwan said, "Our loving Heavenly Father . . . sent missionaries who shared with me the teachings in the Book of Mormon. This latter-day scripture was like dawning light in my dimming life, bringing me precious peace and comfort I needed."[108] At a mission conference in Japan, then–mission president Joseph H. Stimpson said, "The value of the Nephite scripture as an instrument in effective missionary work is recognized by all the missionaries and Saints."[109]

Seven years after joining the Church, Sister Mari Timakov of the Tartu Branch in Estonia received a Book of Mormon in her native language and said, "I have been waiting for the day I could read the Book of Mormon in Estonian. Holding it in your hand, its pages covered with divine counsel, all in your mother tongue—that is something else!" President Dominique Andriamanantoa, the president of the Antananarivo Madagascar Stake, noted that since the Book of Mormon became available in Malagasy, conversion and retention has improved because members are able to read and understand the teachings found in the Book of Mormon. In Tanzania, President William Gideme of the Chang'ombe Branch said the following regarding the Swahili translation: "Finally I can read the Book of Mormon to my whole family with complete understanding. I am so grateful."[110]

In 2014, the Malay Book of Mormon became the 109th language translation of the Book of Mormon. President Bradley Mains, president of the Singapore Mission, said:

> The missionaries and members of the Church in Malaysia have awaited with great anticipation the day they would witness fulfillment of the prophecy that the fullness of the gospel as contained in the Book of Mormon would be available in their own tongue and in their own language. . . . Now that the Book of Mormon is available in Malay, I am confident the work will move forward with greater power to the convincing of many of the gospel of salvation . . . [in] the nation of Malaysia.[111]

On March 26, 1830, E. B. Grandin published the first print version of the Book of Mormon. Almost 185 years later, on March 18, 2015, the Church published the Kosraean Book of Mormon, its 110th translation (see appendix B). The Kosraean (a language spoken on the island of Kosrae in Micronesia) translation was released in digital version first, before printed versions were available. The LDS Church Public Affairs office reported that over 168 million copies have been distributed since 1830, and digital versions were available in 40 different languages online in March 2015.[112] Elder D. Todd Christofferson, member of the Quorum of the Twelve and chair of the Church's Scripture Committee in 2015, said that "members can look forward to several exciting developments regarding the standard works." These developments will include several new translations, more languages available digitally, and "updated style and layout reflected in the 2013 English edition. . . . These updates are meant to make the digital scriptures more personal, more user-friendly, and to provide a deeper study experience." The Church's Scripture Committee has been updating most of the existing translations to make them available online by the end of 2016.[113]

Much effort and devoted service has been rendered to help "flood the earth" with the message of the Book of Mormon. Countless dedicated translators have labored long and hard to fulfill the scriptural mandate to bring forth this sacred volume of scripture to the world. Although it is now available to more people in their own language than ever before, the work will move forward until it is translated and available to "every kindred, tongue, and people."

Notes

1. Note there are 110 translations of the Book of Mormon presently published and distributed by the LDS Church. This does not include the Deseret Alphabet (English) published in 1869 or selections of the Hebrew translation published in 1982 by the LDS Church, which are both out of print; nor does it include the Hebrew translation published in 1988 by the Community of Christ church (formerly RLDS Church); nor other translations by other groups that broke away from the LDS Church. The focus of this article is solely to provide information related to the translations of the Book of Mormon published by and currently distributed by the LDS Church.
2. Robert K. Dellenbach, "The Translation Miracle of the Book of Mormon," *Ensign*, May 1995, 9–10.
3. Royal Skousen, "Book of Mormon Editions (1830–1981)" and "Book of Mormon Manuscripts," in *Encyclopedia of Mormonism*, ed. Daniel H. Ludlow (New York: Macmillan, 1992), 175–76, 185–86.
4. Skousen, "Book of Mormon Editions (1830–1981)" and "Book of Mormon Manuscripts," 175–76, 185–86.
5. Kai A. Andersen, "In His Own Language," *Liahona*, June 1997, 44–47.
6. Lia McClanahan, "To Every Tongue and People," *Ensign*, October 2011, 72–75; "Book of Mormon in American Sign Language Now Available Online," *Church News*, June 30, 2011; "Taking the Scriptures to the World," *Ensign*, July 2001, 24–31.
7. Ryan Kunz, "180 years later, Book of Mormon Nears 150 Million Copies," *Ensign*, March 2010, 74–76.
8. Carrie A. Moore, "Doubleday Book of Mormon Is on the Way," *Deseret News*, November 11, 2004.
9. Church Newsroom, "Church Releases 2013 Edition of English Scriptures in Digital Formats," News Release, March 1, 2013, http://www.mormonnewsroom .org/article/scriptures-digital-2013.
10. "Book of Mormon Reaches 150 Million Copies," *Church News*, April 20, 2011.
11. Ezra Taft Benson, "Flooding the Earth with the Book of Mormon," in Conference Report, October 1988, 5.
12. Joseph Fielding Smith, *Teachings of the Prophet Joseph Smith* (Salt Lake City: Deseret Book, 1976), 176.
13. S. Kent Brown, "The Sesquicentennial of Four European Translations of the Book of Mormon," *Journal of Book of Mormon Studies* 11, no. 1 (2002): 28.
14. Bruce A. Van Orden, *Building Zion: The Latter-day Saints in Europe* (Salt Lake City: Deseret Book, 1996), 5–17.
15. Gilbert W. Scharffs, "Das Buch Mormon: The German Translation of the Book of Mormon," *Journal of Book of Mormon Studies* 11, no. 1 (2002): 35–39, 109; Trent Toone, "Danish: The First Foreign Language Edition of the Book of Mormon," *Deseret News*, February 21, 2012.
16. Richard D. McClellan, "Traduit de L'Anglais: The First French Book of Mormon," *Journal of Book of Mormon Studies* 11, no. 1 (2002): 29–34, 108–9.

17. Scharffs, "Das Buch Mormon," 35–39, 109.
18. Michael W. Homer, "Il Libro di Mormon: Anticipating Growth beyond Italy's Waldensian Valleys," *Journal of Book of Mormon Studies* 11, no. 1 (2002): 40–44, 109–10. Due to opposition, lack of success, and the influence of the Catholic Church on the government, the Italian mission was closed from 1867 to 1966.
19. Ronald D. Dennis, "Llyfr Mormon: The Translation of the Book of Mormon into Welsh," *Journal of Book of Mormon Studies* 11, no. 1 (2002): 45–49, 110.
20. DeAnne Walker, "Iceland—The Saga Continues," *Liahona*, June 1997, 51–55.
21. "Translators and Interpreters Provide Church Content in Multiple Languages," Church Newsroom, August 28, 2008.
22. Kerril Sue Rollins, "The Book of Mormon in Polish," *Ensign*, June 1982, 74–75.
23. Jane McBride Choate, "George Q. Cannon," *Liahona*, February 1989, 34–35.
24. R. Lanier Britsch, "Hawaii," in *Encyclopedia of Latter-day Saint History*, ed. Arnold K. Garr, Donald Q. Cannon, and Richard O. Cowan (Salt Lake City: Deseret Book, 2000), 474–76.
25. R. Lanier Britsch, *Unto the Islands of the Sea* (Salt Lake City: Deseret Book, 1986), 105–7; Choate, "George Q. Cannon," 34–35. Elder George Q. Cannon was later called as a member of the Quorum of the Twelve Apostles.
26. Britsch, *Unto the Islands of the Sea*, 297–99.
27. Matthew Cowley, "Miracles," *Ensign*, October 2004, 44.
28. Britsch, *Unto the Islands of the Sea*, 31–36.
29. Hillary Bowler, "Book of Mormon Translation: Pacific Islands," *Deseret News*, February 22, 2012; R. Lanier Britsch, "Pacific," in *Encyclopedia of Latter-day Saint History*, 883–85.
30. Reid L. Neilson, "Asia," in *Mapping Mormonism: An Atlas of Latter-day Saint History*, ed. Brandon S. Plewe, S. Kent Brown, Donald Q. Cannon, and Richard H. Jackson (Provo, UT: BYU Studies, 2012), 236.
31. Reid L. Neilson, "A Priceless Pearl: Alma O. Taylor's Mission to Japan," *Ensign*, June 2002, 56–59.
32. Alma O. Taylor, journal, vol. 4, July 16, 1904, Mormon Missionary Diaries, MSS 166, L. Tom Perry Special Collections, Harold B. Lee Library, Brigham Young University, Provo, UT.
33. Aaron Shill, "A Classic Dilemma: The Translation of the Book of Mormon into Japanese," *Deseret News*, February 24, 2012.
34. R. Lanier Britsch, *From the East: The History of the Latter-day Saints in Asia, 1851–1996* (Salt Lake City: Deseret Book, 1998), 57–58.
35. Shinji Takagi, "Proclaiming the Way in Japanese: The 1909 Translation of the Book of Mormon," *Journal of the Book of Mormon and Other Restoration Scriptures* 18, no. 2 (2009): 28–37; Reid L. Neilson, *Early Mormon Missionary Activities in Japan, 1901–1924* (Salt Lake City: The University of Utah Press, 2010), 101–2.
36. Diane E. Browning, "The Translation of Mormon Scriptures into Chinese" (unpublished paper, Brigham Young University, 1977).

37. Vernon Poulter, personal letter to Sandy Lee in 2003. Also published by Mark Albright, "Missionary Moment: The Remarkable Story of the Translation of the Chinese Book of Mormon," *Meridian Magazine*, February 4, 2011.
38. Christine Rappleye, "Chinese Translation of the Book of Mormon," *Deseret News*, February 25, 2012.
39. Britsch, *From the East*, 266.
40. Britsch, *From the East*, 181–89.
41. Caresa Alexander, "Translating the Book of Mormon into Korean Was a 'Choice Blessing' for Elder Han In Sang," *Deseret News*, February 23, 2012.
42. Dong Sull Choi, "Korea," in *Encyclopedia of Latter-day Saint History*, 630–31.
43. Britsch, *From the East*, 181–89.
44. Joan Porter Ford and LaRene Porter Gaunt, "The Gospel Dawning in Thailand," *Ensign*, September 1995, 48–53.
45. Britsch, *From the East*, 374–407.
46. Britsch, *From the East*, 374–407; Ford and Gaunt, "The Gospel Dawning in Thailand," 53; R. Lanier Britsch, "Thailand," in *Encyclopedia of Latter-day Saint History*, 1243–44.
47. Britsch, *From the East*, 428–43.
48. R. Lanier Britsch and Richard C. Holloman Jr., "The Church's Years in Vietnam," *Ensign*, August 1980, 24–30.
49. William R. Heaton Jr., "Vietnam and the Restored Church," *Ensign*, June 1973, 34–37.
50. Cong Ton Nu Tuong-Vy, "Out of the Tiger's Den," *Ensign*, June 1989, 45.
51. Cong Ton Nu Tuong-Vy, "Out of the Tiger's Den," 47.
52. E. Dale LeBaron, "Africa," in *Encyclopedia of Latter-day Saint History*, 10–14.
53. Justus Ernst, "Every Man . . . in His Own Language," *Ensign*, July 1974, 23–27.
54. Barbara Jean Jones, "News of the Church: Another Milestone of 100 Reached in 2000," *Ensign*, March 2001, 76.
55. Boyd K. Packer, "Scriptures," in Conference Report, October 1982, 51–53.
56. Jones, "News of the Church: Another Milestone," 76–77.
57. "Taking the Scriptures to the World," 24–31.
58. "Book of Mormon Reaches 150 Million Copies."
59. James E. Faust, "Heirs to the Kingdom of God," *Ensign*, May 1995, 63.
60. "Four New Translations Completed for Book of Mormon, Triple Combination," *Ensign*, February 2007, 77–78.
61. "Translation Work Taking Book of Mormon to More People in More Tongues," *Ensign*, February 2005, 76.
62. "Four New Translations," 77.
63. "Taking the Scriptures to the World," 26.
64. McClanahan, "To Every Tongue and People," 73.
65. Alison Craig, "The Saints in Indonesia," *Ensign*, January 1977, 86–90.
66. Britsch, *From the East*, 484–86, 506–36.
67. Britsch, *From the East*, 365–68.
68. Hillary Bowler, "Book of Mormon Translation: The Philippines," *Deseret News*, February 21, 2012.

69. Giles H. Florence Jr., "City of Angels," *Ensign*, September 1992, 36.
70. McClanahan, "To Every Tongue and People," 72–75.
71. McClanahan, "To Every Tongue and People,"73–74.
72. McClanahan, "To Every Tongue and People," 74.
73. Trent Toone, "The Translators of the Book of Mormon," *Deseret News*, February 2, 2012.
74. Robert K. Dellenbach, "The Translation Miracle," 9–10.
75. Ernst, "Every Man . . . in His Own Language," 25.
76. Dellenbach, "The Translation Miracle," 10.
77. "Translators and Interpreters Provide Church Content in Multiple Languages," Church Newsroom, August 28, 2008; Ernst, "Every Man . . . in His Own Language," 23–27.
78. "Translation—with a Little Help from Our Computers," *Ensign*, April 1979, 30–31.
79. Van Therald, "On Either Side," in *Voice of the Saints* (Hong Kong: Wing Tai Printing Company, March 1966), 35–38.
80. Britsch, *From the East*, 374–407.
81. Boyd K. Packer, "Language of the Spirit," *New Era*, March 1977, 4.
82. Hillary Bowler, "Book of Mormon translation: Pacific Islands," *Deseret News*, February 22, 2012; Grant Underwood, ed., *Pioneers in the Pacific: Memory, History, and Cultural Identity among the Latter-day Saints* (Provo, UT: Religious Studies Center, 2005), 133–41.
83. Allen E. Litster, "I Have a Question: How many languages has the Book of Mormon been translated into and how many copies have been distributed in the years since it was first printed?," *Ensign*, September 1977, 37.
84. Nicole Seymour, "Spirit, Training Help Translators Capture Meaning," *Ensign*, February 2006, 77.
85. The Chinese written language is used by both those in Taiwan and Hong Kong, but the spoken language differs with Mandarin and Taiwanese spoken in Taiwan and Cantonese spoken in Hong Kong.
86. Browning, "The Translation of Mormon Scriptures into Chinese."
87. Britsch, *From the East*, 374–407.
88. Britsch, *From the East*, 484–86.
89. Cong Ton Nu Tuong-Vy, "Out of the Tiger's Den," 46.
90. The Church has discouraged rewriting the Book of Mormon into familiar or modern English, with the exception of the Book of Mormon Reader published by the Church for children. "News of the Church: Modern-Language Editions of the Book of Mormon Discouraged," *Ensign*, April 1993, 74.
91. Craig, "The Saints in Indonesia," 86–90.
92. "Book of Mormon," in *Handbook 2: Administering the Church* (Salt Lake City: The Church of Jesus Christ of Latter-day Saints, 2010), 21.1.8.
93. Rollins, "The Book of Mormon in Polish," 75.
94. "Scriptures," in *Handbook 2*, 17.1.1.
95. Andersen, "In His Own Language," 44–47.

96. Robert J. Morris, "Some Problems of Translating Mormon Thought into Chinese," *BYU Studies* 10, no. 2 (Winter 1970): 173–85.
97. "Translation Work Taking Book of Mormon to More People in More Tongues," *Ensign*, February 2005, 75–76.
98. Kerril Sue Rollins, "The Book of Mormon in Hindi, Tamil, and Telugu," *Ensign*, February 1983, 78–79.
99. Rollins, "The Book of Mormon in Hindi, Tamil, and Telugu," 78.
100. Rollins, "The Book of Mormon in Hindi, Tamil, and Telugu," 79.
101. Jack McAllister, "The Unlikely Daniel Webster Jones: First Spanish Translations from the Book of Mormon," *Ensign*, August 1981, 50–52.
102. Eduardo Balderas, "How the Scriptures Came to Be Translated into Spanish," *Ensign*, September 1972, 26–29.
103. John E. Carr, "Eduardo Balderas: Translating Faith into Service," *Ensign*, June 1985, 44–45.
104. The 84.1 percent of selections from the Book of Mormon in local Filipino languages sold in 1994 and reported in 1995 included 60.94 percent in Tagalog, 19.56 percent in Cebuano, and 3.6 percent in Ilocano. Britsch, *From the East*, 365–68.
105. "Tagalog Selection from the Book of Mormon," Dateline Philippines, Tambuli, August 11, 1988, 6–7; Britsch, *From the East*, 365–68.
106. "Translation Work," 75–76.
107. Andersen, "In His Own Language," 44–47.
108. "Taking the Scriptures to the World," *Ensign*, July 2001, 29.
109. Neilson, *Early Mormon Missionary Activities in Japan*, 101–2.
110. Jones, "News of the Church: Another Milestone of 100 Reached in 2000," *Ensign*, March 2001, 77.
111. Camille West, "Book of Mormon Now in Malay Language," Church News and Events, August 12, 2013.
112. Whitney Butters Wilde, "'A Marvelous Work and A Wonder': A Look Back at the Translation of the Book of Mormon 185 Years after It Was First Published," *Deseret News*, March 26, 2015.
113. Camille West, "Scripture Committee Announces 'Exciting Developments' in Standard Works Translations," *Church News*, March 18, 2015.

Appendix A: Book of Mormon Milestones

1830 First English translation published by E. B. Grandin in Palmyra, New York, translated by the Prophet Joseph Smith.

1837 English edition published by Parley P. Pratt and John Goodson in Kirtland, Ohio, which provided grammatical changes after comparing the first edition with the printer's manuscript.

1840 English edition published for Ebenezer Robinson and Don Carlos Smith in Nauvoo, Illinois (by Shepard and Sterns in Cincinnati, Ohio), corrected errors found between the printer's and the original manuscripts.

1841 First British/European edition. This English edition published for Brigham Young, Heber C. Kimball, and Parley P. Pratt (by J. Tompkins in Liverpool, England). This was basically a reprint of the 1837 edition with British spelling. Additional British editions came in 1849 and 1852, edited by Orson Pratt and Franklin D. Richards, respectively, with minor editing (Richards added paragraph numbers). Subsequent English editions received minor editing but incorporated major format changes.

1851 First non-English edition, Danish.

1855 First Pacific language edition, Hawaiian.

1875 First edition published as Selections from the Book of Mormon instead of full text editions, Spanish.

1879 English edition edited by Orson Pratt, divided long chapters and added scriptural reference footnotes.

1909 First Asian or Far East language edition, Japanese.

1920 English edition edited by James E. Talmage, added introductory material, double columns, chapter summaries, and new footnotes (minor editing in the 1905 and 1911 editions were also included).

1972 First African language edition, Afrikaans.

1981 English edition edited by a committee headed by members of the Quorum of the Twelve, including updated introductory material, chapter summaries, and footnotes. It also corrected textual errors found in the printer's manuscript after comparing it with the 1840 edition and original manuscript.

1982 To clarify and emphasize the purpose of the Book of Mormon, a subtitle was added. The full title reads, "The Book of Mormon: Another Testament of Jesus Christ."

1990 50 millionth copy printed.

1998 Church announced it would discontinue translation of selections from the Book of Mormon for languages and would instead make every new translation a full text edition.

2000 The Book of Mormon was available in 100 languages, and the 100 millionth copy was printed. Church reported that over 90 percent of Church members and 87 percent of the people of the world could read or listen to Selections or the full text of the Book of Mormon in their own language.

2003 Named one of the "20 Books That Changed America" by *Book* magazine.

2004 Commercial English edition published by Doubleday Publishing Company in New York.

2011 150 millionth copy printed.

2013 English edition released in digital format with new photos, updated study aids, maps, chapter and section headings with accompanied online mobile versions. Also available in print.

Appendix B: Book of Mormon Languages in Sequence of First Published (as of March 26, 2015)

	Language	Published	First and Present Editions
1	English	1830	Full book. Revised 1981, 2013
2	Danish	1851	Full book. Rev. 1949, 2005
3	German	1852	Full book. Rev. 1980, 2003
4	French	1852	Full book. Rev. 1998
5	Italian	1852	Full book. Rev. 1995
6	Welsh	1852	Full book. Reprint 2001
7	Hawaiian	1855	Full book. Reprint 1992
8	Spanish	1875	Sel. Full 1886. Rev. 1992
9	Swedish	1878	Full book. Rev. 1958, 2008
10	Maori	1889	Full book. Reprint 1989
11	Dutch	1890	Full book. Rev. 2004
12	Samoan	1903	Full book. Rev. 2011
13	Tahitian	1904	Full book
14	Turkish	1906	Full. Sel. 1983, Full 2001
15	Japanese	1909	Full book. Rev. 1995, 2009
16	Czech	1933	Full book. Rev. 2004
17	Western Armenian	1937	Full book. Selections 1983
18	Portuguese	1939	Full book. Rev. 1995
19	Tongan	1946	Full book. Rev. 2006
20	Norwegian	1950	Full book. Rev. 2002
21	Finnish	1954	Full book. Rev. 2002
22	Rarotongan	1965	Full book
23	Chinese	1965	Full book. Rev. 2007
24	Korean	1967	Full book. Rev 2005
25	Afrikaans	1972	Full book. Rev. 2003
26	Thai	1976	Full book. Rev. 2010
27	Indonesian	1977	Full book. Rev. 2003, 2010

	Language	Published	First and Present Editions
28	Aymara	1977	Selections. Full 1986
29	Cakchiquel	1978	Selections
30	Croatian	1979	Full book
31	Quechua-Peru	1979	Selections
32	Greek	1979	Sel. K 1979, D 1983, Full 1987
33	Hungarian	1979	Sel. Full 1991. Rev. 2005
34	Kekchi	1979	Sel. Full 1983. Rev. 2011
35	Quiché	1979	Selections
36	Bulgarian	1980	Selections. Full 1999, 2004
37	Navajo	1980	Selections. Rev. 1998
38	Quichua-Ecuador	1980	Selections. Full 2011
39	Arabic	1980	Selections. Full 1986
40	Vietnamese	1980	Sel. Full 1982. Rev. 2003
41	Fijian	1980	Full book
42	Quechua-Bolivia	1981	Selections
43	Russian	1981	Full book. Rev. 2012
44	Catalan	1981	Full book
45	Polish	1981	Full book
46	Romanian	1981	Selections. Full 1998, 2004
47	Kuna	1981	Selections
48	Niuean (Niue)	1981	Selections
49	Icelandic	1981	Full book. Rev. 2002
50	Hindi	1982	Full book
51	Telugu	1982	Selections. Full 2000
52	Tamil	1982	Selections. Full 2005
53	Cambodian	1982	Selections. Full 2001, 2007
54	Lao	1982	Selections. Full 2012
55	Swahili	1982	Selections. Full 2000, 2005
56	Guaraní	1982	Selections. Full 2009
57	Maya	1983	Selections
58	Sinhala	1983	Selections. Full 2008

	Language	Published	First and Present Editions
59	Mam	1983	Selections
60	Efik	1983	Selections
61	Chinese (Simp. Char)	1983	Selections. Full 2000
62	Kisii (Gusii)	1983	Selections
63	Hmong	1983	Selections. Full 2000
64	Persian (Farsi)	1983	Selections
65	Haitian	1983	Selections. Full 1999. Rev. 2007
66	Marshallese	1984	Selections. Full 2003
67	Bengali	1985	Selections
68	Bislama	1985	Selections. Full 2004
69	Malagasy	1986	Selections. Full 2000. Rev. 2006
70	Fante	1987	Selections. Full Rev. 2003
71	Zulu	1987	Selections. Full 2003
72	Pohnpeian	1987	Selections
73	Papiamento	1987	Selections
74	Chuukese (Trukese)	1987	Selections
75	Tagalog	1987	Selections. Full 1998
76	Lingala	1988	Selections. Full 2004
77	Shona	1988	Selections. Full 1999, 2007
78	Urdu	1988	Selections. Full 2007
79	Palauan	1988	Selections
80	Kiribati	1988	Selections. Full 2001
81	Chamorro	1989	Selections
82	Ilokano	1991	Selections. Full 1995
83	Cebuano	1992	Selections. Full 1998
84	Tzotzil	1994	Selections
85	Hiligaynon	1994	Selections. Full 2005
86	Pampango	1994	Selections
87	American Sign (ASL)	1995	Full VHS. DVD 2006
88	Waray	1996	Selections
89	Ukrainian	1997	Full book. Rev. 2005

	Language	Published	First and Present Editions
90	Bikolano	1998	Selections
91	Pangasinan	1998	Full book
92	Albanian	1999	Full book. Rev. 2005
93	Estonian	2000	Full book. Rev. 2011
94	Igbo	2000	Full book. Rev. 2007
95	Latvian	2000	Full book. Rev. 2006
96	Armenian East	2000	Full book. Rev. 2006
97	Lithuanian	2000	Full book. Rev. 2006
98	Amharic	2000	Full book
99	Xhosa	2000	Full book
100	Mongolian	2001	Full book. Rev. 2007
101	Neomelanesian	2002	Full book
102	Slovenian	2002	Full book
103	Setswana or Tswana	2003	Full book
104	Yapese	2004	Full book
105	Twi	2005	Full book
106	Yoruba	2007	Full book
107	Serbian	2008	Full book
108	Slovak	2013	Full book
109	Malay	2014	Full book
110	Kosraean	2015	Full book

Total=110		**23 Sel., 87 Full book**
<u>Braille Formats</u>		
Braille (English)	1936	Full book. Rev. 1994
Braille (Spanish)	1995	Full book
<u>Out of Print</u>		
Deseret Alphabet (English)	1869	Full book
Hebrew	1982	Sel. by LDS Church. Full book by RLDS 1988

Appendix C: Selected Questions and Answers on Translating into Other Languages

Answers Provided by the Priesthood Department, The Church of Jesus Christ of Latter-day Saints

Q: What English-language edition do translators currently use?

A: Translators rely upon an English text referred to as the "Translators Copy," which is based on the most current English database. The study aids in the "Translators Copy," such as headings, footnotes, and the Guide to the Scriptures, have not always been exactly the same as the English study aids. When the 2013 English edition of the scriptures was published, many, if not most, of the updates to the headings were harmonized so that the English and non-English scriptures matched each other.

Q: How does the English source text incorporate recent scholarly insights?

A: Translation teams, reviewers, and project supervisors consult tools prepared by the Church to assist them as they translate and review the scriptures. These tools reflect many of the insights which have been shared by scholars both within and outside of Church employment.

Q: Which translators are Latter-day Saints, and which are not?

A: The current practice is that all who work on the scriptures are temple-worthy members of the Church. In some cases in the distant past, some translators or reviewers have not been members of the Church, but this is not the case today, though such may be consulted on various matters.

Q: Are translators today doing so in non-compensated, Church calling capacities, or are they contracted and compensated employees? Is it a mix of both?

A: Translation team members may be volunteers, contractors, or full-time Church employees, depending on various circumstances. Those who perform the doctrinal certification of the translation, called "ecclesiastical reviewers," are all called and set apart and are not paid for their services.

Q: Why are some translators unnamed? Is that a conscious effort by the Church?

A: Scripture translation and associated reviews are performed by many members. As such, the work does not belong to any single contributor.

Q: Why the order of translation in European languages? The larger question is this: how is the decision made as to what language is next?

A: In the Church today, Area Presidencies have the responsibility to address the language needs of their respective areas. They submit requests to the First Presidency and Quorum of the Twelve for approval, who consider global Church needs, resources, and prioritization when giving approvals.

Q: Several translators referred to in the chapter use the word "literal"—the translation must be "literal." What does that mean in this context? How does the Church translation team view "literal" translations? What is the standard for judging "literalness"?

A: Translation work is guided by a policy established by the First Presidency and Quorum of the Twelve. This policy is sometimes referred to as the "literalness policy" because of its emphasis on striving to maintain certain figures of speech and textual features of the original English in the most literal way possible. It is not always possible to do so, particularly if maintaining that literalness makes the translation unusually awkward or detracts in other ways from the acceptability of the translation. At times, a modified literalness is used while still maintaining the correct meaning.

Q: Do translators typically work with English *and* other language versions of the Book of Mormon simultaneously, if they have familiarity with other languages? (So did Estonian or Latvian translators work from English *and* Russian?) Does that still happen today?

A: Translation teams and reviewers will often consult other translations, particularly if the languages are from the same language family. They may use these other languages as resources, but the norm is to translate from the English master.

Q: How does the First Presidency and Quorum of the Twelve Apostles oversee the process of scripture translation?

A: The First Presidency and Quorum of the Twelve approve languages for scripture translation. Ecclesiastical reviewers, who are called and set apart for this work, review the translations. These review committees produce a report certifying that translations meet the requirements set by the First Presidency and Quorum of the Twelve.

Q: Who makes the ultimate decision on what words to use when words need to be invented or as to what tone/tense/terms are too familiar or colloquial?

A: Translation teams and ecclesiastical reviewers make decisions about translations, following the policies and procedures established by the First Presidency, Quorum of the Twelve, and the Scriptures Committee.

Q: How are decisions made to choose words like "older brother" in Chinese, or the word for "priesthood" in Thai? Why those decisions?

A: When the meaning of the English text is either unclear or ambiguous and a language requires otherwise, research is conducted and presented to presiding councils for counsel and direction for that particular language. Previous comments made by Church leaders relating to the passage are also considered. Possible options are given to the presiding councils of the Church who in turn offer direction on these issues. Their decisions become guides to assist the translation effort globally; however, these decisions are not to be regarded as definitive doctrinal statements or commentary on the scriptures. This is the case with the "older brother" passages in the scriptures where the scriptures themselves are either unclear or ambiguous.

Q: The same terminology is used to translate Bible phrases found in the Book of Mormon. Before Book of Mormon translation begins, does the Church designate a standard Bible edition for each language?

A: Yes, wherever possible the Church evaluates existing Bible translations to find one which seems to best represent a translation which is both faithful to the original languages and is rendered in a dignified language style. This Bible serves as a resource for terminology selection in LDS scriptures but does not necessarily determine exact usage of the same terminology if that terminology does not accurately convey the doctrines of the Restoration.

Q: Does the Church now begin with a computer-generated translation that is then reviewed and edited by translators, or does every translation start from scratch?

A: No. The Church does not begin with a computer-generated translation.

Q: What is the typical time for a Book of Mormon translation now? Does the Church have a "goal" timeline?

A: Translations of the Book of Mormon range from 2 to 7 years with an average of about 4.6 years. Additional time is required for initial research and final production. Methods and processes are being considered and implemented to shorten that time frame.

13

"They Are Not Cast Off Forever"
Fulfillment of the Covenant Purposes

Jared W. Ludlow

Jared W. Ludlow is an associate professor of ancient scripture at Brigham Young University.

One of the first purposes of the Book of Mormon we may think of is its purpose to convince Jew and Gentile alike that Jesus is the Christ. While that is certainly a major purpose of the Book of Mormon, the title page also declares that this sacred record will "show unto the remnant of the house of Israel what great things the Lord hath done for their fathers; and that they may know the covenants of the Lord, that they are not cast off forever." The object of this paper is to examine Book of Mormon references that show how the remnant of Israel will be taught about the Lord's covenants and his dealings with their forefathers. Knowledge of these covenants offers the remnant of Israel hope for redemption. The original writers of the Book of Mormon were aware of at least one of God's wise purposes for the coming forth of their record: to teach the remnant of Lehi's posterity of God's covenants so that they would keep these covenants, remain faithful to him, and foster faith in his Son. By coming to know this record, God's power will be revealed to them and they will know that they have not been cast off forever. In order to show how the

Book of Mormon accomplishes these purposes, we will first look at the foundation of these covenants with the house of Israel, then see how they were understood by Book of Mormon writers, and finally examine prophecies concerning the record's deliverance to Lehi's descendants through the Gentiles.

The House of Israel

The Book of Mormon talks frequently of the house of Israel when speaking of the covenant relationship between God and his children. The term "house of Israel" refers back to the descendants of Jacob, whose name was changed to Israel (see Genesis 32:28; 35:10). These children of Israel were the covenant people in the Old Testament. Yet, because of their wickedness and rebellion, the Lord's punishments frequently came upon them, and they were expelled from the covenant land of Israel and scattered among the nations of the earth. Despite these episodes, the Lord promised to gather the house of Israel in order to fulfill his eternal purposes for his children and because of his previous covenants made with Abraham, Isaac, and Jacob (see 1 Nephi 19:15-16; 22:3–12).

Because its primary peoples are descendants of the sons of Jacob, or Israel, the Book of Mormon belongs within the storyline of the house of Israel. Those journeying with Lehi around 600 BC were descended from Joseph through his sons Manasseh and Ephraim (see 1 Nephi 5:14–16; Alma 10:3),[1] and so they have most of the same responsibilities and promises of the biblical house of Israel.[2] Yet their exile from the promised land of Israel could have easily led them to believe that they were cast off from God's covenant family. However, Jacob (Nephi's brother) explained that God had led them to a land choice "above all other lands" for their inheritance and encouraged his people not to hang down their heads, "for we are not cast off; nevertheless, we have been driven out of the land of our inheritance; but we have been led to a better land" (see 2 Nephi 10:19–20). Jacob alludes to the idea that they felt cast off—but since they were in fact a covenant people, God had another plan for this remnant of the house of Israel.

The allegory of Zenos further explores God's dealings with the house of Israel, showing how God will sometimes cast away those branches who have turned wicked, but he always remembers the remnant and preserves the faithful (see Jacob 5:74–75). In the case of Lehi's branch, or remnant, of Israel, they were not scattered or led away from their home in Jerusalem because of *their* wickedness but because of the wickedness and coming punishments of God upon the wicked in Jerusalem (see 1 Nephi 1:13; 2:2; 21:1; 2 Nephi 1:3–4). In this, the Lord preserved a remnant of the seed of Joseph. This remnant of Israel was destined to inherit another promised land, a land far away in the Americas. The Book of Mormon prophets understood that their purpose included encouraging faithfulness in covenants so that their people would not cast themselves away from God. One of the ways these prophets accomplished this mission was by reminding their people of the great things God had done and would continue to do for their people because of the promises and covenants made to their forefathers Abraham, Jacob, and Joseph.

Promises to Abraham, Jacob, and Joseph

The Book of Mormon preserves promises made to Abraham, Jacob/Israel, and his son Joseph during their lifetimes. Although the phrase "Abrahamic covenant" is never used in the Book of Mormon, allusions to it certainly exist. As part of that covenant, Abraham was promised a numerous posterity, lands of inheritance, and the blessings of the priesthood. His posterity was to "bear this ministry and Priesthood unto all nations" (see Abraham 2:9–11), thereby becoming a blessing to all nations (see Genesis 12:3; 22:18). The covenant made to Abraham would be fulfilled in the latter days (see 1 Nephi 15:18), and the Book of Mormon record would help make known the covenants the Father made with Abraham (see 1 Nephi 22:9). In most of the passages referring to the covenants made with Abraham, the writers link those covenants with the covenants passed on through the house of Israel.[3] For example, Mormon 5:20 states that after Lehi's posterity are scattered by the Gentiles, the Lord will remember the covenant "he made unto Abraham and unto all the house of Israel." The resurrected Lord appeared in the Americas and told the people, "Ye are the children of the prophets; and ye are of the house of Israel; and ye are of the covenant which the Father made with your fathers, saying unto Abraham: and in thy seed shall all the kindreds of the earth be blessed" (3 Nephi 20:25). Jesus further states that after being blessed, "then fulfilleth the Father the covenant which he made with Abraham, saying: In thy seed shall all the kindreds of the earth be blessed" (3 Nephi 20:25, 27). This connects Book of Mormon peoples with earlier promises made to Abraham.

Jacob (Israel) also received significant promises related to his posterity. Captain Moroni quotes Jacob's own words, telling us of the promise to preserve a remnant of his son Joseph's seed: "Even as this remnant of garment of my son hath been preserved, so shall a remnant of the seed of my son be preserved by the hand of God, and be taken unto himself, while the remainder of the seed of Joseph shall perish, even as the [other] remnant of his garment. Now behold, this giveth my soul sorrow; nevertheless, my soul hath joy in my son, because of that part of his seed which shall be taken unto God" (Alma 46:24–26).

The resurrected Savior also mentions Jacob during his visitation in the land of Bountiful when he recounts that he will establish "this people" in "this land" in order to fulfill the covenant previously made with Jacob (see 3 Nephi 20:22).

Along with the recorded promises to Jacob are those given to his son Joseph. These promises are found in 2 Nephi 3.[4] Within this chapter, Lehi declares that "great were the covenants of the Lord which he made unto Joseph" (v. 4). These covenant blessings or promises include the preservation of a righteous branch. This branch would be broken off, but it would be remembered in the covenants of the Lord by having the Messiah "manifest unto them in the latter days, in the spirit of power, unto the bringing of them out of darkness unto light—yea, out of hidden darkness and out of captivity unto freedom" (v. 5). As part of the bringing forth of Joseph's remnant into the light, the Lord would raise up a choice seer—Joseph Smith—unto the fruit of Joseph's loins (see v. 6).

The Lord promised the biblical Joseph that this choice seer would do a valuable work among his descendants to bring them to a knowledge of the covenants made with their fathers (see v. 7). This seer would be given power not only to bring forth God's word unto Joseph's descendants but also to convince them of the words or scriptures (the biblical record) that had already gone forth among them (see v. 11). Thus the words of the posterity of Judah would grow together with the words of the posterity of Joseph to confound false doctrines, establish peace, and bring them in the latter days to the knowledge of their fathers and their covenants (see v. 12).[5] The Lord promised that the future choice seer's weakness would be made strong in the day when the Lord would begin restoring the house of Israel (see v. 13).[6] Biblical Joseph also prophesied that the record which would be brought forth by the future seer's hand would bring his people unto salvation (see v. 15).[7] Lehi ended by promising his son Joseph that "because of this covenant thou art blessed; for thy seed shall not be destroyed, for they shall hearken unto the words of the book" (v. 23). By learning of the Lord's covenants, embracing them, and coming unto Christ, they would not be "cast off forever" (see title page).

"Preserved for a Wise Purpose"

The record keepers of the Book of Mormon understood that their work was not their own but followed the wise purposes of God. As Alma the Younger was nearing the end of his earthly ministry, he shared his feelings about how seemingly small things like these records (the Nephite scriptures) could confound the wise and in the end do great things such as bringing about the salvation of many souls (see Alma 37:5–7). Alma went on to explain that these records had already brought many to faith in Christ through the missionary work of the sons of Mosiah among the Lamanites, but he expressed a hope that they would bring even more to the knowledge of their Redeemer (vv. 9–10). Alma then declared: "They are preserved for a wise purpose, which purpose is known unto God; . . . that he may show forth his power unto future generations" (vv. 12, 14). As one of the record keepers of the Book of Mormon, Alma could glimpse the record's significance and role among future generations. He knew that this record would be preserved according to God's wise purpose and in accordance with promises made to their forefathers. He foresaw that when the Book of Mormon testimony would come forth, it would be a means to show forth the power of God by helping many gain a knowledge of the source they could turn to for redemption: Jesus Christ, their Redeemer. Several Book of Mormon writers petitioned God to preserve their record so it could be a blessing to their future posterity, the remnant of the house of Israel, even when those descendants went astray. Mormon implored, "And my prayer to God is concerning my brethren, that they may once again come to the knowledge of God, yea, the redemption of Christ; that they may once again be a delightsome people" (Words of Mormon 1:7–8).

How would Mormon's prayer concerning his brethren be answered? The primary answer is a sequence related to the actual coming forth of the Book of Mormon:

- the preservation of the record from being destroyed by the Lamanites
- the record being buried in the earth and later crying forth from the dust (in fulfillment of Isaiah's and biblical Joseph's prophecies—e.g., Isaiah 29:4; 2 Nephi 3:19)
- the Gentiles bringing forth this record unto the remnant of the house of Israel
- the Book of Mormon initiating and being a sign of the final gathering of the remnants of the house of Israel to their lands of their inheritance, thereby fulfilling God's covenants.

Preserved from Being Destroyed by the Lamanites

In order for Mormon's record to come forth, it first had to be preserved through the centuries until the time of the prophesied "choice seer," Joseph Smith. The Lord's promise to preserve the record was made and prophesied about throughout the Book of Mormon. The Lord promised Nephi that what he wrote would be preserved and handed down to his seed. His posterity would be preserved not only physically (see Alma 46:24–27) but spiritually as well (see 2 Nephi 25:21; see also 2 Nephi 3:23).[8]

Enos, after he had received a promise of forgiveness for his sins, prayed for his brethren the Lamanites. His desire was that the Nephite record would be preserved so that, even if his people were destroyed, it "might be brought forth at some future day unto the Lamanites, that, perhaps, they might be brought unto salvation" (Enos 1:13). God covenanted with Enos that the records would be brought forth to the Lamanites in the Lord's own due time (see Enos 1:16; see also D&C 3:19–20; 10:48–52). Despite the Lamanites' desire to destroy the Nephites' records and traditions, the records were kept safe.

Samuel, a Lamanite, later described that even if the Lamanites should dwindle in unbelief, the Lord would prolong their days until the time of their restoration to the knowledge of the truth, specifically "the knowledge of their Redeemer, and their great and true shepherd" (Helaman 15:11–13). Ammaron, being constrained by the Holy Ghost, hid up the sacred records to the Lord so that Mormon could later retrieve them in order that "they might come again unto the remnant of the house of Jacob, according to the prophecies and the promises of the Lord" (4 Nephi 1:48–49). Mormon prayed and received the assurance that the records would be preserved because of the great things written on them out of which Mormon's descendants and their brethren would be judged (see Words of Mormon 1:11). One can see in all these prophecies a thread that runs throughout the Book of Mormon. In response to the writers' desires to preserve this record, God promised to do so in order to later bring it forth through his own power. Out of great charity, these prophets wanted the record preserved from their enemies so that perhaps it could be a means to bless even their enemies' descendants. Not only is the preserved record a great blessing to the living remnants of the house of Israel, but we as readers are also greatly blessed to be the recipients of this divinely protected spiritual witness.

Preserved to Come Forth from the Ground

As part of this preservation of the record, many Book of Mormon prophets realized that it would be necessary for these records to be literally buried and hid up in order to preserve them for a future time (see 1 Nephi 13:35; Mormon 8:14–16). Nephi taught his people that the prayers of the faithful (for example, Enos, Mormon, and so forth) would be heard, and the remnant of Israel would not be forgotten. He then quoted the prophet Isaiah, relating Isaiah's words to his people: "Those who shall be destroyed shall speak unto them out of the ground, and their speech shall be low out of the dust, and their voice shall be as one that hath a familiar spirit; for the Lord God will give unto him power, that he may whisper concerning them, even as it were out of the ground; and their speech shall whisper out of the dust" (2 Nephi 26:15–16; see also Mormon 8:23–26). Orson Pratt declared:

> Never was a prophecy more truly fulfilled than this, in the coming forth of the Book of Mormon. Joseph Smith took that sacred history "out of the ground." It is the voice of the ancient prophets of America speaking "out of the ground;" their speech is "low out of the dust;" it speaks in a most familiar manner of

> the doings of bygone ages; it is the voice of those who slumber in the dust. It is the voice of prophets speaking from the dead, crying repentance in the ears of the living. In what manner could a nation, after they were brought down and destroyed, "speak out of the ground?" Could their dead bodies or their dust, or their ashes speak? Verily, no: they can only speak by their writings or their books that they wrote while living. Their voice, speech or words, can only "speak out of the ground," or "whisper out of the dust" by their books or writings being discovered.[9]

Mormon was commanded to hide up his records unto the Lord until the Lord felt to bring them forth (see Mormon 5:12–13). As Moroni sealed up the records for the final time, he spoke to "all the ends of the earth," and particularly warned those who would reject the power and gifts of God that they would see him at the bar of God. At that time God would say to them: "Did I not declare my words unto you, which were written by this man, like as one crying from the dead, yea, even as one speaking out of the dust?" (Moroni 10:24, 27). It is indeed a miracle and responsibility to have the Book of Mormon record brought forth out of the ground so that we can hear the powerful testimonies of ancient prophets as speaking out of the dust.

Role of the Gentiles in Bringing Forth the Book of Mormon

Eventually the Gentiles, through the Restoration of the Church and the subsequent missionary program, would be the instruments to uncover these records to share with the world where they "shall hiss forth unto the ends of the earth, for a standard unto my people, which are of the house of Israel" (2 Nephi 29:2; see also 2 Nephi 3:19–20; Moroni 10:28).

The use of the term "Gentile" in the Book of Mormon varies slightly from the Bible. Rather than strictly being the nations who were not Israelites, Gentiles in the Book of Mormon "are generally all those who are not Jews or who did not come from the Jewish people. Thus, by this definition, the Gentiles may include those who are of the blood of Israel but who have lost their identity and been assimilated into non-Jewish nations."[10] In other words, for Book of Mormon prophets looking into the future, the Gentiles appear as non-covenant-abiding peoples living away from the land of Judah (which is what constituted "Jews" for the Nephites), yet in reality they may be literal descendants of the house of Israel. For example, we know that Joseph Smith, the key Gentile figure prophesied to bring forth this record, was actually a descendant of the biblical Joseph and thus a blood member of the house of Israel (see D&C 109:60). But Joseph Smith was a cultural or geographical Gentile leading forth in the "times" or "fulness of the Gentiles."[11] The Book of Mormon also declares that "as many of the Gentiles as will repent are the covenant people of the Lord" (2 Nephi 30:2), so ultimately one's covenant relationship is more important than a lineal one. One of the Book of Mormon's purposes, therefore, is to help all to receive the blessings promised to the house of Israel through covenants, whether originally Jew or Gentile.[12]

In Nephi's early vision of God's future dealings with his people and their land of inheritance (the Americas), he learns from the accompanying angel that the Gentiles will be brought to the Americas and scatter his descendants (see 1 Nephi 13:12–14). Nephi prophesied that after his seed was scattered, the Lord would do a marvelous work through the Gentiles to nourish them in the gospel, thereby blessing his descendants, the Gentiles, and the entire house of Israel as well (see 1 Nephi 22:8–9). As part of this marvelous work, these latter-day Gentiles would bring forth the writings of Lehi's descendants, writings that were "hid up, to come forth unto the Gentiles, by the gift and power of the Lamb" (1 Nephi 13:35). Through this record carried by the Gentiles, Nephi's posterity would not only learn about their fathers but also gain knowledge about Jesus Christ, "and then shall the remnant of our seed know concerning us, how that we came out from Jerusalem, and that they are descendants of the Jews. And the gospel of Jesus Christ shall be declared among them; wherefore, they shall be restored unto the knowledge of their fathers, and also to the knowledge of Jesus Christ, which was had among their fathers" (2 Nephi 30:4–5; see also 1 Nephi 13:38–42; 15:12–14; Ether 12:22).[13] Moreover, they would come to a knowledge of "the covenants of the Father of heaven unto Abraham, saying: In thy seed shall all the kindreds of the earth be blessed" (1 Nephi 22:9). Thus, as "Gentiles" of the last days, ours is the tremendous missionary opportunity to spread these books of scripture and the covenants they contain to all peoples.

One of the initial missionary efforts of the early restored Church was among the Native American tribes in the Kansas Territory of North America in 1830. Terryl Givens has pointed out, "By preaching the Book of Mormon to these Indian tribes, early missionaries had begun the work of conveying to the 'seed' of that New World multitude described in 3 Nephi the record of their own forefathers, fulfilling prophecy, and confirming the advent of the end times."[14] The work that began as a small stone cut out of the mountain without hands continues to fill the earth and bless all nations (see Daniel 2:45; D&C 65:2). The "hastening of the work" further accelerates the efforts of the Church to bring all to the knowledge of God's covenants and thereby fulfill the prophesied role of the Gentiles in the Book of Mormon.[15]

The Lord promises throughout the Book of Mormon that he will remember his covenant with the house of Israel even after (and despite) the role the Gentiles initially play in scattering them. Strong warnings are given to future Gentiles that "the Lord [will] remember the covenant which he made unto Abraham and unto all the house of Israel. And also the Lord will remember the prayers of the righteous, which have been put up unto him for them. And then, O ye Gentiles, how can ye stand before the power of God, except ye shall repent and turn from your evil ways?" (Mormon 5:20–22). Christ, by commandment of the Father, told Lehi's posterity of their descendants' first blessings as a remnant of the house of Israel, as well as the warning for Gentiles to not reject his gospel lest they forfeit the opportunity to receive the same blessings. If they sin against the fulness of his gospel, it will be taken from them and then the Lord will remember his covenant with the house of Israel and bring the gospel to them. "But if the Gentiles will repent and return unto me, saith the Father, behold they shall be numbered among my people, O house of Israel" (3 Nephi 16:13; see also 2 Nephi 6:12 for the promised blessings to repentant Gentiles). Christ's emphasis on these covenant blessings to Lehi's descendants (see 3 Nephi 16; 20–22) helps them realize they are never cast off forever but are heirs to spiritual and temporal blessings.[16]

Lands of Inheritance

A miraculous indication that Lehi's descendants are not cast off forever is that after the gospel has come forth from the Gentiles to the house of Israel, then the entire house of Israel can return to the lands of their inheritance. It is important to note that Book of Mormon passages often speak of multiple *lands* of inheritance rather than the one *land* of inheritance of Israel since Lehi's seed, a broken-off remnant, receive their own promised land.[17] When the Book of Mormon comes forth among the Gentiles, it is a sign that the work of gathering the house of Israel is commencing. Mormon declared that when "these sayings shall come unto the Gentiles according to his word, then ye may know that the covenant which the Father hath made with the children of Israel, concerning their restoration to the lands of their inheritance, is already beginning to be fulfilled" (3 Nephi 29:1; see also 3 Nephi 21:1–7). Elder Russell M. Nelson declared, "In fact, if there were no Book of Mormon, the promised gathering of Israel would not occur."[18] The Book of Mormon not only contains prophecies of the gathering; it also helps bring it about through influencing its readers to "come unto Christ" and embrace the covenants of the gospel (see Moroni 10:30, 32; 2 Nephi 31:17–20; 3 Nephi 27:13–21).

The Lord said through Jacob that once the Jews believed in him, then, because of his covenants with their fathers, they would be restored in the flesh to the lands of their inheritance and the Gentiles would be instrumental in carrying them forth to these lands (see 2 Nephi 10:7–8). In a prophecy of the future New Jerusalem built upon the American continent, Ether saw that not only would the *old* Jerusalem be rebuilt for the house of Israel, but a "*New* Jerusalem should be built up upon this land, unto the remnant of the seed of Joseph" (Ether 13:6; emphasis added).

Nephi summarized his father's teachings on this matter, which included a return to a land of inheritance as well as a restoration of knowledge. Following the scattering of the house of Israel, they would be gathered in *after* the Gentiles had received the fulness of the gospel. Then they would "come to the knowledge of the true Messiah, their Lord and their Redeemer" (1 Nephi 10:14; see also 1 Nephi 15:12–16; Jacob 5:60; 3 Nephi 5:23–26). During his ministry in the land of Bountiful, the resurrected Lord reminded the inhabitants that they were "children of the prophets," "of the house of Israel," and "children of the covenant" (see 3 Nephi 20:25–26). As such, they would help fulfill the promise made to Abraham, "in thy seed shall all the kindreds of the earth be blessed" (3 Nephi 20:27), by being "scattered" and established in a new promised land with a New Jerusalem, where the powers of heaven would be among them, and even Christ would be in the midst of them (see 3 Nephi 20:22). Meanwhile, other members of the house of Israel would be remembered through previous covenants, and they would be gathered together in the Lord's own due time and be given "again the land of their fathers for their inheritance, which is the land of Jerusalem, which is the promised land unto them forever" (3 Nephi 20:29).

Ultimately the gathering would not be just a physical gathering to lands, but a bringing together of all of God's words to his children: the Jews, the Nephites, and the lost tribes, each contributing their respective books of scripture. The Lord promised through Nephi that each group would have the words of the others, and not only would they be gathered into the lands of their possessions, but God's word would be gathered in one. It is another reminder that God will keep his earlier covenant with Abraham and remember his seed forever (see 2 Nephi 29:13–14).

Conclusion

The Book of Mormon is a marvelous work and a wonder. Not only does it recount great things God did for his people during the record keepers' lifetimes and for their forefathers, but its coming forth is a sign of the great things God is doing for the house of Israel, especially Lehi's descendants, in the last days. The Book of Mormon was thus preserved and kept sacred for God's wise purposes so that those remnants of the house of Israel who come in contact with it may know the covenants of the Lord and that they are not cast off forever. One of the key covenant promises is the repeated pledge made to prophets and record keepers (Isaiah, biblical Joseph, Nephi, Enos, and so forth) that this record would come forth in the latter days to serve as an instrument in turning the house of Israel to their Redeemer. In order for this sacred record to come forth, it needed to be preserved from the Lamanites, hid up, and later brought forth to a remnant of their seed through the instrumentality of the Gentiles. In this fashion, all—whether Gentile or of the house of Israel—would have the opportunity to participate in God's covenantal purposes for the house of Israel.

These purposes center on the promised Messiah and his fulfillment of his mission to deliver God's children from physical and spiritual death. Without faith in Christ, the house of Israel and the Gentiles cannot receive the full covenant blessings God has offered them. Moroni, the last of the record keepers, declared that they wrote so that their brethren might be restored to the knowledge of Christ; and this is "according to the prayers of all the saints who have dwelt in the land." He then continued, praying, "May the Lord Jesus Christ grant that their prayers may be answered according to their faith; and may God the Father remember the covenant which he hath made with the house of Israel; and may he bless them forever, through faith on the name of Jesus Christ" (Mormon 9:35–37).

The ultimate goal for the writers of the Book of Mormon record was to help others come unto Christ and receive his redemptive power through making and keeping covenants. These scriptures provide the knowledge of God's covenants, reminders of the great things God has done for his children, and a witness that they are not cast off forever—that they can still participate in the eternal blessings of the plan of salvation through acceptance of Christ.

Nephi summarized it well when he stated, "And at that day shall the remnant of our seed know that they are of the house of Israel, and that they are the covenant people of the Lord; and then shall they know and come to the knowledge of their forefathers, and also to the knowledge of the gospel of their Redeemer, which was ministered unto their fathers by him; wherefore, they shall come to the knowledge of their Redeemer and the very points of his doctrine, that they may know how to come unto him and be saved" (1 Nephi 15:14).

The Book of Mormon has been preserved for *our day* in fulfillment of promises and visions to its ancient record keepers. The invitation and responsibility of every reader of the Book of Mormon, whether of the house of Israel or Gentile, is to accept the covenants contained therein through faith in Christ. Only then can God's purposes be fulfilled and his power revealed. We can then gain the assurance that because of our deliverer, Jesus Christ, we also are not cast off forever.

Notes

1. The fact that Ishmael is a descendant of Ephraim is found in a statement of Erastus Snow recalling the teaching of Joseph Smith. See *Journal of Discourses* (London: Latter-day Saints' Book Depot, 1854–86), 23:184–85. The Mulekites (also known as the people of Zarahemla) descended from Judah through King

Zedekiah (see Omni 1:14–16). The other major people of the Book of Mormon are the Jaredites. Their arrival in the Americas precedes Jacob's life and thus the formation of the house of Israel, although some of the covenants made with them concerning the promised land are the same as those made to the later house of Israel.

2. Steven L. Olsen states that "in Nephi's record, obedience to God's law distinguishes the house of Israel from all other human groups. Membership in the house of Israel is ultimately determined by faithfulness to the covenant with Abraham, including keeping its commandments and receiving its blessings." Steven L. Olsen, "The Covenant of the Chosen People: The Spiritual Foundations of Ethnic Identity in the Book of Mormon," *Journal of the Book of Mormon and Other Restoration Scripture* 21, no. 2 (2012): 19.
3. Or they use a generic phrase like "covenants made to their fathers" (for example, 1 Nephi 19:15; 2 Nephi 11:5).
4. This chapter is the only time Lehi directly quotes from the brass plates and the only time Joseph is singled out from his brother Jacob.
5. Mormon, in his closing words, also understood this close, interwitness relationship between the Bible and the Book of Mormon: "This [the Book of Mormon] is written for the intent that ye may believe that [the Bible]; and if ye believe that ye will believe this also; and if ye believe this ye will know concerning your fathers, and also the marvelous works which were wrought by the power of God among them. And ye will also know that ye are a remnant of the seed of Jacob; therefore ye are numbered among the people of the first covenant" (Mormon 7:9–10).
6. Because of the future writers' faith, any perceived weakness in their words the Lord would make strong "unto the remembering of my covenant which I made unto thy fathers" (v. 21). Biblical Joseph's emphasis on weakness of writing being turned to strength was also brought up by Nephi when he concluded his record (see 2 Nephi 33:4, 11) and Moroni near the end of his writing (see Ether 12:23–27, 40). Thus part of the promise of the future record is that the Lord will make strong whatever weakness in writing the writers felt they had.
7. Grant Hardy includes an insightful chart of correspondences between key terms in 2 Nephi 3 and Nephi's concluding remarks in 2 Nephi 25–33, which seems to indicate that Nephi grew in understanding of the importance of these prophecies in relation to his own record-keeping efforts. See Grant Hardy, *Understanding the Book of Mormon: A Reader's Guide* (Oxford: Oxford University Press, 2010), 80. Hardy also sees Moroni later drawing on biblical Joseph's prophecy to interpret his understanding of the importance and role of this record for the future (see pp. 250–51).
8. Nephi understood that even though he saw the future destruction of his direct seed, a portion of them would be mixed with the seed of his brethren (see 1 Nephi 12–13, 15; 2 Nephi 9:53; 29:2; 30:3–4). Alma prophesied that the future Nephites would become Lamanites, so the promised future opportunities for the Lamanites include Nephite descendants (see Alma 45:13–14). "Thus while the ethnic group called Nephites will not continue forever, his literal descent line will not be completely destroyed." Olsen, "The Covenant of the Chosen People," 17.

9. *Orson Pratt's Works on the Doctrines of the Gospel: The Light of Understanding* (Salt Lake City: Deseret News, 1945), 271.
10. Monte S. Nyman, "Gentile(s)," in *Book of Mormon Reference Companion*, ed. Dennis L. Largey (Salt Lake City: Deseret Book, 2003), 286.
11. "Thus Joseph Smith . . . was the Gentile by whose hand the Book of Mormon came forth, and the members of The Church of Jesus Christ of Latter-day Saints, who have the gospel and who are of Israel by blood descent, are the Gentiles who carry salvation to the Lamanites and to the Jews." Bruce R. McConkie, *The Millennial Messiah: The Second Coming of the Son of Man* (Salt Lake City: Deseret Book, 1982), 233.
12. Grant Underwood concluded that in Church publications before 1846, the most popular topic was "the restoration of Israel" (found 59 times), while the next highest one was "prophecy relating to Gentiles" (37 occurrences). See Grant Underwood, *The Millenarian World of Early Mormonism*, 2nd ed. (Urbana: University of Illinois Press, 1999), 78–79.
13. Grant Hardy wonders what the consolatory prophecies Nephi was receiving must have meant to him: "The Lord had revealed to him that there would be an appreciate audience waiting for him far in the future. In other words, Nephi's mission from God was *not* to unite his family in faithfulness but rather to be a means of 'restor[ing] the preserved of Israel,' to 'be a light to the Gentiles' in bringing salvation 'unto the ends of the earth' (1 Ne. 21:6/Isa. 49:6), and all this would be accomplished through his writing. God had shown Nephi and his book to both Joseph and Isaiah long ago. As Nephi pored over Isaiah 49 and 29, he could say to himself, *I am not a failure; it was part of the plan from the beginning*." See Hardy, *Understanding the Book of Mormon*, 82; emphasis in original.
14. Terryl L. Givens, *By the Hand of Mormon: The American Scripture That Launched a New World Religion* (Oxford: Oxford University Press, 2002), 65.
15. Heather Whittle Wrigley, "Church Leaders Share More Information on Missionary Age Requirement Change," *Church News and Events*, October 6, 2012.
16. Hardy gives a helpful outline of Jesus' instruction about the Father's plan for the salvation of humankind and the role of the house of Israel within it. See Hardy, *Understanding the Book of Mormon*, 199–200. Hardy also sees a shift in Mormon's editing at this point from an "individual salvation" found in the teachings of King Benjamin, Abinadi, Alma, Amulek and others, to "a corporate or collective redemption centered on the restoration of the House of Israel." The resurrected Jesus was there to "save a people, *his* people." (p. 205).
17. The Book of Mormon has many references to Lehi's descendants (seed of Joseph) receiving their own land of inheritance (see 1 Nephi 13:30; 2 Nephi 1:5, 9; 3:2; 10:10, 19–20), including many from the Savior himself when he visited the Nephites (see 3 Nephi 15:13; 16:16; 20:14; 21:22). The Jaredites had earlier been promised this land for their inheritance, but they subsequently lost it due to their unfaithfulness (see Ether 1:38; 2:15). Many passages discuss the *lands* of inheritance when describing the eventual gathering of the house of Israel (see 1 Nephi 22:12; 2 Nephi 6:11; 29:14; 3 Nephi 29:1).
18. Russell M. Nelson, "The Gathering of Scattered Israel," *Ensign*, November 2006, 80.

14

"To the Convincing of the Jew and Gentile that JESUS Is the CHRIST"

Shon D. Hopkin

Shon D. Hopkin is an assistant professor of ancient scripture at Brigham Young University.

There are many purposes identified in the Book of Mormon text for its coming forth (see 1 Nephi 13:40; 15:12–18; 2 Nephi 3:12; 33:4: Ether 8:23–26; Mormon 9:31). The book's central purpose, however, is found on its title page: "to the convincing of the Jew and Gentile that JESUS is the CHRIST, the ETERNAL GOD."[1] Readers can look at each part of this statement—"Jesus is the Christ," "Jew and Gentile," and "to the convincing"—to glean a greater understanding of the Book of Mormon writers' context and purpose in writing. From its first page to its last, it is easy to discern that Jesus is the book's central character and that his divinity is its central message.[2] Truly the Book of Mormon is "Another Testament of Jesus Christ."[3]

"JESUS Is the CHRIST"

The text of the Book of Mormon contains approximately one hundred titles for Jesus. It uses the given name "Jesus" approximately seventy times and the title "Christ" almost four hundred times. What did the Book of Mormon authors mean when they said that Jesus is the Christ or the Messiah?

Book of Mormon writings are unambiguous in defining how the word *Messiah*, and later, *Christ* (the Greek equivalent of the Hebrew *Messiah*) should be understood; the writings are also clear about the kind of Messiah the people should expect. Nephite prophets knew their Messiah not as a powerful leader who would restore their political hopes, but as the "Redeemer" (1 Nephi 10:5) and "Savior of the world" (1 Nephi 10:4). They placed their future hopes for salvation squarely in him (see Mosiah 3:17). The Book of Mormon prophets desired not simply to testify that Jesus is the Christ; they wanted those who heard and read their words to know that he would save them from their sins if they put their trust in him.

The Book of Mormon contains teachings of ancient Israelite prophets such as Zenos, Zenock, and Neum, who taught plain truths about the nature and role of the Messiah. These teachings provide evidence that knowledge about the Messiah existed in ancient Israel (see 1 Nephi 19:10–16 and Alma 33:13–19). Furthermore, Nephite prophets declared that all of the holy Israelite prophets taught about the Messiah (see 1 Nephi 10:5; Jacob 4:4–5; Mosiah 13:33; Alma 33:14; Helaman 8:11–23). Lehi's family's understanding was obtained through direct revelation, either to reinforce existing knowledge, or to provide them with truths that were not known by the majority of Israelites in that day. Before Lehi left Jerusalem (circa 600 BC), he was blessed with a vision of the Messiah (see 1 Nephi 1:9). Lehi later prophesied of the time of the Messiah's coming, baptism, death, resurrection, and mission as Savior and Redeemer of the world (see 1 Nephi 10:4–11).

These early teachings formed the foundation of the Nephite understanding of the Messiah. Visions and revelations given to Nephi (see 1 Nephi 11:20–33) and Jacob (see 2 Nephi 10:3) reinforced and augmented Lehi's teachings and influenced the way that Nephite prophets read and taught the words of Israelite prophets such as Isaiah (see 1 Nephi 19:23; 2 Nephi 11:2). Later prophets such as King Benjamin (see Mosiah 3), Alma (see Alma 33), Samuel (see Helaman 13), Mormon (see Mormon 7), Moroni (see Mormon 8–9), and others continued building upon this early foundation.[4] Jesus' personal visit to Book of Mormon peoples in 3 Nephi fulfilled all earlier Messianic hopes and expectations.

There are many explanations for why the Nephite teachings about the Messiah are so much more pointed and clear than those found in the Old Testament. Nephi explained that he saw the loss of many "plain and precious things" from the biblical record (1 Nephi 13:28). He expressed a preference for "plainness" (2 Nephi 25:4) in teaching that likely influenced later Book of Mormon prophets. Perhaps the greatest influence on the Christ-centered teachings of the Book of Mormon, though, is the book's future-oriented nature. The main Nephite prophet-writers of the Book of Mormon—Nephi, Mormon, and Moroni—saw this day and wrote directly to modern readers (see 1 Nephi 14:23–28; Mormon 7:1–10; Mormon 8:34–35), anticipating their most pressing needs and the best ways to reach them. As stated by President Ezra Taft Benson, "[One] reason why we must make the Book of Mormon a center focus of study is that it was written for our day. The Nephites never had the book; neither did the Lamanites of ancient times. It was meant for us. . . . Each of the major writers of the Book of Mormon testified that he wrote for future generations."[5] The Book of Mormon authors primarily identified this modern audience, as described on the title page, as "Jew and Gentile."

"Jew and Gentile"

What did the titles "Jew" and "Gentile" signify for the Book of Mormon authors? Although the Book of Mormon was written "to the convincing of the Jew and Gentile," elsewhere on the title page and in the Book of Mormon the text broadens this dual designation to include three distinct groups: Jews, Gentiles, and descendants of Lehi (known in the latter days by the title "Lamanites"; see title page; 1 Nephi 13:39). Together these three groups constitute "all men" (1 Nephi 6:4). This three-fold division can be clearly seen in the teachings of Nephi (see 1 Nephi 13:38–39; 2 Nephi 25–26, 30), Mormon (see Words of Mormon 1:8; 3 Nephi 29–30; Mormon 7:1–10), and Moroni (see Mormon 8–9).

The title "Jews" in the Book of Mormon is affixed to individuals from Jerusalem who would be destroyed and taken captive by the Babylonians (see 2 Nephi 6:8; 25:9–10), individuals who would be delivered from Babylonian captivity and return to build up Jerusalem (see 2 Nephi 6:9; 25:11), and individuals who would reject the Messiah and consequently be scattered into all the world (see 2 Nephi 6:9–11; 25:12–16). The Lord would bring forth the Book of Mormon, "convincing them of the true Messiah," the one they first rejected (2 Nephi 25:17–18). Lehi's posterity, who were descendants of Joseph of Egypt, can also rightfully be identified as Jews because they were citizens of the Kingdom of Judah—they came out of Jerusalem (see 2 Nephi 33:8). In this sense Lehi's posterity can be identified as a "subset" of the Jews, and the designation "Jew and Gentile" would then represent all of God's children.

The "Gentiles" are associated with those who were led by God to the Americas (see 2 Nephi 13:12–19), those who persecuted the descendants of the Jews and the Lamanites (see 1 Nephi 13; 2 Nephi 29:5; 3 Nephi 29:8), those who would live in a day of wickedness and apostasy (see 2 Nephi 27:1; 28), those who would receive the fullness of the gospel and carry the Book of Mormon to others (see 1 Nephi 13:38; 15:13–16; 2 Nephi 30:3), and those who would be identified today as Christians (see 1 Nephi 13:19–23; 2 Nephi 26:20). The Gentiles are commanded to "hear the words of Jesus Christ, the Son of the living God" so that they "may be numbered with [Christ's] people who are of the house of Israel" (3 Nephi 30:1–2). Within Nephi's last recorded words in the Book of Mormon, he wrote, "And as I spake concerning the convincing of the Jews, that Jesus is the very Christ, it must needs be that the Gentiles be convinced also that Jesus is the Christ, the Eternal God" (2 Nephi 26:12). For some among the Gentiles, this convincing consists of clarifying and augmenting their knowledge in the true Christ of the Bible, a God who continues to work great miracles according to the faith of humankind (see Mormon 9:6–7).

"To the Convincing": Why?

Why was a scriptural account needed to convince the world of the mission of Jesus the Christ? The Book of Mormon prophetically anticipates a time when "Jew and Gentile" would either not believe in Christ, or would believe in a Christ whose identity had become diluted and distorted. Its prophets recognized a need to "convince" that audience of the true nature of Jesus Christ. As recipients of the Book of Mormon and the teachings of modern prophets, most Latter-day Saints understand Christ's biblical identity through that lens. Although they are aware that most Jews do not believe in Jesus as the Christ, some Latter-day Saints are not aware of how some modern scholarship has drawn varying conclusions regarding the truthfulness and meaning of biblical accounts, based in part on evidence of problems with early biblical manuscripts.

In his best-selling book, *Misquoting Jesus: The Story Behind Who Changed the Bible and Why*, influential biblical scholar Bart Ehrman openly describes the challenge to his faith in the biblical message when he confronted the varying witnesses of ancient texts. Ehrman states:

> In short, my study of the Greek New Testament, and my investigations into the manuscripts that contain it, led to a radical rethinking of my understanding of what the Bible is. This was a seismic change for me. Before this . . . my faith had been based completely on a certain view of the Bible as the fully inspired, inerrant word of God. Now I no longer saw the Bible that way. The Bible began to appear to me as a very human book. Just as human scribes had copied, and changed, the texts of scripture, so too had human authors originally *written* the texts of scripture. This was a human book from beginning to end. . . . It is a radical shift from reading the Bible as an inerrant blueprint for our faith, life, and future to seeing it as a very human book, with very human points of view, many of which differ from one another and none of which provides the inerrant guide to how we should live. This is the shift in my own thinking that I ended up making, and to which I am now fully committed.[6]

Although many biblical scholars remain fully committed to faith in Jesus' divinity, others have viewed differences within the biblical text and among ancient biblical manuscripts as evidence that Jesus' original identity was obscured or altered by later believers; these scholars have made numerous proposals regarding that original identity, including that he was a simple, peasant reformer,[7] a Cynic philosopher,[8] or even a magician.[9]

Because Nephi envisions a time when truths would be lost from the Bible (see 1 Nephi 13:26–27), most Latter-day Saints would not completely reject the claims of these scholars, recognizing that the Bible's message regarding Jesus may be at least partially incomplete, needing support and clarification. The Book of Mormon message was designed by its ancient authors to provide precisely that type of support, clarifying and strengthening the biblical message of Jesus as the divine Son of God (see 1 Nephi 13:40–41). Book of Mormon authors saw and anticipated this need and crafted their message "to the convincing of the Jew and Gentile" in the last days.

The primary goal was not simply to witness that Jesus is the Messiah; it was to *convince* the reader of the truth of that witness. Under the direction of the Lord, the Book of Mormon prophets maintained a clear vision of this goal, and they purposefully and strategically crafted their message to give future audiences the greatest possible chance of being persuaded by that witness. This truth can be seen when tracing the passing of the plates from author to author. The first prophet-writer of the Book of Mormon, Nephi, openly describes his goals early in his account: "For the *fulness* of mine intent is that I may persuade men to come unto the God of Abraham, and the God of Isaac, and the God of Jacob, and be saved" (1 Nephi 6:4, emphasis added). After stating his intent, he gives clear directions: "Wherefore, I shall give commandment unto my seed, that they shall not occupy these plates with things which are not of worth unto the children of men" (1 Nephi 6:6). This "commandment"—to use the plates in order to persuade men to come unto Christ—had a direct impact on the writing of those who would follow. The thread is explicit from Nephi (see 2 Nephi 33:4) to Jacob (see Jacob 1:1–4, 7) to Enos (see Jacob 7:27), to Amaleki (see Omni 1:26), through Mormon's Christ-centered abridgment of the "large" plates of Nephi, to Moroni's closing words (see Moroni 10:30, 32).

"To the Convincing": How?

Book of Mormon authors such as Nephi (see 1 Nephi 6:6), Mormon (see Helaman 3:14; Mormon 5:8; 3 Nephi 26:6), Moroni (see Ether 15:53), and others (see Jarom 1:14; Jacob 3:13) show a sensitivity to space limitations on the plates. Mormon repeats three different times the idea that "this book cannot contain even a hundredth part of what was done" (3 Nephi 5:8).[10] In these statements, they are emphasizing that the concepts that they choose to include are vitally important, and that their choices were made through the filtering lens of their overarching purposes. With these special limitations in mind, the concepts they chose to include regarding Christ take on increased significance, not simply as details included by happenchance, but as purposeful additions targeting precisely those areas in which their audience's understanding of the Savior would need to be strengthened.

How did the various authors of the Book of Mormon carry out their explicitly stated mission to convince and persuade? The remainder of this chapter will provide examples of how the Book of Mormon convinces readers to come unto Christ listed under seven subheadings. The subheadings were conceived through analysis of the interaction between three variables: purpose, audience, and text.

1. Authors affirm key biblical events in Jesus' life, including the virgin birth, his baptism, his miracles, his Atoning sacrifice, his Crucifixion, and his Resurrection.

The Book of Mormon prophets have little to say regarding Jesus' parables or the details of his conflict with the Jewish leaders of his time. The only repetition of teachings from his mortal ministry come directly from Jesus himself during his visits in 3 Nephi 11–28, centering most prominently on the Sermon on the Mount (see Matthew 5–8; 3 Nephi 12–14). When the Book of Mormon prophets do speak of Christ's mortal ministry, they instead choose to confirm its central events. True to Nephi's desire for "plainness" (1 Nephi 13:29), the examples they provide are not ambiguous or open to multiple interpretations. They result from visions (see 1 Nephi 1:8; 1 Nephi 11) or direct revelation, often through the teachings of angels (see 1 Nephi 19:8; 2 Nephi 6:9; Mosiah 4:1). These confirmations are primarily provided by Nephi (see 1 Nephi 11); Benjamin (see Mosiah 3); Abinadi (see Mosiah 15); Alma (see Alma 7); and Jesus himself (see 3 Nephi 11); with key events also affirmed by Lehi (see 1 Nephi 1; 10); Jacob (see 2 Nephi 9); Zenos, Zenock, and Neum (see 1 Nephi 19:10); Amulek (see Alma 34); and Samuel (see Helaman 13).

The book begins with Lehi's vision of "one descending out of the midst of heaven" (1 Nephi 1:9). Nephi, King Benjamin, and Alma all teach of Jesus' descent from heaven and of the virgin birth through his mortal mother, Mary (see 1 Nephi 11:13–21; Mosiah 3:8; Alma 7:10). Lehi also speaks of the ministry of John the Baptist (see 1 Nephi 10:7–8), who would baptize Jesus "in Bethabara, beyond Jordan" (1 Nephi 10:9). Nephi writes of John (see 1 Nephi 11:27), teaching that he would perform Jesus' baptism "by water, to fulfil all righteousness" (2 Nephi 31:5), and that the Holy Ghost would come as a confirming witness "in the form of a dove" (1 Nephi 11:27; 2 Nephi 31:8). Lehi and Nephi both provide witness of the calling and ministry of the twelve apostles (see 1 Nephi 1:10; 11:29; 12:9). Abinadi affirms that Jesus worked "many mighty miracles among the children of men" (Mosiah 15:6). Nephi speaks of the healing of the sick and casting out of devils (see 1 Nephi 11:31), and Benjamin adds that these miracles would include "healing the sick, raising the dead, causing the lame to walk, the blind to receive their sight, and the deaf to hear, and curing all manner of diseases. And he shall cast out devils" (Mosiah 3:5–6).

Book of Mormon prophets testified of the suffering Jesus experienced, in order "to succor" (Alma 7:12) his people, teaching that he "suffereth himself to be mocked, and scourged, and cast out, and disowned by his people," as had been taught by Isaiah (Mosiah 15:5, explaining Isaiah 53). The book emphasizes the depth of his suffering, including "temptations, and pain of body, hunger, thirst, and fatigue, even more than man can suffer, except it be unto death" (Mosiah 3:7; see also Alma 7:11), confirming the witness from the Gospel of Luke (see Luke 22:44) that "blood cometh from every pore" (Mosiah 3:7) due to the depth of his anguish. Most significantly, multiple Book of Mormon prophets affirm the reality of Jesus' judgment at the hands of the Jewish leaders, his crucifixion and death, and his resurrection from the dead (see 1 Nephi 10:11; 11:32–33; 19:10; Mosiah 3:9–10; 15:7; Alma 7:12; Helaman 14:15; 3 Nephi 11:11–15; and others). Such affirmation is one of the ways in which Book of Mormon authors seek to convince readers that Jesus is the Christ.

2. Authors affirm, clarify, and strengthen key biblical teachings regarding the role and identity of Christ, including his divinity, his earthly mortality, and his ability to comprehend all because of his suffering and his substitutionary Atonement.

Although the Book of Mormon's witness of key events from Jesus' life is important as a joint-witness with the Bible, its main purpose in recounting these events is to testify of Christ's identity. The main purpose for teaching of Jesus' descent from heaven and miraculous birth is to witness that he is God (see Mosiah 13:28; Ether 3:14), the Son of God who was born into mortality (see 1 Nephi 11:7; Mosiah 3:8; 15:2; Alma 34:2–5; Helaman 3:28; 3 Nephi 20:31; Mormon 9:22; and many others). Jesus is not only the Son of God, due to his mortal birth, but is also the Everlasting Father (see 2 Nephi 19:6) due to his conception "by the power of God" and his acceptance of his Father's will (Mosiah 15:2–3; 3 Nephi 1:14), his role as Creator (see Mosiah 3:8; 4:2), and his ability through the Atonement to provide spiritual rebirth to fallen mankind (see Mosiah 5:7). Thus, in this context, he is both the

Father and the Son (see Mosiah 15:2–3; Mormon 9:12; Ether 3:14), often referred to as the Son of God, the Father of heaven and earth (see Mosiah 3:8; Helaman 14:12; 16:18; Ether 4:7).

Book of Mormon prophets emphasized his mortal suffering and crucifixion in order to persuade their readers that Jesus had atoned for their sins. The writers emphasized this so that readers could receive forgiveness through faith in his name and so that they would know that there was one who could understand their own sufferings (see Mosiah 15:7; Alma 7:11–12; 34:8–9). The writers repeatedly pointed to the reality of his resurrection so that their readers would believe that he could save them from death (see 2 Nephi 9:5–6; Alma 40:2–3). They regularly used titles for Jesus that point to his role as the one who would rescue humankind, purchasing everyone through the blood of his atoning sacrifice. Clear, pointed titles in the Book of Mormon include "Savior" (12 times), "Messiah" (32 times), the "Lamb of God" (35 times), "Redeemer" (41 times), "Son of God" (51 times), and Messiah's Greek equivalent "Christ" (385 times). Their description of Jesus Christ was designed, much like the Book of Hebrews in the New Testament, to produce awe in his majesty, reverence for his sacrifice, peace and comfort from his suffering, and faith in his power to save. There is no space provided in the Book of Mormon for any debate over identity—he is the Son of God and Savior of the world, not a magician, peasant revolutionary, philosopher, or simply a great moral teacher. Book of Mormon prophets learned of Jesus' identity through vision and revelation. Their witness would either be believed or disbelieved by future readers, but it leaves no room to be misunderstood.

3. Authors speak as true, historical witnesses—witnesses who have either seen Jesus face-to-face or have experienced his miraculous power in their own lives.

An important part of the convincing power of the Book of Mormon prophets is their personal, direct proclamation that they have experienced Jesus' ability to save and that they stand as personal witnesses of his reality. Many of these prophets saw Jesus face-to-face, confirming the New Testament witnesses of Jesus' divinity and his resurrection. Examples of Book of Mormon prophets and other individuals in the narrative who either had personal visions of Christ or who heard his voice include Lehi (see 1 Nephi 1:9), Nephi (see 1 Nephi 11:21; 2 Nephi 11:2), Jacob (see 2 Nephi 11:3), Enos (see Enos 1:10), Alma the Elder (see Mosiah 26:14), King Lamoni (see Alma 19:13), Ammon (see Alma 20:2), Alma the Younger (see Alma 36:22), Samuel (see Helaman 13:3), others named Nephi (see Helaman 10; 3 Nephi 1; 11), Mormon (see Mormon 1:15; 3:14), over 2,500 present during Jesus' visitation (see 3 Nephi 17:25), the brother of Jared (see Ether 3:20), and Moroni (see Ether 12:39). During his discourse on faith, Moroni encourages all to believe that they can also come to know Christ, listing numerous witnesses who have seen him and promising readers that this can be the result of their faith (see Ether 12:7, 8, 12, 19–21, 31, 39).

Not only do they testify that they have seen or heard Christ, the Book of Mormon prophets also regularly record the change that was effected in their own lives or the lives of others through Jesus Christ. For example, Enos related that his sins were swept away because of this faith in Jesus Christ (see Enos 1:5–8). Providing one of the most poignant experiences in the Book of Mormon, Alma the Younger states:

> I cried within my heart: O Jesus, thou Son of God, have mercy on me, who am in the gall of bitterness, and am encircled about by the everlasting chains of death.
>
> And now, behold, when I thought this, I could remember my pains no more; yea, I was harrowed up by the memory of my sins no more.
>
> And oh, what joy, and what marvelous light I did behold; yea, my soul was filled with joy as exceeding as was my pain!
>
> Yea, I say unto you, my son, that there could be nothing so exquisite and so bitter as were my pains. Yea, and again I say unto you, my son, that on the other hand, there can be nothing so exquisite and sweet as was my joy. (Alma 36:18–21)

King Benjamin's people received a mighty change of heart (see Mosiah 5:2), the burdens of Alma the Elder's people were lightened by God (see Mosiah 24:13–15), Zeezrom had a miraculous recovery and discovered joy in Christ (see Alma 15:10–11), Ammon was overcome by his joy in Christ (see Alma 27:17–18), and Ammon's people declared that God took away their guilt (see Alma 24:12).

All of these experiences can be seen as preparatory for the most sublime of scenes in the Book of Mormon—the appearance of the resurrected

Savior to his people. Jesus teaches them, prays with them, and heals their children. He loves them and provides them with unforgettable experiences (see 3 Nephi 11–28).

These witnesses of Christ are provided by real people who understood their joy as coming directly from Christ. They write glowingly and powerfully of their experiences, persuasively giving evidence of the joy and peace that come through Jesus Christ. Reading their stories and experiences personalizes the Christ-centered message of the Book of Mormon for its readers.

4. Authors nuance their discourse depending on their audience, whether Jew or Gentile, to emphasize doctrinal points, evidences, future events, and invitations that will be particularly important to that group.

The Book of Mormon authors purposefully wrote for three future audiences—Jews, Gentiles, and "Lamanites"—and nuanced their message in different ways to focus on the varying needs of those three groups (or those two groups, if the future "Lamanites"—actually a composite of Lamanite and Nephite descendants—are considered a subset of the "Jews"). Since they desired to write to "all men" (2 Nephi 26:27–30), many of their words to each group can be generalized to all, giving all an invitation to come unto Christ. Yet the focus of their discourse to each group shows an awareness of the types of evidences and invitations that will most effectively communicate with each broad group.

To the Jews

As the first author of the Book of Mormon, Nephi shows an awareness of the needs of varying groups early in his record. The account of his family's journey to the promised land connects with exodus themes that would have been particularly familiar to his Jewish audience. Laman and Lemuel do not simply disagree with or fight against the journey, they "murmur" against the journey's designated leaders (see Exodus 15:24; 1 Nephi 2:11–12; 3:5, 31; 4:4; 16:3; 17:17, 22, 49; 18:16; 2 Nephi 5:3). They are led through the wilderness by the Liahona, paralleling God's guidance in the cloud and the pillar of fire (see Exodus 13:21; 1 Nephi 16). Rather than being given manna from heaven and water out of a rock, their meat is made sweet in the midst of their adversities (see Exodus 16–17; 1 Nephi 17:2). Like Moses, Nephi went up on a mount and brought a pattern back down (see Exodus 19; 1 Nephi 17:7–17). There is the crossing of water in a miraculous fashion (see Exodus 14; 1 Nephi 18). They are moving towards a promised land (see 1 Nephi 2:20). Nephi's discourse consistently refers to Moses and the miracles that were wrought at his hands (see 1 Nephi 4:1–5), connecting with future Jewish readers.

Nephi turns almost exclusively in 2 Nephi to discursive efforts of persuasion regarding the identity of Christ. In 2 Nephi 11 he restates his primary goal: "My soul delighteth in proving unto my people that save Christ should come all men must perish" (v. 6). He then quotes extensively from Isaiah in order to provide a foundation for his efforts. This lengthy quotation from the great Jewish prophet prepares the way for his discourse to his "brethren" (2 Nephi 25:20), the Jews.

Nephi begins that discourse (in 2 Nephi 25) by stating that he has lived in Jerusalem, and understands the Jews clearly because of that background (see 2 Nephi 25:1–6). He is thus able to direct his comments to them using the full force of that understanding. He describes the long history of persecution to which the Jewish people have been subjected "from generation to generation according to their iniquities" (v. 9), including the Babylonian destruction and the future return of the Jews to their land. The Jews will fail to recognize the true Messiah for whom they so anxiously wait. Nephi describes who that Messiah is—the one that will be crucified by them and then will rise from the dead (vv. 12–13). He then goes on to describe the Roman destruction of the Jews and their scattering abroad by many nations (v. 15).

Nephi, having come "out from Jerusalem" (2 Nephi 25:5; 33:8), identifies with the concerns of the future Jewish people who find themselves scattered throughout the world, and he then states the solution: God will proceed to do a marvelous work in the last days. The marvel will begin with the publication of "his words [the Book of Mormon] unto them . . . for the purpose of convincing them of the true Messiah, who was rejected by them" (v. 18). He uses messianic examples with which the Jews would identify—the story of the brass serpent and the bringing of water from a rock by Moses—to testify that "there is none other name given under heaven save it be this Jesus Christ, of which I have spoken, whereby man can be saved" (v. 20). After all his efforts to identify who the Messiah is that the modern Jews should worship, this is his most pointed statement: he provides the name by which the Messiah would be recognized in the last days, "Jesus Christ" (v. 19), speaking to the Jews in language that they could recognize.[11] Nephi leaves no space for misunderstanding to whom he is referring.[12]

Other Book of Mormon prophets used Nephi's model for persuading the Jews, using language with which they would identify. They recount the Jews' Babylonian captivity and return, their rejection of the Messiah and subsequent scattering, and call them to believe in Christ in the last days, clearly identifying him as the crucified Son of God (see, for example, Lehi's teaching in 1 Nephi 10:2–11 and Jacob's teachings in 2 Nephi 6–10). Additionally, they rely on Old Testament stories such as the brazen serpent (see Alma 33:19–20; 37:46; Helaman 8:14–15) and Abraham's near-sacrifice of Isaac (see Jacob 4:5), on the Messianic nature of the law of Moses sacrifices (see Jacob 4:5; Mosiah 13:31; Alma 34:13; 3 Nephi 15:4–6), and on the teachings of Old Testament prophets such as Isaiah (see 2 Nephi 7–8; Mosiah 13; 3 Nephi 22) to show that their own prophets of old had foreseen the mission of Jesus Christ, stating that "all the holy prophets" had taught of him (Jacob 4:4; Mosiah 15:11; Alma 30:44; 3 Nephi 1:26; 26:3).

Jacob's use of Zenos's allegory of the olive tree (see Jacob 4–6) and Abinadi's use of Isaiah 53 (see Mosiah 12–15) both stand as exemplary efforts to draw the Jews into the message of the Book of Mormon. After using the allegory of the olive tree to show how the Jews, "after having rejected the sure foundation, can ever build upon it, that it may become the head of their corner" (Jacob 4:17), Jacob concludes with a last persuasive effort. He provides an account of Sherem, one who held rigidly to the precepts of the law of Moses, and who accuses the Nephite Christians of converting "the law of Moses into the worship of a being which ye say shall come many hundred years hence" (Jacob 7:7), mirroring Jewish concerns. In the end, Sherem becomes convinced that Christ will come and confesses the truth of Christ before the people (see Jacob 7:17). Abinadi shows from their own scriptures that the Messiah would suffer the sins of all people (see Mosiah 14:6; Isaiah 53:6) in order to save "his seed" (Mosiah 14:10; Isaiah 53:10).

To the Gentiles

After directly addressing the Jews in 2 Nephi 25, Nephi turns to repeat prophecies concerning the future of the Gentiles that he had already provided from his vision (see 1 Nephi 13–14). Nephi states, "As I spake concerning the convincing of the Jews, that Jesus is the very Christ, it must needs be that the Gentiles be convinced also that Jesus is the Christ, the Eternal God" (2 Nephi 26:12). The nuanced difference is crucial: the Jews need to be convinced that Jesus is the Christ; the Gentiles need to be convinced of the correct identity of Jesus Christ, "the Eternal God."

Nephi begins by recounting how the Gentiles would persecute the descendants of Lehi, and how the Gentiles would be lifted up in the pride of their eyes to build "up many churches; nevertheless, they put down the power and miracles of God, and preach up unto themselves their own wisdom and their own learning, that they may get gain and grind upon the face of the poor" (2 Nephi 26:20). The problem is Gentile apostasy and wickedness, and Nephi again proclaims that the solution is the "marvelous work and a wonder" that will be initiated with the coming forth of the Book of Mormon (2 Nephi 27:26). He foresees all of the reasons why the Gentiles might reject the convincing message of the Book of Mormon: divisive loyalty to their own religious denominations (see 2 Nephi 28:3), a denial of the Holy Ghost (v. 4), a denial of miracles (v. 5), a misunderstanding of God's mercy and justice that denies a need to repent (vv. 7–8), pride (v. 9), false teachers (v. 9), false doctrines (v. 9), and a sense of loyalty to the Bible that does not allow for additional revelation (see 2 Nephi 29:4). His words are designed to counteract these powerful influences, and to persuade the Gentiles to open their hearts to the miraculous, revelatory message of the Book of Mormon. He speaks directly to them, crying out, "O, ye Gentiles" (v. 5).

In fact, Nephi promises that repentant Gentiles can become numbered among the house of Israel (see 2 Nephi 29:2). He then finishes his lengthy, persuasive discourse, speaking of both Jews and Gentiles. He shows how, preparatory to the millennium of peace, the important division will not be between Jew and Gentile, but will instead be between the righteous and the wicked (see 2 Nephi 26:10). Nephi is working to draw both groups together into faith in Christ, so that they can be saved rather than destroyed at the second coming.

Both Mormon (see 3 Nephi 29) and Moroni (see Mormon 8–9; Ether 12; Moroni 10) also speak directly to the Gentiles, repeating themes first introduced by Nephi, warning them of their future state of pride and wickedness, and promising them inclusion with the house of Israel if they will repent (see 3 Nephi 30:2).

5. Authors reveal the weaknesses and challenges of each audience, stating them plainly in ways that could only be possible if God had truly spoken to them, seeking to build trust with that audience in the reality that God exists and knows them.

As discussed, Nephi and other prophets speak plainly to the Jews and Gentiles about their future sins and state of blindness, boldly demonstrating that the writers knew their readers' hearts hundreds of years before any would read their words. This emphasis on a prophetic knowledge of hidden things matches an effective approach used by Amulek, and was possibly included in the Book of Mormon in order to model one of its methods to persuade and convince. When preaching to the hard-hearted Zeezrom, Amulek reveals things about Zeezrom that he could only have known through revelation. Zeezrom is shocked by this evidence that God really does exist and knows him (see Alma 11:46; 12:3). The awareness that his sins are real and are not hidden from God precipitates a crisis of faith for Zeezrom that leads him to be healed by faith in Christ (see Alma 15:5–12).

Both Mormon (see 3 Nephi 29–30) and Moroni's messages to the Gentiles show a detailed awareness of the challenges that the Gentiles will face. In the first of three farewell addresses, Moroni reveals conditions that will exist in the day the Book of Mormon comes forth (see Mormon 8:26–32). In that day there will be murderous, secret combinations (v. 27), and the people will be full of all types of sin (v. 31). Presumably addressing an audience who will be identified as Christians, Moroni foretells that many churches will exist, some designed purposefully for material gain (vv. 32–33). The people will pollute "the holy church of God" (vv. 36–38) and ignore those in true need (v. 39). After briefly addressing a group who does not believe in Christ (see Mormon 9:1–6)—possibly either the Jews or Gentile nonbelievers—Moroni returns to those who believe in Jesus, but deny "the revelations of God," saying that they are "done away." They would also deny the gifts of the Spirit and God's miracles (v. 7). He invites them to repent and to believe in a God of miracles (v. 27). He foresees that some will be tempted to reject his words because of perceived imperfections (v. 31), a concern that is forcefully repeated in his second farewell address (see Ether 12). In Moroni's final farewell (see Moroni 10), he gives a warning, that he—the prophet who knows the desires of their hearts—will meet readers of the Book of Mormon at the judgment day (v. 34). The Book of Mormon prophets' demonstration of a knowledge of hidden things may be—at least in part—an effort to reach a hardened future audience whose sins are exposed by the book in miraculous ways.

6. Through the authors' efforts in recording scripture, in speaking to a future audience, and in seeking revelation on their behalf, they build the audience's trust in their loving message regarding Christ.

The overwhelming sentiment that prevails throughout the Book of Mormon is of loyalty to God and of deep love and concern for those of the last days. Throughout the often momentous challenges of their daily lives, the Book of Mormon prophets struggled valiantly and humbly to engrave scriptures that would not be used by their own people. Deeply aware of their weakness as they worked to engrave their words upon a limited supply of plates of metal, they openly confessed their own flaws (see 2 Nephi 33:1; Ether 12:24) but forged ahead, proclaiming their love for a future generation. Nephi wrote: "I have charity for the Jew. . . . I also have charity for the Gentiles" (2 Nephi 33:3, 8–9). Moroni confirms the love of Book of Mormon prophets for future generations: "And [God] knoweth their prayers, that they were in behalf of their brethren" (Mormon 8:24). Moroni's love is palpable in his final farewell address, pleading with a future people to "come unto Christ, and be perfected in him" (Moroni 10:32). Although they were bold in their denunciation of sin, they understood the principle that Joseph Smith would later teach: "Nothing is so much calculated to lead people to forsake sin as to take them by the hand, and watch over them with tenderness. When persons manifest the least kindness and love to me, O what power it has over my mind."[13]

"Come unto Christ"

7. Authors extend direct invitations, again and again choosing to not let the readers rest comfortably, but

instead confronting them with the need to either accept or reject the invitation to "come unto Christ."

Throughout their record, Book of Mormon prophets do not allow the work to sit as a mere intellectual curiosity for the reader. They constantly challenge the reader to take notice of their message. The miraculous nature of the Book of Mormon prompts the readers to make a choice to accept that the book's message of Christ is true. The writers recognized that many would reject that message because of future barriers to faith and disbelief in miracles, but they reached out from beyond the grave, calling to their readers not simply to believe in Christ, but to act on their faith in Christ. This chapter will conclude with a few of their persuasive calls, provided in the words of the ancient Book of Mormon witnesses:

> **Nephi:** "Hearken unto these words and believe in Christ" (2 Nephi 33:10).
>
> **Amaleki:** "Come unto Christ, who is the Holy One of Israel, and partake of his salvation, and the power of his redemption. Yea, come unto him, and offer your whole souls as an offering unto him, and continue in fasting and praying, and endure to the end; and as the Lord liveth ye will be saved" (Omni 1:26).
>
> **Alma:** "Behold, I say unto you, that the good shepherd doth call you; yea, and in his own name he doth call you, which is the name of Christ. . . . Come and be baptized unto repentance, that ye also may be partakers of the fruit of the tree of life" (Alma 5:38, 62).
>
> **Mormon:** "Hear the words of Jesus Christ, the Son of the living God" (3 Nephi 30:1).
>
> **Moroni:** "I would commend you to seek this Jesus of whom the prophets and apostles have written" (Ether 12:41). "Again I would exhort you that ye would come unto Christ. . . . Yea, come unto Christ, and be perfected in him" (Moroni 10:30, 32).
>
> **Jesus Christ:** "Arise, and come . . . unto me" (3 Nephi 11:14).

Page after page, the Book of Mormon carefully and persistently, even relentlessly, works toward the goal that is finally expressed by Moroni's title page, showing that it was written "to the convincing of the Jew and Gentile that JESUS is the CHRIST."[14]

Notes

1. Moroni has typically been understood as the author of the title page, since he was the Book of Mormon prophet who "sealed up" (title page) the book for future generations. His words, however, closely follow Mormon's statement directed to the book's latter-day readers, found in 3 Nephi 29 (to the Jews) and 3 Nephi 30 (to the Gentiles). See Daniel H. Ludlow, "Book of Mormon, title page of," in Dennis L. Largey, ed., *Book of Mormon Reference Companion* (Salt Lake City: Deseret Book, 2003), 155–56.
2. This paper is not the first to propose the centrality of this message. See, among many others: Jo Ann H. Seely, "Book of Mormon, Purposes of: To the Convincing of the Jew and Gentile that Jesus is the Christ," in *Book of Mormon Reference Companion*, 141–42; Daniel L. Ludlow, "Book of Mormon, Selected Themes of: Come unto Christ," in *Book of Mormon Reference Companion*, 147–49; Jeffrey R. Holland, *Christ and the New Covenant: The Messianic Message of the Book of Mormon* (Salt Lake City: Deseret Book, 1997); John W. Welch, "Jesus Christ in the Scriptures: Jesus Christ in the Book of Mormon," in *Encyclopedia of Mormonism* (New York: Macmillan, 1992), 748–50; Stephen Scharffs, "Unique Insights on Christ from the Book of Mormon," in *Ensign*, December 1988, 8–13; Susan Easton Black, *Finding Christ Through the Book of Mormon* (Salt Lake City: Deseret Book, 1987); Ezra Taft Benson, "The Book of Mormon—Keystone of Our Religion," *Ensign*, November 1986, 4–7; B. H. Roberts, "Christ in the Book of Mormon," *Improvement Era*, January 1924, 188–92.
3. "You should know also that by recent decision of the Brethren the Book of Mormon will henceforth bear the title 'The Book of Mormon,' with the subtitle 'Another Testament of Jesus Christ.'" Boyd K. Packer, "Scriptures," *Ensign*, November 1982, 53.
4. The small plates appear to have shaped the remainder of Mormon's work. Mormon explained what it was about the small plates that drew him to their message: "The things which are upon these plates pleasing me, *because of the prophecies of the coming of Christ*; . . . wherefore, I chose these things" (Words of Mormon 1:4–5, emphasis added). Mormon's first indication of his overarching purposes is found in this section, and is stated almost as clearly as Nephi's had been: "My [Mormon's] prayer to God is concerning my brethren [the latter-day Lamanite descendants], that they may once again come to the knowledge of God, yea, the redemption of Christ" (verse 8). For an in-depth study of the difficult bridges in Words of Mormon, and what they might have meant for the original organization of the text on the plates, see Jack M. Lyon and Kent R. Minson, "When Pages Collide: Dissecting the Words of Mormon," in *BYU Studies* 51, no. 4 (2012): 120–36.
5. Benson, "Keystone of Our Religion."
6. Bart D. Ehrman, *Misquoting Jesus: The Story Behind Who Changed the Bible and Why* (New York: HarperCollins, 2005), 11–13.
7. John Dominic Crossan, *The Historical Jesus: The Life of a Mediterranean Jewish Peasant* (San Francisco: Harper, 1991).

8. Burton L. Mack, *The Lost Gospel: The Book of Q & Christian Origins* (San Francisco: Harper, 1993).
9. Morton Smith, *Jesus the Magician* (New York: Harper & Row, 1978).
10. This nonbiblical saying actually appears to be a type of stock phrase among the Nephites to indicate the editing challenges they faced. It is stated three different times by Mormon (see also Helaman 3:14, 3 Nephi 5:8, and 3 Nephi 26:6) and is repeated by both Jacob (see Jacob 3:13) and by Moroni (see Ether 15:33).
11. In 2 Nephi 10:3, Nephi had already provided the name of Christ, as it had been told to his brother Jacob by an angel. From that point until the end of his writings, Nephi primarily uses the title *Christ*, employing the name fifty-three times in total (compared to *Messiah*, which he only used nine times after 2 Nephi 10).
12. Nephi's discourse also focuses on a subset of the Jews, "my children [descendants of the Nephites], and my beloved brethren [descendants of the Lamanites]" (2 Nephi 26:1; see also 2 Nephi 30:1), showing how their future will intertwine closely with the future of the Gentiles. Since the title page's purpose statement does not explicitly include this group, this footnote will simply acknowledge that the Book of Mormon prophets after Nephi followed his model, including the Lamanites, along with the Jews, as a group who would need to come to believe in Christ, and showing how their future would be enmeshed with the future of the Gentiles (see, in particular, Mormon 7; Moroni 10).
13. Joseph Smith, *History of the Church of Jesus Christ of Latter-day Saints*, 7 vols., ed. B. H. Roberts (Salt Lake City: Deseret Book, 1957), 5:23–24.
14. The author would like to warmly acknowledge his gratitude to Dennis Largey for his help in conceiving and framing this article.

Index

C

D

E

F

G

N

O

P

Q

R

S

T

U

V

W

Y

Z